Alms for Jihad

Giving to charity is incumbent upon every Muslim. Throughout history, Muslims have donated to the poor and to charitable endowments set up for the purposes of promoting Islam through the construction of mosques, schools, and hospitals. In recent years, there has been a dramatic proliferation of Islamic charities, many of which were created in the declining decades of the twentieth century by the infusion of oil money into the Muslim world. While most of these are legitimate, there is now considerable and worrying evidence to show that others have more questionable intentions, and that funds from such organizations have been diverted to support terrorist groups, such as Al Qaeda. The authors of this book examine the contention through a detailed investigation of the charities involved, their financial intermediaries, and the terrorist organizations themselves. What they discover is that money from these charities has funded conflicts across the world, from the early days in Afghanistan when the *mujahideen* (Muslim warriors) fought the Soviets, to subsequent terrorist activities in Central Asia, Southeast Asia, Africa, Palestine, and, most recently, in Europe and the United States. This ground-breaking book is the first to piece together, from a vast array of sources, the secret and complex financial systems that support terror.

J. MILLARD BURR worked for many years in the Department of State and was formerly United States logistics advisor for Operation Lifeline Sudan I. He has worked closely with international charities for more than forty years.

ROBERT O. COLLINS is Emeritus Professor of History at the University of California, Santa Barbara.

They have previously co-authored three books: *Requiem for the Sudan: War, Drought, and Disaster Relief on the Nile* (1995), *Africa's Thirty Years' War: Chad, Libya, and the Sudan, 1963–1993* (1999), and *Revolutionary Sudan: Hasan al-Turabi and the Islamist State, 1989–2000* (2003).

Alms for Jihad

Charity and Terrorism in the Islamic World

J. Millard Burr and Robert O. Collins

CAMBRIDGE
UNIVERSITY PRESS

CAMBRIDGE UNIVERSITY PRESS
Cambridge, New York, Melbourne, Madrid, Cape Town, Singapore, São Paulo

Cambridge University Press
The Edinburgh Building, Cambridge CB2 2RU, UK

Published in the United States of America by Cambridge University Press, New York

www.cambridge.org
Information on this title: www.cambridge.org/9780521857307

First published 2006

Printed in the United States of America

A catalogue record for this publication is available from the British Library

Library of Congress Cataloguing in Publication data
Burr, J. Millard.
Alms for jihad : charity and terrorism in the Islamic world / J. Millard Burr and
Robert O. Collins.
   p. cm.
Includes bibliographical references and index.
ISBN 0-521-85730-9 (hardback) – ISBN 0-521-67395-X (pbk.)
1. Charities – Islamic countries.   2. Terrorism – Islamic countries.
I. Collins, Robert O., 1933– II. Title.
HV435.B87   2006
361.7′5′091767 – dc22   2005024165

ISBN-13 978-0-521-85730-7 hardback
ISBN-10 0-521-85730-9 hardback

Contents

Illustrations

Tables

Preface

This book seeks to unravel and bring clarity to the complex, elaborate, and secret world of Islamic charities that have financed terrorism. It is not an attempt to give the kind of learned discourse on *zakat*, *sadaqa*, or *waqf* that can be found in the *Encyclopaedia of Islam*. Similarly, it cannot provide an extensive analysis of each of the regions where Islamic charities have supported terrorists. Thus, the individual chapters are more an abstract, a *précis*, to provide a succinct explanation of the composition, financing, money-laundering, and management of those charities through which runs their common objective, the establishment of the Islamist state. It must be abundantly clear from the outset that there are thousands of Islamic charities to assist and support the poor, the destitute, the sick, and the refugee that have nothing to do with terrorism. Many of these charities promote Islam for its religious mission, but that is not what this book is about. Our objective was to have the reader, when reaching the last page, have an appreciation for the global extent, ferocity, and determination of the Islamists who are perpetrating crimes against humanity in the name of religion, and the role that certain Islamic charities have played in supporting those Islamists. The rhetoric of revolution to justify terror to seize political power has become a masquerade that denigrates the very spiritual meaning and power of Islam.

Although the authors have had to struggle to select the critical evidence from our many sources to satisfy the practical constraints of publication, the genesis of this book began during the writing of *Revolutionary Sudan: Hasan al-Turabi and the Islamist State, 1989–2000* (Leiden: Brill, 2003). For those familiar with Khartoum, one of the most striking differences between the city in the 1980s and in the 1990s was the appearance of new Islamic charities and their gratuitous proliferation in prominently situated offices. Who were these charities? What was their purpose? Why the Sudan of all places? The more we sought the answers to this phenomenon, the more we realized that Khartoum had actually been transformed from a rather somnolent outpost of the Islamic world into a center of the international Islamist movement, made possible by the enormous amounts of money made available to its leaders by Islamic charities. The search was on before the trail turned cold.

The authors owe a debt of gratitude to Olivier Roy and Steven Emerson, investigators whose lone voices were heard in the early 1990s warning governments that an Islamist revolutionary movement was germinating throughout the western world. Emerson distributed a video to convince those who would look and listen that the Islamists had established in the USA "an elaborate support and recruiting network coast to coast with branches in more than 88 American cities." They served as recruiting centers that supported *mujahideen* operating around the world. Despite the World Trade Center bombing in 1993, the Khobar bombing of the US military barracks in Saudi Arabia in 1996, and the substantial evidence afterward that Islamist warriors had declared war on the USA and now Europe, Emerson was seen as an alarmist, perhaps because of his well-known Israeli bias. Even though certain intelligence officers understood the dangers of *jihad* in the USA, the authors determined as early as 1993 that the FBI was extremely cautious in its investigation of Islamic charities.

A second debt of gratitude is owed Rita Katz, the "anonymous" author of *Terrorist Hunter*, the story of one woman's struggle to expose the activities of seditious operators within Islamic charities functioning in the USA. Like Emerson, she was a *vox clamantis in deserto*, a voice crying in the wilderness, for the abundant evidence she uncovered during a decade of determined investigation. Her book is essential to an understanding of how Islamic charities supported Islamist movements in the USA, but it has been largely ignored by Washington.

We especially want to thank once again Alan Goulty for reading, as he had done for *Revolutionary Sudan: Hasan al-Turabi and the Islamist State, 1989–2000*, the early chapters of *Alms for Jihad* before leaving the UK for demanding diplomatic duties as Her Majesty's Ambassador to Tunisia. We also want to express our appreciation to Steve Humphreys, Professor of History at the University of California Santa Barbara, for his unflagging support in all matters Arabic, and to Sylvia Curtis, the intrepid research librarian at UCSB, who has always come to our rescue.

Spellings can be a curse that can result in chaos, particularly when the documentation for a book, like this one, comes in many languages. Motivated by familiarity, practice, or ethnic pride, Africans, Arabs, Asians, and Europeans have spelled the name of a person, place, or event in a transliteration that reflects their own parochialism, patriotism, and panache. The result is often confusion rather than clarity. The only legitimate principle is consistency of spelling in the text. Consistency, however, is not a universal virtue and does not always guarantee clarity. In the search

for clarity, we have consequently Anglicized or given the English equiva-
lent for people, place-names, and events recorded in different languages.
Place-names are spelled for understanding rather than in the local patois.
Personal names are more precisely retained because they are complex, for
everyone spells his or her name to their satisfaction and not by standard-
ized rules of transliteration. As with place-names, variety can produce
bewilderment in the reader that can best be resolved by consistency.
We have abstained from the use of diacritical marks in transliteration
wherever possible, retaining them only for a very few Arabic words (e.g.
Shari'a) and avoiding them when possible in personal names. Currency is
expressed in US dollars. This is not academic arrogance. It is a practical
response for those who wish to understand what we have written.

   If spellings are a curse, acronyms are a necessary evil. Virtually every
government agency, and certainly most Islamic charities, have very long
names. It would be stylistically cumbersome to repeat this lengthy nomen-
clature at every entry. Although there are 206 acronyms on the list, many
are rarely used in the text while others, because of their frequency, become
instantly recognizable to the reader. When the name of the organization is
first presented, the acronym is placed in parenthesis, e.g. Islamic Countries Educational, Scientific, Cultural Organization (ICESCO). In a few
instances where the acronym appears in a later chapter we refresh the
reader's memory by repeating the full name of the organization, but those
are few.

J. Millard Burr
Rio Rico, Arizona

Robert O. Collins
Santa Barbara, California

Abbreviations

AAIF	Al Aqsa International Foundation (Yemen)
ADF	Allied Democratic Forces (Uganda)
AEL	Arab–European League (Belgium)
AFP	Agence France Press
AFP	Armed Forces of the Philippines
AGI	Agenzia Italia
AHIF	Al Haramain Islamic Foundation (Mu'Assasat al-Haramayn al- Khayriya) (Saudi Arabia)
AIAI	Al Itihad al-Islamiyya (Somalia)
AID	Agency for International Development (USA)
AIP	Azerbaijan Islamic Party
AIU	African International University
AIVD	General Intelligence and Security Service (Algemene Inlichtingen-en Veiligheidsdienst, the former BVD) (the Netherlands)
AM	The Emigrants (Al Muhajiroun) (UK)
AP	Associated Press (USA)
APEC	Asia Pacific Economic Cooperation
ARMM	Autonomous Region in Muslim Mindinao (Philippines)
ASP	Association de Secours Palestinien (Switzerland)
ATF	Bureau of Alcohol, Tobacco, and Firearms (USA)
ATM	automated teller machine
BADEA	Arab Bank for Economic Development in Africa (Sudan)
BCCI	Bank of Credit and Commerce International (Abu Dhabi)
BfV	Office of the Protection of the Constitution (Bundesamt für Verfassungsschutz) (Germany)
BIC	Benevolent International Corporation (Saudi Arabia, Philippines) (see also BIF)

BIDC	Al Baraka Investment and Development Corporation (Saudi Arabia)
BIF	Benevolence International Foundation (in Russia BIF was called Benevolence International Corporation, BIC)
BIF	Benevolence International Foundation (Saudi Arabia)
BND	German Federal Intelligence Service (Bundesnachrichtendienst)
BNP	Bangladesh National Party
BVD	National Intelligence and Security Agency (Binnelandse Veiligheidsdienst) (the Netherlands)
BYL	Bangsamoro Youth League (Philippines)
CAIR	Council of American–Islamic Relations (USA)
CARE	Cooperative for American Relief Everywhere
CBSP	Comité de Bienfaisance et Secours aux Palestiniens (France)
CEO	chief executive officer
CFCM	Conseil Français du Culte Musulman (France)
CIA	Central Intelligence Agency (USA)
CIDA	Canadian International Development Agency
CIPF	Council for International People's Friendship (Sudan)
CIS	Commonwealth of Independent States (former Soviet Union)
CORIF	Conseil de Réflexion sur l'Islam de France
CSIS	Canadian Security Intelligence Service
CSSW	Charitable Society for Social Welfare (USA)
DMI	Dal al-Mal al-Islami Investment Corporation (Saudi Arabia)
DUP	Democratic Unionist Party (Sudan)
EIJ	Egyptian Islamic Jihad (Jama'at al-Islamiyya)
EU	European Union
FATF	Financial Action Task Force (OECD, Paris)
FBI	Federal Bureau of Investigation (USA)
FBIS	Foreign Broadcast Information Service (USA)
FIS	Islamic Salvation Front (Algeria)
FISA	Foreign Intelligence Service Act (USA)
FIU	Financial Intelligence Unit (USA)
FKAWJ	Sunni Communication Forum (Forum Komunikasi Ahlus Sunnah wal Jama'ah) (Indonesia)
FLN	National Liberation Front (Front de Libération Nationale) (Algeria)

FOCA	Friends of Charities Association (USA)
FSB	Federal Security Service (Federal'naya Sluzhba Bezopasnost) (Russia)
FSM	Fondation Secours Mondial (Belgium)
FTATC	Foreign Terrorist Asset Tracking Center (USA)
GDP	gross domestic product
GIA	Armed Islamic Group (Groupement Islamique Armé) (Algeria)
GMT	Greenwich Mean Time (UK)
GRF	Global Relief Foundation (Fondation Secours Mondial) (Belgium)
GSC	Zionist Action Group (Israel)
GSISS	Graduate School of Islamic Thought and Social Sciences (USA)
HAI	Human Appeals International (UAE)
HAMAS	Islamic Resistance Movement (Harakat al-Muqawama al-Islamiyya fi Filistin)
HCI	Human Concern International (Canada)
HLF	Holy Land Fund for Relief and Development (Holy Land Foundation) (USA, France)
HUJI	Jihad Movement of Bangladesh (Harakat-ul-Jihad-al-Islami)
HuT	Hizb ut-Tahrir al-Islami, international Salafist organization
IAC	Islamic African Center (Sudan)
IAP	Islamic Association for Palestine (USA)
IARA	Islamic African Relief Agency (Sudan, USA)
IBC	Islamic Benevolence Committee (Lajnat al-Birr al-Islamiyya, LBI) (Pakistan, Saudi Arabia)
ICC	Islamic Coordinating Council (Pakistan)
ICESCO	Islamic Countries Educational, Scientific, Cultural Organization (France)
ICF	Islamic Charter Front (Sudan)
ICII	International Council for Islamic Information (UK)
ICP	Islamic Committee for Palestine
ICRC	International Commission for the Red Cross/Red Crescent
ICS	Islami Chhatra Shibir (Bangladesh)
IDB	Islamic Development Bank (Kuwait, Saudi Arabia)
IDF	Israel Defense Force
IDPs	internally displaced persons

IEEPA	International Emergency Economic Powers Act (USA)
IHH	Foundation for Human Rights and Freedom, known as the Humanitarian Relief Foundation (International Humanitaire Hilfsorganization) (Turkey)
IIA	International Islamic Aid (France)
IIB	International Islamic Brigade (Afghanistan, Chechnya)
IICO	International Islamic Charitable Organization (Kuwait, Philippines)
IIIT	International Institute for Islamic Thought (USA)
IIRO	International Islamic Relief Organization (Saudi Arabia)
IJMP	Islamic Jihad Movement in Palestine (Harakat al-Jihad al-Islami fi Filistin)
IMA	Islamic Movement for Africa (Nigeria)
IMU	Islamic Movement of Uzbekistan
INS	Immigration and Naturalization Service (USA)
INTERPAL	Palestine Relief and Development Fund (UK)
IPC	Islamic Presentation Committee (Philippines)
IRIC	Islamic Research and Information Center (Kuwait, Philippines)
IRIN	Integrated Regional Information Network
IRNA	Islamic Republic News Agency (Iran)
IRPT	Islamic Renaissance Party of Tajikistan (Hizb Nahda)
IRS	Internal Revenue Service (USA)
IRSA	Islamic Relief Agency (Sudan)
IRS-CI	Criminal Investigations Unit of the Internal Revenue Service (USA)
ISCAG	Islamic Studies for Call and Guidance (Philippines)
ISI	Inter-Service Intelligence Agency (Pakistan)
ISNA	Islamic Society of North America (Canada, USA)
ISRA	Islamic Studies and Research Association (Munazzamat al-Da'wa al-Islamiyya) (USA)
JI	Jammah Islamiyya (Southeast Asia)
KCC	Kurdish Cultural Centre (UK)
KFOR	Kosovo Force
KLA	Kosovo Liberation Army (Ushtria Clirimtare e Kosoves, UCK)
KMM	Kumpulan Mujahideen (Malaysia)

LBI	See IBC
LDK	Democratic League of Kosovo
LJ	Laskar Jihad (Malaysia)
MAK	Maktab al-Khadamat al-Mujahidin al-Arab (Mujahideen Services Bureau) (Pakistan)
MAP	Medical Aid for Palestine (Canada, UK)
MAYA	Muslim Arab Youth Association (USA)
MEMRI	Middle East Media Research Institute
MILF	Moro Islamic Liberation Front (Philippines)
MIRO	Mercy International Relief Organization (Saudi Arabia)
MNLF	Moro National Liberation Front (Philippines)
MSA	Muslim Students' Association of the USA and Canada
MWL	Muslim World League (Rabitait al-Alami al-Islamiyya) (Saudi Arabia)
NATO	North Atlantic Treaty Organization
NCB	National Commercial Bank (Saudi Arabia)
NCIS	National Criminal Intelligence Service (UK)
NDA	National Democratic Alliance (Sudan)
NGO	non-government organization
NIF	National Islamic Front (al-Jabhah al-Islamiyya al-Qawmiyya) (Sudan)
NMCC	National Management Consultancy Center (Saudi Arabia)
NSC	National Security Council (USA)
NSRCC	National Salvation Revolutionary Command Council (often simply RCC) (Sudan)
NSSWO	Non-Sudanese Students' Welfare Organization (Sudan)
NTFIU	National Terrorist Financial Investigation Unit (UK)
OECD	Organization for Economic Co-operation and Development (Paris)
OFAC	Office of Foreign Assets Control (USA)
OIC	Organization of the Islamic Conference
OPEC	Organization of Petroleum Exporting Countries
OPIC	Overseas Private Investment Corporation (USA)
PA	Palestinian Authority
PAIC	Popular Arab and Islamic Congress (Sudan)
PCAPM	Popular Committee for Assisting the Palestinian Mujahideen (Saudi Arabia)

PDF	People's Defense Force (Sudan)
PDPA	People's Democratic Party of Afghanistan
PIJ	Palestine Islamic Jihad
PLO	Palestine Liberation Organization
POW	prisoner of war
PPF	People's Police Force (Sudan)
PRCS	Palestine Red Crescent Society
PULO	Pattani United Liberation Organization (Thailand)
PWA	Palestine Welfare Association
RAFAH	Turkish Prosperity Party
RCC	See NSRCC
RCMP	Royal Canadian Mounted Police
RG	Renseignements Généraux (France)
RISEAP	Regional Islamic Dawah Council of Southeast Asia and the Pacific
RSO	Rohingya Solidarity Organization (Bangladesh)
SAAR	Suleiman Abd al-Aziz al-Rajhi Foundation (Saudi Arabia)
SAMA	Saudi Arabian Monetary Authority
SARCS	Saudi Arabia Red Crescent Society
SAS	Special Air Service (UK)
SAUDIFIN	Saudi Finance Corporation
SCR	Prince Sultan bin Abdul Aziz Special Committee for Relief (Saudi Arabia)
SDA	Party of Democratic Action (Bosnia)
SDGT	Specially Designated Global Terrorists (USA)
SEDCO	Saudi Economic and Development Company LLC
SHCB	Saudi High Commission for Aid to Bosnia
SHIK	Albanian Intelligence Services
SHRC	Saudi High Relief Commission
SIDO	Sub-Saharan International Development Organization (Sudan)
SJRC	Saudi Joint Relief Committee (for Bosnia)
SJRC	Saudi Joint Relief Committee for Kosovo and Chechnya (not to be confused with SJRC for Bosnia)
SPLA	Sudan People's Liberation Army
SPLM	Sudan People's Liberation Movement
SSR	Society for Social Reform (Kuwait)
TANJUG	official Yugoslavia news agency
TMC	Transitional Military Council (Sudan)
TWRA	Third World Relief Agency (Austria)
UAE	United Arab Emirates

UASR	United Association for Studies and Research (USA)
UCOII	Union of Muslim Organizations of Italy
UK	United Kingdom
UN	United Nations
UNESCO	United Nations Educational, Scientific, and Cultural Organization
UNHCR	United Nations High Commission for Refugees
UNICEF	United Nations International Children's Emergency Fund
UNITAF	United Nations International Task Force (Somalia)
UNLU	Unified National Leadership of the Uprising (Palestine)
UNMIK	United Nations Mission in Kosovo
UNOSOM I	United Nations Operation in Somalia I
UNOSOM II	United Nations Operation in Somalia II
UNRWA	United Nations Relief and Works Agency (Palestine)
UNSCR	United Nations Security Council Resolution
UOIF	French Union of Islamic Organizations
UPI	United Press International (USA)
USA	United States of America
USC	United Somali Congress
USF	University of South Florida (USA)
USSR	Union of Soviet Socialist Republics
UTO	United Tajik Opposition
WAMY	World Assembly of Muslim Youth (Saudi Arabia)
WEFOUND	Wisdom Enrichment Foundation (Saudi Arabia)
WHO	World Health Organization
WISE	World and Islamic Studies Enterprise (USA)

Introduction

This confirms that the [Prophet's] Companions were correct to brand as apostates those who refused to pay the alms tax [zakat], and to kill them and imprison their children. God the Most High decreed that unless someone surrenders judgement to the Prophet, he cannot be part of the community of the faithful.

Ayman al-Zawahiri, Egyptian Islamic Jihad, December 2002[1]

The US Department of State estimates that there are some 6,000 legitimate Islamic charities, but that number is surely very conservative. Like hundreds of charities in the West, particularly in the USA, many Islamic charities are modest affairs established by a wealthy individual or family usually for a specific charitable purpose and held accountable only to the founder. In recent years there has been a greater effort by Muslim countries to register their charities, but often the record remains incomplete and there is frequently no organized means to make registered charities account for what they do. Moreover, in the Muslim world there is a deeply ingrained tradition that charitable giving is solely the business of the donor and not the state. The thousands of charities that are the beneficiaries do indeed receive vast sums of assets and money for humanitarian and religious purposes. They are not the subject of this book. Our concern is those charities that have been used as fronts to launder money and assets in order to finance jihadists who believe that only terror will result in the establishment of the Islamist state.

The number of charities that have supported Islamist jihadists and their terrorist activities will never be known, but they were surely a small percentage of the total number of Islamic charities worldwide. Those charities proven by 2004 to have belonged to or to have been associated with Al Qaeda numbered only fourteen (see table 2.2). One can reasonably assume, however, that there are other less obtrusive charities that have helped Islamists committed to terrorism to achieve their ends, but they would be smaller in size and funding than the major charities which are the principal players in the following saga. Moreover, charities for terrorism is not a growth industry since individual national efforts

1

to register, monitor, and hold charities accountable for their activities have been or are being widely adopted by those countries from which most of the terrorists and their sources of funds have originated in the past. Saudi Arabia, Pakistan, Yemen, and other Muslim states have been and are quietly dismantling many of their charities, but in their subsequent silence the causes of closure can only be speculative. The reader, however, should be aware of one very important distinction, for not all charities are alike: although few in number, the charities that have supported Al Qaeda and its offshoots have been among the wealthiest. It is not the number of Islamic charities devoted to Islamist and jihadist terrorism, but their size, outreach, and above all their wealth that has enabled them to have a significant international impact far out of proportion to their numbers, not unlike the Ford and Rockefeller Foundations of the West. The critical difference, of course, is the objective to be achieved, and their sponsorship of terrorism with the aim of bringing about the Islamist state can by no stretch of the imagination be regarded as philanthropic.

The deft synchronization of the suicide attacks by Muslim terrorists that destroyed the World Trade Center and damaged the Pentagon on 11 September 2001 astonished the citizens of the USA and people throughout the world. All of the terrorists were members of Al Qaeda, an international Islamist revolutionary movement of holy warriors (*mujahideen*) founded in Afghanistan in 1988. The leaders of the *mujahideen* were *not* religious fanatics, but men who, with rare exceptions, had received a western secular education that enabled them to use the most complicated weapons and employ the most modern instruments of organization, technology, communication, and finance. The annual reports on terrorism by the Department of State, and evidence obtained about the funding of Al Qaeda during the trial of its members involved in the 1998 bombing of the American embassies in Kenya and Tanzania, have clearly demonstrated that Islamist terrorist organizations raised funds through a variety of methods often opaque and unknown in the West.[2] Some monies were collected through legitimate businesses, but much of the funding to support Islamist terrorist organizations has come, often unwittingly, directly from individuals and from the stream of donations to Muslim charities. Presumably, most donors clearly believed their contributions would assist the needy and promote Islam. Some who gave or established their own charities, however, were committed to the establishment of Islamist states in the Muslim world as well as the conversion of the *kafirin* (unbelievers), beyond the frontiers of Islam. This objective clearly transformed a religious mission into a political cause in which crimes against humanity were believed to be instruments necessary to establish the Islamist state of true believers.

During the 1990s there had been a dramatic proliferation of Islamic charities that began in the late 1970s and accelerated during the 1980s. As many new ones popped up like mushrooms, their presence could no longer be ignored. Most were legitimate, some were not. They were presumably friendly with the older established Muslim charities, but often they were in competition. In time it became abundantly clear that acts of terrorism were being perpetrated by a sophisticated network of Islamist terrorist organizations, funded by individual Muslims and Muslim charitable institutions. By the new millennium numerous Islamic charitable organizations had come to the attention of the Federal Bureau of Investigation (FBI), state, and local law-enforcement authorities in the USA. Their investigations were painfully time consuming. The complexities of Islamic finance and banking were unfamiliar to western officials, and there existed a large number of major Islamic charities – more than forty – that were registered in the USA and supported Muslim activities overseas.[3]

Although the Islamic establishment condemns terrorism, the more radical Islamists have advocated its use in their polemical literature supported by hundreds of Islamic legal rulings (Ar., sg. *fatwa*; pl. *fatawa*) by learned clerics and religious jurists. The writings of the Sudanese intellectual Hasan al-Turabi in the 1990s are a contemporary example. The son of an Islamic judge (*qadi*), he was deeply influenced as a student at the University of Khartoum by the Muslim Brothers (Jam'iyyat al-Ikhwan al-Muslimin), often called simply the Ikhwan, who were devoted to the restoration of Islamic law and a strict interpretation of the Quran in a secular and corrupt Islamic world. After studying law at the London School of Economics and the Sorbonne he returned to the Sudan in 1965 to become Dean of the Khartoum University Law School and patron of the Islamic Charter Front (ICF). In 1985 he founded the National Islamic Front (al-Jabhah al-Islamiyya al-Qawmiyya, NIF) to promote his Islamist ideology and its agenda. By the 1990s he had become one of the recognized intellectual architects of the contemporary Islamic revival that spread like wildfire across the Muslim world after the Soviet invasion of Afghanistan in 1979.

After the coup d'état of 30 June 1989 by Brigadier Omar Hassan Ahmad al-Bashir that brought the NIF to power in the Sudan, Turabi was transformed from an Islamist intellectual into a prominent leader of the global Islamist movement. He argued that the contemporary Islamist movement has evolved through four stages. At first, it was "a mere trend, with no defined organizational structure." The second stage entailed the cohesion of organization "to represent and promote Islam," specifically the Islamic Jihad movement in Egypt and the Al Qaeda organization in

Afghanistan. In the third stage these inchoate groups coalesced to become a "tangible influence in society." Reformist in nature, they sought to achieve the "purification" of Muslim society by returning to the original ideals of Islam and are usually known as the Salafi tendency; such movements have occurred in many places throughout the Muslim world and at many times in the history of Islam such as the Wahhabi (*muwahhidun*) movement in Saudi Arabia in the eighteenth century and the Mahdist revolution in Sudan in the nineteenth. "The fourth stage comes when the Islamic movement assumes the mantle of political leadership of society and takes charge of public policy; an example would be the recent Taliban movement in Afghanistan."[4]

Contemporary Islamist radicals such as Turabi, the Saudi Osama bin Laden, the Egyptian Ayman al-Zawahiri, the Tunisian Rashid al-Gannushi, the Algerian Salafi Brigade for Call and Combat, and countless *mujahideen* regard themselves as Salafist, defenders of a tradition over fourteen centuries old to reform (*islah*) and renew (*tajdid*) Islam to its original purity practiced by the Prophet Muhammad and his followers. Today there are Salafist movements seeking to impose the unity of the pristine and puritanical Islam of the Prophet (*tawhid*) in virtually every Muslim country, including Saudi Arabia. There a number of so-called Salafist crosscurrents flow today just beneath the surface and roil the outwardly calm exterior of the House of Saud which they regard as having corrupted the teachings of the great eighteenth-century purifier of Islam and founder of the Wahhabi movement, Shaykh Muhammad ibn Abd al-Wahhab (1703–1792).[5]

Salafi is derived from the Arabic *al-salaf*, and is usually coupled as *al-salaf al-salih*, the "virtuous forefathers," or companions of the Prophet Muhammad. It literally means keeping the faith with the early generation of Muslims renowned for their piety, and the Salafists regard themselves as the direct descendants of the "best of people" at the founding of Islam. The modern movement was established in the nineteenth century to assert the religious and cultural identity of Islam. Its leaders, Jamal al-Din al-Afghani (1838–1897), Muhammad Abduh (1849–1905), and Rashid Rida (1865–1935), attributed the decline of Muslim societies to secular Islam that had abandoned the original teachings of the Prophet to adopt western ideas of modernity. Thus, the *salafa* (forefathers, Salafists) sought to restore the greatness of the Islamic world by the creation of states ruled by scripture, the Quran and Sunna, and by strict adherence to the founders of the four medieval schools of Muslim law, Hanafite, Malikite, Shafi'ite, and Hanbalite. Moreover, the Shari'a was reinterpreted following two fundamental principles: *maslaha* (the public interest) and *talfiq* (patching, the concept that the sources of Islamic law can be drawn from any of the four schools and not historically just one). Above all, Salafists insisted that Islam was Arab and its language Arabic. Although traditional Salafists believed it is not permissible for Muslims to overthrow a Muslim government, no matter how cruel, incompetent, or secular, contemporary Salafists – the Islamist jihadists – contemptuously reject this belief.[6]

The more "fundamentalist," the more militant and determined is the Salafi organization to recreate an Islam uncorrupted by recent political, economic, and social events. Goals are defined by the Quran, the Holy Book of Islam in which are written the words of God (Allah, an elision of *al-ilah*, "the God") as revealed to the Prophet Muhammad between 610 and 632 CE. The Sunna refers to an ideal pattern of life of the ancestral Arabs within the customary Muslim domain according to the sayings and deeds of the Prophet. After the death of its most famous exponent, Muhammad ibn Idris al-Shafi'i (d. 819 CE), the Sunna of the Prophet (*sunnat al-nabi*) gained widespread acceptance throughout the Muslim world and became the foundation of the Shari'a. Literally *the trodden path leading to a water hole*, Shari'a is God's law transmitted through the Prophet to govern the conduct of the individual Muslim in both worldly and religious matters as defined by one of the four schools of Islamic law. To the Salafist, Shari'a is paramount and must not be confused or corrupted by secular law codes or legalisms adopted from the West.

Determined to purify Islam, the Salafists vehemently denounce the parochialism of Sufism and its corrupt practices. Sufism is usually defined as Islamic mysticism by which a Muslim can become closer to Allah by a combination of theosophical speculation, devotional zeal, and prescribed rituals learned upon initiation into an Islamic order (*tariqa*). Sufism became widely popular in the Islamic revivalist movements of the eighteenth century, but it was regarded by orthodox Muslims as a peripheral and even clandestine phenomenon in the Muslim world. The Wahhabis rejected all forms of Sufism and persecuted its adherents in their efforts to return to the original path of Islam, and the influence of Sufi orders has further declined from the 1930s when confronted by modernist movements drawing on Wahhabi teachings and claiming that Sufism had become dependent on extra-Islamic sources that encouraged passivity to true reform.

In the Salafist pan-Islamic worldview neutrality is impossible. An unremitting and constant struggle (*jihad*) is to be waged against its enemies, both secular and religious. The Salafists still manage to coexist in a tenuous relationship with certain Muslim conservative reformers who seek a return to the pure faith through evolution rather than the Salafist revolution by the use of terror. The most prominent of these is the Muslim Brotherhood, the Ikhwan, founded in Ismailiyya, Egypt, in 1929 by Shaykh Hasan al-Banna (1906–1949). The Muslim Brothers followed the evangelical call to return to the fundamentals of Islam (*da'wa*) by a gradual transition to an Islamic state through education, persuasion, morality and personal behavior. They have survived internal divisions and active repression by the state since 1948. Unlike the Salafists the Brotherhood was a mass movement that followed Banna's message of salvation, a message that was translated into social action through its extensive organization. Banna's ideology lacked the philosophical depth of that of the Salafiyya, but it succeeded in mobilizing a mass following more by clever propaganda than obtuse theology. Although some Islamists often disagree with the tactics employed by the Salafi movements, such as the atrocities inflicted by the Taliban movement in Afghanistan, they do not rule out the use of violence to achieve their ends. Historically, the Salafi leaders have demonstrated no compunction about using terrorism in the pursuit of their Islamist objectives.

Although the UN has been unable to agree on what constitutes terrorism, the FBI has defined it as "the unlawful use of force against persons or property to intimidate or coerce a government, the civilian population or any segment thereof, in the furtherance of political or social objectives."[7] The US government remains convinced that there are more than a dozen major organizations that follow the Salafi tradition and are determined to seize the mantle of political leadership from "unworthy" Muslim rulers in some fifty countries. Where the end justifies the means, terrorism will not only be used, it will be considered justified in order to achieve the purification of Islam.

Late twentieth-century movements determined to revive Islam by the book and the sword also appealed to its founding principles. These included one of the five pillars of Islam, the *zakat* that inextricably involved the principal custodians and dispensers of this tithe, Islamic charities. The linkage between the Islamist movement, terrorism, and the role of Islamic charities confronted authorities in the West with a conundrum and not a little confusion. Muslim religious charities that supported Islamist organizations throughout the world by design, religious obligations, or accident were largely an unknown phenomenon to western governments. In Christian countries institutions seeking financial support for charitable activities have discreetly segregated the secular from the religious, reflecting the historic separation of church and state. Secular philanthropy supported non-religious charities such as the United Way, boys' clubs, museums, cancer societies, the Red Cross. Those devoted to religious purposes – missionary societies, seminaries, church construction,

Christian humanitarian organizations, and the preservation of indigenous languages to promote the propagation of the faith – are separate and discrete from the state.

In contrast, Islam does not distinguish between church and state. Muslims who are obligated to perform *zakat* and individual donors make no distinction between the secular and religious uses to which their donations may be employed. That allows those who administer Islamic charities a great deal of latitude as to how the money is spent and for what purpose. Moreover, the governors of Islamic charities have often a Muslim theological background and are frequently members of the *ulama*, learned clerics with a knowledge of Islam. Historically, these religious scholars were the guardians of religious and legal education, the regulation of Islamic society, and the preservation of Islamic culture. They formed an elite class who vacillated between close cooperation with and fierce independence from the state. They opposed the growing secularism and nationalism of Middle Eastern governments during the nineteenth and twentieth centuries. They directed their influence to Islamist educational and religious institutions that found their political manifestations in the Muslim Brotherhood of Sunni Islam in Egypt and the triumph of the Shi'a *ulama* in the overthrow of Shah Reza Pahlavi and the establishment of the Islamic Republic of Iran in 1979. This historical trust in theological authority had for centuries confirmed the belief that the donation, whether a tithe (*zakat*) or the praiseworthy individual act of giving by wealthy Muslims (*sadaqa*), would be used to support the purposes of Islam without accountability.

Muslims *do* tithe, and one of the most convenient ways to fulfill that obligation is by giving through Muslim charities whose funds have been one of the most dominant aspects of Islamic economics. Billions of dollars are collected annually throughout the Muslim world with little demand for administrative transparency, which permits the distribution of significant funds without the need to create a large administrative infrastructure to decide how, where, and to whom the monies will be spent. Charities, mosques, and schools are not pestered as they are in the West by the ubiquitous tax collector or internal revenue agent, and Muslim governments throughout the world have rarely interfered in the collection of charitable funds. Private and public donors are thus assured considerable confidentiality. Moreover, charitable institutions have traditionally been granted virtual economic autonomy after the funds have been received and in practice are free from government interference. Historically, charitable contributions on the local level, rather than government funds, have been responsible for the financing of Quranic schools, the elementary *kuttab* and the *madrasa*, an Islamic college and center for religious and legal studies. The course of instruction in the *madrasa* was the Quran, Arabic, Islamic theology, and the Shari'a. The graduates of the *madrasa* forged the links between the *ulama*, who were the scholars and teachers of religious education, and the ruling government authorities who financially supported them.

The events of 11 September 2001 (hereafter 9/11) also constituted a dramatic turning point in the ambivalent relations between the USA and the Islamic world. At the memorial prayer service at the National Cathedral in Washington, DC, a week after the destruction of the World Trade Center, President George W. Bush pledged an unrelenting attack on Islamic terrorism, but he carefully called the cabal that produced 9/11 an aberrant minority within the larger Islamic congregation. The *Washington Post* was less generous and more specific. In an article that appeared shortly after 9/11 it quoted a Pakistani "cleric" who claimed that Al Qaeda had "hundreds of well-to-do people almost everywhere in the world" eager to give financial contributions, and what better institution than an Islamic charity? Certainly, the US government was convinced that a portion of the $10 billion that the Saudi leadership showered annually on Islamic organizations through the ministry of religious works had found its way into the hands of Osama bin Laden. Some recipients were certainly individuals, but most were "various international [Muslim] charities" that had "diverted [funds] to terrorism, in some cases with the knowledge of contributors."[8]

In the past Islamic charities in the USA and those established abroad had been regarded by the public with benign indifference and by the more skeptical authorities, with cautious curiosity. Just as national, state, and local governments were loath to probe Christian charities, they had hitherto been reluctant to harass Muslim charitable organizations. September 11 dramatically changed that attitude despite the president's appeal to respect Islam. The very dearth of information about the activities of Muslim charities aroused suspicion, as ignorance usually will do, and spawned a good deal of supposition founded more on imagination than understanding. Some regarded Muslim charities as an integral part of the new geopolitics, or as some put it, "theopolitics." Following the Soviet withdrawal from Afghanistan in 1989 funds and weapons for the *mujahideen* from the US Central Intelligence Agency (CIA) evaporated. However, the FBI became increasingly aware in the early years of the 1990s that Islamic relief agencies in the USA were sending funds to support Islamist *mujahideen* operating in Algeria, the Balkans, Afghanistan, and the Philippines. After 9/11, the Bureau inaugurated a more thorough examination of more than a dozen charities operating in North America that were responsible for the legal and extra-legal movement of funds to recipients abroad. Indeed, for more than a decade millions of dollars had left the USA and Canada in support of "good-will" missions by reputable Muslim charities to assist the impoverished and refugees in Jerusalem, the West Bank, and Gaza and to Islamist terrorist organizations operating throughout the Muslim world.

A week after 9/11 the Treasury Department, which is responsible for all financial matters of the US government, had organized an interagency task force consisting of four Treasury agencies – the Bureau of Alcohol, Tobacco and Firearms (ATF), the US Customs Service, the Internal Revenue Service's Criminal Investigations Unit (IRS-CI), and the Secret Service – all of whom ironically had facilities and personnel who were destroyed at the World Trade Center. The Foreign Terrorist Asset Tracking Center (FTATC) was first located in the Treasury Department's Office of Foreign Assets Control to identify foreign terrorist groups and the people and institutions that supported them, and to disrupt and intercept their funding.[9] Thereafter, FTATC would work closely with the Department of State and the Attorney General to use the authority granted to them by the Presidential Executive Order 13224 to uncover, designate, and direct action against charitable institutions linked to the financing of terrorist groups.

Although the American Islamic community could generally depend on historical American sensitivity to religious organizations and a cultural hesitancy by western intelligence agents to investigate seemingly legitimate Islamic charities, the creation of the Office of Homeland Security nine days after 9/11 could not but focus scrutiny on the Muslim community. The FTATC task force, FBI, and local law enforcement soon found that certain Islamic institutions were operating sophisticated schemes to transfer funds to and from the USA, Canada, and Europe behind a wall of secrecy. Language and cultural mores complicated efforts to unravel their financial transactions or to understand the methods employed by Islamic charitable organizations that enabled them to frustrate investigations into their operations and money-laundering in support of those Islamic terrorist organizations that operated illegally under American law. Moreover, Islamic charities could invariably depend on local Muslims to defend them despite the fact they would never receive or demand an accounting of their donations. Reputable Islamic charitable institutions traditionally devoted to educational and humanitarian works could easily be hijacked by Islamists without the knowledge of the Muslim congregation who disapproved of them.

Assistant Secretary of the Treasury Kenneth Dam made it very clear that Muslim charities, one of the pillars of the Islamic faith, would receive increasing scrutiny despite the fact that FTATC had yet to acquire the necessary evidence to determine which charities had been using funds for uncharitable purposes. "At the same time, there is no denying that some legitimate charities have been penetrated by terrorists or terrorist supporters – possibly by only a few managerial employees – who misdirect a portion of the charity's funds for terrorist ends . . . [and those front charities] primarily organized and directed to abuse charitable status for terrorist ends . . . . [who threatened] not only their targets, but their donors" in their efforts to extract donations. "Our challenge is to prevent terrorists from using charities as a cover for supporting terrorism while ensuring that charitable giving and charitable works continue."[10]

In order for FTATC to begin freezing the flow of funds through charities for Islamist terrorist organizations, it had to build a database. This was extremely difficult, for there were hundreds of Islamic non-government organizations (NGOs) operating throughout the world, and the number of those charities that supported the Islamist revolution could not be guessed. Moreover, like charities in the West, those in the East could be created for a particular purpose and upon completion of the project disappear from the record. Nevertheless, the work of FTATC seeking "transparency and oversight" of Muslim charities was cautiously regarded with favor by the Muslim community and those Islamic governments who were as anxious as the USA to know the operations of Islamic charities in their own countries. The Bush administration announced that it was "gratified by the positive response that these initiatives have received from other governments and the charitable community."[11]

Regulating the industry of Islamic charity and humanitarian assistance is critical to the well-being of Islam in the USA. This is because of the extent to which terrorists operating front organizations have raised funds under the guise of charity and our need to preserve our ability to give of ourselves that tithe on behalf of others without fear that in trying to make the world a better place we actually make it worse.

1 The third pillar of Islam: *zakat*

And they have been commanded no more than this: to worship Allah, offering Him sincere devotion, being true [in faith]; to establish regular Prayer and to practice regular charity; and that is the religion right and straight.
(Sura 98.6)

Of their wealth, take alms [*sadaqa*] so you may purify and sanctify them.
(Sura 9.103)

Establish regular Prayer and give regular Alms, and loan to Allah a beautiful loan.
(Sura 73.21)

Zakat, derived from *zaka'* (thrive, increase, to be pure in heart, righteous, good), is obligatory almsgiving for all adult Muslims who possess at least a minimum of personal wealth. It became one of the five pillars of Islam following the Prophet Muhammad's flight to Medina in 622. It should not, however, be confused with voluntary and spontaneous giving by individuals – *sadaqa* (gifts) – which is highly regarded as an act of piety usually given in money. Indeed, the Quran requires Muslims of all stations to be charitable to the poor, and in one popular Quranic concordance a scholar has listed fifty-one specific references in twenty-four separate *sura* (chapters) of the Quran that refer to spending (*infaq*) and include charitable giving.[1] *Zakat* is specifically mentioned more than thirty times in the Quran, and any Muslim who ignores that obligation would be regarded as a pariah. In a noted Hadith (saying of the Prophet) from Ibn Khuzama, the Prophet Muhammad is quoted as saying, "When you have paid the *zakat* of your wealth you have driven its evil away from you." The first Caliph, Abu Bakr al-Siddiq (d. 635), supporter, confidant, and friend of the Prophet, defined the importance of *zakat*. "In the name of Allah, I will fight those who may differentiate between *salat* [prayers] and zakat; those who may fulfill one act of worship and lapse on another."[2]

Before giving *zakat* one must possess a minimum amount of property (*nisab*) beyond that required for basic daily needs – food, clothing, and shelter, and in the modern age the expenses associated with employment. Annually each Muslim voluntarily calculates his or her *zakat* individually on all other property – gold, silver, cash, securities, loans received, all business profits, and goods, specifically fish, crops, and animals – at the traditional rate of 2.5 percent per lunar year (354 days) except for agricultural crops, which are reckoned at the rate of 5 percent if the harvest is from irrigated or 10 percent from rain-fed land. *Zakat* is also calculated on the value of products that are dried and stored. The tithe for grazing animals may be paid in kind or in value on a sliding scale of the number of animals owned, but it seldom exceeds three animals from a herd of 120. In addition there is a special *zakat* (*zakat al-fitr*) equal to the cost of one day's food for each member of a donor household; it is collected at the end of Ramadan and is used for the fast-breaking celebrations of impoverished individuals and households.

Zakat is calculated annually, usually in a lump sum and often during the month of Ramadan when Muslims, by giving alms and fasting at the same time, can simultaneously fulfill two of the five pillars of Islam. *Zakat* has never been regarded as a tax on wealth. Ideally, it is understood to be an act of individual, voluntary purification to share one's good fortune with those less prosperous. If problems are encountered calculating *zakat*, Muslims consult the Quran, Sunna, and when necessary Islamic law, the Shari‘a. No sharp business practices (*hiyal*) or legal mumbo-jumbo (*hila*) are tolerated.[3] Soon after the death of the Prophet there arose an obvious need to organize the collection of *zakat* and to ensure its distribution to assist the poor and promote Islam. Within a century *zakat* had become institutionalized in most Muslim communities as an integral part of the Islamic state treasury (*bayt al-mal*) from which it was distributed to recipients. Historically, the collection, control, and distribution of *zakat* were the tasks of the Islamic state or the Muslim *ulama* (learned clergy, Islamic scholars). It was obligatory but voluntary almsgiving, and theoretically the only "tax" to be levied on Muslims by an Islamic state. Ostensibly, the Caliph was ultimately responsible "to collect and distribute the *zakat*," but in practice these tasks were delegated to his principal governors or, in those territories that did not recognize the Caliph, to the ruling shaykhs, sultans, or their administrative officials who usually included the *ulama* and Muslim clerics.[4]

Charitable recipients

If *zakat* is required of all Muslims, its recipients are almost as comprehensive because the seven categories of those eligible are very broadly defined: the poor; converts; wayfarers; those in bondage or in debt; those committed to Allah for the spread and triumph of Islam; newcomers whose faith is weak; and new converts to Islam "whose hearts have been [recently] reconciled [to truth]." Moreover, *zakat* may be used to support those who administer it (*amileen*).

Zakat can be given in the path of Allah. By this is meant to finance a Jihad effort in the path of Allah, not [only] for Jihad [but] for other reasons. The fighter (*mujahid*) will be given as salary what will be enough for him. If he needs to buy arms or some supplies related to the war effort, zakat money should be used provided the effort is to raise the banner of Islam.[5]

This explanation is reinforced by the Islamist Khilafah Rashidah, who argued that *zakat* may be spent in "the way of Allah . . . This means spending to facilitate and enhance Jihad. Whenever 'Fi Sabeelilallah' [In the Way of Allah] is mentioned in the Qu'ran it means nothing other than Jihad."[6]

If *zakat* can be used in the path of Allah by *mujahideen*, it also supports Islamic charities and social welfare organizations that address the socioeconomic needs of emerging Muslim societies. Janine A. Clark, a careful observer of Islamic medical clinics in Egypt, the Islamic Center Charity Society in Jordan, and the Islah Women's Charitable Society in Yemen, has examined the structure and dynamics of emerging Islamic institutions and their social and political impact in poor communities. She questions the widespread assumption that such charitable organizations, which benefit both from *zakat* and state financing, primarily serve the poorer classes. In fact, they are managed by and provide substantial assistance to the middle class.[7] Rather than supporting, uplifting, or mobilizing the poor, Islamic charitable institutions with *zakat* monies often play an important role in strengthening the social networks that bind middle-class professionals, volunteers, and clients. Ironically, ties of solidarity that develop along these horizontal lines foster the development of new social networks and the diffusion of new ideas at the expense of impoverished and marginalized Muslims.

Zakat in history

After the death of the Prophet Muhammad his legitimate successors, Abu Bakr, Umar, and Uthman (r. 632–656), were the appropriate collectors of *zakat*. Upon the assassination of the Caliph Uthman in 656, the supporters of Ali ibn Abi Talib (602–661), the cousin of Muhammad, believed that the caliphate should pass only to the rightful descendants of the Prophet. Ali was soon challenged by Mu'awiya ibn Abi Sufyan (c. 602–680), a cousin of Uthman, whose opposition to Ali precipitated the great schism in Islam between Sunni and Shi'ite that remains to this day. When Ali was assassinated in 661, his followers (known as *shi'at*

Ali, the partisans of Ali; hence the terms Shi'ite and Shi'ism), acknowledged the sons of Ali by the Prophet's daughter Fatima, Hasan and
Husayn, to be the rightful heirs. Hasan declined to contest the succession, and Husayn, who agreed to assert his claim to the imamate, was
soon killed by Mu'awiya's Umayyad successor. This provoked opposition
to the Umayyads, the expansion of Shi'ism, and its association with the
descendants of Husayn whom the Shi'ites believed were the only rightful
leaders of the Muslim community, the Imams.

It was during the rule of the sixth Imam, Ja'far al-Sadiq (705–770),
in the mid-eighth century that the rudiments of Shi'a theology were
formed, consisting in the belief that the Imam, presumably a descendant
of Husayn, held the secrets of religious knowledge (*ma'rifa*) and therefore
the supreme authority in all matters of state. The larger Shi'ite group later
recognized that the authority of the imamate passed through twelve successors before the line disappeared. These Shi'ites, known as Twelvers or
Imamis, believe that the last of the twelve Imams will reveal himself as the
leading religious leader (the Mahdi) to reestablish his authority over the
Islamic community and usher in an age of justice and righteousness. The
smaller Shi'ite group, known as Seveners or Isma'ilis, were convinced
that the imamate disappeared with the death of Ja'far's son Isma'il, the
seventh Imam, but that he too will return to establish the virtuous age.

Historically the majority of Muslims, the Sunni, regarded *zakat* as a
special obligation, one of the pillars of Islam, but in reality for them it
soon became just another tax collected by the state. The minority of
Muslims, the Shi'ites, however, do not acknowledge the right of the tem-
poral government to tax and thus regard *zakat* more an act of piety than
an obligation. Whether the Seventh or the Twelfth was the last Imam,
it remained unthinkable to have *zakat*, the very pillar of religious piety,
collected by the state as among Sunni Muslims. The responsibility for the
collection and distribution of *zakat* therefore devolved upon the religious
leaders, the *ulama*, who were the interpreters of the Quran and Hadith
and those judicial scholars who elaborated the principles of Islamic law,
the Shar'ia. As a religious class they regulated Islamic education, trained
teachers, theologians, and officials, and dominated the life of the residential halls of learning, the *madrasas*. As lawyers and judges they regulated Islamic society by matters such as wills, marriage, and trade. It
was no coincidence that all of these profoundly important functions
in the life of the Islamic community were precisely those projects and
pursuits for which *zakat* was intended and logically the *ulama* should
control.

Elsewhere in the Muslim world the collection and distribution of
zakat was undertaken by the state. Anomalies have occurred, such as its

collection during the Ottoman Empire when the collection of tax and *zakat* was farmed out to individuals after they had paid a lump sum to the Ottoman treasury for their franchise. There was much room for corruption in this system, for the collector sought to extract the maximum amount possible. The Prophet or his companions never intended *zakat* to be an onerous imposition, but a reasonable, tolerable, and affordable donation for charitable purposes, rather than a scheme to eliminate poverty or, today, a substitute for a tax based on net income.

Throughout the ages the ambiguities of *zakat* have been discussed and debated by theologians, jurists, and Muslim rulers, but the demands of modernity and the staggering improvement in the means of communication in the latter decades of the twentieth century have transformed the examination of *zakat* from the local and parochial to a subject for debate throughout the greater Muslim world. In the last decade of the twentieth century there were, and there continue to be, a plethora of periodic international Islamic conferences devoted solely to *zakat*, as well as others concerning economics, banking, and charities in which *zakat* is invariably a subject for discussion, particularly the means to modernize its distribution. At the International Conference on Zakat held in Kuala Lumpur in 1990 the participants were unusually candid and admitted that *zakat*, in comparison to secular renewal and welfare programs, had accomplished little to alleviate poverty. In Pakistan some 25,000 inefficient and often corrupt local committees distribute more than six billion rupees from *zakat* to two-and-a-half million impoverished Pakistanis. There has been, however, no diminution of poverty, and the distribution of *zakat* has been unfavorably compared to the programs of private charitable institutions which "have done a much better job of coming to the help of the needy."[8] During the Eighth World Assembly of Muslim Youth (WAMY) held in Amman, Jordan, in October 1998, Crown Prince Hassan bin Talal urged Muslim youth to create an international *zakat* fund to be used in support of refugees, since three-quarters of all the world's refugees are to be found in Muslim countries. At the Fifth International Conference on Zakat held in Kuwait in 1998, *zakat* was not only seen as charity for the poor but as a pool of funds for schemes to employ them. Another concern expressed at the conference were means by which Muslim governments involved in the collection and distribution of *zakat* could work directly with international aid organizations to implement joint programs to benefit the poor and needy. There has also been much concern to improve the cooperation between *zakat* organizations and other Muslim charities working throughout the Muslim world, for despite perennial pleas and proposals there is no single Islamic center devoted solely to the study and research of *zakat*, particularly its distribution and recipients.[9] All of these recommendations led directly to the persistent appeal for an international body to coordinate *zakat* institutions throughout the Muslim world.[10]

Zakat: the Egyptian experience

In recent times the obligatory payment of *zakat* has been implemented by Saudi Arabia in 1951, Pakistan in 1981, and the Sudan since 1982. Elsewhere in the Muslim world Bahrain, Bangladesh, Kuwait, Jordan, and Oman have enacted *zakat* laws and established *zakat* commissions. Nevertheless, the payment of *zakat* still remains voluntary. Several Muslim states have Tax and Zakat Commissions, whose commissioners are usually selected from men known for their honesty and piety, while commission employees are paid by the state.[11] These commissions act as the guardians of *zakat* to see that it is indeed used for charitable purposes and not diverted by the state for purposes never intended – as attempted in Egypt by Gamal Abdel Nasser and his successors. In command of the army and the police, Nasser mobilized the urban masses for his revolutionary schemes of agrarian reform that added millions of the rural *fellahin* to his urban poor supporters in the cities. Social reform to benefit the Egyptian poor required large sums of money, and the Egyptian Ministry of Finance, desperate to tap such a substantial financial resource as *zakat* for social works, sought to take over its collection and distribution because it was a "responsibility of the state, in the framework of its role protecting religion and the earthly policies." This was not just a theological dispute as to who should manage the proceeds of one of the pillars of Islam, but a very practical effort by the state to seize control of E£12 billion (approximately $2.5 billion) annually. With so much money and the concept of *zakat* at stake, the proposal by Egypt's Islamic Economic Center to replace a personal voluntary Islamic obligation by a "tax" from a secular Muslim government was sent to Egypt's supreme religious authority, the Grand Shaykh of Al Azhar. He replied that Islam itself made every Muslim free "to choose the object on which his Zakat will be spent." He reasoned that such a law would be perceived as a tax by many Muslims and would actually "cause people to escape their responsibility of donating their share of the Zakat."[12]

Upon the death of Nasser in 1970 his successor, Anwar Sadat, after eight months maneuvering for power, sought to secure his position as president. He released political and religious prisoners of the Nasser era, returned properties sequestered in the cause of socialism, and in choreographed displays of his own devotion to Islam, tolerated hitherto banned Islamist political groups. Sadat cultivated the Muslim Brothers, commonly known as the Ikhwan (Ar. *ikhwan*, brotherhood), whom Nasser had rigorously suppressed after they attempted his assassination in 1954. Islamist newspapers and cassettes, including lectures and sermons by noted Islamists, were now freely sold to an eager audience, and the Muslim Brothers were let out of jail to support Sadat against the hated former supporters of Nasser. The Ikwan newspaper, *Al-Da'wa*, circulated openly and was perhaps the most popular non-government newspaper. The Muslim Brothers were now free to revive without restrictions their charitable works and in the 1980s began to use *zakat* to finance schools, hospitals, and daycare centers. Their outreach was so powerful that the movement was seen as creating a "parallel social welfare system independent of the state."[13]

In their efforts to consolidate support among the Egyptian masses by a program of social welfare the Muslim Brothers also solicited *sadaqa* from wealthy individuals as well as from Ikhwan in Saudi Arabia, Kuwait, Qatar, and the United Arab Emirates (UAE). In the management of these substantial funds the more militant Ikhwan cells, which Sadat had never embraced in his nascent alliance with the Muslim Brothers, obtained a steady source of revenue. Eventually, Sadat's unilateral peace with Israel, his arrest of most opposition activists, and the failure of his economic program produced a dramatic proliferation of Islamist Ikhwan cells in poor Egyptian neighborhoods. On 6 October 1981 members of one of those cells, al-Jihad, assassinated Anwar Sadat. His successor, Hosni Mubarak, abandoned any thought of making *zakat* a tax and has continued the Egyptian experience of an uneasy balance between the charitable efforts undertaken by the state and those of the Islamic societies. In the Egypt of today, and elsewhere throughout the Muslim world, the payment, collection, and distribution of *zakat* is not fixed in secular or theological cement.

Zakat in the Sudan

In general there has been a scarcity of information regarding *zakat* in precolonial Africa. There were some attempts to introduce a form of taxation based on Islamic law and in accordance with Muslim precepts, but few states adopted any regulated form of religious taxation for any significant period of time. During the Islamic state of the Mahdiya in the Sudan (1885–1898) the Khalifa Abd Allahi introduced and administered a regular system of *zakat* that was abandoned after the British conquest in 1898. A hundred years later, however, the Sudan government, hard pressed for revenue, began the collection of *zakat* as a tax inescapable as death itself. In 1980 a *zakat* fund was legally established. In 1982 the payment was made obligatory for all Sudanese Muslims, and the former Directorate of Taxes became the Chamber of Zakat and Taxes with an official Zakat Board (Diwan al-Zakah). *Zakat* would be paid on salary, professional income, livestock, agricultural products, company earnings, and the sale of personal assets. The funds were then dispersed by the board: 25 percent for the *fuqara*, the poor who do not possess wealth equal to the *nisab*; 25 percent for *masakin*, destitute individuals who must beg for their daily food; 10 percent for employees and administration; 10 percent for converts and debtors; 20 percent for "the way of Allah" (*jihad fi sabeelilli*); and finally 10 percent for wayfarers. The law was rewritten in 1986 and again in 1990 to conform more stringently to the Islamist ideology of the National Islamic Front (NIF) following the coup d'état of Brigadier Omar Hassan Ahmad al-Bashir on 30 June 1989. In 1990 local commissions were created in the eight northern and Muslim-dominated provinces to prepare lists of the needy. A consultation committee of experts in Shari'a rendered "opinions" on the collection and distribution of *zakat*, but its imposition on livestock, supposed to have begun in 1991, was deferred for many years.[14]

In April 2004 the Sudanese of the capital were shocked when the respected President of Ahfad University for Women in Omdurman, Dr. Gasim Badri, was threatened with violence by armed *zakat* police who entered the campus. He was forcefully taken to their waiting car, which was, however, quickly surrounded by his young women students who pelted the police with stones, driving them from the campus. The police promised to return with a larger force to collect *zakat*, but when news of the assault spread through Omdurman and Khartoum, there was widespread indignation and a public outcry the government could not ignore. An official apology was issued, and the Ahfad campus returned to normal, but this crude attempt reminded the Sudanese that in an Islamist state one does not easily avoid the payment of *zakat*.

Sadaqa

Although all Muslims are expected to give *zakat*, individual exemplary Muslims confirm their good fortune, piety, and prestige by giving gifts (*sadaqa*) and larger endowments (*waqf*) for specific causes that are neither expected nor required but given spontaneously in the spirit of Islam to meet the needs of the Muslim community. These voluntary grants (*infaq*) are used to support the favorite charities of the donors and can embrace everything from *jihad* to assisting the poor and feeding the needy. It is assumed that the wealthy, motivated by an "inner feeling of responsibility," will support the congregation of Islam. *Sadaqa* was an individual act and acknowledged throughout the Islamic world as a symbol of piety, generosity, and blessedness – the wealthy merchant, landowner, or official who gives alms to the unfortunate and gifts to the deserving. The *sadaqa* is thus a pious, private, and often secret act given of one's own free will. It is unlike *zakat*, which is expected annually. This spirit of giving does not find its precepts in the Quran or in Shari'a, but in one's heart. From the richest to the poorest Muslim, it is an act of personal devotion and unlike *zakat* is not bound by a percentage of one's wealth.

Throughout the Muslim world, either where a Muslim ruled or where the Islamic community was small or isolated among non-Muslim societies, it was the tradition for the imam (leader of the daily prayer) of the local Muslim community to call for voluntary donations for a variety of causes. In many Muslim states where the administration and distribution of charitable donations were decentralized *sadaqa* rather than *zakat* became the principal source of Muslim charity. In Canada and the USA where the tithe, regardless of whether it be Christian or Muslim, is regarded as a tax rather than a benefice, "the voluntary distribution of alms, sadaqa, was preferred to the institutionalized almsgiving, namely zakat."[15] Private donations of *sadaqa* provided an essential means by which mosques and their outreach programs in support of Muslim communities were able to survive in North America.

Waqf

In Islam, as in Christianity, when a person dies he or she can specifically provide for "ongoing charity" in the same manner that property is left to heirs. Muslim jurists have defined "ongoing charity" to encompass endowments known as *waqf* (pl. *awqaf*), meaning in Islam to hold, confine, and preserve certain property in perpetuity for religious or philanthropic purposes or the alleviation of poverty as specified by the donor. The *waqf*, whether *waqf khayr* (charitable trust) or the *waqf ahl* (family endowment), was the direct result of pious Muslims voluntarily and privately seeking to convert personal assets to serve the public welfare or Islam. The most notable *waqf khayr* is the Islamic Cultural Foundation established by King Faisal shortly before his death to support the Islamic Center in Geneva and thus the spread of Islam in Europe. *Waqf* applies to non-perishable property that cannot be consumed, such as land, buildings, books, or stocks, and it thus forms the third leg of the Islamic charitable triad with *zakat* and *sadaqa*. There are generally three kinds of *waqf*: the religious *waqf* to build and support mosques; the more philanthropic *waqf* to support the interests of the people, such as libraries, education, health service, parks, and roads; and the *waqf* that specifically grants the revenue from an endowment to the poor. The first two *awqaf* were established at the time of the Prophet; the third from his second Caliph, Umar ibn al-Khattab (r. 635–644). The first religious *waqf* was for the construction and support of the mosque of Quba' in Medina in 622. It established the historical principle that a *waqf* should be used for the building and maintenance of mosques. The philanthropic *waqf* was also the initiative of the Prophet when a Muslim called Mukhairiq died in 626, leaving his seven orchards to Muhammad, who made them a *waqf* for the benefit of the poor. Since that time the philanthropic *waqf* has come to embrace a wide range of educational and social activities, not simply the needy. The third kind of *waqf* was established by the Caliph Umar solely to assist the destitute.

Some Muslim jurists have argued that Allah is the real recipient of a *waqf*, but in law and practice the owners are the beneficiaries, although they are not permitted to dispose of the property or use it in any way that deviates from the expressed wishes of the donor. This means that once property is designated a *waqf*, it remains a *waqf* forever. After a lengthy legal process it may be exchanged for a property of equal value, but that is uncommon since those who establish a *waqf* usually provide detailed documentation as to how it is to be used. Such instructions have been supported by Islamic courts for hundreds of years. The combination of the donor strictly specifying the use of the *waqf* and the judgments and precedents from Islamic courts has established the principle of perpetuity in a *waqf*. Any revenues from a *waqf* must be used for the objective stipulated by its founder. If, for whatever reason, the specific purpose is no longer feasible the revenues from the endowment go to the poor and needy. Throughout the centuries most *awqaf* consisted of real estate given by donors, who must be legally of sound mind and body, making a sincere act of charity.

In principle the founder designates how the *waqf* is to be administered and usually appoints an individual known as the *mutawalli* who is responsible for managing the *waqf* in the best interests of the beneficiaries. His or her first duty is to preserve the property; the second duty is to maximize the revenues for the beneficiaries. In return the founder normally decides the compensation for the *mutawalli*, but if by chance this has not been determined the *mutawalli* either volunteers his services or seeks compensation from the courts that are legally responsible for all matters or disputes concerning a *waqf*. As in *zakat*, the Egyptian example is instructive. In the eighth century a judge in Egypt established a special office to record *awqaf* and render judgment in any disputes. In time this office was placed under the overall supervision of the supreme judge. The administration of *awqaf* has also been institutionalized in Pakistan, Sudan, and Turkey and within the minority communities of

India, Kenya, and Uganda, but the "idea is not widely accepted by the rest of the Muslim World."[16] During the 1980s and 1990s an increasing number of *waqf* bequests were managed by one of the Islamic banks such as the powerful Islamic Development Bank Group of Saudi Arabia founded in 1973 to foster economic development and social progress.

The long history of the *waqf*, fourteen centuries after the death of the Prophet, and the permanent nature and management of the institution has resulted in the accumulation of a huge amount of property throughout the Muslim world devoted to religious and philanthropic purposes. In the nineteenth century *waqf* represented one-quarter of all the land under cultivation in Egypt and about one-third in Turkey. In Palestine the number of *awqaf* deeds recorded up to the middle of the sixteenth century was 233, containing 890 properties, in comparison with only 92 deeds of private ownership to 108 parcels of land.[17] Historically, the most frequent purpose of a *waqf* was for mosques, their construction, maintenance, and personnel. This would include salaries for the imam, the prayer leader and preacher of the mosque, and teachers of Islamic studies associated with it. This endowment has had a significant impact on Islamic societies; it has enabled the religious leaders and teachers, secured by a permanent source of income, to advocate social and political positions independent of and often in opposition to the ruling class. Education not specific to the mosque was the second-largest beneficiary from *waqf*. It was a common custom for the government to construct a school to which a *waqf*, either given directly by an individual or assigned by the state, would endow its maintenance, teacher and staff salaries, student stipends, libraries, and books. The *awqaf* of the Ayyubids (1171–1250) and Mamluks (1250–1517) for schools in Egypt are a good example. In 1900 Jerusalem had sixty-four non-religious schools supported by *waqf* properties in Palestine, Syria, and Turkey. Perhaps the most dramatic example is the famous Islamic university, Al Azhar, founded in Cairo in 972. It was funded by *waqf* revenues until Muhammad Ali seized control of the Egyptian *awqaf* in 1812. The use of *awqaf* for financial assistance to students has also had a long and critical impact not unlike that of financial support for religious leaders, for historically *waqf* has created a learned elite quite distinct from the rich and ruling class. Many of these Muslim scholars and teachers came from poor and even slave origins, and often strongly opposed the policies and practices of their rulers.

The third-largest beneficiaries of *waqf* were the poor, needy, orphans, and other marginalized peoples in Muslim society. Health services were particularly popular, and *awqaf* provided funds for construction, salaries for physicians and staff, and indigent patients. The famous Shishli Children's Hospital in Istanbul founded in 1898 is a well-known example.

Waqf was also given to support animals, such as cats and unwanted horses. Other donors specified that their *awqaf* should help the indigent finance their pilgrimage to Mecca, the marriage of young women, and a host of other philanthropic purposes that were special to the donor.

During the colonial period of the nineteenth and twentieth centuries the traditional management of *awqaf* remained undisturbed except in Algeria and Indonesia, but the introduction by all the colonial authorities of a western system of education with its secular emphasis on science and technology opened a cornucopia of economic opportunities that began to undermine, relentlessly and often unintentionally, traditional religious education already funded by *awqaf*. Independence by Muslim nation states from colonial rule, which was frequently accompanied by appeals to socialism, also transformed the long-standing relationship between *awqaf* and the state. Many *waqf* properties were simply confiscated by the state in Algeria, Egypt, Syria, Turkey, and Tunisia to be redistributed in programs of land reform. Other revenues from *awqaf* were used for government economic and social programs. In return the state now assumed the financial responsibility for mosques, religious schools, and Islamic universities.

Although some countries have recently sought to revive the customary *waqf* by new laws to recover former *waqf* properties confiscated by the state and to encourage individuals to create new *awqaf*, the dislocation of *waqf* management and the creation of large sums now distributed to porous charitable organizations has seriously diluted if not destroyed the principle of permanence in favor of grants to agencies whose lax accountability any older, traditional *waqf* donor would denounce with scorn. There is no question that *awqaf* have been channeled through Islamic charitable organizations to support the *mujahideen* and their various jihadist movements. In 1997 Trueco, a Swiss investment firm, was asked to create a *waqf* to support construction of hospitals and schools for the Taliban militia and its supporters in Afghanistan. Trueco could find nothing in the request that would violate Swiss or Saudi law, but under heavy pressure from the Clinton administration, which possessed "evidence" that Saudi trusts had been used to fund terrorist groups, it refused to become involved.[18] Despite this success, the Clinton administration in fact failed to convince the Saudi government to regulate the establishment of *awqaf* more rigorously. Saudi officials were aware that funds from charitable trusts did make their way to terrorist groups, but remained in a quandary as to how to redirect such funds legally protected by the Shari'a.

An example of how a *waqf* can be vulnerable for use to support terrorists was the one created by the Saudi shipping magnate, Abdul Latif Jameel, who left a fortune estimated at $7 billion upon his death in 1993 to fund the charitable aims of militant fundamentalist movements in Algeria, Sudan, Somalia, and in the West Bank and the Gaza Strip. Saudi officials had previously been unable and unwilling to interfere in the distribution of the estate of this respected family until 1992 when, following the Persian Gulf war, King Fahd instituted reforms to control *waqf* donations. The royal family could no longer ignore the danger to themselves when in the guise of Islamic charity *awqaf* were used to finance terrorism. The new Minister of Pilgrimage Affairs, responsible for the provision of facilities for the visits of pilgrims to the Holy Cities of Mecca and Medina, was now placed in charge of all maintenance for mosques throughout the kingdom; thereafter, the administration of land held by religious trusts, the *awqaf*, including the bequest from Abdul Latif Jameel, was monitored by a commission responsible for excluding objectionable groups seeking funds.

Saudi Arabia and Islamic education

The greatest challenge to traditional Islamic education, historically supported by *zakat* and *waqf*, has been the introduction of western secular and scientific education during the late nineteenth and twentieth centuries. The proliferation of government schools whose curricula introduced the sciences and social sciences, in contrast to the *madrasa*s, which emphasized the recitation and interpretation of the Quran and Islamic legal studies, would challenge traditional Islamic education and increasingly isolate Muslim clerics from an ever more secular Muslim society. In reaction, there was a revival of Islam in education during the last two decades of the twentieth century that has strengthened traditional Islamic education promoted by Saudi Arabia. In Saudi Arabia Islam is the cornerstone of all education and the government controls all aspects of the educational system. Committees in the Ministry of Education supervise everything from the curriculum to textbooks, students, and teachers. Saudi Arabia is also the most determined of Muslim nations to disseminate Islamic education, spending billions of dollars "to spread Islam to every corner of the earth."[19] From the most humble *madrasa* in Tajikistan to the first university inaugurated on the island of Zanzibar in 1998, the Saudi government and individual wealthy Saudi notables through organizations such as the Darul-Iman Charitable Association contribute lavishly to Islamic education throughout the Muslim world.

Saudi influence has been pervasive in creating schools, curricula, and textbooks influenced by the teachings of Shaykh Muhammad ibn Abd al-Wahhab (1703–1792) that instruct Muslims to return to the fundamentals of Islam as preached by the Prophet Muhammad. The Higher Committee for Educational Policy of Saudi Arabia insists that the most important aspect of education is to inculcate students with Islamic values that enable the individual to spread the Muslim faith. Saudi students in Saudi Arabia or abroad are expected to accept the mission to propagate Islam worldwide. The Saudi Cultural Mission to the United States has for years distributed *Education in Saudi Arabia*, a book approved and published by the Saudi Higher Committee for Educational Policy that embraces 236 principles to promote Islamic thought and denounces any theology or political philosophy that contradicts Islamic law. When it became clear after 9/11 that former Saudi students were highly committed believers in these principles, the Saudi Minister of the Interior, Prince Naif bin Abd al-Aziz, in defense of Saudi education refused to make any changes in the curriculum. "We do believe in the soundness of our educational curriculum, but we never oppose development of educational methods in a manner that does not run counter to the country's deep-rooted principles . . . We strongly believe in the correctness of our education system and its objectives. We don't change our systems on the demands of others."[20]

The Saudi Minister of the Interior was not the only Muslim to be placed on the defensive in the aftermath of 9/11. When the Sixth International Conference on Zakat was held in 2003, only thirty-eight participants, from fifteen nations, convened in Doha, Qatar. Their discussions were preoccupied with evidence collected in the West in the aftermath of 9/11 which indicated that Muslim charitable institutions, knowingly or unknowingly, were being used to support militant Islamist activities with funds from *zakat*. There were vehement denials that any links between *zakat* and the revolutionary Islamists existed. Many at the conference condemned the USA for unfairly implicating one of the most cherished institutions of Islam in terrorist practices. The radical Egyptian cleric and scholar Dr. Shaykh Yousuf al-Qaradawi, then teaching at the University of Qatar, was the most vociferous in his opposition to claims that *zakat* funded terrorism, and as the head of the European Council for Fatwa and Research, labeled all such prescriptions as "calumnies . . . Charity has everything to do with feeding the hungry and serving the community. Those who make such accusations do not understand that we pursue noble goals required by our religion."[21] In the end the conference completely rejected any allegations that *zakat* had been employed in support of terrorism.

In fact, the investigation of Islamic charities located in Falls Church and Herndon, Virginia, demonstrated that al-Qaradawi was one of the largest shareholders and a board member of Al Taqwa (Fear of God), a Swiss/Bahamian-based financial network whose administrators "have been slapped with terrorist designations by both the United States and United Nations" for support of Al Qaeda.[22] As the lists grow longer, it is not surprising that Islamic charity, the spirit of *zakat*, has been challenged.

> When a man gives Zakah to the poor he cannot stipulate the conditions
> on how the poor man should spend the money. If he spends on some
> evil acts it is not the responsibility of the donor.
>
> Prince Salman bin Abd al-Aziz, Governor of Riyadh Region,
> 8 November 2002[1]

It was the third night of Ramadan, October 2001, and the smell of winter
was in the air. Sayf-al-Adl al-Masri, the Al Qaeda chief of operations
in Kandahar, Afghanistan, awoke just past midnight. The Egyptian was
"feeling anxious and [I] sensed there was a danger close to me." The war
against the Taliban government of Afghanistan had erupted on 7 October,
and he was expecting an attack. He awoke his Al Qaeda brothers who were
asleep in his empty house some distance away and together they heard
the sound of a major explosion. Al-Masri would later write: "I asked the
brothers by telephone and learned that the second house of the Al-Wafa
Charity Foundation in Kandahar had been pinpointed and hit with a
cruise missile." The CIA had been tracking Al Qaeda by their use of
satellite phones and had determined that the Al Wafa house was an Al
Qaeda operations center. The missile destroyed the house and killed a
number of jihadists.[2]

The destruction of the headquarters of the Saudi Al Wafa Humanitarian Foundation (Wafa al-Igatha al-Islamiyya) in Afghanistan went largely
unnoticed in the western media, for the target of this expensive cruise missile was the ramshackle office of an unknown Saudi charity. Al Wafa may
have been little known outside Saudi Arabia, but given the importance of
charitable giving in the Muslim world and the widespread funding support for Islamic charities, it was worth much more than a fleeting notice
in the European and US press.

Charities and charitable donations in Saudi Arabia

In 1979 Saudi Arabia was confronted by new challenges from abroad
and at home. In January the Shah of Iran fled into exile, and the

triumphal return of the charismatic Ayatollah Khomeini on 1 February confirmed the success of the clerical revolution and the declaration of the Islamic Republic of Iran in April. The Shi'ite clerical establishment regarded their seizure of the government of Iran, however, as only the beginning of the revival of Islam throughout the Muslim world under the aegis of Shi'ism, which defiantly challenged the comfortable role of Saudi Arabia as the guardian of the Holy Cities and the heartland of Sunni Islam. Moreover, the revival of Islam could not be left solely in the hands of the Shi'ites of Iran, for the Sunni Wahhabis of Saudi Arabia theologically and historically despised them. At home, and presumably inspired by the Iranian Revolution, a group of Saudi Sunni Mahdists seized the Great Mosque of Mecca during the *hajj* pilgrimage to Mecca in November 1979. Forcibly expelled, they were described as Islamist fanatics. They appeared, however, to be a network with a political as well as an Islamist agenda dedicated to overthrowing the monarchy. These two events shook the somnolent Saudis. Security was strengthened, and Saudi Arabia began to use its vast oil revenues to insure Saudi leadership in the resurgence and spread of Islam. The principal means to accomplish the latter objective was to increase financial support for Islamic – particularly Saudi Islamic – charities. At first the recipients were mainly in Muslim countries, but by the 1980s Saudi funds were spent to support Muslim communities in non-Islamic nations, particularly in Europe and the USA.

The funds for Saudi Islamic charitable institutions were derived from oil. Literally billions of dollars were distributed for humanitarian purposes by individual donors, government ministries, and the royal family. Wealthy individual Saudis – businessmen, merchants, professionals – would support their favorite charities by performing *sadaqa*. During the last two decades of the twentieth century *sadaqa* became an increasingly important source of charitable giving, but the very privacy that accompanies it makes elusive any reckoning of the amount of those donations. Government ministries were somewhat more transparent, and of the nineteen ministries that manage the government of Saudi Arabia, eight are involved, directly or indirectly, in charitable giving: the Ministries of Finance (especially its Directorate General of Zakat and Income Tax), Education, Foreign Affairs, Health, Higher Education, Information, Pilgrimage, and the Ministry of Islamic Endowments and Guidance Affairs. The interest of these ministries in Islamic charities has grown proportionately with the number of important international charities founded in Saudi Arabia after 1979, and the most conspicuous supporter of Islamic charities was the Saudi royal family (see table 2.1).

Table 2.1 *The Saudi royal family and its charitable interests*

King Fahd bin Abd al-Aziz al-Saud	Custodian of the Two Holy Mosques
Crown Prince [now King] Abdullah bin Abd al-Aziz	Prince Abdullah Abdul Aziz Parental Foundation for Housing Development
Prince Sultan Abd al-Aziz	Prince Sultan Foundation for Humanitarian Services; Minister of Defense, Second Deputy Prime Minister; founder (1995), Prince Sultan Humanitarian Society; Regulator, Al Haramain Foundation; member, Special Committee for Relief; Chairman, Supreme Council of Islamic Affairs
Prince Salman bin Abd al-Aziz	Governor of Riyadh region; son of Abd al-Aziz bin Saud; directs activity of IIRO charity; founder (1993), Saudi High Commission for Relief; Chairman, Saudi High Commission for the Collection of Donations/Bosnia
Prince Abdullah bin Khalid	Chairman of the board of trustees of King Khalid Charitable Foundation. Established 2001, directors include family of the late King Khalid
Prince Abdullah bin Abd al-Muhsin al-Turki	Director, Ministry of Islamic Endowments, Dawaa, and Guidance Affairs
Prince Faisal bin Khalid bin Abd al-Aziz	Deputy Chairman, board of trustees, King Khalid Charitable Foundation
Prince Bandar bin Saud bin Khalid Abd al-Rahman	King Faisal Foundation
Prince Saud bin Abd al-Muhsin	Acting Governor of Makkah; acting chairman of Sanabel Al-Khair charity
Prince Bandar bin Sultan	Son of Prince Sultan, and Ambassador to the United States; Saudi National Commission for Relief and Charity Work Abroad
Prince Talal bin Abd al-Aziz al-Saud	Secretary-General, Muslim World League; Secretary General, International Islamic Relief Organization; Arab Network for Non-Governmental Organizations
Prince Turki al-Faisal bin Abd al-Aziz al-Saud	Saudi Ambassador to the United Kingdom; King Faisal Foundation
Prince Naif bin Abd al-Aziz al-Saud	Minister of Interior; Saudi Committee for Support of the Al Quds Intifada; supervisor, Saudi Joint Relief Committee for Kosovo and Chechnya
Prince Alwaleed bin Talal	nephew of King Fahd and Crown Prince Abdullah; numerous education bequests supporting American University of Beirut, American University in Cairo, and various universities in the United States of America

Since 1953 the Kingdom of Saudi Arabia has been ruled by Kings Saud
(r. 1953–1964), Faisal (r. 1964–1975), Khalid (r. 1975–1982), Fahd
(r. 1982–2005), and Abdullah bin Abdul Aziz (2005–). In each case the
most powerful members of the House of Saud have been celebrated for
their support of various charitable organizations. The King is the "Custodian of the Two Holy Mosques" and assumes all the responsibilities for
charitable giving that title demands. King, Crown Prince, and princes
have taken their responsibility to spread Islam throughout the world very
seriously. Many billions of dollars were spent by King Fahd alone on
some 210 Islamic centers; he supported more than 1,500 mosques and
202 colleges, and almost 2,000 schools for educating Muslim children in
non-Islamic countries in Europe, North and South America, Australia,
and Asia. All were to propagate the Wahhabi doctrine with great vigor.
The most powerful members of the House of Saud followed the King's
example, giving generously of their time and money to establish schools
in seventeen countries in the West, eight nations in the Middle East and
South Asia, and in thirteen states in Africa.[3]

The Soviet invasion of Afghanistan in 1979 had a much greater impact
in the Middle East, particularly Saudi Arabia, than the West appreciated.
During the 1980s both private and public Saudi money played a critical
role in supporting the Afghan resistance to Soviet military occupation.
Indeed, Saudi princes and wealthy businessmen were extraordinarily generous in funding various Afghan-Arab movements fighting the Russians,
and many *mujahideen* were Saudi citizens, often from influential families.
Sometimes funds were directly solicited; others were given independently
as *sadaqa*, but a more efficacious means to help the Afghan resistance was
to give through Islamic charities. The established pattern of donations
through the traditional charities was widely accepted, but the distinction between supporting *jihad* to promote the revival of Islam and, later,
sustaining terrorism, became hopelessly blurred. There were, of course,
many legitimate Islamic charities, but there were also those whose objectives and methods were obscure, dubious, and not very humanitarian. In
time the distinction between freedom fighter and terrorist was difficult to
establish. Dr. Anthony Cordesman, certainly no enemy of Saudi Arabia
or its ruling family, has written that senior Saudis privately admitted that
"the Saudi Ministry of the Interior, Saudi Foreign Ministry, and Saudi
intelligence" all failed to comprehend the illegitimate activity undertaken
by many "'Islamic' causes that have received Saudi money."[4]

At the time of the Soviet withdrawal from Afghanistan in 1989 the pattern of giving through Islamic charities to promote the spread of Islam
by resistance movements had been firmly established. It simply continued to flow with unrestricted generosity. This development did not go

unnoticed by the Saudi government, but like western governments it was loath to intervene in the historic and honored tradition of giving to religious charities, particularly when the government was firmly committed to the spread of its Wahhabi ideology. Moreover, the Saudis regarded themselves as the guardians of Islam and were not about to appear less fervent in their support of the Islamic revival than their Shi'ite rivals in Tehran. This head-in-the-sand policy could not, however, be sustained, particularly after the bombing of the World Trade Center in New York in 1993. Under pressure from Egypt and Pakistan, Saudi Arabia had terminated its support for camps controlled by Islamists on the Afghan–Pakistan frontier in 1992, and after the bombing of the World Trade Center a new law was promulgated that gave the Saudi government regulatory authority over funds being raised by Islamic charities. The Saudis were told that their donations would be monitored, and a "set of rules was established to allow the government to be able to trace whatever was going [out]."[5] In 1994 a Supreme Council of Islamic Affairs was created to supervise the distribution of charitable aid, but its management was ineffectual.

Despite some efforts on the part of the Ministry of the Interior, which was responsible for monitoring and enforcing these regulations, it was unable or reluctant to stem the flow of funds to groups that used Islam for their own political rather than charitable purposes. The greatest difficulty was to distinguish between those Islamic charities solely committed to humanitarian relief and those determined to use the institution of Islamic charities to achieve political objectives by appeals to extreme interpretations of *jihad*, terrorism. The end of the Afghan war suddenly released a horde of fanatical *mujahideen* who found the means to continue their jihadist mission as employees in Saudi charities involved in the Balkan wars. By design or default the Saudi Arabian government did little to staunch the flow of riyals and rifles through Muslim charities to the Afghan-Arabs who dominated *mujahideen* activity in much of Bosnia. It would be years before those concerned with counter-terrorism discovered that *mujahideen* financial networks required relentless scrutiny; the Saudi government announced in 2002:

Probably the most significant new action we have taken has been in the area of charitable giving . . . In the past, we may have been naive in our giving and did not have adequate controls over all of our donations. As a consequence, some may have taken advantage of our charity and generosity. With the new steps we are taking, this is now changing.[6]

It was undeniable that for more than two decades funds obtained for charitable purposes and used by reputable international organizations had occasionally been used to support and arm jihadist movements.

Saudi Arabia Red Crescent Society

In June 1859 at the Battle of Solferino, involving French and Austrian armies in northern Italy, a Swiss humanitarian, Jean Henri Dunant (1828–1910), organized first aid for the many thousands of soldiers from both sides who were seriously wounded. He later proposed in his book *Un Souvenir de Solferino,* published in 1862, the formation of voluntary relief societies to care equally for the wounded in war from both sides. Two years later the Red Cross was founded in Geneva and legitimized by the Geneva Convention of 1864. Thereafter, the Red Cross gradually expanded its mission to assist those engaged in naval warfare, prisoners of war, and civilians caught up in the destruction of war. During the twentieth century its mandate became more sweeping to include the prevention and relief of human suffering. From the beginning the Red Cross has been a coalition of national affiliates in which the appellation "Red Cross" was used by Christian countries. After 1906, at the insistence of the Ottoman Empire, the societies in Muslim countries were entitled the "Red Crescent." The organization's official name was changed in 1986 to the International Movement of the Red Cross and Red Crescent with its headquarters in Geneva and a worldwide structure of the International Committee of the Red Cross and the League of Red Cross and Red Crescent Societies. The Saudi Arabia Red Crescent Society (SARCS) is an important member of the 181 country societies of Red Cross and Red Crescent.

Founded in 1933, SARCS has fourteen offices in the kingdom and over 3,000 paid salaried staff members, nearly all of whom are trained in the provision of emergency medical services and disaster preparedness. Its management of the kingdom's ambulance service has been widely praised, and its rapid response to the numerous crises, large and small, that accompany the annual pilgrimage and its seventy *hajj* health clinics has won the gratitude of pilgrims. The official SARCS budget for 2002 was a little more than $10 million, but budgets in Saudi Arabia are frequently disguised, and in reality its revenues were SR249 million ($66 million) for that year. The disparity is attributed to the "many private donors in Saudi Arabia [who] give funds for international relief missions" that do not appear in the official budget. Since 1980 SARCS has been active in Afghanistan, Chechnya, Kosovo, Pakistan, and Palestine; and its contributions in food, medicine, clothing, and shelter for Muslim countries have exceeded a billion Swiss francs ($600 million).[7]

SARCS was one of the first charitable organizations to provide humanitarian assistance for *mujahideen* wounded in the war in Afghanistan, and it soon became deeply committed to assist the growing Afghan refugee population in Pakistan. It worked in the Kachagari refugee camp for more than twenty years where it supported the Palestinian Dr. Abdullah Yusuf Azzam (1941–1989), the "Godfather" of the Afghan *jihad,* who arrived in Peshawar to fight the Soviets for Islam. He soon became the most prominent Islamist in the Afghan *jihad* and its principal promoter, whose famous axiom attracted Muslims from everywhere to become *mujahideen* in the Islamist *jihad: Jihad and the rifle alone: no negotiations, no conferences, and no dialogues.* In 1984 he created the Maktab al-Khadamat al-Mujahidin al-Arab (Mujahideen Services Bureau, MAK) to assist the Afghan *jihad,* and built a global network to recruit Arab *mujahideen.* It became the foundation for Al Qaeda, which began when, in the guest-houses of MAK, volunteers pouring into Pakistan were trained to fight for the *jihad* in Afghanistan. He would write in his *Journey of Maktab Khadamat al-Mujahidin* that the "Islamic foundations" provided support for MAK and its *mujahideen,* including everything from food to arms to ink for his magazine, *Al Jihad.*[8]

Azzam and MAK obtained private donations from Saudi princes, mosques, and substantial sums from the Saudi intelligence service, but also received steady and generous amounts of money from numerous Islamic charities, particularly SARCS and the Muslim World League (MWL).[9] SARCS played an especially important role. A skeptic once questioned Azzam regarding the smuggling of heavy equipment into the war zone, arguing that it would provide easy targets for Soviet aircraft. Azzam responded: "If that happens we shall ask God's pardon, and if not, we shall do our work. We got them into the country in the name of the Mujahidin via the Saudi Red Crescent."[10] Thanks to the generosity of the Saudis and the Central Intelligence Agency (CIA) the cornucopia of cash that overflowed to support the Afghan-Arabs seemed inexhaustible.

A founding member of Egyptian Islamic Jihad (EIJ), Ayman Muhammad Rabie al-Zawahiri, joined the Saudi Red Crescent operation in Peshawar in 1985 and Wael Hamza Julaidan, a close associate of Osama bin Laden and known in Al Qaeda as Abu Hasan al-Madani, left King Abdul Aziz University in Saudi Arabia to be director of both SARCS and the South Relief Agency in Peshawar. He and the other Islamic leaders were avid and successful fundraisers. Just before his death in 1989 Dr. Azzam remarked that his organization had never lacked for funds because "the Saudi Red Crescent and the South Relief Agency headed by [Saudi Prince] Salman Abdel Aziz [had] a budget of 100 million riyals [$27 million] per year."[11] Inventories of weapons and notes from Bin Laden to Julaidan describing "an extreme need for weapons" were found on SARCS stationery, and in a 1999 interview with Al Jazeera television Osama bin Laden personally recognized the importance of Wael Julaidan and obliquely the role of SARCS.[12]

The support of SARCS for *mujahideen* operating abroad was not limited to the war in Afghanistan. When Mansur al-Suwaylim, brother of
the deceased Chechen Jihad leader Samir Salih Abdallah al-Suwaylim
(Abu Khattab), joined the Afghan-Arabs in 1987, he was carrying two
documents. One "was from the director of the Mujahidin Service Office
in Al-Dammam, and the second from a person who had a special status
with the official in charge of the Saudi Red Crescent in Pakistan."[13] By
1993 SARCS was active in the Balkans, as was the Saudi High Relief
Commission (SHRC), which was also providing humanitarian relief in
Bosnia. More than a decade after the Soviet army left Afghanistan some
eighty-nine Muslim relief workers with reported links to Al Qaeda were
expelled by the Pakistan government, including a number who were
SARCS employees.[14] Later, two Red Crescent administrators, also members of Al Qaeda, were arrested in 2001 for planning terrorist attacks
against the US and British embassies in Sarajevo, Bosnia. The impeccable history of altruism by the International Movement of the Red Cross
and the Red Crescent was compromised by the activities of SARCS in the
mujahideen wars in Afghanistan and Chechnya, but in the Middle East
and North Africa Conference of Red Cross and Red Crescent societies
its volunteers have vehemently and sincerely asserted that their objectives
were strictly humanitarian.

Muslim World League

The Muslim World League (Rabitat al-Alami al-Islamiyya, MWL) was
founded in 1962. Among its founders was Said Ramadan, grandson
and spiritual heir of Hasan al-Banna, the father of the Muslim Brotherhood. Following his forced departure from Egypt in 1954, Ramadan
had founded the powerful Geneva Islamic Center. By 1970 the MWL
had become one of the three most powerful charities established in Saudi
Arabia. The league claims to be a non-government charitable organization committed to the propagation of the faith through the tenets of
Wahhabi Islam. The 1960s and 1970s were decades of ferment in the
Islamic world as well as in the West. There was growing concern among
the faithful over the widening gap between the secular and Islamic worlds
and the challenge to Islam from the culture of the West. They demanded
a more modern and aggressive organization to promote Islam than the
clerical and often divided *ulama* who were the historical guardians and
interpreters of Islamic theological and legal thought. There were hundreds of Ikhwan who had fled from Egypt to become residents in Saudi
Arabia, and they were adroit at accommodating their own radical and
Salafist ideology to traditional Wahhabism. Thus, the Muslim Brothers

possessed a profound influence on Saudi students and charities. The subsequent export of Islamist theology from Saudi Arabia to the Muslim world was in many instances the work of Ikhwan preachers and clerics, Saudi and non-Saudi, financed by Saudi charities who were the beneficiaries of the massive influx of petrodollars. At the outbreak of the Arab–Israeli war of 1973, Saudi Arabia continued to be the predominant member of the Organization of Petroleum Exporting Countries (OPEC), founded in September 1960. The dramatic increase in the price of oil produced a seemingly unlimited amount of cash for the Saudi royal family as well as for many new wealthy Saudis that enabled them to fulfill their Islamic obligations by their greater ability to contribute to Islamic charities of which the MWL was a principal beneficiary.

Although a considerable portion of funding for MWL now comes from contributions by wealthy businessmen and *zakat*, the Saudi royal family remains the most substantial and steady donor both as private individuals and as representatives of the Saudi government. In March 1997 the Secretary-General, Dr. Abdullah al-Obaid, who was later appointed President of the first Saudi Arabia National Human Rights Association, thanked King Fahd for his continued support of the MWL, "noting that the Saudi government had officially provided more than $1.33 billion in financial aid to MWL since its founding in 1962."[15] It was, therefore, very difficult to maintain the façade that MWL was a non-government organization as conceived in the West when in fact it is an agency of the Saudi government. Unlike the Red Crescent Society and other large international charities, MWL was ineluctably parochial, linked solidly to the Saudi government and dependent on its royal patronage. The current Secretary-General of MWL, Prince Abdullah bin Abd al-Muhsin al-Turki, is also the Minister of Islamic Affairs, Endowment Call and Guidance and has worked assiduously to promote Islam beyond the Middle East. In July 2002 at the Council of American–Islamic Relations (CAIR) he urged the coordination of Muslim organizations operating in the USA and offered MWL assistance in promoting their Islamic work. After 9/11 Prince Abdullah has consistently denounced terrorists, both officially and unofficially, and has been very careful to disassociate MWL from terrorism despite its past support for Afghan-Arabs in *jihad* movements in North Africa, the Middle East, and the Balkans.

After its founding in 1962 MWL did little to foster Islamist movements until the war in Afghanistan. Afterward, not unlike SARCS, it began to support the recruitment of *mujahideen* and the movement of the materials of war under the guise of humanitarian assistance. The Palestinian Dr. Abdullah Azzam was appointed director of the MWL office in Peshawar where he was soon joined by Osama bin Laden, his former student at the King Abdul Aziz University in Jidda. With funding from MWL Dr. Azzam laid the foundations for what was to become MAK, the nexus for the movement of jihadists from the Muslim world to the war in Afghanistan. Following the assassination of Azzam in 1989, he was succeeded by Wael Julaidan, then head of the Red Crescent in Pakistan, as director of the Peshawar branch of MWL.[16]

International Islamic Relief Organization

Among the most important Saudi charitable organizations is the International Islamic Relief Organization (IIRO, also known as the Islamic Relief Organization, the International Relief Organization, and the Success Foundation), established during the 22nd Session of the MWL held in Mecca in 1975 as its humanitarian non-government organization (NGO), and endorsed by the Saudi royal family shortly thereafter. Its credo was "Provide relief and aid to Muslims as peoples and groups wherever they are, should they face disasters endangering their being, their religious beliefs or their freedom." For years, *zakat* and *sadaqa* were collected by the Al Rajhi Banking and Investment Corporation, for the MWL account number 77700.

Not unlike SARCS, the IIRO mission was to provide assistance to victims of war and natural disasters. However, there was a growing realization that 80 percent of the world's refugees were Muslims, and IIRO soon sought to help them by funding economic development projects, financial and management assistance to small commercial firms, and direct payments to the poor, widows, and orphans. Not surprisingly, as an appendage of MWL the humanitarian mission of IIRO included the protection of Muslim minorities and the sponsoring of programs for teaching and memorizing the Quran. With its headquarters in Jidda, IIRO has over a hundred offices worldwide with most in Africa (thirty-six) and Asia (twenty-four). The remaining thirty offices are equally divided between Europe and South and North America.

IIRO is structured into a variety of departments – Urgent Relief and Refugees, Health Care, Orphans and Social Welfare, Education, and Agriculture – but its central mission is devoted to relief and refugee assistance where it has concentrated its efforts on medical, educational, and religious needs. This worldwide network is funded by charitable donations, including those in fulfillment of *zakat* obligations and gifts from members of the Saudi royal family, which are deposited in the Al Rajhi Banking and Investment Corporation in Riyadh. The funds for its operations outside Saudi Arabia are managed by the Islamic Affairs Department of the embassy of Saudi Arabia in each country.[17] In 1987 IIRO established the Sanabel al-Khair (Seeds of Charity) with its headquarters in Riyadh to provide IIRO with a stable income by investing some of its charitable contributions as an endowment. This ambitious plan was to fund international operations, provide financial stability, and make IIRO self-sufficient. Called Sana-Bell in the USA, Sanabel al-Khair opened its office outside Washington DC in the early 1990s.[18] In 1997, in what had become an annual event, the Governor of Riyadh, Prince Salman, who controlled the disposition of the endowment's funds with an iron hand, opened the IIRO Sanabel al-Khair Charity Festival. Attended by members of the royal family and the heads of international aid organizations, the goal for that year alone was one billion riyals ($266.6 million) for the endowment. Certainly, the campaign would not have succeeded without the enormous financial contributions from the Saudi royal family including King Fahd bin Abd al-Aziz himself and Deputy Prime Minister and Chairman of the Board of Trustees of the Saudi Benevolent Society, Prince (now King) Abdullah bin Abd al-Aziz. There can be no question that the establishment of an endowment, a *waqf*, would guarantee a steady flow of funds into IIRO offices and activities overseas, but the very magnitude of the funds presented problems of policy and accountability that were largely ignored, providing opportunities for abuse and misuse.

The first link that tied IIRO to the Islamist *mujahideen* was a handwritten note on IIRO stationery found in Bosnia. It was an account of a meeting in the late 1980s in which the Secretary-General of MWL informed representatives of Osama bin Laden that IIRO was offering its offices in support of the *mujahideen*. Thereafter, IIRO was suspected of terrorist links in the Philippines, Russia, East Africa, Bosnia, and India. Muhammad Jamal Khalifa, Osama bin Laden's brother-in-law, was the director of IIRO in the Philippines, which supported the Salafi Abu Sayyaf organization. Mohammed al-Zawahiri, brother of Dr. Ayman al-Zawahiri, the confidant of Bin Laden and chief of EIJ, worked for IIRO in Albania during the 1990s. As an engineer, he helped EIJ members "land jobs with charities that were building mosques, orphanages and clinics there."[19] A fellow EIJ leader, Talaat Fouad Abdul Qasim, who was under sentence of death in Egypt for terrorism, had earlier been director of the IIRO office in Peshawar, "specializing in funding Arab militants fighting alongside the Afghan Mujahedeen."[20] Granted political asylum in Denmark, he was seized by US agents when returning to Croatia in 1998. He was handed over to Egypt, tried by an Egyptian tribunal in Cairo, and executed. Another IIRO employee from Bangladesh, Sayed Abu Nasir, led a cell broken up by Indian police; it had intended to strike at the US consulates in Madras and Calcutta. Nasir "explained that his superiors

Table 2.2 *Charitable entities belonging to or associated with the Al Qaeda organization, July 2004*

Name	Location	Listed on
Al Rashid Trust (Aid Organization of the Ulama)	Pakistan	24/04/2002
Al Rashid Trust	Pakistan: Afghanistan, Chechnya, Kosovo	06/10/2001
Al Barakaat	Somalia	09/11/2001
Al-Haramain wa al-Masjed al-Aqsa	Bosnia	28/06/2004
Al Haramain	Afghanistan, Albania, Bangladesh, Ethiopia, Netherlands	06/07/2004
Al Haramain Foundation	Indonesia, Pakistan, Kenya, Tanzania	26/01/2004
Al-Haramain Islamic Foundation	Bosnia, Somalia	13/03/2002
Benevolence International Foundation (Fund)	USA (Canada): Afghanistan, Azerbaijan, Bangladesh, Bosnia, Chechnya, China, Croatia, Gaza, Georgia, Netherlands, Pakistan, Russia, Saudi Arabia, Sudan, Tajikistan, UK, Yemen	21/11/2002
Bosanska Idealna Futura	Bosnia	21/11/2002
Global Relief Foundation (Fondation Secours Mondial)	USA: Seventeen countries	22/11/2002
Makhtab al-Khidamat/Al Kifah	Afghanistan	06/10/2001
Rabita Trust	Pakistan	17/10/2001
Somali International Relief Organization	Somalia	09/11/2001
Wafa Humanitarian Organization	Pakistan, Saudi Arabia	06/10/2001

Source: 1267 Committee, UN, New York, July 2004.

told him of 40 to 50 percent of IIRO charitable funds being diverted to finance terrorist training camps in Afghanistan and Kashmir."[21]

IIRO used its charitable outreach to move funds not only to the Taliban and Al Qaeda but also to Jama'at al-Islamiyya (Egyptian Islamic Jihad, EIJ) in Egypt and Abu Sayyaf in the Philippines. Money also went to causes "with hard-line or extremist elements like the Muslim brotherhood in Egypt and Jordan or Hamas in the Gaza . . . The Saudi government did not begin to properly analyze or control the flow of its funds to movements like the Taliban and extremist groups in South Asia, Central Asia, and the rest of the world until 1998."[22] The flow of charitable funds from Saudi businessmen and even from royal officials was apportioned with remarkable carelessness and little attention paid to the recipients, their objectives, or end use. Accountability and valuation were either deficient or ignored. Thus, Muslim charities had inadvertently created pipelines through which cash flowed to transform ragtag bands of insurgents and jihadists "into a sophisticated, interlocking movement with global ambitions."[23] During the 1990s Islamist organizations had collected between $300 million and $500 million, most of it from Saudi charities and private donors. "Saudi donors alone reportedly moved $150 million through Islamic aid organizations to Bosnia in 1994 alone."[24]

Al Haramain Islamic Foundation

In November 2002 representatives of 241 Saudi Arabian charities, including 23 women's organizations and 23 private foundations, met in Riyadh. Their combined revenue was estimated at SR1.2 billion ($320 million) with expenditures of some SR970 million ($260 million) annually. Dr. Ali bin Ibrahim al-Namlah, Minister of Labour and Social Affairs, announced that the kingdom, in fact, had recorded "264 charitable organizations for helping the poor" with assets "worth SR2.6 billion [$550 million]." Most of this revenue came from wealthy private donors performing *sadaqa* or *zakat*, but Shaykh Saleh al-Hosain, General President of Affairs for the Grand Mosque and the Prophet's Mosque, reported that "the state provides a generous financial assistance to charitable societies at the time of their establishment, in addition to an annual aid of 80 percent of their total expenditures. It also meets nearly 80 percent of the cost of constructing the headquarters of charities."[25] Most of these charities were indeed committed to assisting the destitute, supporting education, health, and refugees, and furthering Islam by *da'wa* and the construction of mosques. Some of these charities, knowingly or not, came to support terrorism and its organizations, but perhaps the most notorious of the larger Islamic charities was the Al Haramain Islamic Foundation (AHIF).

With headquarters in Riyadh, AHIF was founded in 1988 as a branch of MWL at its 22nd Session in Mecca. Endorsed by the Saudi royal family and supervised by the Ministry of Religious Affairs, AHIF, like IIRO, was to "provide relief and aid to Muslims as peoples and groups wherever they are, should they face disasters endangering their being, their religious beliefs or their freedom." Although it spent large sums to promote the radical Islamist agenda, it nonetheless achieved considerable respect for building and restoring mosques and in constructing and funding Quranic schools in impoverished villages. It has printed nearly 15 million copies of Islamic books, established more than 1,100 mosques, schools, and centers, and has dispatched more than 3,000 "missionaries" to spread Islam abroad.[26] There were, however, more sinister motives, for after its founding in 1988 one of its express commitments became financial assistance to the Islamists in Afghanistan, and from there AHIF soon extended its support for Islamists in other countries. By the year 2000 AHIF maintained forty branches in Saudi Arabia with a Zakat Account, account number 6/98998, and an Alms Account, account number 2/9292, well known to most Saudis. It had offices in some fifty countries including those countries where *mujahideen* were involved in *jihad*: Albania, Croatia, Kosovo, and Macedonia in the Balkans; Pakistan and Bangladesh in South Asia; Kenya and Somalia in Africa; and Georgia and Azerbaijan in the former Soviet Union. It was sponsoring 3,000 imams and *da'wa* activists living abroad and maintaining four computer internet sites. American and Saudi investigators later estimated that the Foundation generated about $50 million a year for the *mujahideen*, which included substantial funds for Al Qaeda.

Although the Foundation had been active in the Balkans during the 1990s, AHIF and the mysterious United Aid Committee of Kosovo and Chechnya began to finance the construction of mosques, schools, and terrorism soon after the Muslim revolt in Chechnya. Consequently, in 1999 the Russian Federal Security Service (FSB) openly accused AHIF of wiring funds to Chechen militants using as a false front a branch office of the Foundation for Chechnya. Located in Baku, it worked directly with *mujahideen* active in the Chechen Republic and with "Wahhabi extremists" operating in Makhach-Qala, the capital of the Dagestan Republic, and its second-largest city, Buinaksk. In the same year AHIF established a "Foundation Regarding Chechnya" in Azerbaijan to provide direct support to Chechen terrorists. It was closed by the government in January 2000 "for serious violations of the law," only to reopen, and then was permanently closed after 9/11.[27] The Foundation for Chechnya employed twenty-five agents in regions bordering Chechnya who were responsible for securing supply routes for Chechen military units. AHIF employees Abd al-Latif bin Abd al-Karim al-Daraan and Abu Omar Mohammed al-Seif directed operations from *mujahideen* headquarters inside Chechnya, while other Foundation members were scattered throughout Chechnya with the Chechen insurgents. Abu Seif was both a member of the *majlis al-shura*, the consultative council of Al Qaeda, and its representative to AHIF. Before he was killed in October 2002, he was the conduit through which "the financing of the Chechen fighters was exercised."[28]

When the Saudi government made its first feeble attempt in 1993 to control the end-use of charitable funds for *mujahideen* organizations in Afghanistan, a law was issued requiring that all donations collected by

Muslim charities be deposited in a fund administered by a Saudi prince. It soon proved to be unenforceable, a fact that later became an embarrassment to important members of the royal family.[29] Although there was now no doubt that the Bosnian and Somali branches of AHIF were linked to terrorist funding, for more than a decade AHIF was exempt from investigation, apparently because of its close ties to the royal family. The Bosnia office supplied funds for the Jama'at al-Islamiyya of Egypt, which the USA declared a terrorist organization on 2 November 2001, and it was a signatory to the 23 February 1998 *fatwa* (an opinion on an Islamic legal or religious matter) of Osama bin Laden that targeted Americans and their allies. In Africa the Somali office had been even more active. Some of its employees were members of Al Itihad al-Islamiyya (AIAI), a Somali terrorist organization closely linked to Al Qaeda. Salaries for the employees and a steady supply of funds were funneled through the Al Barakaat Bank, the same institution that provided financial intelligence and money transfers for Osama bin Laden. AHIF funds to AIAI were invariably disguised as donations for the construction of mosques and orphanages, but were used to facilitate the activities of the *mujahideen* in Somalia, including travel to Saudi Arabia.

On 7 November 2001 the USA, Saudi Arabia, and other Middle East states froze the bank's assets.[30] AHIF reacted with outrage. Its Director-General, Shaykh Uqayl bin Abdul Aziz al-Uqayl (aka Aqeel al-Aqeel) issued a *fatwa* condemning cooperation with the "infidel." For months he had dismissed the charges that Saudi charities offered funds and assistance to parties linked to political or terrorist activities as "mere speculation." After the Bosnian and Somali branches were designated by both the US and Saudi governments as supporters of terrorism in March 2002, Uqayl al-Uqayl stated that in the aftermath of 9/11 lawyers had no evidence to convict AHIF in a $1 trillion lawsuit brought against it and other Saudi-based charities by 900 family members of those killed in the 9/11 attack. Al-Uqayl protested that the lawsuit was a "futile exercise." US Secretary of the Treasury, John Snow, thought otherwise. "The branches of Al-Haramain that we have singled out today," he claimed, "not only assist in the pursuit of death and destruction, they deceive countless people around the world who believe that they have helped spread good will and good works."[31] In defiance AHIF reconstituted its Bosnian office, but after a series of raids by local security agents it once again was closed down in December 2003. Although Shaykh Uqayl denied any pressure from his government or the Americans, AHIF decided to close its offices in Albania, Croatia, and Ethiopia in May 2003, to be followed by those in Kenya, Tanzania, Pakistan, and Indonesia – where, however, its large headquarters were put up for rent but quietly "moved to a smaller house down the block."[32] When Shaykh Uqayl announced in October 2003 that AHIF was still active in seventy-four countries and indiscreetly mentioned that Saudi Crown Prince Abdullah had recently sent a check for an unreported sum of money, he was promptly sacked and replaced by his deputy, Dabbas al-Dabbas. In January 2004 the UN officially added AHIF to its list of organizations whose assets were to be blocked for suspected ties to Al Qaeda and invoked a ban on travel and an arms embargo pursuant to United Nations Security Council Resolutions 1267, 1390, and 1455.

Although the AHIF/US won a dubious victory in September 2003 when it forced the *Washington Times* to apologize for a false statement that it had been included in the list of institutions involved in possible terrorist attacks, the retraction did not deter federal agents from searching its Ashland headquarters in Oregon in February 2004. Although the charity's lawyer claimed the office had not received funds from Riyadh, in April 2004 the US Internal Revenue Service (IRS) and the US Attorney's Office for the District of Oregon initiated a search of "property purchased" on behalf of the Foundation pursuant to a "criminal investigation into possible violations of the Internal Revenue Code, the Money Laundering Control Act, and the Bank Secrecy Act." Simultaneously, the Treasury Department's Office of Foreign Assets Control (OFAC) blocked accounts of AHIF, Inc. to insure the preservation of its assets pending further OFAC investigation. In February 2005 the AHIF was indicted in the US District Court for Oregon. Charges were preferred against Soliman al-Buthe, the AHIF international treasurer and Saudi entrepreneur who in 1997 had helped establish the Al Haramain office in Oregon.[33]

Despite earlier denials by Prince Salman that "if some individuals have been attempting to turn charitable work into evil acts, the Kingdom cannot be held responsible," or statements by the Minister of Labor and Social Affairs, Ali al-Namlah, that "we directly supervise the activities of charitable organizations within the Kingdom . . . and we are not responsible for their activities abroad," there was no longer any doubt that certain Saudi charities had been and were still involved in funding international terrorism.[34]

World Assembly of Muslim Youth

The last of the three major charities to receive substantial funding from and through the Saudi royal family was the World Assembly of Muslim Youth (WAMY), with its headquarters in Riyadh. WAMY was founded in 1972 as a Saudi effort to prevent the "corrupting" ideas of the West influencing young Muslims. It was an independent international organization and an Islamic forum to support the work of Muslims and needy communities worldwide. Like other Saudi charitable organizations WAMY was to recruit and educate Muslims, specifically the young, to build schools and mosques, initiate social welfare projects, and provide disaster relief. Saleh al-Shaykh, Saudi Minister of Islamic Affairs, was not only Chairman of the WAMY secretariat but also Chairman of the Administrative Council of AHIF. At the time of 9/11 the Assembly had offices in some fifty-five countries and global associate membership in over 500 youth organizations. Like other charities it would hold annual international conferences where impassioned speeches were the norm and where in recent years Muslim youth have been urged to combat "propaganda" linking Islam with terrorism. The importance of these international conferences is often overlooked. To the cynic they are thought to be an excuse for a holiday, but the annual conferences of Islamic charities have been critically important in bringing together Muslims and Islamists from Morocco to Indonesia, Central Asia, and Sri Lanka. For those members seriously concerned about the humanitarian activities of the Assembly, the annual conference was more social than conspiratorial. WAMY had been especially interested in narcotics trafficking and drug use among Muslim youth, and held international conferences in those countries where that problem was either acute or threatened soon to be.[35] For the young militant Islamists, however, these international conferences were an inspirational opportunity to meet other angry young Muslims, define objectives, and devise whatever means necessary to achieve them. The annual conferences of the WAMY were no exception.

The first branch of WAMY in the USA was established by Abdullah bin Laden, the nephew of Osama bin Laden, and was widely known for the literature it published to promote *da'wa*, Islamic *jihad*, and hatred of the Jews. WAMY Canada managed a series of Islamic camps and sponsored pilgrimages for the youth. A branch office was located in Mississauga, a suburb of Toronto, but was supervised by the WAMY office in the USA.[36] In the USA Fadil Suliman, the Muslim chaplain at the American University in Washington DC, was a director of WAMY USA, and in Britain Dr. Farid Elshayyal, the respected Chairman of the Muslim Investment Corporation of the UK, member of the Center for International Policy Studies in London, and the former Chairman of the Muslim Association of Britain, was a founding member of WAMY. Nevertheless, there appears to have been a dark undercurrent that flowed through WAMY in the UK, and after 9/11 the open challenge presented by terrorism produced an awareness that "as long as 10 years ago" WAMY had been used "as a discreet channel for public and private Saudi donations to hard-line Islamic organisations."[37]

In the USA there was suspicion among federal authorities that WAMY had been funding terrorists since 1996, and after 1999 the FBI began a continuing investigation of its activities. By 2003 Operation Green Quest, the US government's multi-agency investigating money-laundering in support of terrorist organizations, scrutinized the operations of MWL, IIRO, and WAMY only to conclude that the activities of WAMY did not constitute a threat to the USA despite demands from several senators that its offices be closed. Indeed, the Director of WAMY announced plans to open offices in New Zealand, Eastern Europe, and Central Asia to add to the fifty-nine countries in which it already worked, and expected to publish French and Spanish editions of its monthly magazine, *Muslim Youth*.[38] WAMY continued to offer the traditional Ramadan *iftar* (fast-breaking) meals for Muslims in forty countries, and in October 2003 it inaugurated an outreach program to assist poor and needy people during the Ramadan season that included Islamic and Islamist "educational and cultural activities before and after the meals."[39]

Al Wafa Humanitarian Foundation

Although there are a dozen major and visible charities that maintain offices outside Saudi Arabia there are also a number of very small Saudi charities whose provenance is obscure and whose activities are often known only to the donors. Before, but particularly after, 9/11, the infiltration of the large public Saudi charities by terrorists became increasingly revealed by their operations in foreign countries monitored by national security agencies and the elaborate international investigation of terrorist financing networks that was spearheaded by OFAC of the US Treasury. This was not the case for those small private charities in Saudi Arabia, usually founded by wealthy individuals, ostensibly for humanitarian purposes, that could support *mujahideen* and *jihad* undetected. Needless to say, there were many wealthy Arabs who were eager to assist the *jihad* against the Soviets in Afghanistan and were quite sympathetic to the violent Afghan-Arab warriors, whom they would in normal circumstances regard with suspicion if not distaste. Moreover, it was very difficult for Arabs, particularly those in Saudi Arabia who were living in the very comfortable circumstances of their wealth, to resist the deep Islamic belief in charitable giving through *zakat* and *sadaqa* that could easily be diverted from humanitarianism to terrorism.

The dramatic increase in the fortunes of many Saudis, directly or indirectly, from oil revenues in the 1970s and 1980s also spawned the creation of innumerable *waqf* charitable trusts. Consequently, it seems likely that the mysterious Al Wafa Humanitarian Foundation (Wafa al-Igatha al-Islamiyya) of Saudi Arabia may have originally been established as a *waqf khayr*. Al Wafa, which is usually translated as "fidelity and justice," was one of the most malevolent organizations that Saudi money funded along the Afghan–Pakistan border. Headquartered in Saudi Arabia, it maintained unobtrusive offices and mail drops in Saudi Arabia, Kuwait, the UAE, and Pakistan. Its operations remain virtually unknown, but it was commonly believed in Peshawar to have had support from some of the wealthiest Saudi families. During Taliban rule in Afghanistan it served as a reliable supporter of the Al Qaeda network.[40]

When President Bush signed his Executive Order on 23 September 2001 freezing assets in the USA of Specially Designated Global Terrorists (SDGT) that aided, abetted, and supported international terrorism, Al Wafa had the distinction of being first on the list. A US official described the charity as one that does "a small amount of legitimate humanitarian work and raise[s] a lot of money for equipment and weapons . . . [and that] Abdul Aziz, a senior Al Qaeda operative and Saudi citizen, used al-Wafa to finance terrorist activities."[41] The UN would soon follow the lead of the USA and freeze all Al Wafa international assets, impose a ban on travel, and enforce an arms embargo. The Council of Foreign Relations reported in October 2002 that Al Wafa carried out "legitimate work as well as financing more suspect groups," but it was also ominously supporting the Pakistani nuclear scientific establishment.[42] In Pakistan a mysterious Shaykh Abu Abdul Aziz Naqai was supposedly the head of Al Wafa and closely associated with Al Qaeda. Attempts to unravel Al Wafa were made more difficult by the fact that it is a common name widely applied to numerous legitimate organizations, health centers, and hotels. There was an Al Wafa Women's Charity Association in Saudi Arabia. The Al Aqsa Foundation of South Africa supported the Al Wafa Charitable Society and the Al Wafa hospital in Palestine, and the Al Wafa Rehabilitation and Health Center was active in Gaza. Al Wafa institutions were often confused with WAFA, the official Palestine news agency. There was a large Al Wafa center for the mentally ill in Bahrain, Al Wafa Hotels in Aden and Marrakech, an Al Wafa Pharmacy in Tripoli, and the Al Wafa Scrap Copper Recycling Company in Cairo.

After the fall of the Taliban regime in Afghanistan in 2002 the coalition forces carried out an investigation of the Al Wafa premises in Kabul's Wazir Ajkbar Khan district. There they found a laboratory with explosives, fuses, "terroristic guide books," and documents that "showed links between Al Wafa, Al Qaeda and the Taliban." Later additional documentation about Al Wafa was uncovered at the abandoned Abu Khabab Al Qaeda camp outside Jalalabad. Three laboratories under suspicion had been purchased earlier in 2001 by "the Wafa Humanitarian Organization" and their equipment "shipped from the United Arab Emirates to Afghanistan."[43]

Al Wafa remains an enigma to this day. In 2002 US officials were outspoken that Saudi Arabia was "glossing over the terrorist connections of other humanitarian organizations, including the Al Wafa Humanitarian Organization, IIRO, and its parent, the Muslim World League."[44] There was no reported disclosure by the Saudi government, if they knew, of those wealthy Saudis providing funds for Al Wafa.[45] The government of Kuwait denied the existence of any organization called the Al Wafa Humanitarian Organization. There had been an Al Wafa Humanitarian Organization ostensibly operating in Mogadishu, but it used a post office box address in Dubai. Al Wafa also seems to have had an office on the sixth floor of International House in Nairobi, but in 2004 no one seemed to know if it was still active. Unregulated banks in the Cayman Islands were suspected of assisting Al Wafa, but no banks or financial institutions were ever made public. Investigators found an Al Wafa humanitarian group operating in Kurdistan, but there was no relationship with the Al Wafa that operated in Afghanistan. Finally, there was the report that one Abdul Aziz, a Saudi citizen and an important Al Qaeda "financial official" captured in Afghanistan and held in the US prison at Guantánamo, allegedly funneled "large sums of money" to Osama bin Laden through Al Wafa, "a Persian Gulf charity" whose purported mission was to feed and provide medical aid to the poor in Afghanistan.[46] The US government was not ready to publish its findings regarding the Saudi Al Wafa Humanitarian Organization or why it was placed on the list of sanctions by the administration in the days following 9/11. Nonetheless, it is likely that from its inception Al Wafa was an Al Qaeda front and its charitable interests a disguise for its terrorist purposes.

Benevolence International Foundation

In 1987 the wealthy Saudi Shaykh Adil Galil Abdul Batargy (aka Battargee) founded the Islamic Benevolence Committee (IBC; Lajnat al-Birr al-Islamiyya, LBI) in Jidda and Peshawar as a charity to assist the destitute and infirm and provide meals during Ramadan. In fact, its principal resources were publicly committed to support the *mujahideen* fighting against the Soviets in Afghanistan. Its banking relationships were impeccable, including accounts with the National Commercial Bank (NCB), Saudi American Bank, Al Riyadh Bank, Al Rahji Banking and Investment Corporation, and the National Arab Bank. In the following year Muhammad Jamal Khalifa of Jidda, the brother-in-law of Osama bin Laden, founded in the Philippines a separate export–import company, the Benevolence International Corporation (BIC), whose publicly stated purpose was also to support the *mujahideen* in Afghanistan. It acted as a front for Muslim separatists in the Philippines, the Abu Sayyaf Group.[47]

In 1992 Batargy's IBC amalgamated with the BIC creating a Saudi charity, the Benevolence International Foundation (BIF). The Foundation claimed that its purpose was to provide humanitarian assistance to those afflicted by natural disasters, but in fact it had both a public and a private agenda. Suleman Ahmer, a member of the BIF board of directors, drew the distinction between relief and *da'wa*, between humanitarian assistance and the mission to make Islam supreme throughout the world. BIF was not simply a relief agency, but a *da'wa* organization to spread Wahhabism actively throughout the Muslim and western worlds. Taking care of people in distress was subsidiary. In 1999 its "Mission Statement" was quite candid that the purpose of BIF was to make "Islam supreme on this earth."

After the Soviet withdrawal from Afghanistan the principal objective of BIF was to demonstrate the power of Islam by an attack in the USA. It moved its headquarters to Plantation, Florida. As a non-profit charitable trust it solicited funds from wealthy American Muslims. Abdul Batargy selected as the American Director of the Foundation Enaam M. Arnaout (aka Abu Mahmoud al-Suri). Arnaout had lived in Afghanistan, worked with Osama bin Laden, and was perfectly familiar with the aims and operations of MAK on the eastern Afghanistan–Pakistan borderlands. He had first found employment in Afghanistan with MWL, and then with IBC, where his abilities came to the attention of Abdul Batargy. In 1988 *Arab News* published a photograph of Arnaout and Bin Laden together in the "al-Masada" *mujahideen* camp in Afghanistan. Upon arrival in the USA he married an American woman, obtained American citizenship, and moved the headquarters of BIF to Chicago in 1993 where he recruited Jose Padilla and others for Al Qaeda and began to construct the infrastructure and offices in Canada, the Benevolence International Fund, and in Bosnia, the Bosanska Idealna Futura, to support *mujahideen* activity in the Balkans and Chechnya. When the BIF (Bosanska Idealna Futura) office in Sarajevo, Bosnia, was searched by Bosnian authorities and US agents in March 2002, they discovered a "treasure trove" of electrically scanned documents, photographs, and computer disks with photographs of Arnaout and Bin Laden together. Personal letters between the two were also found, including a handwritten note by Bin Laden authorizing Arnaout to sign documents on his behalf.

Late in 1994 Muhammad Jamal Khalifa, who had founded BIC, met with the BIF President Mohammed Loay Bayazid in the USA. Bayazid, a Syrian-American, had lived in Kansas City and sojourned in the guesthouse of Osama bin Laden in a fashionable suburb of Khartoum, before moving to Chicago in 1994. Having received communications from the Philippines that Khalifa was funding Operation Bojinka, a terrorist plot that was foiled on 6 January 1995, the FBI arrested both Khalifa and Bayazid in Mountain View, California, in December. The following January Dr. Ayman al-Zawahiri, leader of EIJ and one of the founders of Al Qaeda and confidant of Osama bin Laden, arrived in Santa Clara on a fundraising trip, where he stayed with Al Qaeda operatives closely tied to BIF. In May 1995 Khalifa was deported to Jordan, where he was acquitted by a Jordanian court and sought refuge in Saudi Arabia. Bayazid was subsequently released for lack of evidence and promptly disappeared.[48]

BIF was soon operating with associated offices in Bosnia, Chechnya, Pakistan, China, Ingushetia, and Russia. In Chechnya it supported Saif al-Islam al-Masri, a member of the *majlis al-shura* of Al Qaeda, and employed him in the BIF office in Chechnya. In 1999 a memorial for a BIF employee killed in Tajikistan wrote that he was the "9th officer to die in the line of duty since 1992," a rather significant rate of mortality for any charity. Arnaout also used Alaa al-Saadawi, a fundraiser who frequented mosques in New York and New Jersey, to move money out of the USA, as much as $650,000 in 2000–2001.[49] After 9/11 the massive search for terrorists and their organizations soon focused on Arnaout and BIF. A search of his home and office convinced US officials that the Foundation was not just a charity to "help those afflicted by wars," but in fact a front to launder and send money to Osama bin Laden to purchase rockets, mortars, rifles, dynamite, and bombs for members of Al Qaeda. On 19 November BIF was declared a terrorist organization, its Chicago office closed, and in February 2003 Enaam Arnaout pleaded guilty to working with Al Qaeda, but in a plea bargain the government agreed to drop its charges in return for information.

Riyadh bombings and Saudi Arabian charities

Throughout the 1990s Israel had pressed Washington to crack down on US-based Islamic organizations that were providing aid to Palestinian HAMAS and Hizbullah. The Clinton administration, which had been reluctant to initiate investigations of any Islamic charities that could precipitate charges of religious bigotry and accusations of ethnic discrimination, or raise constitutional questions, refused to act. Consequently, when US officials visited the Persian Gulf states in January 2000 with a list of more than thirty Islamic charities thought to have links to terrorism, only two were based in the USA. Specific charities were discussed at some length, but the talks were followed by months of delay and drift that lasted well after 9/11.[50]

After 9/11, however, the Saudi government could no longer ignore US diplomatic and political pressure to provide information on the charities of Saudi Arabia, governmental and private. In December 2002 the government announced in Riyadh that all Saudi charities were to be "subject to extensive audits to ensure that the funds provided by donors are used for their intended purposes. In addition, charities whose activities extend beyond Saudi Arabia's borders must now report and coordinate their activities with the Foreign Ministry." To ensure compliance, the government established a High Commission "for oversight of all charities." The Saudi government still had not reached a point where it could "track all donations to and from the charities," but promised such a development so that the "combined changes will substantially decrease its charitable sector's vulnerability to abuse by evil-doers."[51]

Although Saudi officials began to cooperate ever more closely with European and US agents on the trail of terrorists, particularly Al Qaeda, the Saudis appear to have regarded the threat from terrorism as a peculiarly American concern until 12 May 2003, known as 5/12, when suicide bombers blew up a residential compound in Riyadh. The deaths and destruction shook the kingdom just as badly as 9/11 had done in the USA, and brought home to the royal family and its intelligence services that they too were not immune from terrorists. The Saudi government reacted with unexpected vigor. Hundreds of *mujahideen*, who had lived in Saudi Arabia for years, were rounded up, interrogated, and many placed under arrest. Some 2,000 radical clerics were purged from mosques, and warnings were issued among the clerical establishment that the rhetoric of *jihad* would not be tolerated. Their hitherto strident calls for *jihad* from the sanctity of the mosque did indeed become more mellifluous, but "what we are hearing is only a facade. You can smell the disgust they feel in mouthing their new rhetoric."[52]

Several days after the Riyadh suicide bombings a firestorm of debate pitting "conservatives" against "liberals" erupted in the Saudi media. At issue was the role that the Saudi education system might have played in the emergence of terrorism in the country. Abd al-Rahman al-Rashed, the "liberal" editor of the London-based Saudi daily *Al Sharq Al Awsat*, used an acerbic wit to counter the argument that Saudis could not possibly be involved in such atrocities. Using biting sarcasm to pillory the Saudi establishment, al-Rashed wrote:

I also discovered that the Saudis who went to Kashmir, Afghanistan, and Chechnya arrived there by chance; they were tourists who had lost their way . . . It isn't true that the Saudi media and institutions prepared the ground and the mentality for them . . . The charity organizations sent the money only for their tourism and entertainment and that of their Arab and Muslim friends, and not for funding terrorism abroad . . . You must not connect what I said with any bombings heard in your city [Riyadh]; it is only fireworks and American propaganda.[53]

Stung by the growing criticism the government declared it was taking "unprecedented measures" designed to exert "stricter control on charity associations, and at the same time, to guarantee that donors' aids are reaching the rightful beneficiaries." Ostensibly, these measures were to prohibit charities from distributing funds directly to beneficiaries by processing charitable donations through banks that would verify the identity of the donor and the recepient.[54]

Cooperation with the Europeans and the Americans, which had been haphazard at best, now became more earnest. A joint Saudi/US task force to combat the financing of global terrorism was established, and the government imposed stiff scrutiny and restrictions on funds moving out of Saudi Arabia. In addition, an agency was created to coordinate the intelligence services of Saudi Arabia and the USA that provided for the "real-time" exchange of information. An unknown number of terrorists captured in Saudi Arabia were turned over to the USA, and three Saudis, who had assisted the Pakistan Lashkar-e-Toiba and were wanted for trial in the USA, were extradited. Saudi charities, however, remained virtually immune, for Saudi officials claimed they did not have the evidence required by Saudi law to close them down even if it were possible, which was doubtful, and the USA would have to be content with the occasional dismissal of some administrative head of a charity. The kingdom would handle its problem its own way. It would have to. In January 2003 the Arab Human Rights Committee convened a Paris Conference on Humanitarian and Charitable Societies. Considered the "first of its kind," the meeting brought together UN agencies, NGOs, and Islamic charities. The conference was devoted, inter alia, to the impact of globalization on charities. In addition, the performance of international Islamic societies was evaluated, as was their ability to meet humanitarian needs in times of war and peace. Hardly apolitical, the conference preparatory statement argued that 9/11 was a "catastrophe," and that from that event forward the issue of Islamic charities had "changed from just mere harassment into unprecedented actual war [by the United States] against all societies of Islamic traits."[55] In August 2003, Saudi Arabia finally agreed to join the independent Financial Action Task Force (FATF) in Paris consisting of twenty-nine countries, largely organized by the USA, to adopt strict new regulations to interdict terrorist financing. In the months that followed the Saudis froze $5.7 million in questionable funds – that appeared more symbolic than real, for 150 other countries had frozen more than $112 million in terrorist assets worldwide since 9/11. Nevertheless the Saudi government did block the assets of the Al Haramain Foundation offices in Somalia, Bosnia, Kenya, Tanzania, Pakistan, and Indonesia. It also promised to prohibit mosques, schools, and commercial firms from collecting contributions in cash. Saudi charities were ordered to cease all transmittals of cash overseas, and there were even discussions that Saudi charities would be prohibited from operating offices abroad.

Despite these declarations against terrorism, the counter-terrorism policies of the Saudi government remained insufficient and required extensive reform. The State Department sought to modulate the criticism of its vital ally in the Middle East by praising the kingdom's domestic crackdown following the Riyadh bombing. Deputy Secretary of State Richard Armitage declared that Saudi cooperation on those matters "internal to Saudi Arabia has been magnificent"; but many were not so sure. The split between traditionalists and reformers in Saudi Arabia continued to grow. Although there was a desire to maintain contact with the western world for the sake of material wealth, many Saudis believe that all westerners and non-Muslims are infidels. Whether "conservative" or "liberal," however, both 9/11 and 5/12 ironically stimulated an increase in Islamic charitable activities in Saudi Arabia. Despite the misuse of Islamic charities to promote terrorism, the same official Saudi relief organizations that were under investigation after 5/12 entered Iraq in 2003 shortly after the US-led coalition forces had captured Baghdad. IIRO was praised in the Saudi daily *Al-Watan* (The Nation) for its "relief work" in the Sunni triangle of Iraq. Undoubtedly, Muslim generosity has been manipulated, even in Saudi Arabia. Many Saudi donors blessed the militant activity and felt compelled to assist Islamist radicals as long as their generosity remained unknown. The subterranean movement of charitable funds within Saudi Arabia itself finally struck home in 2004 after an indigenous Al Qaeda cell was infiltrated. Captured radicals appeared on Saudi television and acknowledged that they had used funds from two charities to purchase weapons used in attacks within the kingdom. That shocking development was soon followed by the appearance of the WAMY director general on Saudi television, and in a speech he declared that new guidelines were being issued to protect donations. Citizens were assured that they should have no fear that charitable funds could be used to arm radical organizations such as Al Qaeda, and the promise was made that investigations of Saudi charities within the kingdom would continue.

3   The banks

Even the little we know about fundraising shows us al-Qaeda is not an organization run by one man but a global Islamist Internet, with gateways and access points around the world. It has a worldwide operational reach and is better-run financially than many companies you find on the Stock Exchange.

A London banking expert, *The Times*, London, 25 September 2001

As I have said many times, you can't bomb a foreign bank account.

Kenneth W. Dam, Deputy Secretary of the Treasury, 8 June 2002

Golden Chain

The most startling and important document discovered during the raid by US security agents on the Bosnian office of BIF (Bosanska Idealna Futura) in Sarajevo in March 2002 was a computer disk labeled *Tarikh Osama* ("Osama's history"). It chronicled both the activities of Osama bin Laden and MAK in Afghanistan and the subsequent creation of the Al Qaeda organization. The file also contained a list of twenty wealthy donors known within Al Qaeda as the *Golden Chain*. Among the names were seven individuals who gave their considerable donations to Osama bin Laden personally.[1] In Islam the Golden Chain has a much deeper meaning than precious metal. Hadith scholars have long declared that the "golden chain" defined the progression of prophets from Adam through Muhammad, the last Prophet, and among Sufi Muslims the chain (*silsila*) represented the succession of one spiritual master (*murshid*) to another in a Sufi order or brotherhood (*tariqa*). The twenty supporters of Al Qaeda consisted of six bankers, twelve businessmen, and two persons unknown. The net worth of the eighteen was estimated at $85 billion, or approximately 42 percent of the Saudi Arabian gross domestic product (GDP) in 2002. All of them supported charities of one kind or another, and several had founded their own.[2] All the bankers in the Golden Chain were major principals in the National Commercial Bank (NCB), Al Riyadh Bank,

Table 3.1 *The Golden Chain*

Name	Commercial enterprise
Suleiman al-Rashid	Al Rashid Trading and Contracting, Riyadh
Abdel Qader Bakri	Chief Executive Officer, Bakri Group, Jidda
Bin Laden brothers	Saudi Bin Laden Group
Yousif Jameel	Abdul Lateef Jameel Group
Ibrahim Muhammad Afandi	Ibn Baz Foundation; Al Afandi Establishment; African Company-Sudan; Al Amoudi Group
Saleh Abdallah Kamel	Dallah Al Baraka; Al Shamal Islamic Bank; Jordan Islamic Bank; Bank al-Jazira; Ikraa International Foundation
Suleiman A. al-Rajhi	Al Rajhi Banking and Investment Corporation
Mohammed Abdullah al-Jumaih	First Islamic Investment Bank
Abdulrahman al-Sharbatly	Al Riyadh Bank; Beirut Riyadh Bank; Egyptian Gulf Bank; Middle East Capital Group
Mohammed Yousef al-Naghi	Al Naghi Brothers Co., Jidda
Khaled bin Mahfouz	National Commercial Bank; Founder, International Development Foundation
Abdel Qader Faqeeh	Bank Al Jazira; Makka Construction; Ibn Baz Foundation; Savola Group
Salah al-Din Abdel Jawad	United Gulf Industries; General Machines Agencies
Ahmad Turki (Zaki) Yamani	founder, Investcorp; Saudi European Bank
Abdel Hadi Taher	Taher Group; Arab Company for Hotels; Saudi European Bank
Ahmed al-Harbi	Ahmed al-Harbi Trading; Ahmed al-Harbi Group
Mohammad al-Issai	Saudi Research and Marketing Company; Arab Cement Company
Hamad al-Hussaini	Akel Trading Company; Al Hussaini & Co.

Source: www.investigateur.com; Exhibit 5, Government Evidentiary Proffer Supporting the Admissibility of Conconspirator Statements, *USA* v. *Arnaout*, United States District Court, Northern District of Illinois, 29 January 2003.

and the Al Rajhi Banking and Investment Corporation, Saudi Arabia's three largest banks.

Al Qaeda had successfully penetrated the official Saudi banking sector, and members of that loosely knit organization were able to transfer their funds throughout the world with relative ease before 9/11. The financial manager for Bin Laden until 1996 testified that Al Qaeda had "lots" of money in a web of bank accounts in Europe, Asia, and Africa. In the Sudan Bin Laden maintained a personal account at the Al Shamal Islamic Bank, and opened accounts in three other banks in Khartoum under other names. There were also accounts "in Hong Kong and Malaysia and at Barclays Bank in London."[3] Almost a decade later the FBI would confirm that the terrorist Mohamed Atta, who piloted one of the commercial jet-liners into the World Trade Center, "wired money to Mr. bin Laden's former paymaster in Sudan, Shaykh Said al-Masri [aka Mustafa Muham-mad Ahmad] on the eve of the terrorist attacks."[4] "Tens of millions of the $100 million" with which Bin Laden had provided the Taliban since he had arrived in Afghanistan from Sudan in 1996 was "directly traced to Bin Laden entities through banking and other transfers."[5]

When a team of American officials visited Riyadh in June 1999 to discuss the problems of tracking the financial transactions of Saudi char-itable and financial institutions, they were alarmed to learn that Saudi officials seemed generally ignorant and surprised that there was a prob-lem regulating these accounts. Worse, "Saudi police and bank regula-tors had never worked together before and didn't particularly want to start."[6] When Saudi Arabia made no effort to change its banking prac-tices a second task force headed by OFAC of the US Treasury paid a visit to Riyadh in January 2000. The Treasury officials received tea but little sympathy for their appeals to the Saudis to reform their banking regulations.

Investigating the banks

Immediately after 9/11, the US government moved quickly to establish a legal framework to investigate terrorist financial infrastructure. Names and locations of financial institutions through which terrorist organiza-tions banked and moved their money were published. Thus, the USA was the first to launch a determined effort to "follow the money" in order to halt the movement of terrorist funds; other major banking nations were slow to follow. Privacy was valued more than safety. Assets were blocked and regulations were established by executive order under the International Emergency Economic Powers Act that enabled US finan-cial institutions to freeze foreign terrorist accounts. Three months later the EU issued similar regulations, but many difficulties had already sur-faced. The world of international finance had become incredibly compli-cated. Bank secrecy, wire transfers, the myriad of transactions, automated teller machines (ATMs), and the ease and convenience of modern bank-ing could just as readily be exploited by terrorists as legitimate users. The transfer of money could also be disguised by moving small amounts from a variety of sources, and while banking in the USA, Europe, and the Pacific Rim might benefit "both from the presence and the use of sophisticated regulatory laws," the "contrary occurred in the Middle East, Africa, Southeast Asia, and the former Soviet bloc."[7]

In the aftermath of 9/11 the international regulatory community was forced to reexamine its standards. The USA was the first to act. On 24 September OFAC publicized the names of thirty-nine people and organizations on its list of Specially Designated Global Terrorists (SDGTs) whose assets must be "blocked immediately." On the list were Yassin Abdullah al-Qadi, Saad al-Sharif, Ibrahim Salih Mohammed al-Yacoub, and Ali Saed bin Ali al-Houri, all well-known Saudi businessmen from Jidda.[8] Qadi, a man with interests in banks and business throughout the world, had been the former head of the Muwafaq charity which would be accused of channeling millions of dollars from Saudi businessmen to Al Qaeda. A month later, on 24 October, Congress passed with surprising speed the United States Patriot Act, officially known as "Uniting and Strengthening America by Providing Appropriate Tools Required to Intercept and Obstruct Terrorism." That Act established an interagency task force to follow the money-trail. Next, Operation Green Quest combined agents from the US Customs Service, the Internal Revenue Service (IRS), the FBI, and the Secret Service to investigate suspect charities and corrupt financial institutions that funded terrorist activities both in the USA and around the world. Hundreds of agents and intelligence analysts began to discover wire transfers of funds that linked the 9/11 hijackers with terrorist cells in Europe. In Germany a group dominated by Al Qaeda member Ramzi bin al-Shibh had provided both financial and logistical support to the hijackers; the investigation led to the indictment of Zacarias Moussaoui, a terrorist leader.[9] And once the routes used and the dimension of the money flow was understood, it became absolutely essential to proscribe those institutions used by terrorists to fund their operations.

On 29 and 30 October 2001 at an extraordinary Plenary [Meeting] on the Financing of Terrorism held in Washington DC, FATF announced it had begun to crack down on specific institutions.[10] Officials at FATF were determined to expand its mission to "focus its energy and expertise," and a crucial aspect of the FATF effort was to impose severe penalties for financing terrorism, terrorist acts, and terrorist organizations. In addition, UN country members were urged to take immediate steps to ratify and to implement the 1999 United Nations International Convention for the Suppression of the Financing of Terrorism. The UN Security Council and EU responded by promulgating regulations designed to discourage money-laundering and the flow of terrorist funds while expanding the authority of FATF and the European Wolfsberg Group to interdict and halt the flow of terrorist funds.

The UN Security Council adopted Resolution 1373 requiring member states to freeze and confiscate terrorist assets. It published information concerning funds frozen or sequestered, and established procedures to ensure that non-profit organizations were not being used to finance terrorism. It established a Counter-Terrorism Committee to monitor the implementation of the resolution. And following the invasion of Afghanistan by coalition forces and the subsequent defeat of the Taliban regime, the Security Council passed a new resolution (UNSCR 1390) which strengthened the sanctions against remaining elements of the Taliban and Al Qaeda. UNSCR 1390 also established the Al Qaeda Monitoring Group charged with investigating, reporting, and making recommendations against Al Qaeda, Osama bin Laden, and the Taliban. FATF would intensify its cooperation with the numerous financial investigative agencies including those in the UN, the Egmont Group of Financial Intelligence Units, the Group of Twenty, the Basle Committee on Banking Supervision, and the Asia-Pacific Economic Cooperation Forum.[11] Within two months after 9/11 some sixty-six countries, including UAE and Saudi Arabia, together known to be the source of most of Al Qaeda's money, introduced procedures to block the assets of those terrorist organizations identified by the USA. The UK established an anti-terrorist finance unit, and in the EU only Italy was reluctant to introduce transnational financial regulations, and actually enacted a law that hindered any investigation of the flow of funds across its borders.

The United States Patriot Act of October 2001 had given sweeping authority for coordination among intelligence agencies, which had previously been legally circumscribed. The Treasury could now require US financial institutions to "terminate correspondent accounts maintained for foreign shell banks" and ensure that domestic banks would not "indirectly provide banking services to foreign shell banks." Tax Information Exchange Agreements were negotiated with known tax-havens including the Bahamas, the British Virgin Islands, the Cayman Islands, the Netherlands Antilles, and Antigua and Barbuda. The Patriot Act required American financial institutions to have by April 2002 a program in place to prevent money-laundering, and to allay the fears that "intelligence sources and methods" would be compromised, it also permitted in-camera judicial review of classified information used to freeze terrorist assets. These investigations soon led to the Netherlands, UAE, and Saudi Arabia. By then US officials were convinced that Osama bin Laden had "an archipelago of bank accounts" that stretched "from Barclays Bank in London . . . to Girocredit in Vienna to several banks in Dubai." Indeed, UAE was said to be Bin Laden's banking hub of choice because it maintained official relations with the Taliban government in Afghanistan, and thus provided a direct connection to Bin Laden himself.[12]

By 1999 US intelligence services were aware that the Dubai Islamic Bank served as a major conduit for Osama bin Laden's funds. Dubai's lax banking practices were easily circumvented, and funds sent by the Dubai Islamic Bank to Al Qaeda agents were linked to the bombing of the US embassies in Kenya and Tanzania in 1998. Nearly half the $500,000 used by terrorists to prepare the 9/11 attack had been wired to the USA from Dubai banks. Eventually, UAE would enact laws against moneylaundering "within the framework of . . . efforts to fight terrorism in all its forms," which provided for long prison terms and heavy fines.[13] Elsewhere in the Gulf, Kuwait issued an anti-money-laundering law in 2002 and created a Financial Intelligence Unit to monitor local banks and money exchange companies. A year after 9/11 the US Treasury had succeeded "in locating and freezing some $112 million in assets belonging to Al Qaeda and its associates." Terrorist organizations reacted swiftly, and thereafter only a little more than $10 million in additional assets were found and frozen. Cooperating governments reported "having particular difficulty in monitoring and regulating funds collected and disbursed by a number of Islamic-based charities" that "collect billions of dollars each year, using most of it" for beneficent purposes.[14]

The initial tepid response from the Saudis disturbed both the EU and the USA. Nonetheless, the campaign against terrorist financing began to produce a financial strain on the Al Qaeda network. Equally important, it frightened potential donors, who feared being caught funding organizations or individuals on the terrorist lists circulated by the USA, UN, and EU. At the private request of the USA the Saudi Arabian Monetary Authority (SAMA) began to monitor some 150 bank accounts "associated with some of the country's most prominent businessmen in a bid to prevent them from being used wittingly or unwittingly for the funneling of funds to terrorist organizations." SAMA had "sent a circular to all Saudi banks to uncover whether those listed in suspect lists have any real connection with terrorism," and among the accounts uncovered were those at the Al Rajhi Banking Corporation, the Dallah Al Baraka Group, and the National Commercial Bank (NCB), Saudi Arabia's largest bank.[15] Created in 1952, SAMA was largely responsible for enforcing the archaic 1966 Saudi Banking Control Law that regulated the nation's banking system. Since his appointment in 1983 the director of SAMA, Hamad al-Sayari, who was nominally responsible to the Ministry of Finance and National Economy, had enforced a fairly strict set of regulations to ensure the stability of the banking sector; they included regulations that Saudi banks maintain 20 percent of deposits as a liquid reserve, and the prohibition against lending more than 25 percent of their capital to any single customer. In practice, however, al-Sayari would not or could not impose punitive damages against violators without royal approval.

In December 2002 the UN Security Council received a new report that expanded the list of individuals and charities involved with terrorists. It also exposed the close relationship between Al Qaeda and Saudi Arabia. It was prepared by Jean-Charles Brisard, an investigator who had compiled the first extensive intelligence report on the financial network of Osama bin Laden for the 9/11 Families United to Bankrupt Terrorism, the circle of families who had lost relatives in the 9/11 attack and were suing, among others, the Saudi royal family for $1 trillion. Brisard argued that the financial success of Al Qaeda was attributed to the bankers, oilmen, and construction magnates who were "allies" of the USA but who also supported Islamic charities that provided funds for Bin Laden. Although Islamic charities such as the Al Haramain Islamic Foundation, BIF, IIRO, MWL, Rabita Trust, and WAMY all contributed to terrorist organizations, known or unknown by their donors, legitimate Saudi business enterprises and direct "contributions" from wealthy Saudi individuals were also crucial to the Al Qaeda fiscal network. Saudi Arabia could no longer ignore the need for more strict regulations of its charities and the archaic banking laws that gave them virtual autonomy. Consequently, when Saudi Arabia invited FATF and its Working Group on Terrorist Financing to visit the kingdom in April 2003 to conduct a "Mutual Evaluation," Secretary of State Colin Powell was able to announce that "everything we have asked them to do they have done."[16] In Saudi Arabia FATF argued for the establishment of a domestic Financial Intelligence Unit (FIU) to collect real-time intelligence and share such information with local authorities and the sixty-nine FIUs operating internationally. Shortly afterward SAMA issued new guidelines including a "Know Your Customer" program to identify suspicious activity, but the government neither formed an FIU nor agreed to the outside evaluation proposed by FATF.[17]

Saudi banking

Banking, like most institutions in Saudi Arabia, was inextricably intertwined with the House of Saud. In 1744 Muhammad ibn Abd al-Wahhab (1703–1792) allied himself with Muhammad ibn Saud, the ruler of the small town of Dir'iyya in Najd (Saudi Arabia). Ibn Wahhab was an Islamic scholar educated by Islamic clergy in Iraq, Iran, and the Hijaz region of western Arabia. He viewed himself as a reformer insisting that his followers, the *muwahhidun* (unitarians), return to the sources of Islam that

stressed the absolute unity of God and the strict observance of the fundamental meaning of the Quran and the Hadith, the sayings and traditions
of the Prophet. The Wahhabis, as the sect was commonly called, fiercely
rejected the innovations (*bid'a*) then current in Najd, where some Sufi
brotherhoods permitted and promoted polytheism and approved the role
of saints as intermediaries between God and man. Eventually, the alliance
between church and state enabled Ibn Wahhab and Ibn Saud to establish
a state governed by the Shari'a instead of traditional tribal custom. Fired
with the zeal of true believers the Wahhabis spread their movement by the
sword among the tribes of central Arabia, destroyed the Shi'ite shrines of
Karbala in southwestern Iraq, and occupied Mecca and Medina, where
they obliterated the tombs of revered Muslim saints.

As the Wahhabis moved north into Ottoman Syria the Sultan sent his
Viceroy in Egypt, Muhammad Ali Pasha, to suppress the movement. After
years of campaigning in 1822 Muhammad Ali and his sons had finally
destroyed the core of Wahhabi power in Najd, but not the movement
itself. The restoration of the Wahhabi was initiated in the late nineteenth
century by the al-Saud family. In 1902 Abd al-Aziz bin Abd al-Rahman
bin Saud, son of the last Saudi governor of Riyadh, led a daring raid to
recapture Riyadh from the ruling al-Rashids of Shammar and thus restore
his family to power in Najd. Thereafter, he extended his authority, relying
on his own Ikhwan – members of militarized agricultural colonies he
created in 1912 – that would transcend tribal loyalties and adhere strictly
to the puritanical principles of Wahhabism. During the First World War
he received gold and weapons from Great Britain to be used against
the Ottoman Turks and their Arab allies. And though the First World
War ended in 1918, Ibn Saud employed British arms to overthrow his
principal rivals, the al-Rashids. In 1921 he captured their capital, Ha'il,
and in 1924 he occupied the Hijaz, driving Sharif Husayn bin Ali from the
Holy Cities of Mecca and Medina. Two years later the Ikhwan conquered
Asir Province, then under the protection of Imam Yahya of Yemen, but
when prohibited by Ibn Saud to attack Shi'ites under British protection
in Iraq, the Ikhwan revolted against him in 1927. They were suppressed
two years later after hard fighting in their garrison town of Artawiyya,
and Ibn Saud celebrated his victory in 1932 by incorporating the Hijaz
and Najd as the Kingdom of Saudi Arabia, the same year he signed a
concession with an American company to prospect for oil.

Thereafter, Ibn Saud consolidated his power in alliance with the *ulama*,
strictly imposing the Shari'a and promoting the *hajj*, another pillar of
Islam. Although he had subordinated the power of the Ikhwan to his
authority, Wahhabi doctrines had great appeal to Islamic reformers, particularly the Salafiyya Movement in late nineteenth-century Egypt and

in the twentieth the fundamentalist Muslim Brotherhood founded in 1928 by the Egyptian shaykh Hasan al-Banna. The greatest challenge to Wahhabism in Saudi Arabia, however, came in the early 1960s when the impact of phenomenal wealth from oil began to permeate throughout Saudi society. To combat the corrosive influence of these unfettered riches the Wahhabi movement and its *mutawa'in* (religious volunteers and the contemporary name for religious police), who were the successors of the Wahhabi Ikhwan, imposed a strict observance of Wahhabi principles that prohibited the melodious recitation of the Quran, veneration of tombs, desegregation of the sexes, and the appearance of the female form on television. Under Wahhabism the Kingdom of Saudi Arabia became a refuge for Islamic radicals and Muslim Brothers who fled from persecution by the secular, militant pan-Arab rulers, particularly Gamal Abdel Nasser of Egypt. Many found refuge teaching in the new Islamic University of Medina and the King Abdul Aziz University in Jidda. The Muslim Brothers had incorporated their own revolutionary and Salafist propensities with traditional Wahhabism that had a profound influence on students, society, and eventually on charitable organizations. Among them were the hypnotic Muhammad Qutb (the brother of author, Muslim Brother, and Salafist Sayyid Qutb) and Abdullah Azzam. Azzam left a powerful impression on young Saudis, including a student named Osama bin Laden. Indeed, the export of Islamist education was, in many instances, the task of Islamist preachers and clerics financed by Saudi charities.

During the two centuries that followed the appearance of Ibn Wahhab the banking sector was slow to germinate in the Muslim world. Persia introduced western banking in 1889 with the establishment of the Imperial Bank of Persia, but the growth of that bank and other state banks was painfully slow. The reasons were many, some having to do with colonialism, others with Islam itself. When the ruling council of Al Azhar University reaffirmed that usury or interest on loans, the basis of western banking, was *haram* (unlawful, unacceptable) according to the principles of Islamic law, Lord Cromer, the British de facto dictator of Egypt and a member of the Baring Brothers banking family, installed a pliable Grand Mufti who ignored the university council ruling and permitted the practice of usury. In the Persian Gulf the British first introduced western banking in Bahrain, and by the Second World War the Bahrainis themselves had become involved in banking, and the island was soon to become the financial center of the Gulf.

The extraordinary demand for oil after the Second World War provided the wealth that only modern banks could manage efficiently. NCB was the first domestic institution to receive a banking license, to be followed in the 1950s by a succession of foreign banks that were duly licensed. Although oil would soon transform the Saudi economy, the Saudi kingdom was still an impoverished state dependent mostly on *hajj* revenues. The profligate successor to Ibn Saud, King Saud bin Abd al-Aziz (r. 1953–1964), was continually strapped for cash. Thus, when his brother Prince Faisal bin Abd al-Aziz, the Saudi Minister of Finance, approached Salim Ahmad bin Mahfouz, the owner of NCB, for a loan to replenish the royal treasury, he "turned him down flat." Mahfouz had helped the royal family over many a hard time, but Faisal's request far exceeded any previous appeal. In that same year King Saud had squandered his father's patrimony, driving the kingdom to the brink of bankruptcy, with only 317 riyals – less than $100 – in the national treasury. The personally austere Faisal reacted to Mahfouz's rejection by withdrawing his personal finances from the bank, "and told his family to do the same."[18] Within a short time Mahfouz relented. The royal family received their loans, but Faisal never forgot his humiliation and now understood the powerful role that banks played in the financial affairs of his kingdom.

By 1964 the Saud family had lost all confidence in the king for his spendthrift habits and his failed policy of appeasement towards Gamal Abdel Nasser, which had not prevented the Egyptian invasion of Yemen. With the powerful support of the religious establishment King Saud was deposed and replaced by the capable Faisal bin Abd al-Aziz (r. 1964–1975). Faisal's austerity and reforms, which he already had begun as Prime Minister, laid the foundations for a modern government and a social welfare system that benefited from the astonishing increase in oil revenues after 1973. During the Suez crisis of 1956, Faisal, then Finance Minister, had refused demands for an Arab oil boycott of the West, but he could no longer resist another boycott after the outbreak of the Arab–Israel (October) war of 1973. The subsequent boycott by OPEC sent the price of oil soaring, creating serious problems for the Saudi treasury's primitive financial infrastructure, especially in the management of the $34 billion annual infusion of oil revenues, which had been only $8 billion before the October war. Faisal believed that the huge sums deposited in western banks should be invested in development, but the problems of great wealth that seemed to have overwhelmed him were partially resolved after his assassination in 1975. The following year the Council of Ministers decreed that the maximum foreign shareholding in domestic banks could not exceed 40 percent. To survive, seven western banks formed joint ventures with newly created Saudi banks. It proved to be a dynamic stimulant for a domestic banking industry that in 1976 was still in its infancy. A quarter-century later the Saudi banking sector had evolved from a primitive system of little significance into a sophisticated and powerful player in both the Islamic world and the West.

By 1995 Saudi Arabia's twelve commercial banks were flush with oil revenues to rank among the top ten banks in the Arab world. Five of these ten, "measured by tier one capital," were based in the kingdom, and its leading bank, NCB, was well respected in the global financial community. Nevertheless, Saudi banking practices remained somewhat idiosyncratic, for they could not be totally separated from the distinctive characteristics of Saudi government finances. "Until the mid-1980s, Saudi banks had it easy. The phenomenal growth in the economy fuelled by government spending enabled them to make significant profits, [and] there was little pressure to institute good banking practices." There was "a tendency to go in for 'name lending,' whereby loans were made based on the identity of the client rather than being based on an assessment of the credit risk."[19] Thus, the recession that followed the collapse of oil prices in 1986 came as a severe shock to Saudi bankers. They discovered that many of their major borrowers could not, or would not, meet their payments, and large sums had to be written off as defaulted loans. It was not until the mini-boom in oil prices that followed the Iraqi invasion of Kuwait that the domestic Saudi banks recovered to emerge as the strongest group in the six states of the Gulf Cooperation Council, founded in 1981.

By 1993 Saudi banks were making an average return on equity in excess of 15 percent and a return on average assets of 1.5 percent. By the twenty-first century Saudi Arabia had twelve commercial banks, all majority owned by Saudis. In addition there were state development banks that offered soft loans for infrastructure and agriculture projects. Although foreign and offshore bankers did participate in syndicated financing, foreign banks were still not allowed to open offices in the kingdom. In 2003 the Saudi economy ran a record surplus of $12 billion, and beginning in 2004, yet another rise in the price of oil led to an increase in Saudi reserves to nearly $25 billion. US dollars accounted for nearly 80 percent of the total, but in juxtaposition there remained the weight of a huge public debt amounting to nearly $180 billion dollars.

Islamic banking

The introduction of modern Islamic banking in the 1980s owed much to the foundations laid by Hasan al-Banna and the Muslim Brotherhood. He personally promulgated both the theory and practice required to establish an Islamic banking system among the ranks of the Ikhwan. From its very beginnings in 1928 the Brotherhood placed a very high priority on the establishment of an Islamic economic system, and Hasan al-Banna, Sayyid Qutb, Yousuf al-Qaradawi, "and numerous other scholars laid down some of the groundwork for practical theories of Islamic

finance."[20] The Muslim Brothers watched, waited, and learned the management of money that was essential to finance a worldwide organization
devoted to the spread of Islam. To preserve the fiscal independence necessary to achieve their objectives, the only acceptable source of money was
from its own members. Yet another pioneer in Islamic banking was the
Swiss banker François Genoud, who set up Swiss bank accounts for the
various Maghreb liberation movements active in Algeria, Morocco, and
Tunisia. On behalf of the Syrian government, Genoud then created the
Arab Commercial Bank in Geneva, and in 1962 he was named Director of
the Arab People's Bank in Algeria, a predecessor of the modern Islamic
bank.[21] Throughout his long involvement with Islam it was taken for
granted that Genoud was in the pay of the Muslim Brotherhood, but the
Ikhwan appeared in little need of outside help as they spread their movement amongst Muslims all the way to the republics of the former Soviet
Union.

Islamic banking as practiced today is, in reality, a recent phenomenon
attributed to the Egyptian economist Ahmad al-Najjar, who in 1963 created the Mit Cham Savings Bank in Cairo, but it was not until the meeting
of Islamic states in Lahore in 1973 that the first unified Islamic Development Bank was launched. Headquartered in Jidda, the bank's operations
were governed by Islamic principles. Its capital was subscribed by Saudi
Arabia, Kuwait, Bahrain, Pakistan, Bangladesh, Indonesia, and Turkey,
but the Saudi royal family played the predominant role in the funding
of projects that within a decade surpassed $3 billion. Two years later the
Dubai Islamic Bank was founded, and in 1979 Pakistan became the first
country to officially Islamize its banking sector. Since then scores of private commercial Islamic banks have opened for business and begun to
compete with conventional banks in many Arab and then in other Muslim
and non-Muslim countries. By 1983 the Association of Islamic Banks had
helped in the establishment of a dozen banks in new venues, including
Cyprus, Austria, and the Bahamas. From that "genuinely novel development in Islam," Islamic banking would gain "modest market niches by
the nineteen-nineties that began to attract the attention of the international business community."[22] Islamic banks opened in Geneva and the
UK. By the mid-1980s the Ministries of Awqaf of Kuwait and Abu Dhabi
were both important players in international Islamic banking. They were
both shareholders in the emerging Islamic Banking System International
of Luxembourg whose majority stockholder, 25 percent, was the Saudi
Al Baraka Group. Some large international banks, including Citibank,
Dresdner Kleinwort Benson, and ANZ International, offered a range of
Islamic services, and a few launched mutual funds considered unobjec-
tionable by experts in the Shari'a. The British bank Kleinwort Benson

even established an Islamic Banking Research Institute to develop new instruments for Islamic finance of commerce in consultation with Islamic scholars, but in London the Saudi-based Al Baraka Group relinquished its license, permitting it to be a deposit-taking bank in 1993 "rather than undergo expensive restructuring to conform to the requirements of the Bank of England."[23] Islamic finance was introduced into North America in the 1980s, but its promise lagged behind the rest of the world, as "the main problems centered on the existing banking and security laws [in the USA], which were seen as unduly restrictive."[24] In the USA Islamic banking is still in its infancy.

Islamic finance has been considered by one banking expert as the "major laboratory for innovation by Islamists, who are determined by definition to remake or modernize contemporary reality by Islamizing it." To Islamize banking means that Islamic banks should operate according to Islamic principles derived from the Quran and by the exhortations against exploitation and the unjust acquisition of wealth by the Prophet Muhammad, the search for *halal* (religiously permissible) profits. Islam considers objectionable investments in alcohol, gambling, pornography, and other products and services of a similar nature. While creative labor, exchange of goods, common trade, and the quest for profit are not discouraged, Islamic banks cannot give and investors cannot receive a guaranteed rate of return on deposits. Specifically, Islamic banks cannot collect interest (*riba*) on accounts, for such payments are considered to be usury. In order to circumvent this proscription, Muslim legal scholars have devised a banking system wherein depositors can invest in profit-sharing ventures that involve a business risk equally shared by banker and depositor, the profits not being considered interest. Other Islamic financial instruments used to avoid usury include *murabahah* (deferred payment on purchases, often called mark-up financing), *ijara* (leasing), and *ijara wa iqtina* (lease purchase financing). *Mudarabah* (partnerships where one party provides capital and the other labor, often called trust finance) and *musharakah* (equity participation). All are recognized as legitimate use of one's money. Thus, the fundamental difference between Islamic and traditional banking systems is that "in an Islamic system deposits are regarded as shares that [do] not guarantee their nominal value."[25] Shaykh Nizam Yaquby, a graduate in economics from McGill University and presently the adviser on Shari'a to the Arab Islamic Bank in Bahrain, has described the constraints on investment of savings as the maximization of profits within an ethical framework. The greatest challenge for Islamic banks, however, was their inability to make long-term transactions because most of the deposits were short-term ones that required more flexible instruments to comply with *halal*.

By the 1990s deposits in Islamic banks were growing at the rate of 15 percent annually, and most Islamic banks were controlled by private investors, except those in Iran and Pakistan, which were nationalized. Operating in more than fifty countries, Islamic banks could now account for more than $80 billion in savings, but despite this impressive growth the competition from commercial banks that offered many more technologically sophisticated financial services and long-term loans discouraged Muslim depositors: the famed Dubai Islamic Bank required a rescue package in 1998. The greatest single success was in Bahrain, which has long served as the global hub of Islamic banking and whose banking officials have served as a pool for Islamic banking expertise, modernization, and innovation. The total assets of Islamic banks and financial institutions operating in Bahrain were $3.65 billion at the end of September 2003. That strength enabled them to bail out an Islamic bank that threatened to fail in Thailand in 2002 and a "Sharia-compatible" bank in the UK.[26]

Some Islamic states have regarded Islamic banking with considerable distrust, associating its bankers with the secretive Muslim Brotherhood or the financial instrument of the governing elite. Both secular regimes, such as Syria or Iraq, and the traditional regimes of Oman and Saudi Arabia have actively discouraged Islamic banking institutions. In other countries such as Egypt and Jordan, the performance of Islamic banks has been generally disappointing, but Algeria successfully introduced Islamic banking in 1988 and even permitted the establishment of new Islamic banks after the outbreak of the Islamist insurrection in 1992. In 1989 after the coup d'état and its Islamic revolution the Sudan officially adopted Islamic banking practices, which hitherto had been somewhat haphazard. In East Asia Islamic banks have gained a foothold in Bangladesh, and in Malaysia a dual banking system survived thanks to a special partnership between the Malaysian Central Bank and the Bank Islam Malaysia Berhad, founded in 1983, which transacts more than 70 percent of its business in non-Muslim accounts.

In Saudi Arabia the royal family has consistently opposed the introduction of Islamic banking, and for years refused to grant banking licenses to the Dallah Al Baraka and Dar al-Mal al-Islami (Islam's House of Finance), despite the fact that Al Baraka was led by the successful Saudi businessman Saleh Kamel and the Dar al-Mal al-Islami Trust (DMI) was the $3.5 billion holding company for the powerful Faisal Financial SA of Switzerland and the Faisal Islamic Bank. Many assumed that SAMA was "content" to maintain competition between banks at a comfortable level, and that the introduction of the powerful Geneva-based DMI might just destabilize the Saudi financial sector.[27] Cynical observers wondered if the problem was not its secretive operations. Others believed that DMI has survived by distributing subsidies to the royal family. In recent years Muhammad al-Faisal al-Saud, son of the late King Faisal, was a member of the board of directors before becoming its President. The King Faisal Foundation of Riyadh remained a principal shareholder, and true to form DMI shareholders were expected to pay an annual *zakat* on the profits that might accrue from investments. The investigations into terrorist financing after 9/11 discovered that DMI had connections to the Bin Laden family and that Haydar Mohamed bin Laden, a half-brother of Osama bin Laden, served as one of its twelve directors. DMI also held shares in Bank Al Taqwa, registered in the Bahamas and based in Switzerland, which was closed for business in November 2001 after Washington blacklisted it as the centerpiece of Bin Laden's financial network.[28] After 9/11 Islamic banks immediately denied any part, witting or not, in funding terrorism, but the investigations of terrorist financing soon uncovered the fact that the regulatory supervision by central banks and international agencies was badly flawed. At the 2002 World Islamic Banking Conference hosted by the government of Bahrain one speaker argued rather disingenuously that Islamic banks had neither the surplus funds nor the methods of distribution to support terrorism.

Al Rajhi Banking and Investment Corporation

When SAMA finally decided to license an Islamic bank, it selected the relatively small Al Rajhi Banking and Investment Corporation. Why the Al Rajhi Bank was selected remains a mystery, but since so much of Saudi private capital was held and invested in Islamic banks abroad the king may have decided it was time that Saudi Arabia had its own domestic Islamic bank that would enhance the legitimacy of the royal family as the historical caretakers and promoters of Islam.[29] The Al Rajhi was a "traditional" Saudi merchant family whose wealth rivaled that of the Al Sauds throughout the first half of the twentieth century. King Abd al-Aziz had frequently depended on Al Rajhi for financial support, and its comfortable relationship with the royal family lasted until the oil revenues burgeoned in the 1970s to free the monarchy from its financial dependence on wealthy merchants. Founded as "a local money-changing network," the Al Rajhi Bank redefined itself as an Islamic bank.[30]

After a fitful start the Al Rajhi Banking and Investment Corporation began to attract both large and small investors, and by 2001 it had become the third-largest bank in Saudi Arabia, with over 400 branch banks including separate branches only for women. Originally, Saudi Arabia's major banks dealt principally with the royal family and wealthy customers, but Al Rajhi carved its own niche from deposits made by the Saudi middle class.[31] Yousif Abdullah al-Rajhi of the parent Al Rajhi Company for Industry and Trade maintained a close centralized control over its foreign banking operations, particularly in Pakistan and Bangladesh. Not surprisingly, the head of the Al Rajhi family, Suleiman al-Rajhi, was a member of the Golden Chain of wealthy investors who supported Osama bin Laden.

National Commercial Bank

The National Commercial Bank (NCB) was founded as the first Saudi domestic bank in Jidda in 1950 by members of the Kaki family and Salim bin Mahfouz. Like the Bin Laden family, who intermarried with the Mahfouz, Salim was an impoverished Yemeni immigrant from the Hadhramawt who settled in Saudi Arabia in 1930. Mahfouz became a money-changer, from which he amassed a considerable fortune and with the Kaki family convinced King Saud to grant NCB a license. During its first twenty-five years NCB struggled against stiff competition from the preferred foreign banks. In 1976 when foreign banks were forced into joint ventures, it was finally able to compete on a more level playing field. Under the exceptional management of Mahfouz, NCB was organized through a series of holding companies, the most prominent being the Saudi Economic and Development Company LLC (SEDCO), a conglomerate founded in 1976 and based in Jidda. Upon his death in 1986 NCB ranked first in equity and second in assets in Saudi Arabia, and it operated numerous banks throughout the Muslim world and the West. It was already one of the most powerful Arab-owned enterprises in the Gulf and the bank of choice of the royal family.

Following the death of Salim bin Mahfouz he was succeeded by his eldest son, Khaled bin Mahfouz, as President, Chief Executive Officer (CEO), and the largest shareholder of NCB stock. In 1989 he was appointed to the governing council of the Saudi oil giant Aramco by King Fahd, but his good fortune was about to change. In the late 1980s NCB, like other Saudi banks, suffered heavy losses during a recession in the Saudi economy that had forced many creditors to default on their loans. NCB recovered but was again placed in jeopardy in 1990 and 1991 when senior members of the Saudi royal family defaulted on their very large loans, the extent of which was so great that either the debts would have to be repaid or NCB would go under. Even worse, Khaled bin Mahfouz made an unfortunate business decision. He purchased 20 percent of the Bank of Credit and Commerce International (BCCI), founded in 1970 by a Pakistani, Agha Hasan Abedia, with Arab money. The Kakis, who still held a third of the shares in NCB, apparently had no say in the matter.[32]

Unfortunately for the Mahfouz family, between 1986 and 1990 Khaled had agreed to serve as the Chief Operating Officer of BCCI, known as the "Bank of Crooks and Criminals" in the USA. Khaled bin Mahfouz was then accused of "hiding assets and in the cover-up and obstruction of the Senate investigation" which had uncovered a score of its fraudulent practices in July 1992. He was promptly indicted in the USA and charged with participating in a "Scheme to Defraud in the First Degree in violation of New York Penal Law 190.65, in connection with certain of defendant's acts and omissions relative to BCCI holdings and certain related entities." In other words, Mahfouz was charged with embezzlement and violations of American, Luxembourg, and British banking laws by misrepresentations, sham loans, money-laundering, and falsifying his holdings in BCCI.

When BCCI collapsed, the solvency of NCB was threatened and Khaled was forced to resign as CEO in 1992. After a year of convoluted and persistent negotiations NCB settled with the liquidators of BCCI in November 1993; the charges against NCB were dropped, and Michael Callen from Citibank was assigned to reorganize NCB and save it from bankruptcy. Khaled bin Mahfouz agreed to pay a $245 million settlement, including a personal fine of $37 million, to indemnify some of the bank's clients. The Mahfouz family was disgraced, and the Kaki family, who still held a third of the shares of NCB, systematically reduced their holdings to 10 percent and no longer played any significant role in the management of the bank.[33] It was during this turbulent decade that Yassin Abdallah al-Qadi, assistant to Khaled bin Mahfouz, introduced Islamic banking services at NCB and the Al Rajhi Bank with the assistance of the National Management Consultancy Center (NMCC) of which Yassin was Director from 1991 to 2002.

In August 1998 Khaled bin Mahfouz was again in the news when the El-Shifa pharmaceutical plant in Khartoum was destroyed by US cruise missiles in a poorly planned and questionable attack on what was thought to be part of the Bin Laden business empire. In a desperate attempt to justify the bombing, the owner, Salah Idris, was called a "banking protégé" of Mahfouz, and US and UK officials spent substantial time investigating Salah Idris's Capital Trust Bank of New York and London searching for a connection to Osama bin Laden.[34] Then in 1999, SAMA audited NCB and found serious discrepancies in its books. Although family members were permitted to retain 10 percent of the capital and seats on the board of directors, the controlling shares in NCB were transferred to the Saudi state authorities. Under new management NCB recovered to emerge stronger than ever as Saudi Arabia's most important bank with assets of $26.5 billion.[35] There remained, however, deep suspicions in the

West that NCB was being used as a financial conduit that had "funneled millions to charities believed to be serving as bin Laden fronts."[36]

Dallah Al Baraka Group and Bank Al Taqwa

In 1969 Shaykh Saleh Abdallah Kamel founded the Dallah Works and Maintenance Corporation to introduce Islamic principles into its operations that could be adapted to global markets. Born in Mecca in 1941, he was a pioneer in modernizing Saudi Arabian banking institutions, and under his skillful management Dallah grew steadily, expanding into banking, investment, insurance, and lending throughout the Islamic world. By 1995 Dallah Al Baraka Group had absorbed more than 300 companies with 60,000 employees and $7 billion in assets. After 9/11 the US government began to investigate the Group as part of a larger investigation of Islamic banking practices and fiscal transactions that abetted the financial network of Al Qaeda. The possible and possibly unwitting link between Dallah Al Baraka Group and Al Qaeda became more focused in August 2002 when the family members of the 3,000 American citizens killed in the destruction of the World Trade Center brought suit among others against three Saudi princes: Defense Minister Sultan bin Abd al-Aziz al-Saud, former chief of Saudi intelligence services Turki al-Faisal al-Saud, and businessman Muhammad al-Faisal al-Saud.[37] The class-action lawsuit specifically charged the Al Baraka Investment and Development Corporation (BIDC) of Jidda as one of the many companies in the Dallah Al Baraka Group.

BIDC was singled out by US authorities because of questionable investments in two banks suspected of having financial links to terrorist organizations: the Al Aqsa Bank in the Palestinian territory of the West Bank and the Al Baraka Exchange LLC in Somalia. In addition BIDC owned a percentage of Bank Al Taqwa, a "brass plate" finance company based in the Bahamas, Switzerland, and Liechtenstein. Khaled al-Nehdi, Vice President of Dallah Al Baraka Group for public relations, explained that SAMA had not monitored these three accounts, for they were located outside Saudi Arabia. He did admit, however, that the Dallah Al Baraka Group had obtained a 20 percent stake in Al Aqsa in 1999 when "hopes were high for a Palestinian–Israeli peace agreement." He vehemently denied that the Group ever had any association with either Baraka Exchange of Somalia or Al Taqwa.[38] When the UN Suppression of Terrorism list was issued in November 2001, any relationship between the Dallah Al Baraka Group and the Al Baraka Exchange of UAE and the Al Baraka of Mogadishu with headquarters in Dubai was conspicuously absent. That led Shaykh Saleh Kamel to accuse "some irresponsible"

Americans of attempting to blackmail Islamic financial institutions and charities after 9/11. In contrast, Bank Al Taqwa (Fear of God) was a very different story. It was a shell bank whose financial transactions were used primarily to support Islamist organizations. Established in Nassau, Bahamas, in 1988 with financing from the Egyptian Muslim Brotherhood, the bank included among its investors several members of the Bin Laden family.[39] Its two principal directors were mysterious businessmen, Youssef Mustafa Nada and Ahmed Idris Nasreddin.

Youssef Nada was a Tunisian citizen born in Egypt, a member of the Muslim Brotherhood, and Chairman of the Nada Management Organization (aka Al Taqwa Management Organization) of Lugano, Switzerland. In 1954 he had fled from arrest in Egypt to Libya during the reign of King Idris, the deeply religious leader of the Sanusiyya Brotherhood. In 1965, for reasons never made public, he was tried in Egypt in absentia and sentenced to fifteen years in prison. When Colonel Muammar Qaddafi seized power in Libya in 1969, Nada fled once again, this time to Austria where he soon made a fortune dealing in wholesale building materials. He soon became interested in banking and founded the Nada Management Organization, which eventually advised the CA Bankverein of Vienna on its efforts to introduce strict Islamic banking practices in Europe. In 1970, with the help of Egyptian Muslim Brothers, he opened an office in Riyadh, and five years later he transferred his company from Austria to Campione d'Italia on Lake Lugano and took Italian nationality. Nada remained active in Arab banking, and helped Egypt open one of its first Islamic banks. He then created Bank Al Taqwa and used the Bahamas as a false-front headquarters to benefit from its favorable banking laws and tax exemptions. Nada bought full-page advertisements in Egyptian newspapers announcing that he was opening an Islamic bank and displaying the names of 500 Muslims who had opened accounts with Al Taqwa. From then on Nada would divide his time between his commercial operations and Islamic banking.[40]

Ahmed Nasreddin was born in Ethiopia in 1929. He had been an Honorary Consul for Kuwait in Milan where he had substantial financial holdings in his Nasreddin International Group and the Nasreddin Foundation (aka Nasreddin Stiftung), which was yet another shell operation that, inter alia, provided funds for the Islamic Center of Milan. The Foundation was legally dissolved in 1993, but the name was used in business transactions as late as 2000. Nasreddin's financial network provided direct support for Bank Al Taqwa, and the bank was listed by the USA on 7 November 2001 and by the UN two days later. In addition to its Chairman, Youssef Mustafa Nada, the US sanctions list included the bank's Vice Chairman and Muslim Brother, Ali Ghaleb Himmat, and a Swiss citizen, Albert F. A. Huber. Huber had been a political journalist, admirer of Adolf Hitler, and a rabid anti-Semite who converted to militant Islam and was appointed the Swiss director of Al Taqwa, fulfilling the requirement that a Swiss national must be on its board of directors. He publicly acknowledged in 1995 that wealthy Saudi Arabians were large contributors to Bank Al Taqwa, and that one of them, Ghalib Mohammed bin Laden, unsuccessfully sued the bank in 1999 for failure to pay $2.5 million on a *mudarabah* account.

In 1996 Italian intelligence linked Bank Al Taqwa to HAMAS, the Algerian Armed Islamic Group and the Islamic Salvation Front, the Tunisian Al Nahda, and the Egyptian Jama'at al-Islamiyya.[41] However, it was not until two months after 9/11 that US investigations led to the closing of Bank Al Taqwa operations in the Bahamas and Liechtenstein. Swiss authorities moved more slowly. They found nothing irregular despite the fact that Al Taqwa had been providing financial support for Bin Laden and Al Qaeda as late as September 2000.[42] Then in March 2002 an investigative reporter in the USA discovered a previously secret list of names that appeared on an unpublished shareholders' register of Bank Al Taqwa which disclosed their personal holdings as of December 1999. The list revealed previously unpublicized Bank Al Taqwa shareholders, among whom were prominent Arab figures from numerous countries in the Middle East, including Yousuf Abdullah al-Qaradawi, the radical Egyptian cleric and promoter of HAMAS, the Grand Mufti of UAE and five members of his family, a member of the Kuwaiti royal family, and members of the "prominent Khalifeh family of the United Arab Emirates; sisters Huta and Iman bin Laden who lived in Saudi Arabia."[43]

On 19 April 2002 the Treasury then froze the assets of Ali Ghaleb Himmat in the belief that he had long acted as a financial adviser to Al Qaeda. Born in Syria, a Muslim Brother, and Director of the Islamic Center of Munich, he was a member of the board of directors of the Geneva section of the Kuwaiti International Islamic Charitable Organization (IICO) and IIRO. He had banking interests in Munich and had long been under surveillance by the German Federal Intelligence Service (Bundesnachrichtendienst, BND), which reported Himmat's "pleasure" over the news of 9/11.[44] In August 2002 an updated list of organizations having connections with Al Qaeda was prepared by the US Treasury for submission to the UN 1267 Sanctions Committee. It identified twenty-five new terrorist financial institutions, fourteen of which were owned or controlled by either Nada or Nasreddin, including the Akida Bank Private Ltd., whose majority ownership was held by the Nasreddin Foundation.[45] "Lacking a physical presence and sharing the same address in the Bahamas where they were licensed," they were designated by OFAC as shell companies serving as conduits for terrorist funds, and under pressure from the US Treasury the Bahamian government revoked their banking licenses.[46]

Finally, in December 2003 Youssef Nada and Ali Ghaleb Himmat were taken into custody by Italian police after their homes were raided in Campione d'Italia. They were soon released, however, after which Nada admitted he had been in talks with the Swiss Deputy Attorney General. He claimed that the "FBI may have known who the shareholders were for as long as four years . . . since 1997 when I talked to them."[47] In effect, the Swiss authorities had refused to cooperate with international intelligence inquiries into Al Taqwa. Swiss banks were protected by stringent secrecy laws, and the Swiss authorities argued that there was never sufficient evidence to merit a search warrant despite possessing the FBI list of bankers suspected of financing terrorism. Still, the Akida and Al Taqwa banks were closed, but the Al Taqwa Group simply became the Nada Management Organization of Lugano, Switzerland, from where Nada continued to deny funding Bin Laden or any other terrorist group.

Hawala system

After the US Treasury had frozen the assets of sixty-two organizations and individuals associated with Islamic banking and investment in November 2001, federal agents raided a number of their offices in the USA, Europe, and the Bahamas, from which they obtained substantial information on the genesis, morphology, and growth of the worldwide *hawala* banking system used by millions of Muslims. *Hawala* comes from the Arabic word meaning "change" or "transform," and is defined as a bill of exchange or a promissory note. In South Asia it is called *hundi* and is derived from the Sanskrit root meaning "collect." It has the same meaning as *hawala*, i.e., a bill of exchange or promissory note, but adds the connotation of "trust." *Hawala* predates traditional or western banking in South Asia, and was first introduced in Calcutta when the British established the Bank of Hindustan in 1770. A *hawala* operator is known as a *hawaladar* and that of a *hundi* as *hundiwala*. Essentially *hawala* is a remittance system employed as an alternative or a parallel to traditional or western banking practices. There are several other similar systems such as the "chop" or "chit" in China. Together, they are often referred to as "underground banking," but in fact they usually operate in the open with complete legitimacy, and their services are widely publicized. What distinguishes *hawala* from other systems of remittance is the importance of "trust" and the extensive use of connections such as family, ethnic, regional, or business partnerships. Unlike traditional banking or even the "chop" system *hawala* uses only minimal or no negotiable instruments, but it is a very big business. The German Finance Ministry has estimated that the global annual volume of *hawala* cash transfers today is over $200 billion.[48]

Hawala works by transferring money without actually moving it, and to understand *hawala* it is best to follow a single such transfer. Muhammad had arrived in the USA from Dubai on a tourist visa that has long since expired after he got a job driving a taxi in New York. As a cabby he has saved $5,000 that he wants to send to his brother, Faisal, now living in Riyadh. His first thought is a major bank, where he learns several lessons as to how traditional banks transfer money. The bank would prefer he open an account, but Muhammad demurs, for he has no social security number. The bank will still transfer his cash but will sell him Saudi riyals at the official rate of 3.75 riyals to the dollar and charge $25 to issue a bank draft for 18,750 riyals. There will be an additional charge of $40.00 for overnight courier service, for surface mail is unreliable and time consuming. Muhammad believes he can get a better deal through *hawala*. "For many people in remote areas of the world, the nearly untraceable hawala system is faster, cheaper and more reliable than Citibank."[49] He reads in a local Arabic newspaper an advertisement by the "Music Bazaar and Travel Services Agency" in Queens offering cheap tickets, great deals in riyals, movie rentals, video conversions, and pager and cellular activations. Such advertisements are very common in ethnic newspapers. Muhammad calls and speaks with Abdullah, who charges 5 percent to handle the transaction but offers an exchange rate of 4.00 riyals to the dollar (20,000 riyals) with the cost of delivery included. He decides to do business with Abdullah, to whom he gives his $5,000 in cash. Abdullah then contacts *hawaladar* Salim in Riyadh by phone or fax, although e-mail is becoming more common. Salim arranges to have 20,000 riyals delivered to Faisal the next day.

This simple example contains all the vital elements of a *hawala* transaction. First, there is *trust* between Muhammad and Abdullah, who does not give Muhammad a receipt, for he does not record individual remittances, only recording for his own purposes how much he owes Salim. Abdullah *trusts* Salim to make the payment to Faisal – invariably in person – the next day, no later. Abdullah and Salim have done business many times and both belong to a *hawala* network operating on connections that are constructed in several possible ways. One possibility is that Abdullah and Salim are business partners or do business on a regular basis, and *hawala* is just another part of their business dealings with one another. A second possibility is that for whatever reasons Salim owes Abdullah money. Consequently, Salim is simply repaying his debt to Abdullah by paying his *hawala* customers. This is an informal relationship, but one of the most typical for *hawala*. A third possibility is that Abdullah has a "riyal surplus" in Riyadh and Salim is helping him dispose of it. In the last two cases Salim does not have to recover any money by simply repaying a debt to Abdullah or handling money that Abdullah has entrusted to him. In the first case when Abdullah and Salim are business partners a more formal means of balancing accounts is necessary. There are numerous ways to accomplish this, but the most common is an import–export business in which Abdullah imports CDs and cassettes of Arab music, gold, and jewelry from Salim and exports from New York telecommunications equipment to him. To pay Salim, Abdullah simply "under-invoices" a shipment of telecommunications equipment to Salim valued at $20,000 but invoiced for $15,000 so that the "extra value of goods" Salim will receive from the sale of the equipment, in this case $5,000, is the equivalent Abdullah owes Salim. The manipulation of invoices is one of the most common means to settle accounts.

Consumers primarily use *hawala* because it is cost effective and provides its clients with considerable savings. Most *hawaladars* operate out of a rented storefront, not a bank building. They may share space with another business, such as a sari or gold shop, or work from a table in a tea shop. Their employees receive no health insurance and no retirement benefits. Nevertheless, *hawala* is incredibly efficient; remittances never take more than two days, in contrast to a week or so required by international wire transfers to corresponding banks, which are closed on weekends and holidays, and operate in different time zones. Moreover, *hawala* is more reliable than traditional international transactions, which can become frustratingly complex when they involve the client's local bank, its correspondent's bank, the main office of the foreign bank, and then the branch office of the recipient's foreign bank. It is not unusual for large commercial transactions to get lost "in transit" for weeks. Those who use *hawala* remain anonymous, for there is virtually no paper; the *hawaladar* gives no receipts, keeps no accounts, except what he owes or is owed by his correspondent. In addition, *hawala* permits the *hawaladar* to engage in foreign-exchange speculation or black-market currency dealing, which also enables him to turn a profit, for a *hawaladar* can always offer better exchange rates than banks. Obviously, none of this would work without complete *trust* by all parties.

Following Indian and Pakistani usage those who use *hawala* distinguish between "white *hawala*" to describe legitimate transactions such as the one by Muhammad the cab driver and "black *hawala*," which refers to illegitimate transactions, specifically money-laundering for illegal activities: narcotics, fraud, terrorism. *Hawala* can be used in any one of three ways to launder money: "placement," "layering," and "integration." "Place-ment" is the problem of how to introduce large amounts of cash into the financial system, since some jurisdictions require financial institutions to report cash transactions over a certain amount; in the USA it is $10,000. *Hawala* effectively provides a means for placement of large amounts of cash. Most *hawaladars* have a business in which they make deposits into their business accounts that enables them to justify large deposits as the proceeds of a legitimate business or use some of the cash to meet busi-ness expenses. "Layering" takes place when the money-launderer manip-ulates the illicit funds to create legitimacy by transferring money from one account to another. No matter how careful and complicated the manner in which this is done, it can raise suspicions in the traditional banking system and be reported as such. *Hawala*, however, leaves a very sparse trail if any. Even when under-invoicing is used, the mixture of legal goods and illegal money, confusion about "valid prices," and complexities of international shipping make the trail much safer than a wire transfer. "Integration" is the means by which the money-launderer invests the money in his legitimate assets, consumes it for pleasure, or reinvests it in illegal activities. *Hawala*, consequently, becomes ideal for the integration of money by transforming illegal cash into legitimate money that can be easily reinvested in a legitimate business, a financial shell, or a seemingly legitimate front for illegal activities.[50]

Although the basic principles of *hawala* are quite simple, the complexity ascribed to it is produced by the infinite number of variations in its exe-cution. The most consistent indicators of *hawala* activity are *hawaladar* bank accounts that betray significant deposits in cash and checks, usu-ally in the three major financial centers known to be involved in *hawala*: the UK, Switzerland, and Dubai. The Dubai Al Barakaat Bank, which should not be confused with the Dallah Al Baraka Exchange LLC, was a noted *hawala* enterprise whose founder and director was Ahmed Nur Ali Jumale. Jumale had begun his career as a *hawaladar* in Saudia Arabia in the 1970s and met Osama bin Laden during the war in Afghanistan, during which the two had forged a strong personal friendship. In 1988 he opened an Al Barakaat Bank in Somalia. A decade later Al Barakaat was a sophisticated company providing *hawala* services whose extensive transfers amounted to some $500 million a year. Through Al Barakaat Osama bin Laden could transmit intelligence and instructions to Al Qaeda terrorist cells. In addition Al Barakaat skimmed millions of dol-lars which it turned over to Al Qaeda, and it managed, invested, and distributed its funds. On 8 November 2001 it was placed on the US list of institutions supporting terrorism, and the USA and UAE seized Al Barakaat's assets and records. The fears that Al Qaeda had disguised its banking transactions by using alternative means to those of traditional banking, especially the *hawala*, led western investigators down many unknown financial pathways. The systematic exploration of the financial labyrinth of the *hawaladar* world started at the conference of banking experts and government officials held in UAE in May 2002. That meeting has led to more strict licensing and regulation of *hawaladars* operating in such far removed places as Dubai, India, and the USA.

Continuing bank scrutiny

Crucial to the FATF crackdown on money-laundering were directives issued in October 2001 designed to criminalize the financing of terrorism, terrorist acts, and terrorist organizations. Within days some sixty governments had adopted blocking mechanisms. Russia was among the most determined. It had long argued that the Beirut-Ryad Bank of Lebanon, founded in 1958 by Saudi and Lebanese principals, including then Crown Prince and Minister of Defense Saud Ibn Abdul Aziz, had been responsible for funneling funds to the IIRO and WAMY operating in Chechnya and Daghestan. Russia claimed that its modern mastermind was Shaykh Saleh Kameal, whose name had appeared on the Golden Chain list. Kameal's influence could be traced from the Dallah Al Baraka through the Al Shamal Islamic Bank to the Jordan Islamic Bank, Iqraa International Foundation, and other institutions. By Islamic banking standards Beirut-Ryad was quite small, maintaining only twelve branches including a London office. Nonetheless, Russia believed that from the early 1990s it had been a fundamental instrument in assisting the growth of Islamist movements in Central Asia. Its role, according to the Russian intelligence service, was part of a "grandiose plan" directed against Russia, and which visualized the eventual merging of former Soviet republics into a Great Islamic Caliphate.[51] Elsewhere, the Jordan-based Arab Bank Plc, which operated in thirty nations and computed assets of some $27 billion, also received close scrutiny as investigators recognized it as a special favorite for funneling money from Iran, and the Damascus headquarters of HAMAS and Islamic Jihad, to Palestinian jihadists in the West Bank and Gaza.

Following 9/11 the investigation of the Arab Bank's links to terrorist financing extended beyond the Middle East to Europe; according to court documents filed in Spain, an Al Qaeda cell that had helped prepare the 9/11 attacks used the bank to wire money form Spain to associates in Pakistan and Yemen. In August 2005 the US Department of the Treasury imposed a fine of $24 million on the Arab Bank's New

York City branch for 'systemic' failures to operate in accordance with the anti-money-laundering systems and controls demanded by the United States Bank Secrecy Act. The fine was an indication that in the USA the close observation of Muslim banks and banking practices would continue indefinitely.

4   Afghanistan beginnings

> Modern Islamic movements don't believe in schools of jurisprudence,
> they don't define themselves as Shia, or Sunna, or of this Sufi order or
> that Sufi order. They don't want to break with history altogether, but
> they want to go forward and develop.
>
> Hasan al-Turabi, Madrid, 2 August 1994

The beginnings of most Islamist revolutionary movements can be
attributed to the Soviet Union invasion of Afghanistan in December
1979. In Riyadh the royal family leadership was quick to support the
mujahideen, and after the meeting of the Organization of the Islamic Conference (OIC) in Pakistan in January 1980 Saudi money began to mobilize Muslim world opinion against the Soviets. To be sure, there were
secular Muslim revolutionaries in Palestine, militant Islamists in the city
streets of Egypt, and the attenuated belligerent offshoots of the Muslim
Brotherhood, but none of these possessed the commitment, the passion,
or the ferocity of the Salafist cells that were forged in the crucible of
Afghanistan. The inchoate revolutionary movements that later emerged
in Algeria, Bosnia, the Philippines, Chechnya, and Central Asia were
invariably the ideological offspring of those Islamists who had fought for
Islam against infidel communists in the Afghan war led by a hard core of
intellectual clerics and professionals and their Afghan-Arab *mujahideen.*
At the end of the war most them surreptitiously returned to their countries of origin where they founded or joined Islamist groups committed
to overthrowing the government and establishing an Islamist state, but a
handful of these pioneer jihadists remained in Peshawar, committed to a
worldwide Islamist revolution.

Al Qaeda

Between 17 and 20 August 1988 Osama bin Laden had led an intense
discourse among his followers on the following proposition: "Is [our
organization] to serve the governments or the Arabs?" They chose the
Arabs and founded Al Qaeda ("The Base") to lead the Arab Islamist

77

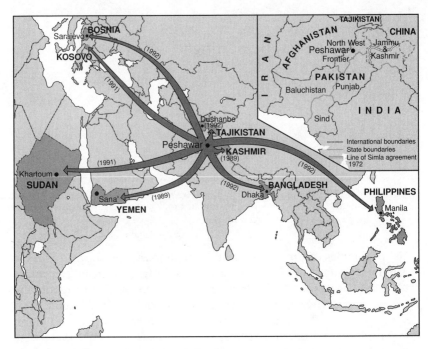

Map 1 The Peshawar–Al Qaeda nexus

revolution by *jihad*. At these beginnings there were only thirty brothers who met the leadership's strict "requirements," to commit themselves to Salafist ideology. The Salafiyya movement was largely the work of Jamal al-Din al-Afghani (1838–1897), Muhammad Abduh (1849–1905), and Rashid Rida (1865–1935), who attributed the decline of Islamic societies in contrast to the West to the fact that contemporary Muslims had abandoned the original teachings of the Prophet. Thus, the *salafa* (forefathers, Salafists) sought to restore the greatness of the Islamic world by the creation of states ruled by scripture, the Quran and Sunna, and strict adherence to the founders of the four medieval schools of Muslim law: Hanafite, Malikite, Shafi'ite, and Hanbalite. Moreover, the Shari'a should be reinterpreted following two fundamental principles – *maslaha* (the public interest), and *talfiq* ("patching"), whereby the sources of Islamic law can be drawn from any of the four schools and not as in the past from just one. Above all, Salafists insisted that Islam was Arab and its language Arabic. Although traditional Salafists believed that it is not permissible for Muslims to overthrow a Muslim ruler no matter how cruel, incompetent, or secular, contemporary Salafist Islamist jihadists have contemptuously rejected this belief.[1]

Clandestine by design, Al Qaeda was only made open to those who swore the traditional oath of loyalty, the *bay'a*. Each was given an alias using Abu as a first name followed by a descriptor, e.g. *Abu al-Kanadi* (Abu the Canadian).[2] In fact, the name "al-Qaeda" appears not to have been used by Osama bin Laden or other members until it became widely employed by the CIA and then the media. Al Qaeda had broad roots, for its members came from the larger circle of Afghan-Arabs who had come to Pakistan from all over the Arab world, but particularly from the Armed Islamic Group of Algeria and EIJ, which worked closely with another Egyptian revolutionary movement, Jama'at al-Islamiyya, rapidly emerging from its moribund Muslim Brotherhood chrysalis. The gestation of Al Qaeda had taken more than two decades and involved three Afghans educated in the 1960s – Burhanuddin Rabbani and Abdul Rab Rasul Sayyaf, who had studied at Al Azhar University in Cairo, and Gulbuddin Hekmatyar, educated in Afghanistan. Within a year of the invasion of Afghanistan by the Soviet Union they led the three most resolute *mujahideen* forces in the *jihad* against the Russians. They were acquainted with one another and had in common their reverence for the writings of the deceased Egyptian and Salafist intellectual Sayyid Qutb (1906–1966). Sayyid Qutb had been a literary critic in Cairo when he journeyed to the USA in 1948, where he remained for two years, during which time he was appalled at the moral and spiritual degeneracy of the West – even castigating the fundamentalist Christian churches for the laxity between men and women. Thoroughly radicalized he returned to Egypt, joined the Muslim Brothers in 1951, repudiated his earlier more secular publications, and rejected everything western, including the royal Egyptian government and after 1952 its secular successor, Gamal Abdel Nasser.[3] His outspoken views against the theological corruption of the secular revolutionary government of Egypt made him anathema to Nasser, and he was arrested in 1954 during a purge of the Muslim Brotherhood.

In prison Qutb was horrified by the barbaric treatment of the devout Muslim prisoners by Muslim guards, but during the next eleven years of imprisonment he had ample time to reflect and develop his ideas, which he published in a prodigious outpouring of religious polemics that were widely read. He not only produced his thirty-volume *Fi Zilal al-Quran* (*In the Shade of the Quran*), committed to the "unconditional demands" of Salafism, but the book that had much greater influence, *Ma'aallim Fittareek* (*Milestones*), published in 1965. Although a thin volume compared to *In the Shade of the Quran*, *Milestones* was the principal proof used by the prosecution in his trial and subsequent hanging in 1966. It was later translated into English and published in Damascus in 1980, by which time, however, it had become "a classic manifesto of the terrorist wing of Islamic fundamentalism."[4] His works filled an ideological vacuum for the Muslim Brothers that had existed since the assassination of Hasan al-Banna in 1949.

His radical contribution to Islamic jurisprudence was his justification for Muslims, in certain circumstances, to assassinate a Muslim ruler, which had hitherto been strictly forbidden in Islam. He argued that any ruler of a Muslim nation who does not firmly implement Muslim law, Shari'a, is not a true Muslim but – even worse – an infidel, *kafirin*, who can be killed with impunity. Sayyid Qutb relied on the writings of an early Salafist, Ibn Taymiyya (1268–1328), who wrote a treatise advocating the same reasoning when the Mongols invaded Muslim territory and many Arabs fell under the tyrannical rule of Mongol rulers. He skillfully equated Ibn Taymiyya's struggles against Mongol rulers with his own condemnation of the Nasser regime in Egypt. Moreover, Qutb redefined the Islamic concept of *jahiliyya*, which hitherto had referred to the time before the revelations of Muhammad as a period of "ignorance." Qutb now adopted the terminology of Abu al-'Ala al-Maududi (1903–1979) to call *jahiliyya* "barbarism," to be destroyed by true Muslims who had not compromised their belief in the all-powerful oneness of God. Applying this concept to contemporary times, he argued that secular society by its implementation of non-Islamic laws had overridden the wishes of God and violated His sovereignty. He was, in effect, providing an ideological framework whereby Muslims could use the principles of Islam rather than dictatorships, democracy, socialism, or communism in the holy war against these secular and unjust governments. Fifteen years after his death, in 1981, President Anwar Sadat was assassinated by the Salafist Lieutenant Khalid Ahmad Shawki al-Islambuli of the Islamist Jama'at al-Jihad (Society of Struggle) in 1981.

Not surprisingly, Sayyid Qutb deplored the corruption of one of the five pillars of Islam, *zakat*, by the dearth of any definition as to who should collect and distribute this charitable giving. He argued that in order to meet the demands of the *bayt al-mal* (the state treasury), the government should collect the *zakat* and distribute it to the poor. His opponents argued that such a procedure was not Islamic but socialistic, for traditionally Muslim governments refrained from interfering in the payment of *zakat* and *zakat al-amwal al-batina*, gold, silver, and commercial goods that can "be hidden," and therefore *zakat al-amwal al-batina* can be given only if the donor does so voluntarily, without coercion for its distribution by the government. Qutb dismissed these arguments with derision. To him *zakat* was a tax, and since the government collects the nation's taxes, so too must it collect *zakat*, including *zakat al-amwal al-batina*. He radicalized the traditional Islamic concept of *zakat* as a charitable gift that takes place between two individuals face to face, arguing that it is not an individual gift or alms that are passed over from hand to hand, but a tax paid to the government. His concept of charitable giving did not stop with *zakat*, for he also insisted that Islamic governments should also manage *awqaf*. To him the wishes of the deceased for the use of the *waqf* were subordinate compared to the obligations of the Muslim state to advance the fundamental tenets of Islam. Indeed, Sayyid Qutb was a Salafist who visualized Islam as a movement permanently in the *jihad* against unjust Muslim governments and their rulers, with *zakat* providing the resources that enabled Islam to wage war against them. There can be little doubt why Qutb was "regarded as the father of modern [Islamic] fundamentalism."[5]

Qutb and the Afghans

It is not surprising that Qutb was the single most important Islamic influence upon the Afghan leaders Burhanuddin Rabbani, Abdul Rab Rasul Sayyaf, and Gulbuddin Hekmatyar in their struggles against the Soviet invaders. Burhanuddin Rabbani was born in the rugged Badakhshan Province of Afghanistan where he attended school before going to the Darul-uloom-e-Sharia (the Abu Hanifa religious school) in Kabul. From Abu Hanifa Rabbani became a student in the school of law and theology at Kabul University for the next four years, where he was deeply influenced by the writings of both Qutb and Sayyid Abu al-'Ala al-Maududi, a contemporary of Hasan al-Banna. Invited to join the faculty at the university as professor in 1963, he sought further study at Al Azhar University in 1966 where he received his master's degree in Islamic philosophy two years later and returned to Kabul University. Here he was given the task of organizing the university students, and among his contemporaries he was the most intellectually accomplished, having translated Qutb into Dari, an Afghan version of Farsi (Persian) and one of the two official languages of Afghanistan. By his learning, works, and active support for Islam he was selected head of the High Council of the Jama'at-i-Islami (Islamic Society) Party of Afghanistan in 1972, whose outspoken demands for an Islamic state led to an attempt to arrest him in 1974. With the help of his students he eluded the police and escaped to Pakistan where he converted the Jama'at-i-Islami into a successful *mujahideen* fighting unit.

Like Burhanuddin Rabbani, Abdul Rab Rasul Sayyaf earned a degree in religion from Kabul University and then traveled to Al Azhar where he too earned a master's degree in religion. During his Cairo years he was much influenced by the writings of Sayyid Qutb, and even more than Rabbani adopted a fierce hatred for the West and the USA. Returning to Afghanistan in 1969 he founded, with Rabbani and Gulbuddin Hekmatyar, the radical Akhwan-ul-Muslimen in Afghanistan, which had strong ties with the Muslim Brotherhood. Although not the intellectual equal of Rabbani, he was certainly his military superior, organizing the Pashtun Ittihad-i-Islam-Baraye Azadi Afghanistan (the Islamic Alliance to Liberate Afghanistan) which under his leadership became one of the most successful *mujahideen* militias in the Afghan war. Numerous disciples of Abdul Sayyaf were to play dominant roles in spreading Salafism throughout Muslim Southeast Asia.

Another Pashtun, Gulbuddin Hekmatyar, was originally from Baghlan and first studied at the military academy but switched in 1968 to the engineering department of Kabul University. Although he is sometimes referred to as "Engineer Hekmatyar," he never graduated from the university, becoming an outspoken member of the People's Democratic Party of Afghanistan (PDPA), a Communist Party of the Parchami and Khalqi groups. In 1972 he was imprisoned for killing a Maoist student, escaped, and fled to Pakistan where he abandoned the communists to become a devout Muslim and founded Hezb-i-Islami (Islamic Party). He subsequently received financial assistance and extensive training from the Americans and the Inter-Service Intelligence Agency (ISI) of Pakistan, which provided Hekmatyar and his Hezb-i-Islami with millions of dollars of military and financial aid. Usually described by Pakistani officials as "power hungry, cunning, and a ruthless fanatic," he could count on 30,000 dedicated *mujahideen* and support from Pakistan's Jama'at-i-Islami movement, the Islamic Resistance Party of Tajikistan, Islamists in Kashmir, and the Hizb-i-Wahdat, a *mujahideen* collection of nine Shi'a groups in Iran.

The USA was slow to react to the Soviet invasion of Afghanistan, preferring to wait on events and observe rather than act. This passive policy soon changed after the election of Ronald Reagan to the presidency in 1981. He was determined to build up the USA armed forces and undermine where possible Soviet interventions throughout the world, and Afghanistan was a top priority. The Special Coordination Committee of his National Security Council (NSC) recommended that the USA give financial and military assistance to the "Peshawar Seven" that comprised the original Afghan resistance. These seven groups together with a host of independent *mujahideen* forces had been the creation of ISI and its director, the Pakistani General Hamid Gul. Washington supplied the cash and the weapons and was not about to question arms deliveries to militant Islamists, for they were the highly motivated *mujahideen* who usually fought fiercely. In Afghanistan the need was for short-term results with little thought given to the aftermath of a Soviet withdrawal. Little or no consideration was given to the fact that Hekmatyar had close ties with Iran, or that the forces of Abdul Rasul Sayyf would seek Islamist revolutions throughout Southeast Asia.[6]

Declaring Pakistan a "frontline state" in the war against Soviet aggression, the USA funneled its financial support and military aid, particularly the deadly Stinger anti-aircraft missiles, to the *mujahideen* from operational centers in Islamabad and Cairo. President Anwar Sadat, and, after his assassination in 1981, President Hosni Mubarak provided camps and equipment to train *mujahideen*, and arms for *mujahideen* in Afghanistan were flown to Pakistan from Egyptian military airfields. Saudi Arabia contributed hundreds of millions of dollars annually through a secret bank account held jointly with the CIA in Switzerland. The British Special Air Service (SAS) worked closely with ISI in Pakistan to train *mujahideen*, and at the end of the war in 1989 over 10,000 Afghan-Arabs had been housed, fed, and given medical treatment from a host of Islamic charities. In the end more than $4 billion had been provided by the USA and Saudi Arabia alone for the war in Afghanistan.[7] How much of that money was funneled through Islamic charities will never be known, but it was substantial.

Emir of Jihad

When Soviet forces crossed the Afghanistan frontier, Dr. Abdullah Azzam (1941–1989) was one of the first Arabs to join the Afghan *jihad*, where he was known as Shaykh Abdullah Azzam. Born in the village of Ass-ba'ah in Palestine in 1941, Azzam was reared in a humble, pious home. He was a precocious child whose abilities were recognized and nurtured in the village schools. The youngest graduate from Khadorri Agricultural College, he taught in a village school in South Jordan. His piety convinced him to seek religious training at the Shari'a College of Damascus University where he obtained a bachelor's degree in Islamic law in 1966. Deeply angered by the Israeli capture of the West Bank in 1967 he fled to Jordan and joined the *jihad* against the Israeli occupation. When that *jihad* collapsed, he fled to Egypt and graduated with a master's degree in Islamic law from Al Azhar University. Returning to Jordan in 1970 he accepted a teaching position at the University of Jordan in Amman, but having won a scholarship he returned the following year to Al Azhar where he obtained his doctorate in the "Principles of Islamic Jurisprudence" in 1973. During his years in Egypt he was a frequent visitor at the home of the deceased Sayyid Qutb.

During the 1970s Azzam rejoined the Palestinian *jihad*, but he became increasingly disillusioned when he discovered that the Palestinians did not regard their revolution as inspired by religion. His compatriots appeared more interested in cards and music than liberating Palestine. One day "he rhetorically asked one of the 'mujahidin' what the religion behind the Palestinian revolution was, to which the man replied, quite clearly and bluntly, 'This revolution has no religion behind it.'" As a Muslim Brother committed to *jihad*, this revelation convinced him to abandon the Palestinians. His vocal opposition to the secular policies of the university soon made him unwelcome, and he fled to Saudi Arabia and a professorial appointment at King Abdul Aziz University with the deep conviction that only by means of organized force could the Islamist state be established. *Jihad* and the gun became his way of life, a life devoted to a single goal: the restoration of the caliphate and the "establishment of Allah's Rule on earth." Borrowing much from Sayyid Qutb, Azzam's Islamist state would be ruled by a theocrat devoted to the pure faith; a man who would unite the attributes of an *imam* (theologian) and an *amir* (political and military commander). In the Islamist state corruption would be eliminated and only the *zakat*, authorized by the Quran, would be collected by the government as a tax. He preached that every Muslim had two obligations – *jihad* and the obligation to "arouse" the believers. *Jihad* was the path to "everlasting glory" and was not to be abandoned until the "occupied lands" were restored, the "oppressed peoples" freed, and "Allah alone" worshiped by all mankind; that was to be accomplished by the gun: "One hour spent fighting in the Path of Allah is worth more than seventy years spent in praying at home."[8]

In 1979 he and his family moved first to Islamabad, where he had accepted a post at the university shortly before the Soviet invasion of Afghanistan, and then later to Peshawar sixty miles from the Afghan border in the Northwest Frontier Province of Pakistan. There he administered the activities of MWL until his assassination in 1989. He began his personal effort to support *jihad* by opening a storefront, the Bayt Ashuhada (House of Martyrs) in Peshawar, as a one-man welcoming committee, and was soon overwhelmed when the trickle of arriving Arab jihadists became a flood. In order to accommodate hundreds of *mujahideen* recruits he established the famous Maktab al-Khadamat al-Mujahidin al-Arab (Mujahideen Services Bureau, MAK) in 1982 to offer all possible assistance to the *mujahideen*; it eventually became the headquarters of Al Qaeda. Azzam also gave refuge to hundreds of radical mullahs from the Arabian Peninsula who were bent on purifying the faithful while spreading Wahhabi theology: no fellowship with Christians, Jews, or other *kafirin* – not in Afghanistan, Pakistan, or elsewhere. In Peshawar he became famous for his many declarations in the mosque on the justification for the *jihad* and honored by the sobriquet the "Emir of Jihad" for his Friday sermons.

Never shall I leave the Land of Jihad, except in three circumstances. Either I shall be killed in Afghanistan. Either I shall be killed in Peshawar. Or either I shall be handcuffed and expelled from Pakistan.

I feel that I am nine years old: seven-and-a-half years in the Afghan jihad, and one-and-a-half years in the Jihad in Palestine, and the rest of the years have no value.

Jihad must not be abandoned until Allah (SWT) Alone is worshipped. Jihad continues until Allah's Word is raised high. Jihad until all the oppressed peoples are freed. Jihad to protect our dignity and restore our occupied land. Jihad is the way of everlasting glory.

As the director of MWL in Peshawar he was employed coordinating the activities of Islamic relief agencies, whose vehicles were often used to transport *mujahideen* and arms from one province to another along the eastern frontier, including trucks of IIRO, whose administrator in Peshawar, Talaat Fouad Abdul Qasim, a member of EIJ, had been sentenced to death in absentia by an Egyptian court. IIRO was a self-proclaimed, sophisticated humanitarian organization pledged to "alleviate human suffering worldwide" by providing support to the Afghan-Arab *mujahideen* in the field and to their families in the camps. The Dar al-Mal al-Islami Bank, the Dallah Al Baraka Bank, and BCCI, which had offices in Lahore and Peshawar, funneled the necessary funds to twenty non-government organizations (NGOs) operating in Pakistan, the "most famous of which was the IIRO."[9] The Red Crescent, Islamic Da'wa, and the Lajnat al-Birr al-Islamiyya (The Islamic Benevolence Committee, IBC) were all very active providing support for the *mujahideen*.

By the mid-1980s Peshawar had been overrun by Islamist agencies, including thirteen major charities and a plethora of minor ones such as the shadowy Islamic African Relief Agency (IARA), founded in Sudan to support Arab *mujahideen*. To bring order from this chaos and competition the Islamist assembly of Peshawar headed by Azzam created an Islamic Coordinating Council (ICC) to sort out who would do what for whom, but by 1984 Shaykh Abdullah Azzam had begun to neglect his directorship of MWL in order to spend more time raising funds for MAK. As for Azzam himself, he saw clearly the path to follow: "It is also possible for loftier models, people with mature abilities and wiser, more mindful propagators to come to the land of jihad. Thousands of such people could bring about a tremendous revolution in the reality of Afghanistan, and in the inhabited regions thereafter. Those thousands may change history."[10]

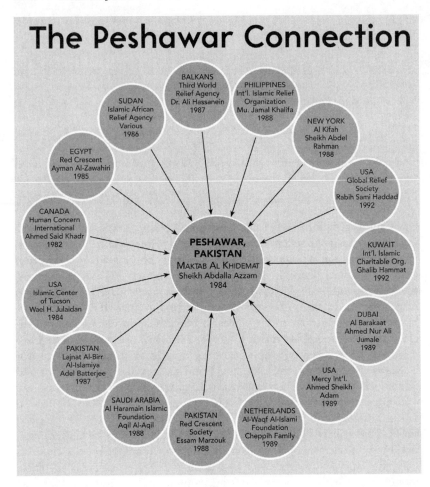

Figure 1 The Peshawar Connection

As his Friday sermons became more strident and implacable in the cause of *jihad* so too did his enemies in the government of Pakistan and among the rival *mujahideen* factions. In mid-1989 a bomb planted beneath his pulpit for his Friday sermon in the mosque failed to explode, but on 24 November while he was driving to the mosque with his two sons his car stopped momentarily on the road in time for a planted bomb to destroy the car and its occupants. It is said that Shaykh Abdullah Azzam was found whole but dead with only a trickle of blood befitting the martyrdom he seemed to crave. The charitable said that ISI did him in; the uncharitable that it was the CIA.

Osama bin Laden and MAK

By 1982 Azzam was managing numerous projects in Peshawar, among them MAK. As director of MWL for Pakistan he was presumably responsible also for supplying food and shelter for some of the more than 1.4 million Afghan refugees that had arrived in Pakistan by 1981. Hundreds of thousands of Afghans lived in ramshackle camps around Peshawar, the first of which was Akora Khattak, a city of tents and mud huts in a barren desert erected mostly by Islamic charities. During the flood crest of refugees the camp city held over 250,000 people.[11] Although it appears that Azzam took little interest in refugees, he used MWL as a cover for a very different charity that began as a guesthouse for Afghan-Arabs which was protected by Gulbuddin Hekmatyar and his Hezb-i-Islami. Hekmatyar himself had a house nearby, and when Azzam traveled through Afghanistan he was accompanied by Hekmatyar's guards. When Osama bin Laden arrived in Peshawar in December 1979, he went first to see Azzam, his former teacher at King Abdul Aziz University, who had had a profound influence on the formation of Osama's ideas concerning *jihad*. Osama bin Laden was an energetic, inquisitive twenty-two-year-old much too young and inexperienced to be given organizational command of any aspect of the *jihad*, but under the patronage of Azzam and the protection of his *mujahideen* Bin Laden was able to obtain a thorough understanding of the role of the *jihad* in Pakistan and Afghanistan.

At Peshawar the decision was made to receive recruits for advanced military training at the Al Qaeda al-Askariya (Military Base) outside Peshawar, while Bin Laden personally took charge of the finances, including a dependable relief agency (Hay'at al-Igatha) to manage donations collected by the brothers as well as the funds given by legitimate Islamic charities ostensibly for strictly humanitarian reasons. The first important task Azzam assigned to Bin Laden was to assist him in establishing "the Sidda camp for the training of Arab Mujahideen who came for Jihad in Afghanistan" to be followed by the construction of a second training base, the Ma'sadat al-Ansar (Lion's Den), inside Afghanistan.[12] There was little reason at this time for US intelligence agents to pay attention to Bin Laden, for construction was his business and that of his family. Milton Bearden, who ran the covert actions of the CIA in Afghanistan from 1986 to 1989, knew of Bin Laden but claimed the CIA "had no relationship with him" and presumably no suspicion of his motives, for he was donating innocuous heavy machinery and was only one of many raising funds for the same cause as the CIA.[13] Dr. Saad al-Fagih, a Saudi physician and director of the Movement for

Islamic Reform in Arabia, which had supported Bin Laden, claimed that during his early years in Afghanistan, "nobody noticed that he was there."[14] During his frequent visits to Saudi Arabia he preached *jihad* in the mosques, collected funds to support the war effort, and sold cassettes in which he urged the youth to take up *jihad*. When in Peshawar Osama stayed in Azzam's guesthouse where he helped in planning for the administration of MAK, the organization that inspired him to found Al Qaeda.

Azzam was never a rich man, and consequently he welcomed financial support from his wealthy friend. Certainly, Bin Laden was not hesitant in pledging his own resources to the movement, and throughout the 1980s his construction company built camps and roads, including a secret pathway from the Pakistan frontier to within twenty kilometers of Kabul. When he was not constructing camps, Bin Laden was active in collecting funds that enabled Azzam to publish magazines and books that urged a call to action, including *The Defense of Islamic Countries as an Inherent Duty*, which soon became the Islamist strategy for *jihad*. Both Bin Laden and Azzam would travel widely seeking acolytes for their inchoate jihadist movement, all the while preaching the "mentality of *jihad*."[15] Traveling, printing, and spreading the cause of *jihad* costs money. The government of Saudi Arabia channeled hundreds of millions of dollars to support the *mujahideen* through secret bank accounts in Switzerland. Prince Turki al-Faisal, who directed Saudi Arabia's intelligence apparatus from 1976 to 2001, admitted that he had personally met Osama bin Laden four or five times in the 1980s, but he has been conspicuously silent about Azzam.[16] "Money flowed into the Service Bureau" from the Muslim Brotherhood, "but the heaviest funding" came from Saudi Arabia – some directly from the Saudi government, some from mosques, and some from Saudi princes and members of the kingdom's financial and business elite. Some believe that Prince Turki's relationship with Bin Laden at this time was more than casual, and he worked closely with Osama "to coordinate both the fighting and relief efforts."[17]

There were other contributors to the *jihad*. Prince Salman bin Abd al-Aziz, Governor of Riyadh, was chairman of a committee specifically set up to fund *mujahideen*. Another big donor was the Grand Mufti, Shaykh Abdul Aziz bin Baz, who chaired MWL which was even then "the main conduit for Saudi government funds to Islamic cause worldwide."[18] Both Bin Laden and Azzam realized the importance of having a charitable foundation as a front and as an umbrella for Islamist jihadist activities; that convinced Bin Laden to found in Saudi Arabia the shadowy Islamic Salvation Foundation and its satellite, Al Kifah (Struggle).[19]

Al Kifah

Al Kifah (aka Makhtab al-Khadamat/al-Kifah) was the charitable out-reach of MAK that operated secretly to support the *jihad* in Afghanistan, and was founded by Bin Laden who was its "financial sponsor." When the offices of Al Kifah were opened in Peshawar, its activities were kept quite separate from those of MAK, and within five years the fundraising abil-ity of Bin Laden, Azzam, and a handful of Islamist companions enabled them to open Al Kifah "recruiting offices [for the *jihad* in Afghanistan] in 35 countries."[20] Between 1985 and 1989 Azzam and his companion, the pudgy Shaykh Tamim al-Adnani of Palestine, who would die from a heart attack during a visit to Orlando Disney World in 1990, traveled throughout the USA seeking both funds and recruits. Azzam visited a dozen cities, raised funds, enlisted *mujahideen*, and held an open forum to meet other Muslims and jihadists active in the USA. In 1988 he attended the First Conference of Jihad held at the Al Farouq Mosque in Brooklyn where Al Kifah Refugee Services had a small office, the Al Kifah Refugee Center, which was the work of Egyptian Islamist militants Mustafa Rah-man and Shaykh Omar Abd al-Rahman, the latter well known as the "spiritual leader" of the Egyptian Jama'at al-Islamiyya (Islamic Group) revolutionary movement. They opened the Center in 1987 ostensibly to provide financial assistance for orphans and widows of jihadists, but in fact they recruited some 200 jihadists to fight in Afghanistan. Al Kifah offices were gradually opened in every country in the Middle East, Great Britain, France, Germany, and throughout Scandinavia as well as in thirty US cities.[21]

Some have claimed that there were only "three people outside the US government who ever knew exactly what role Al Kifah really played [in the United States]." One was Azzam; the second was Mustafa Shalabi, Azzam's confidante and Al Kifah director in Pakistan who was murdered in 1991, and the third was Osama bin Laden.[22] There was, however, another man who most likely knew a great deal about the activities of the Al Kifah Refugee Center in Brooklyn: Dr. Ayman al-Zawahiri, the rabid anti-American and leader of the clandestine Egyptian Talaa al-Fateh (Vanguards of Conquest), a small, clandestine organization that had historical ties to both the Muslim Brotherhood and EIJ. A radical Islamist movement, its members were involved in the assassination of Egyptian President Anwar Sadat in 1981.

Ayman al-Zawahiri

Hundreds of Afghan-Arab jihadists, young and old, followed Bin Laden to MAK. Some were drawn to the war by *Al Jihad,* a magazine published by

MAK that openly recruited *mujahideen* for the war; others were inspired to serve by appeals, subtle and fierce, in mosques during the Friday sermon. Among those who arrived in Peshawar was Dr. Ayman al-Zawahiri, on the run from the Egyptian authorities. He seemed a most unlikely *mujahid*. When Dr. Rabie al-Zawahiri and his wife Umayma moved with their son Ayman to Maadi, a middle-class suburb of Cairo, in 1960, they belonged to two of the most prominent families in Egypt. The Zawahiri clan comprised an Egyptian medical dynasty. Rabie was a professor of pharmacology at Ain Shams University in Cairo as one of the thirty-one family members who were doctors, chemists, and pharmacists. There were also an ambassador, a judge, and a member of parliament in the extended family, but the Zawahiri name had been most closely associated with religion. In 1929 Ayman's great-uncle Muhammad al-Ahmadi al-Zawahiri became the Grand Imam of Al Azhar University, the historical center of Islamic learning, where his great- and great-great-grandfathers had been Islamic scholars. Moreover, his mother, Umayma Azzam, was also from a distinguished, wealthy, and somewhat notorious clan. Her father was the President of Cairo University, founder of the King Saud University in Riyadh, and at various times the Egyptian ambassador to Pakistan, Yemen, and Saudi Arabia. Her great-uncle had been the first Secretary-General of the Arab League, and her uncle, Mahfouz Azzam, was a dedicated Egyptian nationalist and was implicated but never tried in the assassination of Prime Minister Ahmad Mahir.

The Zawahiri family, with five children, of whom Ayman and his twin sister Umnya were the first born on 19 June 1951, lived modestly on a professor's salary. They were a very conservative and religious island in the cosmopolitan and secular life of Maadi. Ayman attended the state secondary school, rather than the elite Victoria College, where he was an excellent and pious student and following in the family tradition graduated in 1974 from the University of Cairo Medical School. At fourteen he had joined the Muslim Brotherhood and was later implicated in a failed attempt to assassinate Gamal Abdel Nasser and imprisoned. Upon his release two years later he joined the outlawed fundamentalist EIJ and ultimately became its leader. In the summer of 1980 he was working at a Muslim Brotherhood clinic in Cairo when its director "invited" him to take a four-month tour in Peshawar caring for Afghan refugees "under the auspices of the Red Crescent Society."[23] It is not known if Zawahiri met Azzam at this time, but given his interests and the limited society of Peshawar, it seems very likely.

In March 1981 Zawahiri reappeared at Peshawar for two months, working again with the Red Crescent.[24] He returned to Cairo, where a few weeks later he was charged, tried, and convicted for the possession of weapons but not for being involved in the plot that assassinated President Anwar Sadat in 1981. He was sentenced to three years in prison. At his trial he had been filmed shouting, "We are Muslims who believe in our religion . . . We are here, the real Islamic front and the real Islamic opposition. We're trying our best to establish an Islamic state and Islamic society."[25] Perhaps he was not executed because of the Zawahiri name and his influential family, but he did not waste his time in jail. His charisma and fluent English earned him an international reputation as the spokesman for the imprisoned militant Islamists, and he now had the leisure to study the Islamism of the Ayatollah Khomeini and reform EIJ.

After his release from prison Zawahiri opened a medical clinic in Cairo, but soon disappeared. In 1985 he was in Jidda, where he may have met Osama bin Laden.[26] He then reappeared in Peshawar again but now as a member of SARCS. He arrived back in Cairo in 1986 for a few months before traveling through Saudi Arabia to Peshawar, never to return to Egypt. Once again he served as a surgeon but this time for the Kuwait Red Crescent, a legitimate employer in the Pakistan borderlands that was often used for illicit purposes by the *mujahideen*. He also opened an office for EIJ in Peshawar, and with Ibrahim al-Mekki, a former Egyptian colonel and Islamist who fled the country after the Sadat assassination, he transformed EIJ into a true revolutionary, clandestine Islamist movement.[27] Among his patients in Peshawar was Osama bin Laden, who apparently was suffering from health problems associated with diabetes.

Shaykh Omar Abd al-Rahman

Born in 1937 in the Egyptian Fayoum, Shaykh Abd al-Rahman was blind almost from birth. Largely self-educated, his persistence and brilliance earned him admission to Al Azhar, where he graduated with a doctorate in religious law and theology. He had joined the Muslim Brotherhood in his youth, and after graduating from Al Azhar his reputation for learning and piety was instrumental in his appointment as "adviser" to the Ikhwan's "Guiding Bureau"(Maktab al-Irshad), one of whose responsibilities was to issue *fatwas*, literally legal opinions but often regarded as religious judgments from reputable scholars of great trust. Among his subsequent *fatwas* was one that permitted Afghan-Arab *mujahideen* to assassinate "Muslim opponents in their respective countries who had violated the Shariat, or Islamic law."[28] His provocative *fatwa* was characteristic of the blind cleric who had served for years as an *alim* (adviser, spiritual leader) to Egyptian Islamist revolutionaries – the original al-Jihad and to its terrorist offshoots, the Islamic Jihad, the New Jihad Group, and the dangerous Vanguards of Conquest, a mysterious organization that included Dr. Ayman al-Zawahiri, and the radical Jama'at al-Islamiyya.

Egyptian intelligence was convinced that his *fatwa* was the justification for EIJ assassination of Anwar Sadat. He was arrested, "charged with providing the inspiration for the murder," tried three times before being acquitted for lack of evidence, and released in 1984. He soon appeared in Peshawar where he became close friends with Bin Laden, Abdullah Azzam, and Gulbuddin Hekmatyar.[29] Acting on his advice, Jama'at al-Islamiyya sent some 300 *mujahideen*, including his two sons, to fight courageously in Nangarhar Province, and he himself visited the jihadists operating inside Afghanistan on numerous occasions. During the next five years he served as the chief propagandist for Islamic Jihad in Afghanistan, Egypt, Saudi Arabia, and Islamic centers in Germany, the UK, and Turkey. He made several tours in the USA and preached *jihad* at the Al Kifah Center in Brooklyn where the Afghan Refugee Services Inc. at the time was raising funds for *mujahideen* operations in Peshawar.

Although the Egyptian authorities could not prevent his return to Egypt, they followed his movements, and particularly his sermons in the mosques of Cairo and Upper Egypt. Returning to Egypt from his trip to the USA to attend an Islamic conference in 1987, he was seized and placed under house arrest for three years. In 1989, while still under house arrest, he was charged with inciting a riot in his hometown, Fayoum, and jailed for three months, and then tried. He was acquitted for lack of evidence. Upon his release, he fled to the USA in 1990. This prompted the Egyptian government to try him in absentia, and it succeeded in winning a conviction.[30] Like Ayman al-Zawahiri, Shaykh Omar was determined that the various Egyptian jihadist movements should be united; EIJ should join with the Jama'at al-Islamiyya, and those two with the Muslim Brotherhood, which had survived clandestinely using the "Da'wa and Shari'a" organizations as cover to send Egyptians to Afghanistan.

Peripatetic *mujahideen*

The Soviet departure from Afghanistan was a stunning victory for the Islamists in their never-ending *jihad* against the *kafirin*. Afghanistan, a small, economically underdeveloped country of 15 million people and an army that was a rabble in arms, but with strong support from Pakistan and weapons, stinger missiles, and cash from the USA, had forced the Soviet Union to abandon the ill-fated mission to expand its domination of Central Asia. The *jihad*, however, was not to end with the Soviet departure in 1989. As far as the *mujahideen* were concerned the *jihad* remained unfinished, for the installation of an Islamist government in Kabul had to be fulfilled. The Marxist President Mohammad Najibullah, installed by the Soviets before their departure, realized the danger and offered his services to the USA in what he perceived to be "the new struggle against the radical Islamic threat." He warned that if the *mujahideen* captured Afghanistan they would turn it into a "'center of world smuggling for narcotic drugs,' and a 'center for terrorism.'"[31] In May 1988 Najibullah had been willing to sign an agreement with the UN that would have allowed western aid agencies to operate in those regions of Afghanistan not under the control of Kabul as a counterweight to Islamist relief agencies supporting the *mujahideen*, but nothing ever came of his proposal.[32] There was also confusion in Peshawar over the meaning of the Soviet departure. Unproven rumors circulated that Zawahiri was seeking to "undermine" the role played by Shaykh Azzam. Others whispered that Azzam and Bin Laden had fallen out over the direction of the Islamist revolution. On the one hand, some thought that Azzam was determined to impose an Islamist state upon Afghanistan as a base from which to launch attacks against secular governments in the Muslim world. On the other hand, some believed that Zawahiri, Bin Laden, and others had lost interest in Afghanistan. Although the strength of their infrastructure and connections in Pakistan had deteriorated, Al Qaeda continued to use it as a base to attack secular governments in Egypt, Yemen, and, as the Soviet Union disintegrated, to infiltrate themselves from Pakistan into the new Muslim republics of Central Asia.

Azzam was determined to gain victory in Afghanistan. Zawahiri was determined to win in Egypt. Zawahiri always took the longer view that the purpose of the *jihad* was to replace the governments of major secular states, such as Egypt, with Islamist governments rather than become preoccupied with an immediate victory over inconsequential states such as Afghanistan. He was prepared to support the worldwide Islamist revolution so long as it did not divert his focus on Egypt. Osama bin Laden had originally come to Afghanistan to drive out the Soviet invaders, but in Peshawar he fell under the influence of both Azzam and Zawahiri and began to consider the founding of a movement that, after Afghanistan, would continue the *jihad* in Algeria, Egypt, and the republics of the crumbling Soviet Union. When Shaykh Abdullah Azzam and his two sons were killed by a car bomb in November 1989, it was well known that Ayman al-Zawahiri had had a falling out with Azzam over philosophical disputes and that Bin Laden and Azzam had had an increasing number of heated arguments over administrative matters.[33] After the death of Azzam Bin Laden appeared undecided whether to remain in Pakistan at MAK, move to Afghanistan, or go elsewhere. When the Afghan factions began fighting amongst themselves soon after the Soviet withdrawal and the Marxist government in Kabul managed to survive, he turned his back on Afghanistan and the *mujahideen*, perhaps in disgust, and returned to

Jidda. Here his interests turned to developments in Islamist Iran while his ill-disguised contempt for the Saudi royal family earned him the street name "the Saudi ayatollah." It would be only a matter of time before he openly clashed with Saudi authorities.

On the night of 30 June 1989 a select group of Sudanese Islamist army officers in Khartoum led by Brigadier Omar Hassan Ahmad al-Bashir overthrew the civilian government of Prime Minister Sadiq al-Mahdi. At first their coup d'état appeared to be yet another of the many that have afflicted post-colonial Africa, but within a short time the coup became a revolution as the officers installed an Islamist government. The Sudan, with one-third of its population non-Muslim and non-Arab, seemed a most unlikely country to become the first Islamist state in the Arab world and Africa, but Osama bin Laden, unsure of his old MAK base in Peshawar and distrusted in Saudi Arabia, opened discussions with the Sudanese revolutionaries in Khartoum. He began investing in the Sudan soon after the coup in 1990, and the following year purchased a house and a spacious guesthouse in the fashionable Khartoum suburb of Riyadh and a farm and stable for his horses south of Khartoum on the Blue Nile. To finance all these purchases and conduct business he opened an account and deposited $50 million in the Al Shamal Islamic Bank and later other accounts in the Tadamon and Faisal banks in Khartoum. His commercial headquarters were located in a nondescript office on Mek Nimr Street, and by 1992 Bin Laden had set up two holding companies, Taba Investments and Laden International; his Al-Hijra Construction Company employed 600 Sudanese building the major arterial road from Khartoum to Port Sudan.

Socially he was a familiar figure around Riyadh, where he quickly established a close personal relationship with Hasan al-Turabi who was the ideological patron of the Islamist government. He married Turabi's niece as his third wife, and in return Turabi arranged for Bin Laden to import construction equipment duty free. Making Khartoum and the Sudan his home he and Al Qaeda members moved freely in and out of the country on Sudanese passports. His guesthouse was always open to Islamist revolutionaries – members of Al Qaeda, Egyptians from Jama'at al-Islamiyya, Algerians from FIS, Libyan and Yemeni insurgents, HAMAS – and Bin Laden would hold court on the second-floor reception room. On Thursday evenings the Al Qaeda leadership met at the farm where heavy construction equipment brought from Afghanistan was stored and used in the Sudan to build twenty-three camps to house and further train Afghan-Arab *mujahideen*.[34] By 1991 Osama bin Laden had abandoned his dealings in Pakistan, and his assiduous secretary, Wadih al-Hage, transported his last personal effects to Khartoum.

Table 4.1 *Islamist terrorist organizations*

Country	Date	Organization	Leader
Afghanistan	(1999)	Al Qaeda	Osama bin Laden
Algeria	(1997)	Armed Islamic Group (GIA)	various
	(1998)	Salafi Brigade for Call and Combat	various
	(2004)	Dhamat Houmet Daawa Salafia	various
Egypt	(1997)	al-Gamaat al-Islamiya	Taha Musa
	(1997)	al-Jihad (Talaa al-Fateh)	Dr. Ayman al-Zawahiri
Lebanon	(1997)	Hizbullah	Imad Mughnaya, Hasan Izz al-Din, Ali Atwa
	(2001)	Usbat Al Ansar	Al Qaeda alliance
Pakistan	(1993)	Harakat ul-Jihad al-Islami and Harakat ul-Mujahedin merge	various
Kashmir	(2001)	Harakat ul-Mujahedin (ex-Harakat ul-Ansar)	Farooq Rehman Khalil
	(2001)	Lashkar-e-Toiba	Prof. Hafiz Mohammed Saeed
Pakistan	(1997)	Jamaat ul-Fuqra	Shaykh Ali Gilani
	(2000)	Jaish-e-Muhammad	Masood Azhar
Palestine	(1997)	HAMAS	Muusa Abu Marzouk
	(1997)	Palestine Islamic Jihad	various
	(1999)	PIJ-Shaqaqi Faction	Ramadan al-Shallah
	(2001)	Al Aqsa Martyrs Brigade	Marwan Barghouti
Philippines	(1997)	Abu Sayyaf Group	Abdurajak Janjalani
Southeast Asia	(2002)	Jammah Islamiyya	Abu Bakar Bashir, Riduan Isamuddin
Uzbekistan	(2001)	Islamic Movement of Uzbekistan	Juma Namangani

Sources: *Report on Foreign Terrorist Organizations,* Office of the Coordinator for Counterterrorism, Department of State, Washington DC, various years; *Patterns of Global Terrorism,* Office of the Coordinator for Counterterrorism, annual report, 1997–2002.

Although the Sudan was the perfect base from which to infiltrate Islamist terrorists into Egypt, as the Egyptians well knew, Zawahiri did not immediately follow Bin Laden despite a steady flow of Egyptian Afghan-Arabs arriving in Khartoum. Since Osama bin Laden was no longer readily available to supply financial assistance, Zawahiri began his extensive fundraising tours in the USA. In 1991, using a false passport in the name of Dr. Abdel Muez, he arrived in California where he visited at least three mosques to collect money for EIJ, claiming it was to be used "for Afghan widows, orphans and other refugees."[35] From the USA he traveled on to Bosnia on French and Swiss passports and lived for a time in Denmark with EIJ leader Talaat Fouad Abdul Qasim before being granted asylum in Norway. Later Zawahiri returned to Peshawar where he was joined by Abdul Qasim, who once again became director of IIRO. By 1991, however, the government of Pakistan had decided to rid the country gradually but firmly of troublesome Afghan-Arabs, and Jama'at al-Islamiyya was at the head of the list as its members returned clandestinely to Egypt from their safe havens in the Sudan. Since most Afghan-Arabs expelled from Pakistan were already wanted fugitives in their homelands, many used Iran as a transit point to the Sudan while others came through northern Iraq where Kurdish revolutionaries protected them until they could filter into other countries in the Arab world.

Zawahiri was a frequent visitor to Khartoum, but despite the growing hostility of the Pakistani government he remained quietly in Peshawar until 1993 when the expulsion of Egyptian "undesirables" followed the failed assassination attempt on Prime Minister Benazir Bhutto. No longer able to charm ISI, Zawahiri finally moved himself and his headquarters to the Sudan where he had considerable influence in the Sudanese Islamist movement led by Hasan al-Turabi. Within a year he was reported to have arranged "security for a meeting in Sudan between Bin Laden and the leaders of the Egyptian Islamic Jihad, Hizbullah, and the Iranian government."[36]

Foot-soldiers

Khaled Shaykh Muhammad, the son of an expatriate Baluchi who had settled in Kuwait, was among the most notorious Islamist foot-soldiers to arrive in Pakistan to follow Azzam and Osama bin Laden. Muhammad had joined the Muslim Brotherhood as a teenager in Kuwait, and he may have visited Afghanistan as early as December 1982 on a Pakistani passport. He enrolled in North Carolina A&T College in the USA, from which he graduated in 1986. During his studies he led clothing and food drives for shipments to the Afghan *mujahideen*, and six months after graduation arrived in Peshawar, his airfare reportedly paid by Osama bin Laden. Here Muhammad remained for five years as a member of Bin Laden's circle, working for various charities, and reportedly present at the founding of Al Qaeda. In 1993 he would play a major role in the bombing of the World Trade Center in New York, and thereafter as Al Qaeda's "chief of operations" he was personally involved in virtually every major attack by the Al Qaeda network including the recruitment of operatives to work with his nephew Ramzi Yousef in the Philippines, the financing of Operation Bojinka, a plot to destroy a dozen airliners over the Pacific Ocean, and the mastermind of the destruction of the World Trade Center on 9/11.[37] Ramzi Yousef himself had also made his way to Peshawar in the early 1980s where he stayed for a time at the Bayt al-Ashuhada (House of the Martyrs). When Bin Laden and Azzam rented a house in Peshawar, the Bayt al-Ansar (the House of the Faithful), he became a loyal follower working like his uncle, Khaled Shaykh Muhammad, in various Islamic charities that were assisting the *mujahideen* over the border in Afghanistan. After the Soviet withdrawal Yousef, now a member of Al Qaeda, emerged in Southeast Asia where he worked in association with the Indonesian terrorist Hambali (aka Riduan Isamuddin) who had also been a *mujahid* in Afghanistan and a known associate of Osama bin Laden, Ayman Zawahiri, and Muhammad Jamal Khalifa, brother-in-law to Osama bin Laden.[38]

Ahmed Said Khadr (aka Abu al-Kanadi) was born in 1946 in Egypt, where he was educated before immigrating to Canada in 1977. He became a Canadian citizen and director of Human Concern International (HCI), a Canadian charity whose activities seemed so innocuous that by 1997 it had received $325,000 in grants from the Canadian International Development Agency (CIDA). After the Soviet invasion of Afghanistan Khadr traveled to Peshawar in the early 1980s as a volunteer in the *jihad* against the Russians. Here he came in contact with Osama bin Laden, long before the Al Qaeda terrorist network was created in 1988. In Peshawar Khadr worked with BIF and was later a "key figure in the Canadian al-Qaeda network."[39] He became a close associate of Bin Laden and a senior leader in Al Qaeda.

From the very beginning of the war in Afghanistan Yemen had become a principal source of Afghan-Arab *mujahideen*, among whom the dominant figure was Shaykh Abdul Majeed al-Zindani. During the 1980s he reportedly was responsible for recruiting between 5,000 and 7,000 Arab Yemenis for military training in Saudi Arabia and "religious teaching under his guidance" in Pakistan.[40] He himself seldom went to the front, serving rather as a spiritual father for the *mujahideen* from the Yemen and the leader of Yemen Islamic Jihad. Shaykh Zindani had known Bin Laden since the 1970s and in Afghanistan in the 1980s, and was instrumental in raising money from Saudi charities. In 1984 he successfully convinced MWL to establish a Commission on Scientific Signs in the Quran and later received funds for *jihad* from the Al Haramain Foundation, where he was chosen to spearhead the "It-is-Truth" internet campaign. In Yemen he assumed the leadership of the Islah (Islamic Reform Party), and in 1995 he founded the radical Imam University in Sanaa where he taught thousands of students radical *jihad* against the West and its most infamous alumnus, John Walker Lindh.

Shaykh Muhammad Umar, an Afghan and the youthful leader of a small mosque in Karachi, occasionally visited Peshawar where he stayed at MAK. In 1983 Bin Laden provided financial support for his mosque and even bought the shaykh a house. A decade later Shaykh Umar returned the favor as head of the Taliban movement taking control of the government in Afghanistan, by assisting Bin Laden in his search for a refuge in Afghanistan.

Wadih al-Hage (aka Abu al-Sabbur; Norman; Wa'da Norman; Abu Abdullah al-Lubani; The Manager) was born in Sidon, Lebanon, on 25 July 1960 and immigrated to the USA where he became a citizen and graduated from University of Southwestern Louisiana with a degree in urban planning. In 1983 he arrived in Peshawar at the age of twenty-three where he was employed in the office of MWL. By this time Shaykh Azzam had relinquished most of his duties with MWL to concentrate his efforts on MAK. In 1984 he returned to the USA, only to travel back to Peshawar in 1986, where he was assigned to the MAK field office in Quetta, Pakistan. During these years he became a confidant of Osama bin Laden, entrusted to arrange the transportation of the last of Bin Laden and the family's belongings from Peshawar to Khartoum in 1990. In 1993 Bin Laden made him his personal secretary, and he provided false documents for Al Qaeda members and devised plans for an Al Qaeda cell in Nairobi. He was then sent to Nairobi in 1996, masquerading as a representative of Africa Help – supposedly a German humanitarian charity, but unknown to the German authorities. In Nairobi he also set up several bogus companies in Kenya and Tanzania as covers for his activities, including a fraudulent mining concern, Tanzanite King, under Aadil Habib (aka Abu Ubaidah al-Banshiri), a top military commander in Al Qaeda, who died in a boating accident on Lake Victoria in 1996. Later al-Hage would be arrested and tried for his part in the bombing of US embassies in Nairobi and Dar es Salaam, during which he testified that Bin Laden "was the financier" for MAK before he was sentenced to life imprisonment.

Born in 1965 and educated as a money manager in the Sudan, Jamal Ahmed al-Fadl arrived in Peshawar in the 1980s, where he was befriended by Osama bin Laden and was given considerable responsibility in his commercial firms. He was among the first to take the *bay'a* (oath of allegiance) to Al Qaeda in 1989, after which he was sent to the Sudan to purchase offices, land, and housing for the brothers who were about to move from Afghanistan to Khartoum. During these years he traveled back and forth between Pakistan and the Sudan, making arrangements for Bin Laden's business ventures and family before finally joining Osama bin Laden permanently in Khartoum in 1991. Fadl, who had spent some time in the USA during 1988–1989, was a frequent visitor to the Al Farouq mosque in Brooklyn. He described its activities there in just a few words: "We bring donations to the office and they send donations from Brooklyn to Afghanistan."[41] In 1996 Osama bin Laden dismissed Fadl when he could not repay the $100,000 he had stolen from one of his construction companies.

Abu Zubayda (aka Zain al-Abidin Muhammad Husayn; Abu Gazawi) was born in Riyadh in 1973 to a wealthy Palestinian family from Gaza. Uninterested in politics until he met Osama bin Laden, he became obsessed by Bin Laden's ideal of the Islamic Caliphate. After the leadership left Afghanistan in the early 1990s the charismatic Abu Zubayda remained behind, training volunteers and screening potential jihadists in the Bayt al-Ashuhada compound in Peshawar. He personally interviewed every recruit and either accepted or rejected him, handled much of the camp's logistics, and controlled its finances. He was one of the few Afghan-Arabs who mastered all of the military skills taught in the Al Qaeda camps, from explosives to armor-piercing cartridges to booby-traps. Once volunteers were finished with the battle of the warlords raging in Afghanistan they would return to Pakistan where Abu Zubayda would send them to cells around the world. He was the instructor of Jamal Beghal, the ringleader of an Al Qaeda European network in France and Belgium. He was responsible for planning unsuccessful bomb plots in Jordan, Canada, and the USA during the millennium celebrations, for which he was sentenced to death in absentia by a Jordanian court and later captured in 2002 by the CIA.

Mohammad Nazzal, a West Bank Palestinian, was another important Afghan-Arab. He earned a degree from the University of Karachi in computer science before becoming a *mujahid* in Afghanistan. When the Soviets withdrew, he returned to the West Bank and joined the Islamic Resistance Movement, known as HAMAS, and became a member of its Political Bureau in 1992. With the support of HAMAS, he founded the Jaish-e-Muhammad (Muhammad's Army) in 1991 to launch a campaign of terrorist attacks to overthrow the Hashemite Kingdom of Jordan. After a series of bombings in Amman the Jordanian authorities retaliated in August 1999 by arresting twelve HAMAS activists, closing the Amman bureau of *Felastine al-Muslemah*, a HAMAS-affiliated magazine, and issuing a warrant for the arrest of Mohammad Nazzal, who managed to evade the police and remain at large.

Other *mujahideen* leaders, including Mahmoud Abouhalima, an Egyptian Afghan-Arab, and his accomplice, the Afghan-Arab Ahmad Ajaj, entered the USA on fake Pakistani passports carrying bomb-making manuals and other material for the Trade Towers bombers. A third accomplice, Sudanese Siddiq Ibrahim Siddiq Ali, had been with Abouhalima in Afghanistan in 1988–1990. All were thought to have used the Al Kifah Refugee Center in Brooklyn as a safe haven, including Ali Mohammed who was a staff sergeant in the Special Forces of the US Army at Fort Bragg, North Carolina. On the weekends Ali would travel to New York to distribute Islamist pamphlets and give instruction in weapons and explosives at the Al Kifah Center and to fledgling Egyptian jihadists who were forming their own terrorist group at the Al Farouq Mosque. It was the Center that provided Ali Mohammed with an introduction to Osama bin Laden during his trips to Peshawar.[42] When Ali left the army in November 1989 he moved to California where he accompanied Ayman al-Zawahiri on his fundraising trip, on which he traveled as Dr. Abdel Muez, representing the Red Crescent Society.

Wael Hamza Julaidan and the Rabita Trust

Wael Jamza Julaidan was born into a wealthy Medina family in 1958, and like many others he was appalled by the Soviet invasion of Afghanistan. With assistance from MWL he shortly arrived in Pakistan, and by the mid-1980s he was the director of SARCS in Peshawar.[43] He was personally close to Shaykh Abdullah Azzam who undoubtedly introduced him to Osama bin Laden in Peshawar. They became close friends, and using the alias Abu Hasan al-Madani he was one of the original founders of Al Qaeda at the meeting held in Peshawar 18–20 August 1988. Upon his return from Pakistan in 1989 Julaidan cultivated his reputation as a cultured businessman representing MWL. He was often given the innocuous title of "fundraiser," and fundraise he did. Julaidan was later one of the principal members of the Saudi Joint Relief Committee for Kosovo and Chechnya (SJRC) and maintained close personal connections with the Al Haramain Foundation. His name was on the list of the Golden Chain as an intermediary with Saudi plutocrats Suleiman al-Rashid of Riyadh, and Abdel Qader Bakri, Salah al-Din Abdel Jawad, and Abdel Hadi Taher from Jidda.[44]

He was well known for his Salafist views, however, and his friendship with Osama bin Laden was largely regarded with indifference by the Saudi authorities until they declared Bin Laden persona non grata and consigned him to permanent exile in 1993. Nevertheless, Julaidan continued the friendship, which did not seem to jeopardize his rise in the bureaucracy of MWL. When the USA and UN indicted Julaidan for supporting terrorism on 6 September 2002, the US Treasury and the government of Saudi Arabia froze his assets and those of the Rabita Trust, of which he had been Director-General since 2000. When he was put on the US list of SDGT for funding Al Qaeda and other terrorist organizations, however, most Saudi Arabians were shocked. The Saudi Interior Minister and head of Saudi intelligence services, Prince Nawaf bin Abd al-Aziz, expressed his "surprise" and hoped the report was "untrue because it would be unfortunate if a Saudi businessman was assisting and funding terrorism."[45] Prince Nawaf argued that Julaidan, who had worked for MWL for more than a decade, was innocent, but his defense of Julaidan was not sufficient to prevent the Saudi representative to the UN, Prince Naif bin Abd al-Aziz, from placing before the Security Council a letter requesting that "Julaidan be added to the Committee's consolidated [terrorism] list." Julaidan, however, remained a free man, and the Rabita Trust was relocated in Pakistan under the name of the Aid Organization of the Ulama.

The Rabita Trust for the Rehabilitation of Stranded Pakistanis, known simply as the Rabita Trust, had been founded in July 1988 by Dr. Abdullah Omar Naseef, Secretary-General of MWL during the administration of Pakistan President Zia-ul-Haq and funded by MWL. Although the Trust was ostensibly "a popular, international, Islamic and non-governmental organization at which Muslims from all over the world are represented," it was, in fact, one of the financial arms of the Pakistani MWL, in which Saudi money gave them de facto control of the organization.[46] Its original purpose was to assist 260,000 Biharis stranded in Bangladesh to return to Pakistan, but it was soon providing funds for Kashmir terrorists. Although President Musharraf of Pakistan was a patron of the Rabita Trust, it is unclear whether he was aware of its funding terrorism, but it was well known that the Al Akhtar Trust, a Rabita Trust subsidiary founded in Pakistan in 2000, was openly Islamist and providing financial support for two Pakistan terrorist organizations, Lashkar-e-Toiba and the Jaish-e-Muhammad. The government eventually froze the Al Akhtar bank accounts, but even that did not deter its members from continuing a close relationship with the Al Rashid Trust of Karachi.[47]

Pakistan and the Al Rashid Trust

In the secular Pakistan of 1957 there were only 150 religious schools (*deeni madrasa*); when the Soviets left Afghanistan in 1989 there were more than 3,000 *deeni madrasas* with over 100,000 students. This phenomenal growth in religious education continued throughout the 1990s as the government of Pakistan disbursed "millions of rupees" to religious schools "as government donations from zakat money." Also huge sums of money from Saudi Arabia, which hitherto had helped finance the *mujahideen*, were now transposed to support Salafist groups in Pakistan, the *deeni madrasas*, and the Banuri Deobandi *madrasa* complex in Karachi.[48] Founded in 1947 by Maulana Yusuf Banuri, the school was located on twelve sites and annually enrolled some 3,000 students. Banuri was home to the former *mufti* Nizamuddin Shamzai, author of more than 2,000 *fatwa*s, including a declaration of war against the USA after its invasion of Afghanistan in 2001. It was also at Banuri that Osama bin Laden met Mullah Omar, the Afghan religious leader who would one day rule Afghanistan as head of the Taliban organization. Its most famous jihadist, however, was Maulana Masood Azhar who taught at Banuri for two years before leaving in 1989. Maulana Masood was the organizational genius behind the amalgamation of Pakistani Islamist movements into the umbrella Harkatul Ansar and would later take personal charge of Pakistan's Jaish-e-Muhammad. The Jaish was later designated a terrorist organization by the USA in October 2001, followed by the UN Security Council Sanctions Committee on 24 April 2002.

As a close personal friend of Osama bin Laden and the Al Qaeda leadership, Maulana Masood was active with Al Qaeda forces in Somalia in 1993 and was reported to have clandestinely met with Bin Laden in Medina the following year. Consequently, when Bin Laden returned to Afghanistan from the Sudan in June 1996, Masood helped him establish the Al Rashid Trust as a charitable organization with the approval of ISI and the government of Pakistan as a charity in compliance with the Income Tax Act. Maulana Mufti Rasheed Ahmad (1928–2002), co-founder with Maulana Yusuf Banuri of the Banuri Deobandi *madrasa*, became its Director and Mufti Abu Lubaba its ideologue; these were the only two having direct access to Osama bin Laden. The Al Rashid Trust soon had forty branches, and by 2000 was the second-largest charity in Pakistan. The Trust was not only "one of Osama's many sources of income," but it had close ties to the Taliban in Afghanistan and jihadists fighting in Kashmir. It had funded Qari Saifullah Akhtar, a graduate of Banuri *madrasa*, who became leader of the Islamist Harakat ul-Jihad al-Islami (HUJI) forces and "one of a number of madrasa-trained Pakistanis who helped the Taliban seize power in Afghanistan in 1996." After the Taliban established their government in Afghanistan Akhtar served as adviser to its leader, Mullah Shaykh Muhammad Omar. His *mujahideen*, "the Punjabi," would fight for both the Taliban and Al Qaeda from their bases in Kandahar, Kabul, and Khost and were the spearhead of the *mujahideen* invasion of Uzbekistan, Tajikistan, and Chechnya.[49] The threat to Uzbekistan and Tajikistan was substantially reduced following 9/11 and the presence of US forces in Central Asia. Akhtar was arrested in Dubai in 2004 and extradited to Pakistan.

Before being banned by the Pakistan government after 9/11 the Al Rashid Trust, during its short life, had provided financial and legal assistance to Islamists in jail, established a network of *madrasa*s and mosques in Afghanistan, and coordinated its activity with the Wafa Khairia, an Afghan charity "largely funded by bin Laden."[50] Its trucks regularly hauled weapons, ammunition, and supplies from Pakistan to the Taliban forces in Afghanistan, and when the Taliban destroyed the ancient statues of the Buddha of Bamiyan, "parts were handed over to the Rashid Trust so they could sell them to art smugglers and use the proceeds for operations."[51] The Indian government was quite convinced that Al Rashid may have collected funds for the poor and needy, but in reality it was primarily a front organization for the Taliban with close ties to three Pakistan terrorist organizations, the Dharb-i-Mumin, Lashkar-e-Toiba, and Jaish-e-Muhammad. Many of its *mujahideen* had been trained in Al Qaeda camps. When the Al Rashid Trust became one of the first charities recognized for funding terrorist organizations after 9/11, it resisted any investigations and discreetly changed its name to the Aid Organization of the Ulama and remained active in Pakistan.

During the Afghan war Pakistan had at first welcomed a plethora of Muslim charities. Once the war ended, however, the government had second thoughts and in 1993 began to close those known to be fronts for Islamist *mujahideen*. In 1993 attempts in Egypt to assassinate the Interior Minister, Hassan al-Alfy, in August and the Prime Minister, Atef Sedki, in November were blamed on Egyptian Afghan-Arabs from Pakistan and the Sudan, and under Egyptian pressure Pakistan signed a treaty of extradition promising "to return" 1,800 Egyptian Afghan-Arabs. This effectively ended the Al Qaeda cell in Pakistan. Its members fled to Afghanistan, scattered around the world, or simply disappeared underground. The Islamists strongly protested the closures of the charities and threatened violent demonstrations. Important military officers, including Lieutenant General Javed Nasir, who had led ISI during the Afghan war, urged the government to cease and desist, which it did. When the UN requested information from the government of Pakistan about the Al Rashid Trust, its officials declared that "it has proven particularly difficult to pierce the charity veil and uncover the deep pocket donors, including business entities that provide such funding."[52] After the Al Rashid Trust was prorogued it soon reemerged outside Pakistan as the Al Akhtar Trust International. However, that organization was listed by the US Treasury Department in October 2003 after it was learned that a member of its board of directors was implicated in the kidnapping and murder of *Wall Street Journal* newsman Daniel Pearl.

Under great pressure from the USA a symbolic 100 aid workers were expelled, but it was not until the government was faced with growing internal violence and President Pervez Musharraf narrowly escaped several attempts to assassinate him that the Pakistan National Economic

Council announced in January 2004 a $100 million program to administer the religious school curriculum and reform some 8,000 *madrasa*s. This was denounced by the clerics as appeasing the USA who "were concerned that private Islamic charities finance the madrasas, where . . . radical Wahhabi theology is taught promoting militancy and jihadi sentiment among Muslim youth." The Pakistan media were skeptical that government intervention would result in any substantive changes, for throughout history Islamic charitable institutions had "always remained free from government intervention and have functioned independently."[53]

Islamic charities and the revolutionary Sudan

Foreigners are now required to register with the police within three days
of arrival, and a permit should be obtained for movement from one
region to another.

Sudan Minister of Interior, April 1995

When Osama bin Laden and his Al Qaeda cabal had settled into the
Sudan in 1991, the Islamist revolution was only a year old. The Sudan
was the second government after Iran to adopt Islamist principles for its
constitution, but unlike Iran it did not possess ethnic homogeneity or a
single common language, and a third of its inhabitants are non-Muslims.
Iran fought a fierce war with its neighbor Iraq for eight years (1980–1988),
but until 2005 the Sudan had been mired in an even more debilitating
and tragic civil war in the south and now in the west, in Darfur, that the
NIF regime in Khartoum had not been willing to end if the price to be
paid would compromise its Islamist ideology.

The Sudan is the largest country in Africa, a million square miles,
the size of the USA east of the Mississippi, straddling "the Afro-Arab
divide between northern and central Africa" on the frontier of Islam.
In 1991 some 25 million Sudanese were represented by nineteen major
ethnic groups and hundreds of smaller ones speaking some four hundred
languages. Arabic is the lingua franca in the urban enclaves, but English
is often the preferred language of the elite. Unfortunately, it was only
too true that "religion in the Sudanese political context [was] no longer
a matter of personal ethics, piety, spirituality or morality; but a lethal
weapon in the power struggle" between Arab North and African South.[1]
It was that power struggle, and the first emerging Arab Islamist state,
that attracted Osama bin Laden to the Sudan. There was, in addition, the
long tradition of private and government support for Islamist movements,
a tradition continued by Sudan's Islamist leader and champion of Bin
Laden, Hasan al-Turabi. Although Khartoum was generally regarded as
an African and Arab backwater, its very lack of visibility appealed to the
Islamists as a safe haven for the headquarters of those Islamic charities

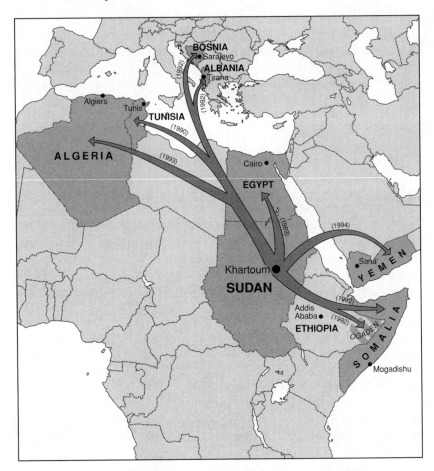

Map 2 The Khartoum–Al Qaeda nexus

over which they had administrative control. Moreover, the presence of
Islamic banks in the capital would prove useful for the quiet laundering
of charitable funds for uncharitable causes.

Banking in the Sudan

Perched marginally on the frontier of Islam, the Sudan had received little
assistance from the Islamic Development Bank (IDB) with its headquarters in Kuwait, and banking in the Sudan did not receive any significant
financial stimulus until 1975 when the Arab Bank for Economic Development in Africa (BADEA) established its headquarters in Khartoum.

BADEA hoped to exploit the vast areas of Kordofan being opened to Arab investors for large-scale mechanized farming designed to make the Sudan the "Bread Basket of the Middle East." By 1977 BADEA, which received broad support from members of the Arab League, was the principal lending institution in the Sudan. It further consolidated its position in banking circles by absorbing the Saudi-sponsored Special Arab Aid Fund for Africa. The commendable purpose of BADEA was the promotion of "Arab–African friendship and solidarity" by providing funds for economic development in Africa.[2] It was very active in the countries of the Sahil and savanna of the medieval Bilad al-Sudan, the great African plain that stretched from Port Sudan on the Red Sea to Dakar on the Atlantic, and where Saudi money went Islam would follow. Its financial assistance was employed to support Arab governments, as well as Idi Amin in Uganda and African Muslim leaders, particularly in West Africa – Sékou Touré in Guinea and Ahmadou Adhijo in Cameroon.[3]

The Sudan was not only the home for Middle Eastern economic development banks, but its government publicly encouraged private banks to open in Khartoum. It offered generous terms to the Nilein Industrial Bank in 1961, the Unity Bank in 1970, the National Bank of Abu Dhabi in 1976, and later the Saudi-Sudanese bank, founded by the Saudi banker Khaled bin Mahfouz in 1984. During these years the Sudan also became the center for one of the first attempts in the Muslim world to introduce banking based on Islamic principles. The Faisal Islamic Bank (Sudan) was founded in 1977 and opened the following year in Khartoum.[4] Next, the Tadamon Islamic Bank of Sudan was established in November 1981 and commenced operations in 1983 under its Chairman, Dr. Hassan Osman Abdalla; and finally the enigmatic Al Shamal Islamic Bank, created in 1988, opened for business in 1990. By 1985 the rapidly expanding Islamic Banking System International of Luxembourg, which was 25 percent owned by the Al Baraka Group, operated a branch in Khartoum, and listed the Kuwait Finance Group, the Ministries of Awqaf of Kuwait and Abu Dhabi, and the Tadamon Bank of Sudan as shareholders. Other Sudanese Islamic banks were less successful: the Islamic Solidarity Bank and the Islamic Company for Investment, both founded in 1983, failed to attract investors.

Of all such banks, the Faisal Islamic Bank held a special and privileged position in Khartoum. It had been founded by Saudi Prince Muhammad al-Faisal al-Saud, and after passage in the national assembly of the Faisal Islamic Bank Act of the Sudan in 1977, it had served as principal patron of the Sudanese Muslim Brothers. The Sudanese Ikhwan and the political coterie surrounding the Islamist politician and ideologue Hasan al-Turabi played a prominent role in the enactment of that Bank Act, and both had representatives on the board of directors. Moreover, the Faisal Islamic Bank, which enjoyed the patronage of the Saudi royal family, which controlled 40 percent of its shares, also enjoyed the protection of Sudanese President and dictator Ja'far al-Numayri. Whether for political or personal reasons al-Numayri had become committed to applying Islamic doctrine to all aspects of Sudanese life. He therefore bestowed on the Faisal Islamic Bank privileges denied other commercial banks, including exemption from taxes on assets, profits, wages, and pensions. He also guaranteed that the bank would not be subject to either confiscation or nationalization.

From the 1990s the Islamic banks played an important role in the political life of the Sudan, and particularly the Islamist-dominated NIF. Founded in 1986 after the overthrow of Ja'far al-Numayri in 1985, NIF was an outgrowth of the Muslim Brotherhood but sought a broader base for the popular mobilization of a political agenda of the Islamization of Sudanese society. It received substantial funding from the Islamic banks – Faisal, Tadamon, Dar al-Mal al-Islami Investment Corporation, and the Kuwaiti Zakat Fund – and through its members it gained control of the currency exchange market. Well before the Islamist coup d'état of 30 June 1989 NIF, with funds from the Islamic banks, had laid the foundations for the "internationalization of Islamism."[5] The Muslim political opponents of NIF, the Ansar and the Khatmiyya religious brotherhoods and their political parties, the Umma and the Democratic Unionist Party (DUP), found themselves checkmated when they tried but failed to introduce their own Islamic banking systems. Thus the appeal of the Islamic banks prior to June 1989, as well as government support and patronage thereafter, enabled the institutions to acquire an estimated 20 percent of Sudanese deposits by 1992. In June 1991, at the time when Osama bin Laden was transferring his operations to Sudan, the Faisal Islamic Bank had twenty-six and the Tadamon Islamic Bank eighteen branches operating in the Sudan, and most commercial banks allowed depositors to conduct their financial transactions on Islamic principles.[6]

After the 30 June Revolution the public and private Islamic Sudanese banks were expected to support the Islamist revolution and the Islamist development of the Sudan, particularly after the Sudanese economy was hopelessly mismanaged by military officers who were illiterate in economic affairs. In March 1991 a presidential decree (No. 239) introduced by fiat an "Islamic Shariah Support Fund" to insure the implementation of Shar'ia by deepening Islamic faith and practices, spreading and encouraging holy war (*jihad*) to protect the Islamic community. Specifically, the Fund was used for the mobilization and training of a people's defense force, a paramilitary organization, "and providing for martyrs' families." The martyrs were, of course, the jihadists who had lost their lives fighting a losing war against the Sudan People's Liberation Army (SPLA) in the southern Sudan. The government of Sudan contributed a small donation of £Sd100,000, and ministers gave a month's salary, but the commercial banks were expected to contribute, and indeed generally did. Abdel Rahim Hamdi, a Muslim Brother, Minister of Finance and Economic Planning, and member of the board of directors of the Faisal Bank, donated £Sd20,000, and his bank added more than £Sd7 million followed by another £Sd5 million from the Tadamon Bank. Even the innocuous Al Shamal Islamic Bank chipped in £Sd7 million. Although these amounts appear to be generous donations, the drastic depreciation of the Sudanese pound in the early 1990s reduced these impressive gifts to a pittance when converted to US dollars. Nevertheless, the banks contributed more for the *jihad* than the government or any company or individual.[7] In March 1997 the Secretary of the Sudanese Information Ministry, Muhammad al-Bashir Muhammad al-Hady, boasted that the government "had completely Islamized the financial sector."[8]

Enter Osama bin Laden

Even before the arrival of Osama bin Laden, Al Qaeda had already investigated and found the Sudan a most suitable location from which to continue its *jihad*. After all, the government of the Sudan was the only one carrying out a *jihad* to create an Islamic republic south of the Sahara, and needed all the help it could get. Shortly after Bin Laden appeared in Khartoum, Yunnis Khalis of Hezb-i-Islami, operating from Al Qaeda's Al Jabal camp, issued "An Appeal to Support the Holy War in Sudan."[9] Even before his arrival in Khartoum Bin Laden established relations with a bank upon which he could depend to carry out his wishes. He invested $50 million in the moribund Al Shamal Islamic Bank, which then had only two branches in Khartoum.[10] In addition, he opened an account in his own name in the Central Bank of Khartoum, and although never verified, it was implied that the account included his own money and funds deposited by many Islamic charitable organizations, "especially from the Gulf."[11] Undoubtedly, the Al Shamal bank was now largely capitalized by Bin Laden and Saleh Abdallah Kamel, a wealthy financial and media personality in the Arab world. Kamel was the chairman of the Dallah Al Baraka Group; ironically, its Al Baraka Bank, established in the Sudan in 1984, was privately held and operated as a traditional western bank. Moreover, the Al Shamal board of directors appears to have included wealthy members of NIF, Saudi Prince Mohammed al-Faisal, and a member of the Bin Laden family.

There is little doubt that Bin Laden wanted his "personal" bank in the Sudan, given the recent problems his family had encountered with their personal investments in the Banque Al Saoudi. That bank had only been saved from bankruptcy in 1989 by the Banque de France and then assimilated by the Banque Indosuez, and its name changed to the Banque Française pour l'Orient. "Generally speaking," the same set of shareholders, "Salem bin Laden, Khalid bin Mahfouz, Salam Ahmed Bogshan, Saad Khalil Al Bahjat, Taha Baksh, etc." had invested in the Banque Al Saoudi and the Saudi Arab Finance Corporation in Paris, the Saudi Finance Corporation (SAUDIFIN) in Geneva, and the Saudi Arab Finance Corporation International in Luxembourg. Osama bin Laden was certainly no novice when it came to moving money and no stranger to the Saudi banking families.[12] Although he undoubtedly had a controlling interest in the Al Shamal bank, Bin Laden was careful to make it difficult if not impossible to block all his funds by maintaining smaller accounts in the Tadamon and Faisal banks and in the little-known Bank of Almusia. He also controlled bank accounts in London, Malaysia, and Hong Kong, from which he routed funds through an account listed under another name at Giro Credit in Vienna. For reasons of both privacy and secrecy, however, the Al Shamal Islamic Bank remained his bank of choice.

Despite its relative insignificance – or perhaps because of it – the Al Shamal bank was used to transfer large sums of money. During the trials in the USA of Al Qaeda members accused of participating in the bombing of the American embassies in Kenya and Tanzania in 1998 an Al Qaeda collaborator, Essam al-Ridi, testified that Bin Laden had used the Al Shamal bank to transfer $230,000 from the Sudan to a bank in Arizona in order to purchase a plane to fly Stinger missiles from Pakistan to the Sudan. In another case, Bin Laden worked with the Abu Ali Group, an Al Qaeda affiliate operating in Jordan, to transfer $100,000 from the Al Shamal bank to an account in Amman by a courier traveling on a Sudanese passport under a false name. By 1993 Al Qaeda regularly used the Al Shamal, Tadamon, and Faisal banks to create an intricate business and financial network based on Islamic practices with funds from "dozens of 'charities'" that raised "money for jihad from the rich and faithful around the Gulf."[13] Despite his many investments in the Sudan and the cost of road building and maintaining a 600-man payroll, Bin Laden was still able to create a financial network in the Balkans in 1993 using charities "that provided comprehensive social and welfare services. Not only did these charities raise money, they were also effective in building popular support for militant Islam."[14]

Islamic charities and the Sudan

The earliest Islamic charitable outreach to make any significant impact in Africa began in 1962 with the founding of MWL in Saudi Arabia. The League was a creation of the Saudi royal family, designed to coordinate and spread Islam throughout the world. For years it remained as the supreme authority in the Islamic world on various theological issues, reviewed the progress and problems of Islam, and reported on events in a monthly magazine that received wide distribution. Two decades later MWL was funding training centers for Islamic leaders in Mauritania, Nigeria, Indonesia, France, and the USA, and seminaries in Mecca and Brussels that sent graduates to Africa.[15] The Sudan was fertile ground for MWL because its Muslim north and African south had historically been divided between Islam and the traditional African religions and Christianity since the nineteenth century. Here on the frontiers of Islam was the opportunity for Islam to advance into the heart of Africa. The thin veneer of secular toleration introduced by the British was slowly being stripped away after independence – internally by Islamists such as Hasan al-Turabi and externally by Muslim Brothers fleeing the secular Egypt of Gamal Abdel Nasser. By 1984 MWL had provided over two million copies of the Quran for the conversion of non-Muslim Sudanese.[16]

The Islamic Call Organization (Munazzamat al-Da'wa al-Islamiyya, aka Islamic Call, Islamic Da'wa), is a more modern but equally powerful outreach institution in Africa: *da'wa* is commonly used to describe Islamic missionary efforts, e.g. the Grand Imam of the Al Azhar mosque in Cairo is customarily named the "Chairman of World Islamic Council for Da'wa and Relief." Islamic Call itself was founded in May 1973 by Muammar Qaddafi of Libya, who was determined to spread the message of Islam throughout sub-Saharan Africa. In 1980 the organization suddenly moved its headquarters to Khartoum, and the reasons for leaving Libya have never been disclosed. Although the erratic Qaddafi had created numerous problems with his fellow Arab states, he also had his own home-grown dissidents, Libyan Islamist revolutionaries.[17] After moving to the Sudan in 1980, Islamic Call proclaimed itself a "non political organization." Its Executive Director was a Sudanese Islamist, Abd al-Salaam Sulayman Saad, who led a sixty-member board of trustees representing the governments of Saudi Arabia and the Gulf states. One of its members admitted, "Since its inception Munazzamat al-Dawaa worked hard on maintaining Islamic Identity and protecting [the] existence of Islam in Africa in particular and also in Eastern Europe and Asia with a view to fighting dangers of colonization and Christian missionary activities which exploit conditions of poverty and ill health which prevail in a number of Muslim communities."[18] Not surprisingly, after Islamic Call moved to the Sudan it initiated a determined proselytizing effort, especially in the southern Sudan among those practicing indigenous religions and Christianity. The southerners regarded it with ill-disguised hostility. It was seen as an unwanted intrusion that was determined to organize, finance, and direct Islam-oriented projects – particularly those concerned with what Islamic Call named the Islamic Civilization Project for Africa.[19]

Shortly after the relocation of the Islamic Call Organization, a satellite, the Islamic African Relief Agency (IARA), was founded in Khartoum. Its initial purpose was to provide assistance to Africans threatened by flood and drought in the southern Sudan and Uganda. These praiseworthy humanitarian efforts, however, were soon of less importance than assisting the hundreds of thousands of Muslim Ethiopian and Eritrean refugees in the Sudan.[20] By 1985 Islamic Call and IARA were implementing a strategy to penetrate all of Africa. The continent was divided into six regions, and plans were devised to establish communications and information centers in as many African states as possible.[21] Serving as an "outreach" organization of MWL, IARA had the use of its offices in some forty Muslim countries and field missions in a score of African states. Its progress, like other Islamic charities in the developing world, would be facilitated in large part from the substantial funds provided by the governments of the Arabian Peninsula.[22]

By 1990 IARA served as the perfect cover through which Sudanese intelligence agencies could provide assistance to Muslim revolutionary movements in the Horn of Africa. It would eventually serve as an umbrella organization coordinating efforts by the many Islamic charities working with *mujahideen* in the Sudan, the Horn of Africa, and the Middle East. At the time when offices of IARA began to spread throughout Africa, yet another charity, the Islamic Relief Agency (IRSA), sprouted from the fertile riverine soil of the northern Sudan. Its principal mission was to act as a counterpoise to the many Christian and western charities operating in the famine-stricken Sudan from 1984 after the devastating floods in Khartoum, but it did not establish a permanent office in the country until 1991. Nevertheless, IRSA collected funds for Islamic charities in the Sudan, but it was even better known for its close relationship with the Afghan-Arabs fighting in Afghanistan. In the mid-1980s it joined with other Islamic relief agencies to form the Peshawar Islamic Coordinating Council (ICC), chaired by Shaykh Azzam. Nearly two decades later, when Pakistan deported eighty-nine Arab aid workers in October 2001, four Sudanese working at the "Sudan-based Islamic Relief Agency [IRSA]" were among those sent back to the Sudan.[23]

The Sudan also became a safe haven for the education and training of Islamist jihadists as well as Islamic scholars. With financial support from the Gulf states the Sudan provided hundreds of scholarships to the Islamic African Center (IAC) located a few miles south of Khartoum, to which Saudi Arabia also made substantial contributions.[24] Working with both Islamic Call and IARA the IAC by 1983 had become the third partner in what would prove to be a determined Islamist outreach.[25] After the 30 June Revolution the Center evolved into the African International University (AIU), and Colonel Faisal Ali Abu Salih, the government's first Minister of Interior, compatriot of President Bashir, a committed Islamist and former IAC student, served as an AIU sponsor. A visitor to AIU, who was jailed for his curiosity, labeled it "the school of choice among radical Muslims looking for a career in terrorism."[26] Undoubtedly, AIU was a training ground for religious teachers, but by 1992 it was renowned for the number of East and West African Islamists who had graduated from the university. In 2004 one IAC graduate, an Al Qaeda terrorist from the Comoro Islands, carried a $1 million price tag on his head.

Revolutionary Sudan

In the aftermath of the 30 June Revolution the Islamist military leadership in the Sudan sought to reduce the influence and activities of western relief agencies operating in the country, and to make certain that those Islamic charities in the Sudan were properly Islamist. Despite their claims to the contrary, within a year IRSA, IARA, Islamic Call, and later the Muwafaq (Benevolence) Foundation strongly supported the revolutionary government and used their resources to assist Sudanese Islamists creating the Islamic Republic of the Sudan. The leader of the new Islamist regime, General Omar Hassan al-Bashir, was a close friend of General Abd al-Rahman Muhammad Siwar al-Dahab, the former Chief of State and director of the Transitional Military Council (TMC), who had led the coup in 1985 that ended the dictatorship of his former boss, General and President Ja'far al-Numayri. General Siwar was a well-known Muslim Brother, and after TMC was replaced the following year by the elected government of Sadiq al-Mahdi, he was appointed Chairman of the Board of Islamic Call. Under his leadership Islamic Call became ever more conservative. After the June Revolution it would "organize, finance and direct, various Islamic oriented projects, especially those concerned with the Islamic Civilization Project" undertaken by NIF activists to impose on all Sudanese – Muslims, Christians, and Traditionalists alike – Islamic institutions and Arab-Islamic traditions, speech, customs, and religion.

They were dedicated to transform the Sudan "into an Arab-Islamic civilized Nation-state by the year 2000."[27] By 1990 all Islamic charities and NGOs operating in the Sudan had been registered by the Ministry of Social Welfare, and their directors were interrogated by the various intelligence agencies of the Islamist, military, revolutionary government – except for IRSA, whose members included the well-known Islamist Hasan al-Turabi.

Of all the relief agencies in the Sudan the Sudanese Red Crescent, which was considered the most secular and even-handed, was abruptly dissolved by presidential decree shortly after the National Salvation Revolutionary Command Council (NSRCC, or simply RCC) seized power in June 1989. It would be reformed under government auspices a year later with an Islamist board of directors, and continued to work with UN organizations as in the past but avoided any cooperation with western aid agencies. Moreover, the new Islamist government soon attracted the attention of other Islamic charities, which swiftly established themselves in the favorable religious and political environment surrounding Khartoum. The Islamic Benevolence Committee (IBC), founded in Peshawar by Adil Galil Abdul Batargy, had provided assistance to both Afghan refugees and the Afghan-Arab *mujahideen*. The Muwafaq Foundation was new and largely unknown, but it had the firm support of the powerful Khaled bin Mahfouz. Islamic Call expanded its outreach; IRSA was very active, led by its Chairman of the Board of Trustees, Dr. al-Juzuli Dafalla, the conservative former Prime Minister of the TMC government, and its equally conservative Director General, Dr. Said Abdallah. Like IARA and Islamic Call, IRSA administration had been stocked with Islamists well before the 30 June Revolution, and by 1993 its former members were well placed in the Ministry of Health and the somewhat dubious Peace and Development Foundation. All three charities were also actively proselytizing in prisons, implementing the Shari'a Implementation Support Fund, and administering "peace villages" where displaced Sudanese from the Nuba Mountains were forced into concentration camps.

Under the Minister of Social Planning and powerful leader in NIF, Ali Osman Taha, all government institutions were expected to carry out a Comprehensive Da'wa Program to renew and revitalize the "spiritual life" of the Sudanese by a "framework of comprehensive social harmony." Armed forces and police officers were also trained and received diplomas for studies in *da'wa*.[28] In addition, a People's Police Force (PPF), a constabulary, was created to serve as guardians of public morals. Until his death in a helicopter crash in 1993 Sharaf al-Din Ali Mukhtar, the brother of RCC member Brigadier Kamal Ali Mukhtar and former Director of IRSA in Jidda before being expelled from Saudi Arabia in April 1991 for seditious activity, served as an intelligence agent attached to General Headquarters in Khartoum, whose mission was to watch and report on the activities of western relief agencies in the Sudan.

People's Defense Force

When the SPLA had, in several fierce battles, defeated the regular army in 1984, Siwar al-Dahab, then chief of staff to Numayri, was the first to arm the wild *murahileen* in southern Kordofan with automatic weapons to stem the advance of the SPLA. At the insistence of the Minister of State for Defense, Fadlallah Burma Nasr, a Baqqara from Lagowa, Prime Minister Sadiq al-Mahdi continued the practice in order to strengthen his position in negotiations with SPLA. The result was massive devastation and the methodical slaughter of the non-Muslim Dinka and Nuer, particularly the young men, in the northern Bahr al-Ghazal and western Upper Nile. The success of the *murahileen* confirmed the belief within the RCC, which had seized power on 30 June 1989, that it must create a more organized militia, the People's Defense Force (Difa' al-Sha'bi, PDF), to defend the state and spread the faith when it could no longer rely on the army to defeat the southern Sudanese insurgents.

The paramilitary PDF was designed to protect the 30 June Revolution from armed opposition in the North and to suppress the non-Muslim rebellion in the South. As the ideological guide of NIF, Hasan al-Turabi continued his efforts to instill Islamist ideology in the new members of PDF. He had long argued in private and public that it would be impossible to "Islamize" the Sudanese army because its professional officers had already been "secularized." Thus, in order to achieve "consensus," an Islamic Sudan should create "a small standing army and a large popular defense force" that would come from an "Islamized" society.[29] Many of the senior officers of the army were arrested or purged, and those unit commanders who remained in the army deeply resented the creation of a rival, but they could hardly object. During the early months of 1989 before the Bashir coup d'état that army had fallen further into disgrace by another series of defeats by the SPLA as demoralizing as those suffered in 1984. In response the Bashir government renamed its militias the People's Defense Force in November, only four months after coming to power in Khartoum. It then announced that all first-year students enrolled in Sudanese universities had to undergo PDF training. The shaven-headed, slogan-spouting students were not particularly enthusiastic to engage in combat, but their appearance managed to send a chill through the inhabitants of Khartoum.[30] Many parents used their influence and their cash to seek deferments for their sons. The Council of Ministers, which succeeded the RCC, responded by announcing in March 1991 that all Sudanese between the ages of eighteen and thirty would be subject to three years of compulsory military service.

PDF recruits, who were conscripted from this universal and very unpopular draft, numbered 150,000 by the end of 1991. They were introduced to weaponry by instructors from the army, but their indoctrination was more religious than military and included interminable lectures on Islam delivered by known members of NIF and the Muslim Brothers. The indoctrination itself was entrusted to Ibrahim al-Sanoussi, a confidant of Hasan al-Turabi. He frequently lectured at PDF camps, and his speeches and Islamist propaganda were widely distributed. The fanatical Issa Bushra, another ally of Hasan al-Turabi and the former IARA director in El Obeid, was specifically responsible for training PDF in the strategic region of South Kordofan. It was soon no secret that the Sudanese PDF would become neither an effective revolutionary guard nor an efficient paramilitary organization. It was a rabble in arms used by the Sudan army in its southern civil war as cannon fodder, whose depleted ranks had to be filled by force and unpopular conscription. Other newer PDF units consisting of urban youth experienced their first test in battle in the Blue Nile Province where they suffered heavy casualties at the hands of SPLA to the consternation of many professional families in Khartoum and Omdurman.

The revolution, however, needed to have its Islamist praetorian guard, and in time the most dependable and most fanatical PDF units were deployed not in the rural areas where SPLA fought but in the major cities and, therefore, under civilian NIF control. Such armed units were more dependable than the police if civilian or student protests threatened to get out of control. In 1992 *The Times* of London reported that four PDF camps were being run by "Iranian and Arab" instructors trained by the "Hizbullah in Lebanon"; both Sudanese expatriates and the Egyptian government claimed they had proof that Iranian advisers were involved in paramilitary training of PDF auxiliaries and the indoctrination of civilian cadres.[31] Since it was virtually impossible to distinguish between those who were PDF recruits and those who only received military training in PDF camps, reports circulated in the Sudan and abroad that some of these camps were, in fact, used as special centers for the training of Sudanese Muslim Brothers and NIF cadres, and as safe havens and schools for international terrorists, including Afghan-Arabs ready to lead the Islamist revolution in Tunisia, Algeria, Libya, and Egypt.

During the war between the Muslim northern Sudan and its African South the Islamist government made no distinction between civil and military activity. Thus, Islamic charities were expected to assist and support the paramilitary PDF and, when called upon, the army. Agencies such as IBC and the Muwafaq Foundation worked closely with the government military and paramilitary forces, and the Nidda al-Jihad (Call for Jihad), yet another new "charity" approved by the government, helped fund PDF training camps and supported "the costs of military expeditions." In 1992 the Islamic NGOs were "well along in carrying out a highly politicized and highly directed relief operation that dovetails with the [government] programs to gradually exclude non-Islamic NGOs from working in Sudan," and all received government funds obtained through collection of *zakat*.[32] Thus, Islamic charities operating in the Sudan might receive donations honestly given and charitable pledges from wealthy families of the Arab and Muslim world, but they were still subservient to a government that used them for its own purposes and not for the poor. In contrast, the non-Muslim foreign NGOs were regarded by the government of the Sudan as a nuisance whose activities must be circumscribed and their numbers drastically reduced. By spring 1991, of the eighty-three expatriate agencies that had operated in the Sudan prior to the 30 June Revolution only twenty-three remained, and most of those worked in the southern Sudan far from any association with the northern Sudanese.

Turabi's presence

During the eighteen months after the 30 June 1989 coup d'état Hasan al-Turabi received little attention from the government-controlled media, and he maintained a low profile. Although Turabi was an intellectual and Islamic legal scholar, he was certainly better known than the new Sudanese president, Omar Hassan Ahmad al-Bashir, and his works were read throughout the Muslim world. Almost unnoticed, Turabi appeared in Chicago in December 1990 to attend a conference entitled Islam: The Road to Victory, where he supported the little-publicized Islamic Committee for Palestine (ICP). ICP described itself as a charitable organization, but it would later be "identified by experts as part of a support network for terrorist groups."[33] Also present at Chicago were his friends and a "Who's Who" of the Islamist movement, including Rashid al-Gannushi of Tunisia, Shaykh Abd al-Aziz Odeh of the Palestine Islamic Jihad (PIJ), Khalil Shaqaqi of Al Najah University in Nablus, Shaykh Said Shaban of Lebanon, Shaykh Omar Abd al-Rahman from Egypt and Brooklyn, and Muslim Brothers from Egypt and Jordan. Publicly, they all supported the continuation of the Palestinian revolt (Intifada) and the liberation of Palestine, but they spent much of their private meetings discussing the prospect of an invasion of Iraq by the West, which they vehemently opposed.[34]

After Iraq had been driven from Kuwait, Turabi organized the first Popular Arab and Islamic Congress (PAIC) in April 1991, a conclave of 300 Sudanese and 200 delegates from 45 states. Like the great *habub*s (sandstorms) that periodically engulf Khartoum, Islamists, mullahs, and terrorists from the Muslim world made their way to the capital of the Sudan and the office of Hasan al-Turabi. Here they met with young men captivated and aroused by a spiritual experience unknown since the early years of the Muslim Brotherhood to lead the revival of Islam. Some sought to eradicate all western influence. Others were determined to destroy the state of Israel. There were intellectuals who argued that the insidious spread of western secularism had corrupted the true meaning of Islam and the incontrovertible union between Islam and the state. Pragmatic, ideological, jurisprudential, and theocratic, Turabi believed that the Islamist movement, symbolized by PAIC, was born at a time when the European, African, and Asian Muslim world was in confusion and turmoil. It sought to offer a universal Islamic religious structure to residents of secular Muslim states. With Hasan al-Turabi in the chair, the members of the General Assembly discussed, debated, and urged Muslims to turn away from the secular, hedonistic, and selfish proclivities of the West. They sternly rejected the morals and mores of the "Neo-Crusaders," which would continue to corrupt and erode the fundamental faith and meaning of Islamic culture. All the delegates rallied "to set the foundations for the establishment of the Armed Islamist International – the umbrella organization of the Sunni Islamist international terrorism affiliated with Teheran." Yasir Arafat played a leading role at the congress, and at the end its delegates established a permanent secretariat with Turabi as Secretary-General.[35]

By 1991 Turabi's essays, tape recordings, videos, and radio broadcasts has made him a popular *alim* whose name was esteemed throughout the Muslim world. He thought of himself as navigating "a course of history" that made the establishment of Islamic states "almost inevitable." He believed that as more states became Islamic, many in the West would realize that Islam cannot be stopped, "and they will cease interfering."[36] As founder of the PAIC General Assembly Turabi soon became a commanding figure in "the rejectionist front" that consisted of individuals and organizations controlled by Islamists and funded by Muslims who endorsed his call for the regeneration of Islam. His role as mediator in the HAMAS–PLO peace talks had demonstrated the power of his personality, ideology, and political presence. At first PAIC was dismissed, incorrectly, as simply another aspect of a growing "nationalist phenomenon" symbolized by the creation of Muslim institutes, media outlets, and think tanks that served as outreach agencies of the Islamic movement. Muslim governments had discovered the prestige that accompanied the sponsoring and funding of such institutions and their inevitable conferences. Turabi, however, had no intention of turning PAIC into just another Muslim debating society; its General Assembly and its permanent secretariat provided him with the instrument he needed to establish his political and religious influence throughout the Islamic world. He would proudly declare, "I am close to, I know every Islamic movement in the world, secret or public," and he regarded himself as the head of an Islamist movement dedicated to the "resurgence of new [political] action."[37] He was in contact with the Ikhwan and shaykhs active in Tajikistan and with the secretive Nahda parties in the other former Soviet republics of Central Asia, and corresponded with the *mujahideen* in Afghanistan and Kashmir.

Strange political and religious bedfellows would come to meet with him in Khartoum. Sunni Sudan would join Shiite Iran to spread the message of the Islamist revival from West Africa to Mindanao. Turabi would keep apprised of Islamist warriors: Nur Hashim in the Philippines, Abd al-Quddus, the Burmese leader of the Arakan Liberation Front, and Islamist friends in the disintegrating Socialist Federal Republic of Yugoslavia. In the Horn of Africa he was the patron of the Islamic Ogaden Union that sought to overthrow the Christian Amhara–Tigrean Ethiopian government of Meles Zenawi. He closely followed the activities of Shaykh Omar Abd al-Rahman in the USA, and welcomed to Khartoum Louis Farrakhan, the American black Muslim leader. Turabi soon became involved in the alliance between Al Qaeda and Hizbullah. Ironically, before relocating to the Sudan Al Qaeda had demonstrated little interest in cooperating with Shi'ite Iran until their relations improved immeasurably after a meeting between Osama bin Laden and Shaykh Nomani, the Iranian representative in Khartoum organized by Ahmad Abd al-Rahman Hamadabi, a Sudanese Sunni and scholar close to Turabi. Shortly thereafter a Bin Laden aide was instructed to arrange for Al Qaeda "militants" to receive "advance explosives" training for the destruction of large buildings in the Iranian-sponsored Hizbullah camps in Lebanon.

After the success of the PAIC conference in 1991 Turabi took revenge on his political rivals. He was determined to immobilize the powerful Sudanese Sufi brotherhoods and their leaders – the Ansar of the Mahdi family, the Khatmiyya of the Mirghani, and the conservative Ansar Sunna sect – that over the years had opposed him in matters political, religious, and theocratic. Their followers grumbled but could only watch helplessly as the government imposed Islamist rule upon them. One well-informed journalist wrote that Turabi would "go to the last meter and even beyond it. As far as political power is concerned, he is as hard as steel."[38] Under the PAIC banner Turabi became the master of his Islamist revolution, whose influence could be found from Bosnia to the Philippines, and in the Muslim Chechnya region of Russia. In November 1993, when Chechen President Dzhokhar Dudayev publicly "urged the Islamic World to form an alliance against the West," Turabi and his PAIC were eager to help.[39] An Al Qaeda operation to support the Chechen rebels was promptly organized, and *mujahideen* trained in Khartoum were funneled through Al Qaeda guesthouses and Islamic aid agencies in Ankara and Baku to training camps in Dagestan.

In May 1991, one month after the first PAIC conference had come to a close, Hasan al-Turabi attended a congress of Algerian Islamic fundamentalists. Returning to the Sudan he made "a tour of some Arab and Islamic countries with the aim of coordinating the efforts of the fundamentalist organizations and parties in the Arab region."[40] Given his views and his growing friendship with Bin Laden, who was now firmly in residence in Khartoum and had married Turabi's niece as his third wife, he surely knew of the support by Al Qaeda for the insurrection of the Armed Islamic Group (GIA) against the Algerian government. It was also common knowledge that he assisted the passage of Afghan-Arabs through the Sudan to Algeria. When the Islamic Salvation Front (FIS), a party of both moderate and radical Islamists, won a round of parliamentary elections in December 1991, the National Liberation Front (FLN), a socialist party that had ruled Algeria since independence from France in 1992, nullified the results and banned FIS. The outcry soon turned violent and the paramilitary wing of FIS, which had begun to target the security forces, soon broke up into splinter groups, one of which was the GIA. Although GIA has never articulated its political goals with any precision, it was "rabidly anti-foreign, anti-Christian and [an] even more militant version of the FIS" in its determination to replace the secular Algerian regime with an Islamist state.[41] The hard core of GIA were some 1,500 Afghan-Arabs who operated in autonomous groups of fifty to a hundred *mujahideen*. GIA included such well-known Afghan-Arab *mujahideen* as Sid Ahmed Mourad (aka Jaafar al-Afghani, Kamar Kharban, Aissa Messaoudi, Tayeb al-Afghani), a former smuggler who led a famous but failed raid on a police station near the southeastern border with Tunisia in November 1992. It was said that he had funds from Bin Laden as another manifestation of the covert assistance by Al Qaeda and from the Sudan government for those *mujahideen* headed for Algeria.

As Algeria disintegrated the US State Department became increasingly concerned about the dangers of a massive immigration of North African Muslims into Europe: "Events in Algeria have inspired a young radical movement in many of Europe's slums and working-class suburbs where North African Muslims abound."[42] Much of this festering discontent coalesced in mosques from Norway to Bosnia and could be measured by the increasing participation in the use of charities to fund Islamist movements. Throughout the mid-1990s the governments of Egypt and Algeria "repeatedly asked Gulf governments to monitor the activities of charities that they said were funding Islamist militants."[43]

Yassin Abdullah al-Qadi and Muwafaq

Yassin Abdullah al-Qadi, a Jidda businessman, was an individual to whom coincidences seemed ordinary rather than unusual. When a delegation of influential Saudi businessmen, which included powerful men such as Ibrahim Effendi, Saleh Kamel, and Suleiman al-Rajhi, and was headed by Prince Faisal, visited the Sudan early in 1990 Yassin al-Qadi was hardly noticed. A friend and associate of Khaled bin Mahfouz, al-Qadi surprisingly won a bid to operate a scrap-metal project from the Islamist government, which only made awards to those who met with its full approval. To manage his affairs in the Sudan he founded Leemount Limited in 1992 and registered it on the Isle of Man. Once accepted by the Sudanese Islamists, al-Qadi invested heavily in oil, banking (the Saudi-Sudanese Bank), and sesame sales. He opened accounts with Al Shamal, the bank of the Islamist insiders, claiming that its return on investment was far greater than that achieved by the Faisal Islamic Bank. Despite the fact that every Sudanese Islamist knew what was happening in Khartoum, he would later assert he was never aware that Bin Laden had invested in the Al Shamal Islamic Bank, and that he had made no personal use of Al Shamal after 1994.

After al-Qadi had used NMCC to assist Khaled bin Mahfouz to introduce Islamic banking services at NCB, he began to move in the highest circles of Saudi Arabian finance. Bin Mahfouz had witnessed the challenging growth of the Al Rajhi bank, and used al-Qadi and NMCC to compete with his rival. It remains a mystery why Bin Mahfouz singled out al-Qadi, but after the latter's successful reorganization of NCB, he seemed to be the indispensable man. And when Khaled bin Mahfouz decided to found a charity in the Sudan in memory of his parents, he chose al-Qadi despite the fact that he had no previous experience in charitable work or charitable institutions. According to al-Qadi, Bin Mahfouz suggested Muwafaq Foundation (Al Muwafaq Al Khariyya, Benevolent Foundation) for its name, and perhaps it was just a coincidence that in 1991 al-Qadi had already registered his own Muwaffaq Ltd. (with the alternative spelling) on the Isle of Man as another "brass-plate" home for tax dodgers. Al-Qadi then used Muwaffaq Ltd. to establish Shifa International Hospitals Ltd. of Pakistan.

The Muwafaq Foundation of Bin Mahfouz, a charitable trust, was registered in Jersey in 1991. Both Bin Mahfouz and al-Qadi chose to register their charities outside Saudi Arabia, and Jersey was an ideal site, a "self-governing island" that did not have a charities commission and did not require charities to register or issue reports, as required by the UK and Saudi Arabia. Officially, the Muwafaq Foundation did not really exist. Nevertheless, it had six trustees including al-Qadi, Abdul Rahman bin Mahfouz (the son of Khaled, aged twenty), Rais bin Mahfouz, a family member and doctor, and three other trustees appointed by al-Qadi. Strangely, Khaled bin Mahfouz refused to be a member of the board, but his son would act on his behalf. An obscure Sudanese, Siraj al-Din Bari, administered the Muwafaq program in the Sudan to provide food and assistance during a series of famines in 1991 and 1992, but the Muwafaq Foundation confined itself to the Muslim northern Sudan, leaving the delivery of food aid and other assistance in the non-Muslim southern Sudan to the western aid agencies.[44] Muwafaq employees in 1992 were seen wearing military uniforms along the Ethiopian border where they supported PDF units in the Upper Nile. They also proselytized among the southern Sudanese in the Mayo Internally Displaced Camp located south of the Khartoum airport. Inexplicably, Muwafaq was not officially recognized until April 1993 when it signed an agreement with the Commissioner General for Voluntary Agencies in the Sudan. Nevertheless, from the moment it began to work in 1992 the charity openly supported Sudan's Islamist government and had interests in the Chad, Ethiopia, and Eritrea borderlands. Although Muwafaq was not registered in Chad, authorities there were convinced that its local director was providing funds for Islamist extremists.[45]

Shortly after Muwafaq opened in Khartoum in 1992, another office was established in Mogadishu, Somalia. There its purpose was defined as "general development" and consisted of transporting weapons and ammunition to Islamists in the city. Muwafaq also signed an agreement with the Ethiopian government in April 1993 but did little relief or rehabilitation work. Al-Qadi also established Muwafaq offices in the Balkans. He had visited the region in the early 1990s and registered the Muwafaq Foundation in Zagreb, Croatia, in November 1992. He then opened an office in Sarajevo the following year. From 1992 to 1996 the Muwafaq Foundation in the Balkans was managed by Director-General Chafiq Ayadi. Ayadi had been introduced to al-Qadi by the omnipresent Wael Julaidan, who was also involved in "relief work" in Croatia, whom he had known since the 1980s. When Ayadi was kidnapped in 1994 by angry Serbians who argued he only assisted Muslims, Yassin al-Qadi paid his ransom. Other Muwafaq Foundation offices were opened in Albania,

Austria, and Germany in 1993. In the USA, Muwafaq was registered in Delaware in January 1992, and then in Holland and Belgium, but was not known to have established an active program in these countries.

During the 1990s Yassin al-Qadi had been a very busy man. He was on the board of directors of the Al Haramain wa al-Masjed al-Aqsa (Two Holy Shrines and Al Aqsa) charity, registered in Saudi Arabia, and active in Sarajevo where he had been investigated by Bosnian authorities in 1992, who froze his assets, and later in Albania where he was suspected of financing indigenous *mujahideen*. His greatest predicament, however, was a report in *Africa Confidential* in July 1995 that a Muwafaq employee had been involved in the failed attempt to assassinate Hosni Mubarak in Addis Ababa on 26 June 1995 during his state visit to Ethiopia.[46] The article reported that Ethiopian authorities had "arrested a Sudanese, Siraj Mohamed Hussein, who claimed to work for the Addis branch of Moafak el Hairiya [Blessed Relief]," which was described as an "agency" of the NIF government in the Sudan.[47] Shortly thereafter, the Ethiopian government ordered all Sudanese charities out of Ethiopia.

Within the year al-Qadi officially terminated the Muwafaq Foundation, handing over its Sudan operations to the Sub-Saharan International Development Organization (SIDO) under Siraj al-Din Abdel Bari, who had previously headed Muwafaq. Once this was done Khaled bin Mahfouz sued *Africa Confidential* for libel. In August 1995, a British firm that specialized in libel cases issued a writ on behalf of six Saudi businessmen against Blackwell Publishers, the owners of *Africa Confidential*. The Saudis claimed that the article defamed them because they were the trustees of the Muwafaq Foundation registered in Jersey and the Muwaffaq registered on the Isle of Man. The plaintiffs were, however, very chary in providing information that would establish their own connection to the Muwafaq and their relationship to the offshore brass-plate offices registered in Jersey and the Isle of Man, or to the Muwafaq operating in Sudan, Ethiopia, Somalia, and Bosnia. Al-Qadi blamed all his and Muwafaq's problems on *Africa Confidential*, and the case dragged on in the British courts for six years until the judge found for the plaintiffs, who were granted costs and received a public apology from *Africa Confidential* in court. Al-Qadi would later assert that the "foundation sued the newsletter and won."[48] Ironically, when the suit was settled al-Qadi denied transferring Muwafaq to SIDO despite the fact that the UN office in the Sudan reported SIDO as the "former" Muwafaq and continued to provide $1.4 million for Muwafaq after the office had been closed. Khaled bin Mahfouz also brought a libel suit in London against US author Rachel Ehrenfeld. Ehrenfeld countered by bringing a suit in the US District Court, New York City, against Bin Mahfouz, who had objected to passages in her book *Funding Evil*, published in 2003. This important case was still being decided in mid-2005.

In 1998 the FBI discovered that al-Qadi had transferred $820,000 to HAMAS through the Quranic Literacy Institute, a Chicago-based Islamic charity, but he denied that any funds from Muwafaq went to Bin Laden. "According to my records, I don't believe there is any chance any money has gone to bin Laden at any time."[49] After 9/11 the Foreign Assets Control Department of the US Treasury conducted its own investigation of Yassin Abdullah al-Qadi, whom they called a "wealthy businessman" used "by wealthy Saudi businessmen to transfer millions of dollars to Bin Laden." His assets in the USA were then frozen.

Sudanese charities in Somalia

Various Saudi charitable institutions had been working and spending substantial funds in Somalia from the 1980s, but during the next decade acrimonious tensions developed between the indigenous Islamic leaders and the new Islamists arriving from, of all places, the Sudan. Most mullahs in northern Somaliland, the former British protectorate that declared itself the Republic of Somaliland, resented the ideology and pretensions of the Sudanese Islamists, and after a long struggle, which continues to this day, they generally managed to retain their indigenous Islamic traditions despite the efforts of the Sudanese to change the character of traditional Islam in Somalia. In the south, it would be a different matter.

The first Islamic institution to have any major impact on the Somali Republic following its independence in 1960 was MWL, which asserted its supreme authority on all Islamic issues by establishing centers for training Islamic mullahs.[50] Islam had been confined to the mosque during the regime of Socialist President Mohamed Siad Barre (1976–1991), but he lost control of the Democratic Republic of Somalia in January 1991. Thereafter, Somalia dissolved into chaos and civil wars as the clan-based militias fought one another in the political vacuum to gain the powers and privileges previously enjoyed by Siad Barre. By the end of 1991 a dozen clan elders or warlords whose infighting nearly destroyed the capital, Mogadishu, had wreaked havoc in the countryside, already devastated by famine from the continuing drought.

Shortly after his arrival in Khartoum Osama bin Laden was the first of the *mujahideen* in the Sudan to take any interest in Somalia. After a succession of reconciliation conferences had failed to end the "battle of the warlords," by 1992 Bin Laden was eager to fill the political vacuum in southern Somalia. In Mogadishu General Muhammad Farah Aideed, an unpredictable and unorthodox Muslim, held the advantage, and it was to Mogadishu that Bin Laden sent three teams to determine if Al Qaeda could help establish an Islamist regime. In northern Somalia the Afar demonstrated little interest, for they were conducting their own *jihad* against Ethiopia in the Ogaden, led by graduates from Islamic universities, especially the Islamic University of Medina. In southern Somalia, however, Al Qaeda agents were more successful in establishing cordial relations with the friendly Ittihad al-Islami *mujahideen* and the Um Rehan clan, whose turf extended from Mogadishu to the Kenya border, which enabled them to set up cells in Somalia and nearby Kenya with support from hardcore Islamists in the Sudan government. In March 1992 the sinister Abd al-Bagi Muhammad Hassan was appointed Sudanese ambassador to Somalia, and the Sudanese embassy in Mogadishu soon became the center of Islamist operations and hostility against the UN. Ali Mahdi Muhammad, the former interim president of the United Somali Congress (USC) and the most powerful opponent of Muhammad Farah Aideed, publicly hailed the new relations between Somalia and Sudan and thanked Khartoum for food aid sent at a time when hundreds of thousands of Sudanese were starving in their own country from the drought.[51]

By the New Year 1993 widespread famine and endemic banditry galvanized the UN to approve Security Council Resolution 794, which authorized the delivery of food, medicine, and other assistance to a million Somalis in the south and required the UN to restore order in a failed state. Hitherto the efforts of the international relief agencies had been blocked by the warlords defending their own territory. This forced the UN, members of Congress, and the western relief agencies to realize that military force would be required to protect the distribution of food in an increasingly violent region, where the number of Somalis dying from starvation would rapidly escalate. Led by US Marines in Operation Restore Hope, the UN launched the United Nations International Task Force (UNITAF), which quickly secured all seaports, airports, and delivery routes into Somalia to be followed in May 1993 by the United Nations Operation in Somalia II (UNOSOM II) with a broad mandate to facilitate national reconciliation and rebuild the country's shattered economy. UNOSOM II failed dismally, and in March 1995 the UN withdrew from Somaliland.

The anarchy in Somalia was grist for the Islamist mill. On behalf of Al Qaeda Ayman Zawahiri "first set up Bin Laden's East Africa networks," and by 1993 "such organizations [networks] had been used to disguise Bin Laden's presence in the south of Somalia."[52] Al Qaeda was now moving arms and men between Khartoum and Mogadishu, for there was a "coincidence of interest" between the Islamists and the USC Hawiye clan led by Ali Mahdi against Farah Aideed, for whom

Al Qaeda had little respect.[53] Despite support from Ali Mahdi's forces and other *mujahideen*, however, Al Qaeda failed to dislodge Aideed from his redoubt in Mogadishu's northern quarter, but he was so threatened by Al Qaeda that he began portraying himself as "a born-again Muslim fundamentalist." Given the fragile and volatile nature of Somali society, where Islamist groups offered the best-organized social support structures, "any alliance between Aideed and radical Islam" created a "potentially very dangerous engagement indeed."[54] William Millward, a Canadian government anti-terrorism expert, was among the first to appreciate "the rising tide of Islamic fundamentalism" in the Horn of Africa by an incipient Iran–Sudan network. He reported in April 1993 that there were "signs of expanding joint Iranian/Sudanese contacts with Islamic militants in Somalia."[55] Seemingly from nowhere, the warring clans were by 1993 armed with automatic weapons, mortars, grenades, and landmines, and the last vestiges of law and order disappeared.[56]

In January a UNICEF doctor was killed at Bossaso and a CARE representative wounded by "fundamentalists who were well-trained, armed, financed and equipped, apparently with Iranian and Sudanese money."[57] At the time there were as many as forty-nine UN and expatriate NGOs operating in Somalia, far outnumbering the Islamist aid agencies working independently from the UN. As in Afghanistan in 1989 and the Sudan in 1990, every effort was made by the Islamists to eliminate the western NGOs in order to ensure, undisturbed, the work of Islamic relief agencies. Although the Sudanese charities could not "match even private Saudi financial resources," they were determined to assist the foreign charities, including Islamic Call, Mercy International from Ireland, IARA, IIRO, and the Muwafaq Foundation. In Khartoum the government used its Council for International People's Friendship to extend brotherly financial aid to Somalia, and other Sudanese organizations, including the Sudan Peace and Development Foundation and the National Youth Organization Association, were active in Somalia as early as December 1992. In 1992–1993 the Sudan government had sent 100,000 tons of food aid to Somalia and supposedly provided scholarships for 10,000 Somali students.[58] Khartoum's support for Aideed predated the Somali famine, and for more than a year the Sudan was the only government to oppose UN intervention. From the initial UN involvement, the Khartoum regime argued that only Islamic relief agencies should operate in Somalia. By late 1992, relief supplies were arriving at Merca, a minuscule port just south of Mogadishu. There, Red Cross barges were met by Red Crescent personnel. Aid shipments were guarded by armed Islamic Union Party (Al Ittihad) *mujahideen*, who had eliminated the problem of looting relief supplies.

Despite a succession of operations dominated by the UN presence in southern Somalia – UNOSOM I (August–December 1992), Operation Restore Hope (UNITAF, December 1992–April 1993), and UNOSOM II (initiated May 1993) – both the UN administration and the US military and civilian leaders were appallingly ignorant of the activities and objectives of the Islamist aid agencies, whose operations were naively regarded as legitimate humanitarian relief programs. Among the seven principal Kuwaiti charities, whose objectives were the spread of Islamist movements, the Committee for Helping Muslims of Asia and Africa operated only in Somalia.[59] After the departure of US forces and the marginalizing of the UN, southern Somalia, for all practical purposes, had become Islamist. *Mujahideen*, led by the "militant Muslim leader" Ahmad Bille Hassan, received support from Al Qaeda and were reported to be receiving arms through the Sudan.[60] Other Somali Islamists, supported by Osama bin Laden and Hasan al-Turabi, plotted the progressive Islamization of northern Somalia, the self-proclaimed Somaliland.

By 2000 the "presence and influence of radical Islamists [was] felt everywhere" in the north, and the governing element in Hargeisa was considering the adoption of Shari'a. "Feeding centers for the displaced are eagerly funded by wealthy Saudi fundamentalists; Koranic academies run by Somali fundamentalists are sprouting throughout the country to educate a significant percentage of the school-aged population; and clandestine centers training 'Islamic warriors' are reputedly scattered in various locations."[61] After the departure of Osama bin Laden from the Sudan in May 1996 Sudanese assistance to the Somali warlords soon declined and education became the center of its charitable works. Scholarships were provided for Somali students to attend Sudanese schools and to assist them upon their return to acquire positions of influence which they could use to benefit the Sudan. The Non-Sudanese Students' Welfare Organization (NSSWO), a branch of Islamic Call, provided room, board, and tuition, and Somali students were eligible for WAMY funds for education at AIU in Khartoum.

Al Qaeda and Islamic charities in East Africa

During his years in the Sudan Osama bin Laden had adroitly used Islamic charities to further the projects of Al Qaeda. In 1992 he ordered Ali Mohammed to seek possible US targets in East Africa, and upon his return to Khartoum Bin Laden was particularly interested in his photographs of the American embassy in Nairobi. Mohammed was immediately sent back to Kenya to establish an Al Qaeda cell in the capital, where he opened a fishing business, a luxury auto lot, and a store selling precious gems as cover for at least twelve Al Qaeda members who joined him. Bin Laden wanted to bomb two US embassies simultaneously for maximum shock value, and those in Nairobi and Dar es Salaam were found to be vulnerable. On 7 August 1998 the plan succeeded when a truck carrying bombs crashed through the barriers at the US embassy in Nairobi, killing 224 people and injuring thousands. The Al Qaeda bombers had used the Kenya office of Mercy International as cover, and Osama bin Laden regularly contacted its Director, Ahmad Sheik Adam, by satellite phone. Wadih al-Hage, who planned the embassy bombings, kept his files in the Nairobi office that contained a rolodex with the business cards of Mercy International personnel in Kenya and the USA.

Although US, Kenyan, and Tanzanian agents were quite successful in rounding up the *mujahideen* responsible for the atrocities, Al Qaeda activity in East Africa was not finished. In 2003 members of the Tanzanian branch of the Saudi charity Al Haramain Islamic Foundation planned but failed to bomb several hotels in Zanzibar; that led to international financial sanctions against the Tanzanian and Kenyan branches of the Foundation. Both the Kenyan and Tanzanian offices were linked to Osama bin Laden and Al Qaeda, and were in contact with *mujahideen* in Somalia.[62] In Uganda Alirabaki Kyagulanyi (aka Shaykh Jamil Mukulu), who worked out of locations in London, Saudi Arabia, Sudan, and Kenya, actively recruited jihadists from the Allied Democratic Forces (ADF). ADF leadership was dominated by Islamists, and during the 1990s it sent jihadists to Osama bin Laden training-camps in Afghanistan and elsewhere in the Middle East.[63] In Malawi the Director of the Prince Sultan bin Abdul Aziz Special Committee for Relief (SCR) was among five people arrested in 2003 "on suspicion of channeling money to the Al-Qaeda terrorist network." He was the "manager of religious affairs in the Saudi Army" and a Major General who was also responsible for SCR charities in Mali and Nigeria. He and a second individual, "a Sudanese director of the Islamic Zakaat Fund," were deported, interrogated, and released in the Sudan. With great indignation Saudi Arabia demanded an apology but closed the SCR office.[64]

Islamic charities in West Africa

When Osama bin Laden moved to the Sudan in 1991 the Islamist penetration of West Africa, unlike eastern Africa, was insignificant. Hasan al-Turabi and his PAIC had attracted radical Muslim clerics from Nigeria, Senegal, and Mauritania but their influence and followers were regional rather than national: "The true Islamic state has remained an ideal so far in the African setting because, in most cases, some pre-Islamic habits, traditions and beliefs" are deeply rooted. There is little information on obligatory almsgiving in West Africa because *zakat* was not widespread among Muslim African societies in the Western Sudan. There is even less known about permanent endowment in property or money (*waqf*) to support mosques, hospitals, or schools. Thus the "third pillar" of Islam was "based on voluntary almsgiving, or *sadaqa*, and not *zakat* nor *waqf*."[65] In those patriarchal communities in West Africa where Muslims were in the minority or intermixed with other religious practices, "almsgiving was not a voluntary act or private moral obligation, but part of the public sphere." Within this "sphere of communities of believers within a society of non-believers" the collection of *zakat* was handled in the way the Quranic ideal had prescribed, i.e. "being collected from all members by the imam or shaykh who disbursed it among the poor, needy, wayfarers and collectors."[66]

In the few instances where regular collection and distribution of alms did occur, MWL, which appeared in West Africa shortly after its founding in 1962, was very active. As was the case in Somalia, it sought to coordinate and spread Islam throughout the region by constructing hundreds of mosques and establishing Islamic centers in Mauritania and Nigeria. Twenty years later in 1982 the Dar al-Mal al-Islami Investment Corporation (DMI) under the chairmanship of Prince Faisal of Saudi Arabia began a determined effort to increase the influence of Islam in West Africa by the introduction of Islamic banking. DMI founded *masraf*, as local banks were called, in Guinea, Senegal, and Niger. Each had an authorized capital of $20 million, and DMI retained a majority of shares. "Along with any *masraf*, the DMI always sets up a *takful*, or insurance company, and a Business Group, or investment company." Its first major success occurred in Guinea where Saudi-sponsored activity attracted both foreign and local investment in various projects, including an oil refinery.[67]

In Nigeria foreign support for Islamic charitable works first began in 1983 with the visit of a pan-Islamic delegation organized and led by Prince Faisal representing DMI. Businessmen from Pakistan, Britain, and Ireland who accompanied the prince established a fund of $650,000 to assist the Nigeria Islamic Foundation, founded in 1971, to build more *madrasas* and provide teachers and scholarships in religious and Arabic studies.[68] Still, foreign assistance generally came from the banking sector, and the banks themselves were run on western banking principles although lending was generally limited to the Islamic community alone. Nigeria as a center of Islamic *da'wa*, education, and teacher training was given added impetus in 2002 when the Islamic Movement for Africa (IMA), ostensibly a non-political, non-governmental, and non-profit

Islamic organization, was founded "to serve as the institutional base for the promotion of Islam in Africa." Three Egyptian scholars were present, including an official from the Al Azhar Islamic Research Academy, Professor Abdul Satar Abdul-Haq al-Halwagy. Al-Halwagy represented two opposing themes of Islamic outreach in Africa. He had been the recipient of the King Faisal International Award for Islamic Studies in 1998, and he was a representative of an Egyptian government that had never denounced pan-Africanism and that traced its roots to the secular socialism of Gamal Abdel Nasser.

6   Islam at war in the Balkans

> There can be no peace or co-existence between the "Islamic faith" and non-Islamic societies and political institutions . . . Islam clearly excludes the right and possibility of activity of any strange ideology on its own turf. (p. 22)
>
> The Islamic movement should and must start taking over the power as soon as it is morally and numerically strong enough to not only overthrow the existing non-Islamic, but also to build up a new Islamic authority. (p. 43)
>
> Alija Izetbegovic, "Islamska deklaracija" (Islamic Declaration), 1970/1990

Alija Izetbegovic was born on 8 August 1925 in Bosanski Samac, Bosnia-Herzegovina, into a wealthy family that moved to Sarajevo in 1928. He grew up in a multicultural society and was educated at a German Gymnasium where, at the age of sixteen, he founded the Muslim Youth Society of Bosnia, modeled on the Muslim Brotherhood of Egypt. Seemingly innocuous but designed to be secretive, the Society concealed its more subversive activities by charitable works. He graduated from the Gymnasium in 1943 and studied agriculture for the next three years. Despite his bookish manner he worked assiduously to promote Islam by publishing, with Nedzib Sacirbey, the journal *Mujahid*, which immediately brought both of them to the attention of the communist authorities in Yugoslavia, whose motto, "Brotherhood and Unity," did not permit any dissent by Muslims. He and Sacirbey were imprisoned in 1946 for three years, and upon his release in 1949 the government sought to contain Izetbegovic's Islamic activities by cracking down on the Muslim Youth Society for their activism, sentencing four members to death and imprisoning many more. Izetbegovic quietly tempered his pan-Islamic rhetoric, having learned in jail that he could be of greater help to his fellow Muslims by knowing and using the Yugoslav legal system. He graduated in 1956 with a law degree from the University of Sarajevo to become a moderate Muslim lawyer working as a legal adviser to trucking firms in Sarajevo and representing his fellow anti-communist Muslims in the courts.

Somehow Izetbegovic managed to survive, despite his Islamist views and his widely distributed "Islamic Declaration" of 1970 which urged true Muslims to seize power from secular Islamic governments, after which western institutions would not be tolerated. Bosnian Muslims (officially known as "Bosniaks") were to abandon any idea of a multi-ethnic secular society and, instead, work for a federation of Balkan Islamic States.[1] He was imprisoned again in 1983, sentenced to fourteen years on the charge of disseminating "Islamic propaganda" aimed at turning Bosnia into an Islamic state. Like his hero, Sayyid Qutb, he wrote his seminal work, *Islam Between East and West*, in prison. It condemned the West for its denial of Islam, for ignoring the contributions to civilization made by Muslims, and offered a critical comparison of secular and Islamic civilization using examples from art, morality, culture, and law. Smuggled out of prison in 1984, the book was banned in France, but it became an instant best-seller throughout Europe during the 1980s. After serving five years, he was released in 1988. His defense of Muslims in the courts, his advocacy of Islam, his writings, and his imprisonment had won for him a large following among the Bosniaks, particularly in the rural areas where he became a father figure reverently called "Deedo," Grandpa.

Journalists and diplomats alike were beguiled by Izetbegovic's professed reverence for democracy and human rights in a multi-ethnic society. Behind this fatherly façade, however, lay a complex man – intelligent, calculating, and strong in his convictions that Islam would prevail "in every field in the personal life of the individual, in family and society . . . and the establishment of a unique Islamic community from Morocco to Indonesia" that would not tolerate equality or coexistence with non-Muslims. No sooner had he been released from jail than he sought to exploit his fame politically by founding the Muslim Party of Democratic Action (SDA). He argued that in the future of Yugoslavia, Slobodan Milosevic would speak for the Serbs and Franjo Tudjman for the Croats, rallying Bosniaks with the slogan "Who will speak for you? Alija Izetbegovic!" In the multiparty Bosnian elections of 1990 its Muslims, 44 percent of the population, elected Alija Izetbegovic President of Bosnia-Herzegovina.

When Serbia and Croatia declared their independence from the Socialist Federal Republic of Yugoslavia and the federation began to disintegrate in May 1991, Izetbegovic at first assumed a stance of moderate neutrality that satisfied few. He then sought to resolve the issue by a referendum on the independence of Bosnia-Herzegovina. The Bosnia Serbs boycotted the referendum, and on 3 March 1992 Izetbegovic proclaimed Bosnia-Herzegovina an independent republic. The Bosnia Serbs, led by Radovan Karadzic, rebelled, seized 70 percent of the country, and then enforced a policy of ethnic cleansing to "purify" the country by expelling the Bosniaks. Supported by fellow Serbs from the new Republic of Serbia the Bosnia Serbs wreaked havoc among the Bosniaks, driving them from their homes as 2.5 million Muslims fled into refugee camps while others were confined in Serbian concentration camps, where torture and rape were common. An estimated 350,000 Bosniaks were killed. From his sandbagged office and apartment in Sarajevo Izetbegovic sought to rally his people. The West saw this terrible conflict as a clash of cultures; the Muslim world understood it to be a *jihad*.

Afghanistan in Bosnia

In the early months of 1992 the Islamists, determined to come to the rescue of their fellow Muslims in Bosnia, utilized the lessons – military, political, and religious – they had learned in Afghanistan. Throughout the Muslim world, but especially from Afghanistan, Pakistan, the Sudan, and Yemen, *mujahideen* were on the move to Bosnia. They were followed by military advisers, mullahs, Islamic bankers, and Islamic charities. Assistance from Saudi Arabia began to arrive in Bosnia in 1993. In December 1992 King Fahd had met with Izetbegovic and promised the Bosniak leader unstinting Saudi support. A Supreme Committee for the Collection of Donations for the Muslims of Bosnia was established, and Prince Salman bin Abd al-Aziz, Governor of Riyadh, assumed the coordination of seven major Islamic charities – MWL, Al Haramain, IIRO, WAMY, SARCS, the Islamic Waqf Organization, and the Makkah Humanitarian Organization – which operated in Bosnia through offices in Zagreb, Sarajevo, and Tuzla. Millions of dollars from Saudi charities poured into Bosnia in support of the Bosniaks and *mujahideen* jihadists who had come to fight for them. "Fundraising" weeks were common throughout Saudi Arabia and the Islamic world. Two-thirds of the funds that passed through Prince Salman's Supreme Committee were delivered directly to the Bosniak government, "either through a dedicated bank account, through the Bosnian Embassy in Riyadh, or by delivery to President Izetbegovic personally." The remainder purchased supplies "without the requirement of accountability" and was given to needy individuals and the eight Bosnia centers supported by the Supreme Committee.[2]

From the outbreak of the conflict in the Balkans and for the next decade, the Saudi Supreme Committee was the largest fundraiser in the Muslim world. Saudi assistance for the Bosniaks could be compared favorably to Islamic charitable funds that had supported the jihadists in Afghanistan. Between 1992 and February 1996 King Fahd bin Abd al-Aziz was personally responsible for $103 million of the total Saudi donations for the Bosniak government of $356 million.[3] By 1997 the Muslim states and "various extremist groups and informal institutions" had reportedly sent more than $1 billion in military and humanitarian aid to Bosnia.[4] Later, according to estimates supplied by the Saudi embassy in Sarajevo, the Supreme Committee, now renamed the Saudi High Relief Commission (SHRC) for Bosnia, was responsible for donations in excess of $561 million by 2000. A Bosniak government investigation on its own initiative determined that SHRC had actually spent an estimated $800 million in support of *da'wa* and humanitarian projects in Bosnia.

A small number of Afghan-Arabs had arrived in Bosnia in the first few months of 1992, to be followed by many of the Islamic charities that had been active in Peshawar. The lightly armed Bosniak army was soon overwhelmed by Serbian artillery and tanks, and by the autumn of 1992 President Izetbegovic was appealing to his fellow Muslims for arms and men to fight the Serbs. There were thousands of Afghan-Arabs in the Middle East ready and willing, and in his appeal he made it abundantly clear that this was not just a fight for the Bosniaks but for Islam. An experienced diplomat with many years in the Balkans succinctly rendered his judgment of Alija Izetbegovic: "There is no doubt that he is an Islamic fundamentalist . . . He is a very nice fundamentalist, but he is still a fundamentalist. This has not changed. His goal is to establish a Muslim state in Bosnia, and the Serbs and Croats understand this better than the rest of us."[5] In October Izetbegovic met with Iranian leaders in Tehran to thank them for their "over-all support," but with winter approaching he required not only more arms but food and fuel.[6] At the same time in the mountains of western Herzegovina a contingent of Afghan-Arabs led by Abu Abdul Aziz of Al Qaeda numbered in the hundreds and protected the Saudi volunteers of the Ibrahim bin Abdul-Aziz al-Ibrahim Fund. The volunteers were working to build a road from Split on the coast to the hills near Sarajevo that would skirt the Serbian fortified positions and provide food and blankets for the Muslim refugees who had swarmed into Travnik. Its headquarters were little more than an "office with a brass plate on the door" at the Inter-Continental Hotel in Zagreb, Croatia.[7]

Although some $70–100 million in food aid and cash from Saudi Arabia were funneled into Bosnia during the early months of the war, the Saudi government firmly refused to become involved in any direct shipment of arms. It left that task to others, just as it had in Afghanistan.[8] While the Saudis supplied cash, construction crews, and trucks for Izetbegovic, Iran had already begun to provide the guns. In 1992 it was the only Islamic state caught breaking the UN arms embargo imposed on all of Yugoslavia when its officials at the Zagreb airport inspected a gun-running Iranian 747 supposedly carrying relief supplies. At the meeting of the Organization of the Islamic Conference (OIC) held in December 1992 Iran advocated a "Final Declaration" allowing Islamic states to arm the Bosniaks if the UN and "the West" did not take action to end the fighting by mid-January 1993.[9] In January the Italian navy intercepted a major Islamic arms shipment near the port of Rijeka, Croatia; it was a new route for arms and considered more dependable than the older overland route from Salonika on the Aegean Sea through Macedonia.[10] The following month a secret meeting was held in Tehran by the principal Islamist terrorist groups determined to provide the men, weapons, and relief assistance to save the Bosniaks. The fighting between the Muslims of Bosnia, on the one hand, and Christian Serbs and Croats, on the other, had already taken 20,000 lives and more than 1.6 million were classified as homeless "Internally Displaced Persons (IDPs)." Another 150,000 Muslims were threatened with starvation, including thousands huddled in the ruins of Sarajevo.[11] Ominously, there were rumors that Russia was prepared to provide $360 million in weapons to Serbia that would obviously find their way to the Serbian-controlled areas of Bosnia and Croatia.[12]

By April 1993 Muslim volunteers had begun to trickle into Bosnia, and by June the numbers of Afghan-Arab *mujahideen* had substantially increased. Veterans from the war in Afghanistan and volunteers from the Sudan and other Muslim countries arrived posing as Islamic aid workers. In May, at a ceremony in Tehran, the first Ambassador from the Muslim government of Bosnia-Herzegovina presented his credentials and publicly praised Iran for its "relief assistance" – which in fact consisted of large shipments of arms and little or no food.[13] Then a large consignment of weapons from Iran via the Sudan disguised as humanitarian aid for Bosnia was discovered by UN officials at the Maribor airport in Slovenia. The find confirmed the role Sudan was playing in illegal arms shipments; this not only violated the UN arms embargo affecting the warring parties in Bosnia, it also implicated members of the Slovenian secret service and, indirectly, the Austrian Ministry of Interior. In fact a Slovenian "economic team," which included the Minister for Transportation and Communication and officials of the Slovenian national airline, had just visited Iran where three agreements were signed, including the establishment of air and sea links between the two republics.[14]

Austrian journalists investigating the illegal arms shipment at the Maribor airport soon learned that both Slovenian security agents and the Austrian Ministry of Interior were providing funds for the Muslim government of Alija Izetbegovic in Sarajevo.[15] Although the Austrian Foreign Minister, Alois Mock, strongly urged that "the only solution" to end the slaughter of Bosniaks by the Serbs was "military intervention by the international community," he also argued that the right of self-defense should be ensured, "and that Austria was both willing and able to help the beleaguered Bosnian Muslims."[16] That policy was not solely driven by humanitarian concerns, however, for the Austrian Ambassador to Iran succinctly pointed out in 1993 that Iran was Austria's "third biggest business partner," and he affirmed that "his country, too, is a reliable partner for Iran."[17]

The fact that Shi'ite Iran had taken over supplying weapons to the Bosniaks deeply troubled the less militant Sunni members of OIC who called an extraordinary meeting at Islamabad in July to discuss the problem of Bosnia-Herzegovina. The Sudan boycotted the OIC meeting, which was historically dominated by the Sunni Saudis, and offered instead the PAIC of Hasan al-Turabi as host and Khartoum as a more suitable venue than Islamabad. The sixteen ministers attending the OIC meeting ignored the Sudanese invitation and urged the UN to lift its arms embargo; they offered to send a 17,000-man Islamic peace-keeping unit, including 10,000 troops from Iran, which would double the proposed UN peace-keeping force of 7,600 troops, for which only France had pledged men and materiel. The UN, however, thought that the arrival of a Muslim force would only exacerbate the situation, and the OIC proposal was not accepted, nor was the arms embargo lifted.[18]

In September 1993 a Turkish newspaper reported that 1,300 *mujahideen* from Iran and other Muslim countries were already fighting in Bosnia, but the figure was certainly conservative.[19] A few months later the UK Home Office, not wishing to give the impression of accepting the presence of the Afghan-Arabs in Bosnia, refused to grant visas to representatives from "the Islamic movement" in Bosnia, Lebanon, Palestine, Albania, Tunisia, Malaysia, Nigeria, and the Sudan who were bound for London to hold a meeting on Bosnia. Ayatollah Ahmad Jannati, a member of Iran's Council of Guardians, was also refused entry as was Shaykh Iz al-Din, the Hizbullah Party foreign minister. By 1994 more than 500 Afghan-Arabs from South Asia alone had arrived in Bosnia, congregating near Muslim-held Zenica, and there were an increasing number of military firefights involving Afghan-Arab *mujahideen*. A British humanitarian aid worker was murdered near Zenica in January 1994, and shortly afterward three *mujahideen* carrying fake Pakistani passports and representing a Muslim charity were killed by Bosnian military police at a roadblock near Sarajevo. By the early months of 1994 *mujahideen* and money were pouring into Bosnia.

Like Saudi Arabia the Gulf states were particularly generous in providing substantial funds for the Bosniaks. The UAE Red Crescent Society
was especially active, and its wealthy shaykhs a soft touch, but the total
amount donated would never be known, for they dealt mostly in cash.[20]
The UAE Human Appeals International (Hayat al-Amal al-Khariyya,
HAI) opened offices in Zagreb and Tuzla and collected funds for Bosnia
in such disparate places as Khartoum, Nouakchott, Mauritania, and
Denmark. Its headquarters was in Dubai, and HAI had a direct connection with the Palestinian HAMAS and maintained ties to both the
Muwafaq Foundation and the Qatar Charitable Society. The latter's office
in Khartoum was used on occasion by Al Qaeda members while Osama
bin Laden was active in the Sudan.

The Islamic World Committee (Lajnat al-Alam al-Islami), the Social
Reform Society of Kuwait, and the International Islamic Charitable
Organization (IICO) founded in 1986 were all Kuwaiti charities sus-
pected of supporting *mujahideen*. The Social Reform Society (Jamiyat
al-Islah al-Ijtimai), established in 1982 and closely associated with the
Kuwait Muslim Brotherhood, had by 1995 offices in Sarajevo, Tuzla,
Zagreb, Albania, Bulgaria, and Austria. Of the fifty major indigenous
charities in Kuwait, it was the most strongly suspected of supporting ter-
rorists. (It was declared a terrorist operation by the Russian Supreme
Court in 2003). Another suspected charity was the Lijnat al-Da'wa, a
Kuwaiti charity active in the Balkans. It had operated from Peshawar in
the 1980s under Zahid Shaykh Muhammad, brother of Khaled Shaykh
Muhammad who had planned the 9/11 attack on the World Trade Center. The support given by these four charities remains unknown, for as a
Kuwaiti succinctly put it: "We believe charity should not be given publicly. No receipts, no donor lists – giving charity for recognition devalues
it. The organizations who keep books and follow the rules are the ones
being wiped out. The ones who work in the traditional way – you'll never
know who they are."[21]

Al Muwafaq Brigade

After a visit to Bosnia, the journalist Robert Fisk traveled to Khartoum
late in 1993 to interview the elusive Osama bin Laden. After Fisk obtained
a meeting with Hasan al-Turabi, and perhaps through Turabi's intervention, Bin Laden granted a rare interview to a western reporter. When
Fisk informed Bin Laden that "Bosnian Muslim fighters in the Bosnian
town of Travnik had mentioned his name to me," the Saudi expatriate
added laconically that only a small number of *mujahideen* had gone to
fight in Bosnia because "the situation there does not provide the same

opportunities as Afghanistan."[22] The ease with which one could cross back and forth between Pakistan and Afghanistan did not exist in the Balkans, for the Croats had made it difficult for the Afghan-Arabs to pass through their country. Whether Bin Laden himself had ever traveled from the Sudan to Bosnia is not clear, but he had been issued a Bosnia-Herzegovina passport in 1993 by the Bosnian embassy in Vienna.

In 1992 the El Moujahed (Al Mujahideen) unit, consisting of Afghan-Arabs, was organized and loosely attached to the Bosniak army. It soon acquired a reputation for ferocity that even frightened Bosnian jihadists, and within months attracted to its ranks "volunteers from all over the Islamic world whose passage to Bosnia was facilitated by Al-Qaeda. El Moujahed was the nursery from which an international terrorist network spread to Europe and North America."[23] By June 1993 the Afghan-Arab El Moujahed had established themselves near Travnik, where they formed a "Mujahideen Battalion," known as the Al Muwafaq Brigade, which operated throughout Bosnia's Zenica region. Consisting of 750 Afghan-Arabs, the Brigade had Iranian "advisers" and was commanded by an Egyptian Afghan-Arab.[24] Perhaps by coincidence the Al Muwafaq Brigade had taken the same name as the Muwafaq Foundation established in the Sudan in 1991 by Khaled bin Mahfouz, which, not surprisingly, was reported to have ties to the Al Muwafaq Brigade.

By 1995 the Muwafaq Foundation was only one of many Islamic charities operating in Bosnia with offices in Zagreb, Sarajevo, Split, Zenica, Tirana, and Tuzla, but by then it had become well known that the Foundation was supplying money for the Al Muwafaq Brigade and at least one camp in Afghanistan training *mujahideen* for Bosnia. In March 1995 the Foundation opened an office in Karlsruhe, Germany, ostensibly to collect funds for Bosniak refugees. The office moved to Munich the following year and worked in tandem with an office in Vienna that had been established in 1993. On 31 July 1995 a US Foreign Broadcast Information Service (FBIS) report indicated that the Muwafaq Foundation office in Zagreb was a front for Osama bin Laden's operations. Six months later, in February 1996, *Al Watan Al Arabi*, a Paris-based Arab journal, published what it claimed was an interview with Bin Laden who listed the "Muwafaq Society" in Zagreb as part of a network of humanitarian organizations he supported. Yassin al-Qadi, the Foundation's administrator, strongly denied any involvement with the *mujahideen*. He added that the Al Muwafaq Brigade had already ceased to exist as a combat unit, and its jihadists were reduced to weapons instructors. Two years later, in 1998, the Muwafaq Foundation closed its office in Bosnia, and its only other project, an Islamic school in Risala, was turned over to a Bosnian corporation.

Sudanese connections

When Al Tayib Zein al-Abdin, a shadowy Sudanese intelligence agent and principal liaison officer for the Iran–Sudan task force in Somalia during 1992–1993, appeared in Bosnia in June 1994, veteran volunteers from the Sudan had already been incorporated into the Bosniak army. Sudanese C-130s, which had been used to transport Iranian arms from Port Sudan to small airfields in Somalia, were now making clandestine flights from Khartoum to airfields in the Balkans. The Islamic Relief Agency (IRSA) headquartered in Khartoum and controlled by NIF, had opened offices in Sarajevo, Zagreb, Tirana, Tuzla, and Germany. The IRSA office in Zagreb was particularly active supplying weapons to the Bosniak army. The Sudanese opposition, the National Democratic Alliance (NDA), active in the UK, published Sudan government documents to embarrass Bashir and NIF which proved that Khartoum was a major conduit for the flow of arms from Afghanistan to Bosnia. Regular Boeing 707 cargo flights loaded with weapons from Afghanistan were arriving at Khartoum airport in August 1993, the same month the US Department of State added the Sudan to its list of countries involved in state-sponsored terrorism.[25] Reporters discovered that the name "Osama" was listed on the flight log. It was, of course, a curious coincidence that the reclusive Osama bin Laden was a resident in Khartoum surrounded by scores of Afghan-Arabs. The flight documents also revealed that the arms destined for Bosnia followed a secret meeting in June at Tehran between the intelligence services of Iran and the Sudan and several militant Islamist organizations.[26] The flight documents had been endorsed by Dr. Mustafa Osman Isma'il, a NIF stalwart, former Minister of State, Turabi disciple, and the Secretary-General of the Council for International People's Friendship (CIPF). Created by Sudan's President Ja'far al-Numayri in 1980, CIPF was supposed to foster political and cultural ties with the Islamic world, and it seemed an innocuous organization of no particular international standing. When President Bashir announced in 1993 that all foreign aid from institutions, foundations, and Islamic charities in the Sudan had to be approved by the CIPF office, the Council generously "extended brotherly financial aid to the Mujahideen of Afghanistan, the Bosnia Muslims, Somalia" and other countries "facing severe difficulties."[27] While CIPF appeared to work openly, it obviously supported covert projects involving every major Sudanese charity in Bosnia.

In the secret world of Sudanese charities it is difficult to judge the impact of their efforts to help the Bosniaks. The controversial Yossef Bodansky, Director of Research of the International Strategic Studies

Association and Director of the Task Force on Terrorism and Unconventional Warfare of the House of Representatives, was convinced it was in the Sudan that the use of indiscriminate violence in defense of the *umma*, the Muslim peoples, became the foundation of the Islamist movement. A *fatwa* issued at a conference held in El Obeid in the Kordofan province of the Sudan in April 1993 served as the "precedent-setting text for legislating relations between Muslims and non-Muslims in areas where the infidels" were unwilling to accept subjugation "by the Muslim forces."[28] Although the *fatwa* originally appeared to have been a product of the war in the southern Sudan, it was used to give legitimacy for Sudanese and Al Qaeda support for the Bosniaks and the murder of Serbian civilians, and later appears as the justification for jihadists' acts of terror in Algeria, Chechnya, Palestine, Kashmir, Tajikistan, and the Philippines.

Third World Relief Agency

In June 1994 the Austrian government invited President Bashir and Mahdi Ibrahim, confidant of Hasan al-Turabi and head of the all-important Political Department of the Sudan Foreign Ministry, and President Museveni of Uganda to Vienna in the hope that the Sudanese and Ugandan leaders could, perhaps, resolve their hostile relationship. Despite the benevolent mediation of Austria, nothing came of this initiative. Bashir, however, did use the visit to meet with "members of the Sudanese community" whose large numbers came as a complete surprise to the Austrians.[29] Among the Sudanese who met with Bashir and the Sudanese delegation was a mysterious "diplomat," al-Fatih Ali Hassanein. Hassanein was a devout Muslim and, as a medical student at the Belgrade School of Medicine in the 1970s, had met Alija Izetbegovic. He had stood by him during his 1983 trial in Sarajevo for fostering Muslim nationalism. In 1987 he had founded, with his brother, Sukarno Hassanein, the Third World Relief Agency (TWRA), an Islamic charity with headquarters in Vienna.

TWRA eventually became *the* principal humanitarian front for moving arms to Bosnia. After the Bosnian declaration of independence in March 1992 President Izetbegovic had contacted his old friend through the Zagreb Mufti, Hassan Cengic. Hassenein was urged "to collect funds" for Bosnia from Muslim countries. When he agreed to facilitate the purchase of arms and launder money, President Izetbegovic guaranteed Hassanein's credentials with the Erste Bank Österreich (First Austrian Bank). TWRA was soon transformed from an obscure NGO into a major relief agency involved in warehousing and transporting arms;

"AK-47 rifles and missiles were shipped to Bosnia in containers marked as humanitarian aid."[30] Hassanein worked closely with the Bosniak security organization, the Agency for Information and Documentation; as a stalwart follower of Hasan al-Turabi and a member of NIF he was able to maintain contact from Europe with Turabi, Bin Laden, and Shaykh Omar Abd al-Rahman in New York. Among other activities TWRA became the agent for Shaykh Omar to market his videotapes and sermons in mosques around Europe. Hassanein also opened small offices in Budapest, Moscow, and Istanbul, and to give his charitable front some credibility he sponsored innocuous projects in the Balkans such as a chicken farm and a women's sewing center. At the same time Hassanein had become heavily committed to the illegal arms trade. He obtained a Sudanese diplomatic passport, probably through the intervention of Hasan al-Turabi, that allowed him "to transport large amounts of cash through Austria and into Croatia and Slovenia without being subjected to police checks." If nothing else these activities were in violation of the Vienna Convention governing diplomatic missions.[31]

The inner circle that surrounded President Izetbegovic, including "former Zagreb Imam Deputy Defense Minister Hasan Cengic, the Cengic clan, and the Austrian citizen Dieter Hofmann," used "the Third World Relief Agency as a conduit for funds and supplies from the Islamic world, principally Iran . . . to encourage the rebirth of Islam in Eastern Europe and the then Soviet Union."[32] Included among the members of the TWRA board of directors was Hassan Cengic, an Islamic cleric and the Mufti of Zagreb who, having lived in Tehran, negotiated the acquisition and shipments of arms from Iran to Bosnia, and was known as the "godfather" to Afghan-Arab *mujahideen*. Irfan Ljevakovic, a founder of Izetbegovic's Party of Democratic Action, and Huso Zivalj, Bosnian Ambassador to Austria between 1992 and 1995, were also involved in numerous questionable transactions by TWRA, including the delivery in 1993 of a Bosnian passport to Osama bin Laden. Zivalj personally used the embassy to assist the "Zima 94–95" (Winter 94–95) TWRA fundraising campaign.

By 1993 TWRA accounts had been opened in Liechtenstein and Monaco to launder money. Some $80 million was remitted on a Vienna account in the First Austrian Bank in 1992 and $231 million the following year. Substantial sums were "spent on corrupting Croatian authorities" after Bosnia's Croatian nationalists initiated their own struggle against the Muslim government in Sarajevo. In 1994 and 1995 some $39 million from Saudi Arabia, Iran, Sudan, Pakistan, Brunei, Malaysia, and Turkey passed through TWRA accounts and a "large portion of money was used for the purchase of the weapons for Bosnian Moslems."[33] Hassanein continued to operate despite having to surrender his Sudanese diplomatic passport in 1993. He moved to Istanbul in 1994 to escape an Austrian investigation of TWRA money-laundering, and then received a gold medal from the Bosnian government in Sarajevo for his "humanitarian" efforts.[34] In Istanbul Hassanein had played host to President Izetbegovic during his private visit to Turkey and "organized several encounters between Izetbegovic and Sudanese officials."[35] By 1994 TWRA had laundered more than $300 million to Sarajevo for the "purchase of arms for Bosnia," and to "cover the expenses of the international tours of the Bosnian Moslem politicians and their propaganda campaigns."[36]

By the autumn of 1993 western intelligence agencies were well aware of Hassanein's activities. Still, the USA took no action either to publicize or block TWRA fundraising or arms purchases. Critics of the Clinton administration would later argue that Hassanein must have received the blessing of its National Security Council (NSC), for there was considerable sympathy for the plight of Bosnian Muslims in the USA, where a host of charities for the relief of Bosnia had sprouted like mushrooms.[37] Others charged that the arms transfers had helped "turn Bosnia into [a] Militant Islamic Base, in violation of the arms embargo initially demanded by the US and behind the back of its European allies Clinton had approved Iranian arms to Bosnia."[38] Ironically, the USA continued to turn a blind eye to Balkans arms trafficking and the role the Sudan played despite the fact that in August 1993 the State Department had added Sudan to its list of nations involved in state-sponsored terrorism. Eventually, a senior western diplomat familiar with the Balkans claimed that the Clinton administration knew what TWRA was up to in Bosnia but "took no action to stop its fund-raising or arms purchases, in large part because of the administration's sympathy for the Muslim government and ambivalence about maintaining the arms embargo."[39]

As late as April 1995 the Clinton administration was apparently unaware of the meetings of Egyptian terrorists held in Khartoum to plan an increase in the combat readiness of *mujahideen* operating in the Balkans. EIJ was already active in Albania, but the organization, hardpressed for funds, had urged Ayman al-Zawahiri to visit the USA on a fundraising mission. Certainly, Zawahiri was welcome in America where a score of charities, such as Al-Nasr International (Worth, Illinois), were collecting cash for the American Bosnia-Herzegovina Relief Fund. Al-Nasr maintained offices in San Carlos, California, Saddle Brook, New Jersey, and Falls Church, Virginia, and worked directly with the Mission of Bosnia and Herzegovina to the United Nations.[40] As the war in Bosnia was coming to its dismal conclusion in September 1995, the Austrian police finally raided the headquarters of TWRA in Vienna to discover a treasure-trove of documents. When asked why it took so long to close a bogus charity, Austrian officials claimed they could not end the TWRA charade because it was not illegal to negotiate a weapons deal on Austrian soil so long as the transfers took place elsewhere. The TWRA ledgers, however, gave a full accounting of the transfer of huge sums for arms trafficking through the First Austrian Bank.

Although officially shut down by the police, TWRA continued to operate for some months, transferring arms and repatriating Bosniak refugees from Macedonia and Kosovar refugees from Bosnia to Kosovo until 1996.[41] Hassanein had countless contacts in the Islamic world, and in the latter months of the conflict in Bosnia served as intermediary with the Turkish Humanitarian Relief Foundation (IHH, aka Foundation for Human Rights and Freedom), founded in Istanbul in 1995 specifically to provide support for the Bosniaks. IHH raised immediate suspicions among the Turkish authorities, and was eventually closed for a time in 1998 after investigators found bombs in its Turkish office and again in August 1999 when funds for Turkish earthquake victims were found to be missing. As with TWRA the USA labeled IHH as nothing more than a "cover-up" organization to forge documents for "infiltration" by *mujahideen*.[42]

Aftermath in Bosnia

When the Dayton Peace Accords were signed in 1995 all "foreign soldiers" were required to leave Bosnia. Some *mujahideen* did. Others did not, and in the summer of 1995 there were an estimated 3,000 Muslim *mujahideen* who had fought either with the Bosniak army or as separate units. Among those who stayed behind were a hundred *mujahideen* of the Seventh Muslim Brigade, mostly Algerians who had occupied the former Serbian village of Bocinja Donja, sixty miles north of Sarajevo, near the city of Zenica in central Bosnia.[43] Algerian Afghan-Arabs and Kamar Kharban, leader of the Algerian Islamic Salvation Front, were seen in Bosnia on various ceremonial occasions. The Bosniak government bestowed "Bosnian citizenship to several hundred Arab and other Islamist volunteers," eliminating their "foreign" status before the Dayton Accords took affect in 1995, and in the early months of 1996 there was still a large number of *mujahideen* in the Balkans where the influence of Iran had already been "detected behind the wave of new Islamic schools which have sprung up across central Bosnia."[44] When nine Iranians were arrested in Zagreb in February, Nicholas Burns, spokesman for the Department of

State, warned that the continued presence of some 300 "foreign fighters" in Bosnia threatened future military assistance approved by the Dayton Accords.[45]

In Bosnia over a million people were dead, wounded, or living abroad in refugee camps. The government was weak, impoverished, and decentralized, needing massive assistance from the international community and its humanitarian agencies; yet TWRA, having accomplished its task, ignored all appeals for help, closed its offices, and departed, leaving the legitimate Islamic charities, particularly charities from the Gulf, to provide hundreds of millions of dollars in aid. The Party of Democratic Action of President Alija Izetbegovic continued to receive funds directly from Saudi Arabia and the Gulf States. Additional assistance came from a half-dozen major Islamic charities that had previously backed the President and the *mujahideen*. In autumn 1996 these Saudi charities were hard at work assisting Muslim refugees to return to Bosnia, and the Saudi High Commission for Aid to Bosnia (SHCB), also founded by Saudi Prince Salman bin Abd al-Aziz, was spending millions repatriating over 100,000 Bosnian refugees from Turkey, Croatia, Macedonia, and Slovenia back to Bosnia.[46]

Of the 250 NGOs active in the Balkans in 1996, fifty were Islamic; thirty of these were known to have terrorist connections but were ignored by the new multi-ethnic national police force. Among the most active of those thirty was the Kuwait Joint Relief Committee (General Committee for Refugee Assistance) whose office in Zagreb was headed by Shaykh Abu Adil Uthman al-Haydar, a known Muslim Brother and HAMAS agent. The Iranian Red Crescent Society (aka Helal Ahmar) and the Iranian Humanitarian Aid Organization, with offices in Sarajevo, Split, Tuzla, and Zenica, had previously moved arms to the *mujahideen* and continued to do so. IBC had offices in Zenica and Zagreb, as did MAK in Zagreb and Sarajevo and the Al Haramain Foundation in Zagreb, Rijeka, and Belikoj Gorici, Albania. All assisted the *mujahideen*. Zenica was also the headquarters of the Egyptian Jama'at al-Islamiyya (EIJ), whose leaders used UN High Commission for Refugees (UNHCR) credentials to move freely throughout the Balkans. The *mujahideen* who remained in Bosnia after the war years (1992–1995) were no less committed to continue the *jihad*, and from their relative obscurity they began to discuss and plot the Islamist penetration of Europe and America. They "wanted to use Bosnia as a logistical base . . . and tried to radicalize the Muslim population," but their call to arms made little impression upon the Bosniaks who were exhausted by war, and were too secular, or accustomed to "a tolerant form of Islam that abhors terrorism and fundamentalism."[47]

Although TWRA would disappear other charities remained, including the Bosnia branch of BIF (aka Bosanska Idealna Futura), which supplied the travel documents permitting Mamdouh Salim, a "key bin Laden associate" charged as an accomplice in the bombing of US embassies in Tanzania and Kenya, to travel to Bosnia in 1998 with all expenses paid.[48] Two years later the Bosnian office of "Mothers of Srebrenica and Podrinje" sent a letter to Prince Salman of Saudi Arabia, asserting that the Director of the Sarajevo office of SHRC that coordinated the work of Islamic charities in Bosnia had diverted $100 million collected specifically for the relatives of the victims of the slaughter of Muslims after the fall of Srebrenica in July 1995. The financial police of the Bosnian Ministry of Finance then searched the SHRC office and uncovered documents that demonstrated without any doubt that it was "clearly a front for radical and terrorism-related activities."[49]

In 1998 French troops serving in Bosnia began to suppress the activities of the *mujahideen*. Islamic charities were raided, Afghan-Arabs arrested, and Iranian diplomats expelled. The French intervention brought to a halt the regular shipments of C-4 plastique from Bosnia to EIJ cells in Europe and disrupted plans to harass US and European troops in Bosnia and Albania. Again many *mujahideen* were on the move, silently slipping out of Bosnia. In December 1999 Ahmet Ressemi, an Afghan-Arab Algerian national who had fought in the Al Muwafaq Brigade and who was in contact with Al Qaeda cells in Bosnia and Germany, was arrested at the Canada–USA border while driving a carload of explosives and bomb-making materiel meant for an attack on the Los Angeles airport. In April 2000 troops of the UN Mission in Kosovo (UNMIK) raided a house rented by the SARCS in Pristina to discover it was an Al Qaeda safe haven paid for by former directors of the Red Crescent including a founder of Al Qaeda, Wael Julaidan, who at the time was the Secretary-General of the Rabita Trust in Pakistan. In July that year three Egyptian Afghan-Arabs with close ties to Osama bin Laden were arrested in Sarajevo by the Bosniak Muslim–Croat Federation police. They had fought with the Bosniak *mujahideen* and like many others had been able to obtain Bosnian citizenship – either as a reward for their services in the Bosniak army, where they were generally used as instructors, or by marriage to Bosnian women.

In 2000 a highly classified State Department report warned that the Muslim-controlled portions of Bosnia had become a safe haven and "staging area" for Islamist terrorists protected by the Muslim government of Izetbegovic, but after the investigations into the activities of BIF in Chicago following 9/11 there was no longer any doubt that, following the Dayton Accords, Islamists had found a home in Bosnia from which to plan and execute terrorist plots. The discovery in the BIF office in Sarajevo in March 2002 of the "Golden Chain" list with the names of wealthy Saudi sponsors appeared to confirm that Al Qaeda was alive and well in the Balkans. These suspicions resulted in the Bosnian Ministry of Internal Affairs closing the Bosnian offices of three Islamic charities: BIF, the Global Relief Foundation (GRF), and the Al Haramain Foundation.

Albanian imbroglio

During the forty-six years of xenophobic communist rule (1944–1990) Albanian Muslims, who comprised 70 percent of the population, were at best restricted in their observation of the rituals of Islam and at worst persecuted. By the 1990s some had abandoned Islam, and many had simply let the practice of their religion lapse, to the dismay of the Islamists. They were determined to restore Islam in Albania on Islamist principles, and in 1990 "a number of Islamic groups" began to visit Albania. Proselytizers from the Gulf, Turkey, and Iran soon followed in greater numbers to revive the religious enthusiasm of lapsed Albanian Muslims. An "aid scheme" was agreed to with Turkey. In Tetovo Saudi Arabia funded the construction of a large *madrasa*, and Saudi charities shipped more than half a million copies of the Quran to Albania. Kuwait offered badly needed economic aid, but on condition that it could construct several mosques.[50] Iran was also a major donor, and in Scutari (Skadar), a famed Albanian town, Iranian agents opened the Ayatollah Khomeini Society; at Prizren, a city in Kosovo close to the Albanian border, Iranians founded a society funded by the Iranian Culture Center in Belgrade and selected groups of Albanians to receive scholarships for the study of theology in Iran.

After the elections in March 1992 installed a democratic government to replace the last of the doctrinaire communists, the impoverished government of Albania, in conjunction with the Islamic Development Bank of Jidda, invited a Saudi delegation to a conference to plan and organize economic assistance for Albania. The Netherlands Alislamic Aluok Foundation, IDB, and ISRA all offered economic assistance. In 1993 the largest charity operating in Albania was the Islamic Charity Project International, an association of more than a dozen Islamic charities including the Muwafaq Foundation and the Ayatollah Khomeini Society of Iran. The Islamic Relief Organization sponsored a medical clinic, and the Eastern European Muslim Youth worked in coordination with WAMY. By 1994 officials in several western European countries had become "deeply suspicious of [President Sali] Berisha's motives, fearing that Albania could become Islam's advance-post in Europe," yet ironically the Muslim President enthusiastically supported the efforts of the CIA to reorganize the inchoate Albanian intelligence service (SHIK).[51] Thereafter, CIA agents working with SHIK monitored the activities of Muslim charities and Islamist militants from Tirana. They would check travel plans, phone calls, "and contacts of various charity workers with suspected links to extremist groups from Egypt, Algeria, and other countries." Among the first of the *mujahideen* they spotted in 1992 was Mohammed al- Zawahiri, an employee of IIRO and the younger brother of Ayman al-Zawahiri. He had taken command of the terrorist cells in Albania and found jobs for the members of EJI who were attracted to Albania by "the availability of paying jobs with the Muslim charities."[52]

Zawahiri immediately hired Mohammed Hassan Tita who arrived in Tirana in January 1993 to work for IIRO, "to find the jihadists jobs in Islamic charities," and collect "zakat amounting to twenty percent of the salary from the Jihad members."[53] Zawahiri subsequently organized his own cell with more than twenty *mujahideen* including the EIJ Afghan-Arab Mohamed Ahmed Salama Mabrouk, a jihadist who had served seven years in jail for his part in the assassination of President Anwar Sadat in 1981. Mabrouk had been sentenced to death in absentia for his role in a plot to blow up Cairo's Khan al-Khalili bazaar in 1995. He directed the Saudi Center for Research and Revival of Islamic Heritage funded by smaller Saudi and Turkish charities.[54]

While at IIRO, Tita's most important hire, perhaps, was Shawki Salama Attiya, a forger who in the early 1990s had been an instructor at Al Qaeda camps in Afghanistan, and now worked for the Islamic Heritage orphanage in Albania. He arrived from the Sudan in August 1995 within days of the attempted assassination of President Mubarak in Addis Ababa. His job at the orphanage paid him $700 a month, a fortune in Albania or elsewhere in the Middle East, and was but one example why the fiscal fortunes of EIJ had become precarious. During a meeting of EIJ leaders in Sanaa, Yemen, in December 1995 Ayman al-Zawahiri reported on his visit to California to solicit funds for EIJ in Albania. Zawahiri was a noted fundraiser, but he failed to find any wealthy patrons, especially after EIJ was implicated in the bombing of the Egyptian embassy in Pakistan and the failed assassination in Ethiopia of Egyptian President Mubarak. Following the October 1995 bombing of the Egyptian embassy in Islamabad the Pakistan security forces moved rapidly to expel Arab-Afghans from their bases in Pakistan. This action placed intense funding demands on the Afghan Support Committee and the Al Kifah Refugee Center, as hundreds of *mujahideen* were shipped off to Bosnia. At Sanaa Zawahiri delivered discouraging news. EIJ was nearly broke. According to Ahmed Ibrahim al-Naggar, who attended the meeting, Zawahiri had said, "These are bad times." A month after the conclave EIJ outfitted Naggar with a plane ticket, laptop computer, and $500 to join Tita, Mabrouk, and Attiya in Tirana. There this trained pharmacist from a

Cairo slum found a job with the Al Haramain Foundation, the Saudi charity that operated out of a three-story villa in the center of Albania's dilapidated capital. Zawahiri and the cash-starved EIJ worked quietly and without much success until "Iranian and Saudi representatives opened foundations to provide patronage," and an Islamic bank opened in Tirana.[55]

Toward the end of the Bosnian war IIRO identity cards (*ingatha*) were found on *mujahideen* killed inside Bosnia, convincing evidence that a functioning jihadist cell was in Albania. Next the Macedonian government closed the IIRO office in Skopje in March 1995, and its regional financial accountant, an Egyptian, was detained by Croatian police after a raid on the IIRO Zagreb office in April. Not only was EIJ the most active *mujahideen* organization in Albania, its members provided a safe haven for Al Qaeda. The Albanian newspaper *Republica* reported that Bin Laden himself carried an Albanian passport and was a majority stockholder and founder of the Arab-Albanian Bank located in the central square of Tirana. Al Qaeda recruited young Albanians by setting up soup kitchens and providing medical supplies, all in the name of Bin Laden, who was cast in the role of the "Benevolent Arab." The recruits were first given military training in-country, and the good prospects were then sent for "further instruction in Islamic law and religion in Saudi Arabia."[56] Although the extent to which radical Islam has been imposed in a region formerly dominated by communist governments remains unclear, there are certainly Islamist organizations now entrenched in virtually all Balkan countries where there were none before the Saudis became involved.

As early as 1993 employees of Human Concern International (HCI), with its headquarters in Ottawa, Canada, had close ties with Algerian and Egyptian Salafists. The office of its subsidiary in Albania, Human Relief International, was closed without comment by Albanian authorities in April 1995. The following year the Iranian Revolutionary Guards joined forces with Al Qaeda and EIJ to support the Albanian insurgency in Kosovo, and by 1997 their Albanian network was sending *mujahideen*, known in Kosovo as "muj," to train the Kosovo Liberation Army (KLA, Ushtria Clirimtare e Kosoves).[57] Although Albania was thrown into chaos early in 1997 after the collapse of a bizarre pyramid investment scheme that bankrupted thousands of Albanians and forced President Berisha out of office, the new government continued to support those CIA operations he had approved. From the phone taps agents learned that Al Qaeda and EIJ had merged, and Zawahiri's financial difficulties were resolved. Thus, when the Albanian cell became an ever more active threat to the US presence, the CIA decided to terminate Al Qaeda operations in Albania in spring 1998. Although the government was skeptical "that the Muslim charity workers posed a serious threat," it could not prevail against the advice of its own security services, SHIK, the CIA, and the Egyptian government.[58]

Five Egyptian members of the EIJ cell in Tirana, who worked ostensibly for the Islamic Revival Foundation of Kuwait, were arrested. Organized in 1992 and active from Britain to Bangladesh, the Foundation was based in Peshawar, and its funding was managed directly by Al Qaeda. According to the Tirana press "the Egyptian terrorists had infiltrated 'volunteers' as the Kuwait people themselves do not prefer to be employed in poor countries, like in Albania."[59] The "US authorities considered the Tirana cell among the most dangerous terror outfits in Europe," and the CIA believed its tracking of the jihadists to be "one of the agency's great successes."[60] Nevertheless, the demise of EIJ did not end Islamist activity in Albania. In 2002 Albanian authorities seized the fifteen-story twin towers under construction in the heart of Tirana by the Karavan Construction Company owned by the ubiquitous Yassin al-Qadi. Al-Qadi had been active in Albania since the arrival of the Muwafaq charity and had been suspected of laundering some $10 million in support of Al Qaeda. Other Islamic religious charities came under investigation by SHIK for "illegal operations." Teams specializing in money-laundering pursued new cases, and Prime Minister Ilir Meta reported: "We identified the financial entities active in our country that are financially linked to the Al-Qaeda network."[61] In October 2002 a list was sent by the USA to the Albanian government urging the closure of the Active Islamic Youth, Al Haramain, Al Furkan, and SHRC offices in Albania. In the end, Saudi charities found that to broadcast the seeds of Salafist Islam on rocky ground was a bootless task.[62]

War in Kosovo

Kosovo, an international protectorate administered by the United Nations, remained part of Serbia and Montenegro, but its legal authority resided with the UN Interim Mission for Kosovo (UNMIK). The Kosovo Force (KFOR) – the NATO police force – and UNMIK were unable to halt the destruction of Christian churches, the region's widespread narcotics trafficking, and the infiltration of radical Islamists, many of whom were involved in mosque construction. In 1989, when President Slobodan Milosevic abolished the autonomous status of Kosovo and imposed direct rule from Belgrade, Dr. Ibrahim Rugova founded the Democratic League of Kosovo (LDK), the first non-communist party in the province. At first the LDK sought recognition for Kosovo as a full Yugoslav republic. However, upon the disintegration of the Federal

Republic of Yugoslavia Rugova declared the independence of Kosovo in 1993. It was an independence no one recognized.[63] Some Muslim Albanian Kosovars – who numbered 1.7 million, against 200,000 Christian Serbs – argued that they should emulate the Muslim Croats and Bosniaks and go to war. President Rugova believed this would be a terrible mistake that could only result, as in Croatia and Bosnia, in the massive flight of tens of thousands of Muslim Kosovar refugees into Albania. Instead, Rugova and the other political parties representing the Serbs established parallel structures of government, health care, and education. This unique experiment appeared to work, for the Serbs preferred the popular and pacifist Rugova to the hardliners among the Albanian Kosovars. Unfortunately, after the signing of the Dayton Accords in 1995, the Albanians were shocked to learn that Kosovo had been ignored in the settlement, and any expectation they may have had that the West would recognize their independence quickly vanished. When Rugova's popularity began to sag and his pacifism was denounced as passivity, the clandestine Albanian Kosovo Liberation Army (KLA: Ushtria Clirimtare e Kosoves, UCK) decided in 1996 to achieve by arms in Kosovo what the Bosniaks could claim they had won at Dayton.

Founded in the early 1990s, the KLA first killed individual Serbs and their Albanian collaborators, and then, emboldened, they attacked Serbian police stations and army units, capturing large quantities of arms. Albanian émigrés in Europe and the USA opened their checkbooks to supplement funds raised by smuggling and drug-running. Ibrahim Rugova condemned the actions of KLA, but refused to denounce them as terrorists as demanded by the USA. The media portrayed KLA as a liberation movement to free Albanian Kosovars from the tyranny of Slobodan Milosevic. Unfortunately, like other militia movements in the Balkans KLA's program was ethnic separatism – driving the Serbs, Macedonians, and other ethnic minorities from Kosovo. Beginning as a small, uncoordinated guerrilla group, by 1999 KLA had evolved into a substantial fighting force of 50,000 men equipped with some sophisticated weaponry captured from the Serbs or looted from armories in Albania during the civil war that erupted after the fall of President Sali Berisha. KLA soon received support from the USA whose Secretary of State, Madeleine Albright, intervened to see that its leader, Hashim Thaci, and not Rugova appeared as the head of the Kosovar delegation at the negotiations held in Rambouillet in February and March 1999. That meeting resulted in a US and NATO decision to intervene militarily in Kosovo, first clandestinely and then directly with money, arms, and training. As early as May 1998, NATO began to strengthen its military capabilities in Albania and Macedonia, and by October the USA was prepared for direct intervention. By then KLA had control of a third of Kosovo. On 15 January 1999 the supposed "Serb massacre" of the inhabitants of the village of Racak provoked both the USA and NATO to impose demands upon Milosevic, and, when he refused to accept them, NATO launched its seventy-nine days of bombing from 24 March to 10 June 1999. Within a week 300,000 Albanian Kosovars had fled across the borders into Albania and Macedonia, and by June 850,000 Kosovars, overwhelmingly Muslim Albanian refugees and IDPs, had fled their homes and villages.

Islamic charities from Saudi Arabia were the first to respond. They had arrived in Tirana in December 1998, and had soon been joined by aid agencies from Kuwait and UAE. In fact, refugees fleeing from fighting between KLA and Serb security forces had begun to trickle into Albania as early as May 1998. They were cared for by the Islamic Coordinating Council (ICC), which oversaw the work of some twenty Islamic relief groups operating in Albania. As the river of refugees rose in flood SHRC was authorized by royal decree in April 1999 to create a separate Saudi Joint Relief Committee for Kosovo and Chechnya (SJRC – Kosovo and Chechnya). It would coordinate the operations of the seven Saudi relief organizations for Kosovo and Chechnya that had previously been active in Bosnia. SJRC – Kosovo and Chechnya maintained a bank account at NCB which was managed personally by Suleiman Abd al-Aziz al-Rajhi. Within five months SHRC had received $45.5 million in cash, services, and supplies. The Kuwaiti and Saudi charities devoted their resources to assisting refugees, while charities from the Gulf states concentrated their efforts on the repair and reconstruction of some 200 of the 600 mosques and *madrasa*s in Kosovo that had been badly damaged or destroyed by Serbian militias. New mosques were constructed with "a zeal that has often come at the expense of the mosques' historic character, or of the mosques in their entirety" but that represented, however, a considerable infusion of cash into an impoverished region.[64]

Islamic charities from the Arab countries soon found themselves embroiled in the internal differences between the Kosovo Muslims and the *mujahideen* as to the concept of *jihad*. Muslim Kosovars were unconventionally Sufi, and when Arab Sunni volunteers "tried to similarly graft their concept of jihad to the KLA struggle" against the Serbs, they failed.[65] Members of the Iranian Revolutionary Guards, Al Qaeda, and *mujahideen* from at least half a dozen Middle Eastern countries were now crossing into Kosovo from bases in Albania to infiltrate the KLA. Alerted by the CIA–Albanian intelligence operations the USA, which had guaranteed the safety of Albanian Muslim Kosovars, met in Geneva with the leaders of KLA to insist they reject the jihadists. KLA eventually agreed, to the anger and disbelief of some of the Islamic charities in Kosovo. One of them complained: "The moderate Kosovar Albanians expelled or betrayed Arab militants who came to Kosovo with the aim of Islamizing ethnic conflicts."[66] Members of the militant Finsbury Park Mosque in London "bitterly recalled the betrayal" of *mujahideen* they had sent to Kosovo.

SHRC, however, was not easily discouraged, and persisted in opening *madrasas*, closing Sufi shrines, and creating separate schools for boys and girls. It occupied a building in Pristina sufficiently large to be used as a prayer hall, and continued its role as the umbrella organization representing several Saudi charities. It would spend "over $100 million on caring for and resettling refugees, on rebuilding schools and houses, and on health care" during its four years.[67] The Saudis built mosques in Rahovec, Peja, and Gjakova, all handsome stone structures in the Wahhabi architectural tradition, which stressed simplicity in distinction to the historically ornate Balkan mosques, until the Department of Culture of UNMIK intervened to halt construction of the Gjakova mosque, insisting that the Saudis would have to conform more to the Balkan traditional architecture with mosques built with local materials and historically appropriate designs. The Saudis also angered the Muslim Kosovars by the destruction of tombstones, graveyards, and monuments to Islamic saints in Vushtrri, Peja, and Gjakova that were anathema to Wahhabi beliefs. The Islamic community of Kosovo, established in 1912, should have prevented the desecration but remained aloof, more interested in the Saudi money pouring into the community than in architectural style, but the Wahhabi activities became so egregious that the Mufti of Kosovo requested SHRC either reduce its presence in Kosovo or leave.

Charities from UAE in Vishtrri in north-central Kosovo also tended to be immune to local sensitivities. The Zayed Bin Sultan Al Nahyan Charitable and Humanitarian Foundation had restored mosques, built a hospital, and refurbished over 1,200 damaged houses, but the 1993 construction of a new Islamic cultural center in the heart of Vushtrri offended the residents. The center did not "allude in any way to the 15th-century mosque that once stood on the site," and locals argued that the charity was "trying to promote religion" while the population at large was "eager to distance itself from anything that smells of 'fundamentalism.'"[68] In 1999 the Zubayr Philanthropic Foundation, an unknown Sudanese philanthropic organization, began sending planeloads of food, blankets, and medicine to Muslims in Kosovo, and a Sudanese Financial Committee for Supporting the Kosovo Muslims collected money for *da'wa* in Kosovo.[69] It was just one of the many charities collecting funds, but its concern for Kosovo was somewhat perverse when there were hundreds of thousands of poverty-stricken Sudanese who were desperate for the assistance Islamic charities could provide.

After 9/11

The effort to mobilize Muslim charities in the USA to support the incipient *jihad* in the Balkans began after Suliman al-Ali, who had lived in the USA, joined IIRO, and personally solicited over $500,000 during his first year in Saudi Arabia as an IIRO fundraiser. Impressed by his abilities to raise money, in 1991 "the Saudis sent al-Ali back to the United States to open IIRO's official office in the Washington DC area."[70] His arrival coincided with a realignment of "the Saudi-relief infrastructure" from Afghanistan to Eastern Europe and the Balkans for *jihad*. The Al Kifah Refugee Center in New York, which had previously raised funds for use in Afghanistan, now devoted its energy to humanitarian operations in Bosnia. Suliman al-Ali did the same, and in the years that followed he funneled untold millions through his charity to support Bosniak and Albanian Muslims. In addition, al-Ali completed some unusual money transfers to Mercy International Canada, a branch of Mercy International (originally HCI). Other transfers were made to an Islamic charity based in Michigan, and to a Chicago chemical company run by a director of Mercy International. Throughout the 1990s US authorities did little or nothing to impede the flow of donations from Muslim charities in America to the Balkans, but these sums were by no means comparable to those sent from Saudi Arabia to Bosnia.

In June 2000 Alija Izetbegovic stepped down after ten years as President of Bosnia. He declared that his reason for leaving was the determination by the international community to dilute the Islamic essence of Bosnia that to him was its reward to the Serbians for ethnic cleansing. "The international community is pushing things forward in Bosnia . . . but it is doing it at the expense of the Muslim people. I feel it is an injustice . . . These are things that I cannot live with."[71] The change of government in Sarajevo did, indeed, lead to the investigation of Islamic charities by Bosnian Financial Police. Accompanied by agents from NATO, they soon discovered accounts that had been used for illegal activities in the Balkans. Most surprising, anomalies were found in the Sarajevo office of SHRC for aid to Bosnia. An audit undertaken in October 2001 found unaccountable cash on hand, suspicious money transfers through personal bank accounts, and little or no accounting of money spent. Moreover, the Bosnian and NATO investigators uncovered a wealth of information on past and present terrorist activists in Bosnia and incriminating evidence, including photographs of the World Trade Center, the US Embassies in Kenya and Tanzania, and the USS *Cole*. There were maps of government buildings in Washington and instruments to forge State Department identification badges. After the raids had "revealed inappropriate materials that appear to indicate terrorist activity," including a "plot" against the US embassy in Sarajevo and apparent "planning materials for terrorist strikes throughout Europe, Bosnian officials threatened to close SHRC, one of the largest Islamic charities in the world."[72]

Early in 2002 Bosnian police raided the BIF (Bosanska Idealna Futura, aka Bosnian Ideal Future) offices in Sarajevo and Zenica, where they seized weapons and instructions on how to make bombs, booby-traps, and forge bogus passports. BIF was a safe haven and an integral part of the Al Qaeda money-laundering network. When the very next day a bomb threat was received by the US embassy in Sarajevo, the Bosnian police quickly arrested Munib Zahiragic, a Bosniak, and charged him with espionage. Zahiragic was a former member of the Bosnian Muslim secret police from 1996 to 2000, after which he had been appointed director of BIF in Sarajevo. He had in his possession more than a hundred secret files on Middle East and African *mujahideen* who had escaped arrest and were still in Bosnia. As a result police were able to arrest twelve members of a Bosnian Al Qaeda cell including six naturalized Bosnians, five Algerians, and a Yemeni, all of whom worked for Islamic charities and who were planning to bomb the US embassy and other government buildings in Sarajevo. One member was in direct telephone contact with Osama bin Laden, another had numerous blank western passports at his home in Zenica, and a third was the administrator at SHCB, a "$9 million complex, which includes a mosque that can accommodate 5,000 people."[73]

In possession of this incriminating evidence the Bosnian Financial Police immediately launched investigations into several foreign Islamic charities that implicated employees and officials of SHCB, BIF, the Al Haramain Foundation, Human Appeals International, and IIRO in illegal activities. When the Bosnian police raided the Al Haramain headquarters in March 2002, its officials had already destroyed its financial records for 1994–1998, but those for 1999–2001 recorded that $1.59 million had been withdrawn from its charity account and then vanished. The Director of the sister organization to Al Haramain, Al Haramainwa wa al-Masjed al-Aqsa Charity Foundation, could not explain how the charity had spent $3.5 million in 1999, the year its Director was in contact with Al Qaeda. Nor could it explain the transfer of funds to Yassin al-Qadi and Wael Julaidan, both on the US list of designated terrorists. The BIF and Al

Haramain were closed, and the regional commander for NATO reported sententiously in July 2002: "We detected a pattern here . . . for terrorist cells and those who aid and harbor them to operate behind the shield of legitimate humanitarian . . . organizations. They were preaching good, and sometimes doing good, while plotting evil."[74]

7   Russia and the Central Asian Crescent

> Islamist movements are first of all about national liberation, not indi-
> vidual liberties; they are about power before politics; their populism is
> a form of mass mobilization, not participation.
>
> Hasan al-Turabi, quoted in Kramer, "The Mismeasure of Political Islam"

The collapse of the Soviet Union in 1991, ironically, enabled revolutionary Islam, which had been anathema to communism, to establish Salafist
radicalism in the now independent Soviet republics of Central Asia. Kyrgyzstan on the border with China in the east and Azerbaijan on the shores
of the Caspian Sea in the west were the hinges of a giant door opening
to expose the heartland of Central Asia to the Islamists. Historically, this
region, which stretches in a great crescent more than 1,800 miles from
east to west, had been the traditional frontier between the Russian heartland and the states and societies of the Asian steppe. It remains so to
this day. In the west the volatile region of the Caucasus was inhabited
by numerous ethnic groups with disparate cultural traditions, long histo-
ries of mutual animosity, and a veneer of Soviet communism. They were
now open for Afghan-Arabs and Islamists to spread their jihadist message
among Muslims of the former Soviet Chechen-Ingush Republic and ever
northward into Russia. When the Red Army withdrew from Afghanistan
in 1989, followed by the dissolution of the Soviet Union in 1991, the
emerging Muslim states possessed their own unique blend of Islam characterized by many local beliefs and rituals that resulted in varying degrees
of susceptibility to the invasion by Afghan-Arabs, Salafists, and Al Qaeda,
all seeking to export the Islamist revolution.

During the second PAIC conference, held at Khartoum in December
1993, the prominent Russian Islamist Geidar Jemal took the opportunity to discuss the problem of Muslims in Russia with Hasan al-Turabi.
Turabi was a sympathetic listener, and publicly denounced the "traitorous
policies" of Russian Foreign Minister Andrei Kozyrev, who he said had
produced a "huge tragedy for the Islamic world" by allowing the emergence of a world dominated by the USA. Turabi proposed that an Islamic

committee for Russia should be established with Jemal as its chairman to make the committee "an organ representing the religo-political will" of Russian Muslims.[1] Turabi had good reason to urge his fellow Islamist to action, for the Turks and Saudis had already sent proselytizing missions into Central Asia to consolidate and spread traditional Sunni Islam and Wahhabism. Turkey was as interested in cultivating its historical cultural and linguistic ties as it was in spreading Sunni Islam, for it had a linguistic affinity with the Azeri, Kazakh, Tatar, Uzbek, Kyrgyz, Turkmen, and Uighur peoples; by 2000 there were more than 10,000 students from Central Asia studying in Turkey.

Saudi Arabia regarded the demise of the Soviet Union as a unique opportunity to launch *da'wa* and spread Wahhabi Islam among the Muslims of the new republics; after more than a half-century of communist rule, they had abandoned Islam or were perfunctory practitioners in the mosque with no sense of unity or ideological commitment.[2] In the past Saudi Arabia had been excluded from any meaningful presence in the Soviet Union; it had been forced it to enlist the diplomatic, religious, and commercial channels of UAE, Kuwait, and Pakistan to further its diplomatic and Islamic objectives. With the demise of the USSR *da'wa* became the mission of the employees of Saudi international Islamic NGOs whose activities were supervised by Prince Turki al-Faisal, head of the Saudi General Intelligence Service.[3] By the mid-1990s the various Saudi and Muslim agencies – WAMY, Rabita Trust, IIRO, the SAAR Foundation, and IDB – "regularly [made] contributions" to religious, educational, and public health programs in Central Asia.[4]

During the Afghan war combatants from the various tribes of Central Asia and the *mujahideen* in Afghanistan had set aside their historical ethnic, linguistic, and religious differences, but once the Soviets departed those differences quickly reemerged in Afghanistan as the various Islamist warlords began to fight among themselves. The Hezb-i-Islami of Gulbuddin Hekmatyar were supported by the Sunni Pushtuns of central and northern Afghanistan; Ahmad Shah Massoud's Jama'at-i-Islami was commanded by a Persian-speaking Sunni Tajik; the Hizb-i-Wahdat was led by Shi'ite Hazaras; the Jambesh-e-Melli of Abdul Rashid Dostum were Uzbeks. And then there was the Taliban ("student," an Urdu word derived from Arabic) movement, which practiced a strict Salafist Islam that was unacceptable, and even considered heretical, by many Afghans. Thus, the stage was set for internecine war. Elsewhere in Central Asia following the dissolution of the Soviet Union in 1991 five independent states, the "Stans," were created – Turkmenistan, Uzbekistan, Tajikistan, Kyrgyzstan, and Kazakhstan. Although Muslims were in the majority in each, they differed dramatically in character, history, and language from the Muslims of the Middle East and North Africa, and even from one another. Moreover, under communism Islam had been contained and persecuted for nearly seventy years by a determinedly atheistic communist regime. In the late 1920s severe restrictions had been placed on the Islamic community of Central Asia, and its Muslim leaders were carefully selected by the Soviets to enforce the will and regulations of the Russian government. Authorities forbade the collection of *zakat*, prohibited the *hajj*, closed mosques, and at one time Stalin even ordered the execution of any Muslim who owned a Quran. The Soviets were confident that ethnic and religious differences were bound for extinction.

From the Caspian Sea to China the Soviets had divided the Turkic-speaking Muslims into the Soviet Socialist Republics of Uzbekistan, Kirghizia, Turkmenistan, and Kazakhstan. The border between Uzbekistan and Tajikistan, however, was drawn in such a fashion as to divide Tajiks, who speak a language akin to Persian (Farsi). The Turkic-speaking people, ethnic Tatars, and Bashkirs each had their separate Tatar and Bashkir Autonomous Republics. The Soviet control of Islam was insured by four Islamic Spiritual Directorates, each led by a Soviet-approved Mufti. The first comprised Central Asia and Kazakhstan, with its seat in Tashkent; the second, at Ufa, incorporated European Russia and Siberia; the third controlled the Caucasus and Dagestan from Makhach-Qala; and the fourth administered the Muslims in the Transcaucasus from Baku.[5] Despite determined efforts by the Soviets to contain orthodox Islam in the expectation of its eventual demise, the Islamic religion had survived in these regional directorates as Muslims gravitated underground to the less visible Sufi brotherhoods (*tariqa*) with their secret rituals and self-proclaimed mullahs. In these brotherhoods the practice of Islam has, historically, acquired many idiosyncratic and syncretistic rituals – such as in Turkmenistan and Uzbekistan, where the worship of Muslim saints, shrines, and tombs, anathema to orthodox Islam, was sustained thanks to the surviving Sufi brotherhoods. Sufi individualism also remained undiminished in the countryside where indigenous practices included the ecstatic dervish dance combined with secretive, ceremonial, and non-doctrinaire customs. Even the pre-Islamic cults of ancestors and shamans were observed, as were magical ceremonies that attended marriages and funerals. Submerged within the Soviet Union, Islam did not become more visible until the late 1980s when Muslims of the Soviet Union were allowed much greater freedom to practice their religion during the war in Afghanistan, so that when the five "Stans" became independent in 1991, the Islam that emerged was an amalgam of the old, the obscure, the modified, and the new.

Those leaders who had inherited control of the governments in the new Central Asian republics had little understanding and less appreciation for the Islamist crosscurrents that had emerged in modern Islam, and the practices of their own people differed significantly from the Salafism that influenced the jihadists who had fought against the Russians in Afghanistan. The Central Asian secularists, however, had absorbed the history of Soviet totalitarianism and its use of political power. They soon perceived that Salafist Islam was a direct challenge to their own survival, and the best means to quarantine it was to adopt the constitutional principles of a democratic society, in particular the separation of church and state, but the legal codes adopted after independence were simply insufficient to regulate Islamic movements, charities, or international Islamic NGOs. Similar problems beset the emerging states of Azerbaijan and Georgia in the west. Although they were secular by choice, there was a dramatic increase in the creation of the *mahalla* (neighborhood organization), voluntary giving through *waqf*, and even the collection and distribution of *zakat*, and each of the Central Asian states became full members of the politically conservative OIC.

Outsiders begin to arrive

In 1989 Saudi Arabia initiated a dynamic program to rebuild Islamic religious institutions in Central Asia. It subsidized the pilgrimage to Mecca, built mosques, and provided scores of scholarships for students to attend *madrasa*s in Saudi Arabia, where they were exposed to Wahhabi practices of Islam and the doctrines of Salafist theology. In the first four years after independence the number of mosques, *madrasa*s, and seminaries in Tajikistan and Kyrgyzstan alone quadrupled as "various kinds of religious missionaries flooded into the cities and towns."[6] The first radical Islamist group to appear in Central Asia was the clandestine and secretive Hizb ut-Tahrir al-Islami (Islamic Liberation Party, HuT) whose members were to be found in the nascent Islamic Movement of Uzbekistan (IMU). HuT had been founded in Palestine in 1951 by Shaykh Taqiuddine an-Nabhani al-Falastini, a Quranic scholar, author, politician, Muslim Brother, former Al Azhar student, and *qadi* in the Court of Appeals in Jerusalem. An Islamist in the line of Hasan al-Banna and Sayyid Qutb, Nabhani not only opposed the *kafirin* and the Soviet atheists with equal vigor, he was the unflagging enemy of Muslim secularists such as Gamal Abdel Nasser. Until his death in 1977 Nabhani was determined to transform the Islamic world by imposing Shari'a and eliminating secular governments. His organization was secretive, and the name of its *amir*, Abdul Qadeem Zalloum, who led the organization in the early 1990s from a secret location, was unknown for years. HuT had played a part in the coups d'état that failed in Jordan and Syria in 1968, in Egypt in 1974, and Iraq and Tunisia in 1988, where in the latter forty of its members were tried by a military court in secret and executed.

Nabhani and his successors claimed that HuT "does not engage in charity works or armed actions"; rather, its presumed peaceful intentions were based on the "texts" of the Shari'a.[7] They sought to project the perception that HuT was devoted to the gradual evolution of society through *al-da'wa al-Islamiyya*, "as opposed to *al-thawra al-Muslimin* [the Muslim Revolution] camp," which sought change "through rapid and often violent means."[8] Thus, it was not a charity and did not pretend to be one. It was a political movement "supported initially by the Saudi-based radical Islamist Wahhabi movement" operating from London, but the extent of Saudi support has remained a mystery and the organization is currently banned in Saudi Arabia.[9] HuT first infiltrated into Tajikistan, "setting up its first cells in Tashkent and the Ferghana Valley." There it was declared an "extremist" movement in 1995 by the government in Dushanbe, and soon afterwards all the Central Asian republics proscribed the organization, forcing it underground. Although HuT claimed to have "more than 60,000 supporters" in Tashkent alone and "tens of thousands in other cities," its leadership claimed no ties to Saudi Arabia or the Wahhabis.[10]

The HuT movement does not appear to have spread after Tajikistan agreed to allow Russia to station troops in its territory for ten years; this greatly reduced the possibilities of a coup d'état against the government of President Imomali Rakhmonov.[11] In 2000 scores of HuT members were put on trial in Dushanbe and charged with "illicit activities," including the formation of "organizations advocating racial, ethnic, and religious bigotry." It was also charged with plotting to overthrow the secular government. Indeed, the HuT movement was "active in various parts of the Islamic world" and its goal remained to resume the "Islamic way of life by reestablishing the Islamic State."[12] Throughout the Central Asian Crescent thousands of HuT members were arrested, but the clandestine organization was hard to crush given its network of cells, often numbering no more than three members, and the leadership remained unrepentant: "Whenever there is a Muslim Amir who declares Jihad to enhance the World of All and mobilizes the people to do that, the members of Hizb ut-Tahir will respond in their capacity as Muslims in the country where the general call to arms was proclaimed."[13] After 9/11 the US anti-terrorist campaign against the Taliban government and the occupation of Afghanistan by coalition forces contributed greatly to the stability of both the political and economic condition in Tajikistan, and the threat from HuT virtually disappeared.

Although the Russian Federal Security Service (FSB) had reported "Wahhabite propaganda" during the last days of the Soviet Union, diplomatic relations were established for the first time between Russia and the Kingdom of Saudi Arabia in 1990. Embassies were subsequently opened in their respective capitals. The Russian–Saudi detente and diplomatic recognition were "preceded by a secret visit" from Tariq bin Laden, younger brother of Osama, representing the Saudi Bin Laden Group. He appears to have been instrumental in facilitating the establishment of the Saudi diplomatic mission in Moscow. Shortly thereafter the embassy was opened with a very active "Department of Islamic Affairs, with the collaboration of the World Islamic League (Saudi Arabia), [and] the Ministry for Islamic Affairs Organization." The Voice of Saudi Arabia "became one of the major channels for financing subversive elements in the Russian Muslim community," and the diffusion of Wahhabite theology appeared first "in Daghestan and in Chechnya" in the Caucasus.[14] Russian critics, who perceived that the Salafist Islamists were dividing the world into the *dar-ul-islam* (the realm of Islam) and the *dar-ul-harb* (the realm of war), argued that Islam had declared war on Russia.

Russian intelligence was soon very concerned that agents from the Saudi General Intelligence Service were supervising the activities of the Muslim employees of Islamic charities.[15] FSB was especially interested in Ikraa (*Laa ikraa-haa fid-deen* – "There is no compulsion in religion," Quran 2:256), a mysterious charity with headquarters in Jidda whose president, Mohammed Abed al-Yamani, had close ties with the Saudi royal family and with Saudi financial circles, particularly the Bin Mahfouz family. Ikraa sent Wahhabi clergy from the Gulf to apply pressure on the traditional Islamic clergy in Central Asia and in Moscow, Volgograd, Ulyanovsk, Astrakhan, and Yakutsia to adhere more closely to Wahhabi Islamic principles. Their more overt efforts were made in the Caucasus, especially in Dagestan, where Ikraa opened its first *madrasa* in February 1992. It also financed a printing house administered by Servakh Abed Saad from UAE, who began printing Islamist material at Pervomansk. Ikraa publications spread quickly through the Caspian region, and Ikraa *mujahideen* were "trained in Saudi Arabia, Egypt, Pakistan, and Afghanistan."[16] Saad redoubled his propaganda and sent reports to the Saudi embassy in Moscow as the violence in the Caucasus escalated, before moving on to war-torn Chechnya in August 1999.

Islam in Tajikistan

In September 1991 the Supreme Soviet proclaimed Tajikistan an independent state. Three months later Tajikistan and ten other former Soviet republics banded together in the Commonwealth of Independent States

(CIS). Along with other Central Asian republics, Tajikistan had histor- ically been a drain on the resources of both imperial Russia and the Soviet Union. And like its neighbors, Tajikistan formed part of the Islamic cultural sphere, a world far removed from the Christian, parliamentary republics of Russia, Belorussia, and the Ukraine.

Prior to the departure of Soviet troops from Afghanistan in 1989 the Afghan-Arab *mujahideen* had provided support to Tajikistan *mujahideen*. Thereafter, Afghan-Arabs allied with the Hizb Nahda (the Islamic Renaissance Party of Tajikistan, IRPT), which was formally established in 1990. The rapid evolution of an indigenous Islamist movement had begun with the perestroika of Mikhail Gorbachev, which loosened the hitherto tight control over the Soviet republics by Moscow. A respected Sufi and mullah, Akhbar Turajanzade, the *kazikolon* (Muslim leader) of Tajikistan, assumed an important role in its development. Despite the prohibition against Muslim political movements, IRPT was a dynamic Islamist move- ment when Tajikistan became independent in September 1991. It was defeated, however, in Tajikistan's first election in October by the move- ment of Rakhmon Nabiev, the former head of the Tajik Communist Party. Claiming election fraud, IRPT initiated hunger strikes. In March 1992 it led anti-government demonstrations in Shahidon Square in the capi- tal, Dushanbe, while pro-communist demonstrators opposed them from nearby Ozodi Square. Violent clashes and bloodshed followed, and the situation was only temporarily stabilized by the intervention of the 201st Division of the Russian army. A coalition government soon collapsed, and the conflict between the pro-communist Popular Front based in Kulobi and IRPT escalated into open warfare throughout the autumn of 1992.

On 18 November 1992 the different Tajik factions held a conference in the northern city of Khujand, which had witnessed no violence, at the end of which the Supreme Soviet, which in effect acted as a parlia- ment, appointed Imomali Rakhmonov, who had previously been just a mid-level official and the leader of the Kulobi Soviet People's Deputies, head of state. Rakhmonov inherited a Tajikistan overwhelmed by a ruined economy, its administration destroyed, and a fragmented society of com- munists, democrats, and Islamists. The government supporters were determined to "fight to victory" against the Islamists; the opposition were determined to crush communism in order to establish the Islamist state. Rakhmonov chose to distance himself from the extremists in either group, and sought the intervention of CIS, Russia, Iran, and the UN to establish a ceasefire and open negotiations between his government and the United Tajik Opposition (UTO) which had joined IRPT. UTO con- sisted of some 10,000 *mujahideen* led by the Saudi Commander Khattab, who just arrived in Afghanistan in 1987. He had returned home only to come back to Peshawar as an employee of a Saudi charity. Khattab's Tajik *mujahideen* had gained notoriety by launching several assaults against Soviet outposts on the Tajikistan border. By 1989, he was receiving substantial financial support from Pakistani and Saudi charities.

As these events unfolded the economic and political chaos that had overwhelmed Tajikistan led many Tajik, particularly the young men who had been deeply influenced by the conflict in Afghanistan and the Islamist *mujahideen* who had fought there, to seek answers for their spiritual and economic impoverishment in the certainties of Salafism, a disciplined theology that forced one to live in accordance with Islamic practice at the time of the Prophet Muhammad. Tajikistan was a hospitable place for redundant Sunni Afghan-Arabs because four of five Tajiks were Sunni. Only the Tajik of Badakhshan, located far to the east, were members of the Isma'ili sect of Shi'ite Islam, but they did not count for much. Not surprisingly, Al Qaeda had been welcomed by IRPT whose leadership had come from clandestine Islamist youth organizations influenced by the Muslim Brotherhood and the writings of Sayyid Qutb. In the subsequent civil war the rebels were an amalgam of a small group of indigenous Tajik religious extremists joined by Afghan-Arab jihadists and *mujahideen* from Afghanistan.[17]

The Islamists were led in Tajikistan by Mullah Akhbar Turajanzade and by Mohammadsharif Himmatzoda, chairman of IRPT, who continued to operate from his base in Afghanistan. The latter received arms and assistance from Gulbuddin Hekmatyar and, after 1996, from the Taliban, who vigorously collected donations – mostly from opium producers and traffickers. The same pattern of support through Islamic charities that had worked so well in Afghanistan was now widely applied throughout the Central Asian crescent. Charities were usually run by Muslim outsiders and members of Al Qaeda to provide arms, cash, and supplies to *jihad* movements. From its offices in Peshawar the ubiquitous ISI of Pakistan quietly coordinated the activity of several Islamic organizations including HuT, the Ikhwan, and the Saudi Ibrahim bin Abdul-Aziz al-Ibrahim Fund. It provided cash for the camps where "about 400 fighters from Uzbekistan and Tajikistan mostly from Ferghana Valley were trained in Pakistan."[18]

In 1996 Russia and Iran acted jointly to secure a ceasefire in the civil war. As mediators they opened negotiations in Dushanbe involving the government and UTO/IRPT. The thorny question that dominated the agenda was power-sharing. Was the government prepared to sacrifice the principle of secularism, which most Tajiks favored, to accommodate the Islamist demands for a share of state power? A compromise was eventually reached in 1997 whereby IRPT was given legal recognition, but secularism remained the central principle of the Tajikistan constitution. Ultimately a 70–30 power-sharing percentage was agreed by which the government retained 70 percent of government positions. President Rakhmonov willingly agreed to build a broad-based Movement for National Unity and Revival involving all ethnic groups in an effort to overcome the traditional clientist and regional networks that had dominated Tajik political life. Both Russia and Iran agreed to be the guarantors of the 1997 General Agreement to end four years of civil war that had taken over 60,000 lives. The Afghan-Arabs faded away, including Commander Khattab, who later surfaced in the Caucasus. The process of refugee resettlement began as thousands of Tajiks returned from Uzbekistan, but the dilemma of secularism or Islamism remained unresolved.

Heartland of Central Asia: Uzbekistan

Modern Uzbekistan, a country of some 25 million people, lies in the ancient cradle between the Amu-Darya and Syr-Darya rivers with borders on all the other "Stans." Historically, it has been the center of empires and commerce. Its conquest by Alexander the Great about 330 BCE superimposed the culture and language of the Greeks, and the region soon became the crossroads of Asia, and the meeting place of Persian, Indian, and Greek cultures. Thereafter, Uzbekistan was swept by tidal waves of invaders, Huns and Turks between 484 and 1150 CE followed by the Turkic Mongols of Genghis Khan in 1220, and Timur (Tamerlane). From his center at Samarkand between 1370 and 1405, he devastated and plundered the lands and empires from the Mediterranean to China, enabling him to construct mosques, minarets, and *madrasa*s of stunning beauty in Samarkand and Bukhara and control the commerce that passed along the ancient "Silk Road." Uzbekistan was incorporated into Russia in the late nineteenth century, and after stiff resistance was made a Socialist Republic of the Soviet Union in 1924.

In western Uzbekistan the Soviets introduced the cultivation of "white gold" (cotton) and grain by extensive irrigation that depleted the supply of water in a semi-arid land, shrinking its rivers and consequently the Aral Sea. Boundaries were drawn to divide and rule its ethnic groups. The Soviets developed the Ferghana Valley, home to a third of the population of Uzbekistan who live on the fertile flood plain of Syr-Darya around the city of Ferghana, founded on an ancient site by the Russians in 1876. Uzbekistan combines both the old and the new in Islam. The archaic contains the famed Islamic cities of Bukhara and Samarkand, whose intellectual, cultural, and religious life was known and revered throughout the Islamic world. Both cities were allowed to quietly decline during the seventy years of the Soviet occupation. They decayed despite the fact that Bukhara, the more renowned and older of the two, was the center of the Naqshabandi (literally engraver of wooden stamps) Sufi *tariqa*, founded in the fourteenth century by Shaykh Bahauddin Naqshabandi, whose mausoleum is located six miles east of Bukhara. During the Soviet era the site was defiled and used as a storage shed for fertilizer.

Bukhoro-ye sharif (the noble Bukhara) is often called Islam's second city, with 350 mosques and a hundred *madrasa*s. The Soviets made it the center of their "Arab World" *madrasa*, where they carefully indoctrinated the future Muslim leaders in the USSR. However, the students were few, and under communism Islam presented no serious religious challenge to the state. This began to change dramatically after the dissolution of the Soviet Union in 1991. Pilgrims now came in ever-increasing numbers to visit the fabled mosques and holy shrines of Bukhara and Samarkand, and the Sunni Islam of the Hanafi religious school was now vigorously taught in the *madrasa*s of these holy cities. Bahauddin Naqshabandi's shrine was restored, and the name of the main thoroughfare in Bukhara was changed from Lenin to Bahauddin Naqshabandi Street. Situated far to the west of the former communist capital, Tashkent, the two cities seemed isolated in a world of their own where language differentiated the proud Persian-speaking inhabitants from the rest of the country, but since one-quarter of the Uzbek population are members of the Naqshabandi Sufi order, the government very early perceived that the movement could be a constructive alternative to the puritanical teachings of the Wahhabi Islamists.

As in Tajikistan, resurgent Islam in Uzbekistan was the result of perestroika, and the Soviet government had made no move to prorogue the nascent Salafist movements led by Muhammad Radjab, Hakim Kor, and Abduwal Mirza. Thousands of Qurans printed in Saudi Arabia suddenly appeared, young people began to enroll in religious rather than state schools, and wealthy Uzbeks, who had migrated from Bukhara to the Ferghana Valley, returned to build mosques to honor their ancestors. This religious effervescence was "exploited by international centers disseminating ideas of fundamental Islam." They had reacted more quickly to exploit local conditions than either the government or the official Muslim *ulama*, which resulted "in the increase in influence of the radical Islamic views."[19] On 24 March 1990 the first secretary of the Communist Party of Uzbekistan, Islam Abduganievich Karimov, was elected President of the Uzbek Soviet Socialist Republic, and the following year, along with the other "Stans," the Supreme Soviet proclaimed the independent Republic of Uzbekistan. In December 1991 Karimov became its President in a very dubious election, and the rival Erk and Birlik political parties were soon crushed and their leaders driven into exile.

Although the Uzbek constitution provides for freedom of religion and the observance of religious holidays, the restoration of mosques and the reopening of Islamic colleges and religious foundations were registered and monitored by a State Committee on Religious Affairs. The Islamic clergy of Bukhara and Samarkand generally ignored the presence of the new Islamists and seemed oblivious of the Salafist revival in Tajikistan to the east and the Sunni renaissance in the Ferghana Valley. The Salafist Adolat (Equity) Movement in the Ferghana Valley, which in 1991–1992 sought to impose Islam as the state religion and with it the Shari'a, was driven underground and eventually shattered, as was HuT, which had a considerable following in Namangan, Ferghana, Andizhan, and Tashkent.

Islamic charities from Pakistan, Turkey, Afghanistan, Saudi Arabia, and Iran were at first permitted to fund projects of "Islamic philanthropy" ranging from the construction and maintenance of mosques and *madrasa*s to regional road construction. In the capital, Tashkent, the extent of that assistance was impossible to assess given the informal practices by which financial transfers were made. The stringent Law on Public Associations in 1991 was passed to control NGOs, and the registration of charitable organizations resulted in their careful surveillance. In August 1992, some seventy Islamic "scholars" from Saudi Arabia were deported for having maintained close relations with radical elements, and in 1993 the government cracked down on its own indigenous Islamists, forcing the opposition to leave for Afghanistan and Tajikistan where the Salafists founded the Islamic Movement of Uzbekistan (IMU). To combat IMU President Karimov continued with greater vigor his policy to build a secular state, while supporting an evolutionary growth in a regulated Islamic community under the orthodox, moderate *ulama*, but the appearance of IMU and other radical Islamist movments "exacerbated the problems facing Russian-speaking Uzbeks." Between 1991 and 1998, "around 600,000 of them emigrated – around half of them Russian." Unfortunately, the majority of émigrés belonged to "the educated classes, people with professional training and reasonably high qualifications."[20]

IMU and HuT, which had begun to spill over from Tajikistan, were prorogued. Many mosques constructed by funds from the Gulf states were closed, and the activities of the surviving 2,000 mosques and various religious groups were monitored closely by Uzbekistan's intelligence service. The government organized committees of moderate Muslim leaders and scholars to preach and teach in the towns and villages to dissuade Uzbeks from joining or supporting Islamist movements, singling out teachers and graduates from Wahhabi institutions, the followers of the reactionary Imam Nazarov of Tashkent, and members of IMU. IMU was a special target, for the Islamist movements in Tajikistan and Uzbekistan were in a close alliance and their *mujahideen*, when hounded by the authorities, could always retire to safety in Afghanistan. In 1996 the Taliban openly sponsored IMU insurgents along the Amu-Darya River in the region of Termez, and when Osama bin Laden returned from the Sudan to settle in Afghanistan, Al Qaeda provided arms and trained Uzbek rebels. During the final stages in the war of the warlords in Afghanistan IMU joined the victorious Taliban movement while cooperating with the "Arab brigade 055" of Osama bin Laden, the extremist anti-Shi'ite Sipah-e-Sahaba, and the Lashkar-e-Jangvi of Pakistan. In the same year IMU became much more active under the leadership of Juma Namangani, a former Soviet paratrooper and *mujahid* with close ties to the Taliban, Osama bin Laden, and ISI. Two years later Namangani became a deputy to Osama bin Laden. With an infusion of funds from drug trafficking Namangani plotted to overthrow all secular governments in Central Asia and began with a failed attempt to assassinate President Karimov in February 1999.[21] The estimated numbers of IMU *mujahideen* active in Afghanistan increased from 500 in 1999 to 1,000 by 9/11, and in Uzbekistan IMU units began combat operations in the Ferghana Valley, Tashkent, and Surkhandarya. After the US invasion of Afghanistan IMU fought alongside the Taliban, and suffered heavy losses including the death of Juma Namangani in a US airstrike in November 2001.

By 2001 Bukhara and Samarkand appeared secure from the Islamists, and in the Ferghana Valley, which had at one time seemed vulnerable to infiltration by Taliban/Al Qaeda, all seemed quiet. Still, the low standard of living in that region, the lack of economic development, and high unemployment among the youth led to the clandestine growth of Akromaya, a youth movement in the Ferghana Valley, and HuT. After the expansion of the American presence in Uzbekistan that came after 9/11, HuT became ever more radical. The Mufti of Uzbekistan, probably acting on orders from the President, responded by publishing a *fatwa* forbidding Muslims to have any contact with members of HuT. Nevertheless, Islamic institutions continued to support Islamist goals, and in fact collected *zakat* to finance the Islamic opposition to President Karimov. This led him to complain in October 2000 that the opposition dreamed of a caliphate to "take our country back to the Middle Ages, the age of obscurantism, as if we are not living in the 20th Century."[22] He continued to ban opposition parties, muzzled the press, and used the threat of radical Islam to stamp out dissent. Between 1998 and 2000, some 4,000–5,000 Muslims were imprisoned, and after 9/11 the Karimov government warned foreign NGOs to refrain from supporting Uzbekistan political organizations.[23] Muslim charities were not the only ones told to stay out of politics, for the government also singled out the Open Society Institute of American billionaire George Soros and three other American NGOs, warning them not to become involved in local politics. When a decree issued in December 2003 required some seventy-three aid and charitable institutions to re-register with the Justice Ministry, two Uzbek opposition parties were refused official recognition and the Uzbek parliament adopted a law banning all political parties from receiving any foreign assistance as President Karimov consolidated his dictatorship.

The Islamists responded by attacks in Tashkent, but still the government remained unmoved and refused to permit mosques to reopen in Andizhan and other cities in the Ferghana Valley inhabited by the most devout Muslims in Uzbekistan.[24] In April 2004 there were further religious-inspired incidents in Tashkent and eastern Uzbekistan, once again threatening peace in the Ferghana Valley. Mosques were ordered to tighten controls over their own activities and a decree was issued, "ordering local government authorities to check up on the financial transactions of any Muslim religious institutions located within their area." In March 2005 Pakistan President Pervez Musharraf signed an agreement in Tashkent in which he promised to crack down on IMU terrorists still in Pakistan from launching attacks against Uzbekistan: "I have assured President [Karimov] that Pakistan will not allow the use of its soil by any terrorists from Uzbekistan."[25]

Turkmenistan and Kazakhstan

Although Turkmenistan, like Tajikistan and Uzbekistan, bordered on Afghanistan, its trans-Amu-Darya (Oxus) River region was relatively untouched by Afghan influence. Turkmenistan looked to the west, its lifeline the Caspian Sea where the bulk of its 5 million people are congregated, leaving its southern region near Afghanistan sparsely populated. Unlike Uzbekistan and Tajikistan, however, the government of Saparmyrat Niyazov (Nyyazow), who seized the presidency in 1992 for life, was decidedly secular and enforced the separation of state and religion. Declared a Soviet Republic in 1925, during the ensuing years its Muslims had been administered by the Spiritual Administration for Muslims of Central Asia located in Tashkent and headed by a Kazi approved by the Soviet Union. After the collapse of the USSR in 1991 the Spiritual Administration was replaced in June 1992. Kazi Hajji Nasrullah ibn Ibadulla officially registered the kaziate of Turkmenistan to replace it. The Turkmen Ministry of Justice duly approved the kaziate, but the government closely watched the activities of Khezretguly Khan, the chief Imam in the capital of Ashgabat.

Under Article 3 of the Turkmenistan constitution "the freedom to profess a religion" or personal conviction is only restricted when "necessary to safeguard public safety and order." However, Article 6 declares that while religious practice is free to all, private religious instruction, whether in an Islamic *madrasa* or a Christian seminary, is prohibited. A cadre of officials from the Ministry of Justice vigorously enforced Article 6, in which they demonstrated little tolerance for the many mullahs who had profoundly suffered under the Soviet regime. Xenophobia reached new heights in February 2004 when President for Life Saparmyrat Niyazov, the Great, who enjoys the title Turkmenbashi (leader of the Turkmen), fired 15,000 people in the health-care sector and replaced them with conscripts from the Turkmen army and by ill-educated civil servants. In the private sector the government would no longer recognize the degrees of doctors, lawyers, and teachers. The Turkmenbashi patiently explained that these draconian decrees were necessary to dissuade people from sending their children abroad for a university education, a practice commonly employed when higher education was reduced to just two years.[26]

Needless to say, under such a regime with a President obsessed by the cult of his personality, there was little room for dissent and only limited Islamic charitable giving in Turkmenistan. Islamic and Christian charities were circumscribed, which is perhaps why they cooperated with one another. When the American Red Cross arrived in Ashgabat in 1992, it worked closely with local Islamic charities and even shared office space in the building that housed the Turkmenistan Red Crescent Society. Activity that had been tolerated but restricted in the past was further circumscribed in May 2004 when the government imposed major restrictions on religious freedom – not only for Muslims, but for Christians as well. The Islamic community, in a pattern similar to that imposed in Libya by Colonel Muammar Qaddafi and his self-deification in the *Green Book*, was forced to regard the *Ruhnama* (*The Book of the Soul*), written by Niyazov, as "a sacred work on a par with the Koran." It is mandatory reading in all the schools.[27] Meetings at the government Ruhyyet (Spirituality Palace) were carefully orchestrated, and Niyazov shrewdly managed to reduce the importance of WAMY, the Islamic youth organization, by subordinating it to the Magtymguly Youth Association of Turkmenistan. He also pre-empted the role of the traditional Muslim *waqf* by using his own multi-million-dollar charitable fund to support his own political objectives.[28] In his usual abrupt fashion President Niyazov revised his policy in June 2004, perhaps realizing that some assistance was better than none and "eased restrictions on charity aid for religious groups." He created new legal guarantees for religious freedom and freedom of worship, and he improved the legislation that had greatly circumscribed the activity of religious organizations.[29] Few took his actions seriously.

Kazakhstan, potentially the richest of the emerging Central Asian states, also limited the activity of Islamic institutions, political parties, and politico-theological movements. After independence in 1991, Turkey – not the Arab states – assumed responsibilities for "cultural and Islamic integration" in Kazakhstan and provided substantial financial assistance. Still, when the pan-Turkic Nurji sect, banned in Turkey, failed to achieve influence in Kazakhstan, a window of opportunity opened for the Gulf Islamists to make their presence felt. The national newspaper, *Kazakhstanskaya Pravda*, soon reported that the South Kazakhstan Humanitarian Academy (formerly the Kazakh–Kuwait Humanitarian Academy) at Shymkent, the administrative center of southern Kazakhstan, was receiving questionable financial assistance from the Kuwait-based Jamiyat al-Islah al-Ijtimai (Social Reform Society). The students observed strict Islamic rules and were "instructed to grow beards and wear long dresses in line with the 'unwritten rules.'" The tuition-free academy could "well have been mistaken" for a *madrasa*, and its lecturers were a varied crew, "coming from Turkey, Sudan, Jordan, Morocco, Tunisia, and Egypt." The Kuwaiti society was aggressively building mosques and "using sadaqa to help the poor." Its "goals" were unclear and its educational curriculum "a bit dubious."[30]

Kuwait was not alone in its interest in Kazakhstan. Saudi Arabia used financial investments and Islamic charities to spread its influence. Tablih missionaries, who constituted a loose network of itinerant preachers calling for a return to the teachings of the founding fathers of Islam, arrived from Pakistan; Al Azhar sent Egyptians to teach in Islamic schools. The Egyptian Ministry for Religious Affairs and Waqf signed an agreement with the government of Kazakhstan to further religious education, and the Egyptian government sponsored the construction of the Nur-Mubarak Academy in Almaty. These official overtures to orthodox Islam did not obscure the determination of the government to crush clandestine Islamist movements in the late 1990s, beginning with HuT. HuT had moved into southern Kazakhstan from Uzbekistan where the movement had been charged with a variety of illegal activities including inciting revolution and fostering religious discord. It had begun to infiltrate the *zhamaghat* (Islamic communities), the education system, the police, and the professions. Unlike Uzbekistan, Kazakhstan did not place the HuT on its list of banned organizations, but by 2004 its survival depended on the ability of its members to circumvent a 1998 religious law that made it illegal to distribute printed materials or proselytize without government approval. In 2004 the government reported that the "current situation around Islam does not raise any serious concerns."[31] Yet it remains to be seen if the influence of HuT, which is now especially strong among the Kazakh youth, will threaten the survival of the Kazakhstan secular state.[32] The Muslim Religious Office for Kazakhstan remained vigilant, even investigating the activities of officially registered mosques and charities and the various independent Islamic *zhamahgat*s. Also closely scrutinized were the efforts of Saudi Arabia to "change the face of Islam in Kazakhstan" by introducing Wahhabite doctrines and in particular the activities of Islamic centers and their sponsors, the "Islamic charity funds."[33]

Kyrgyzstan: door to China

After the Supreme Soviet proclaimed the Republic of Kyrgyzstan in 1991, Kyrgyzstan enjoyed nearly ten years as an island of stability and democracy among the "Stans" of Central Asia. Historically, the Kyrgyz were a Turkic pastoral people following their herds across the mountain massif of the Tien Shan that dominates 95 percent of the country. During the twentieth century, both under the Tsars and then the Soviets, large numbers of Russians colonized Kyrgyzstan, where they received the best agricultural land and introduced modern farming in the south that forced many of the southern Kyrgyz to abandon their nomadic culture. Nevertheless, cattle breeding continued to dominate the economy of the northern region and seemed a perfect economic match for the agriculture of the south, encouraging the Kyrgyz to vote overwhelmingly for free-market reforms in 1994. Kyrgyzstan did not possess the profound Islamic heritage of its neighbors; during the Soviet era religious freedom was a reality despite the fact that Islam had been contained, the Muslim clergy restrained, and those mullahs who were not registered with the authorities imprisoned. After independence Islamists exploited the Republic's religious freedom to penetrate into the southern region from Uzbekistan and Tajikistan, where a number of schools and mosques came under their control.

   In general the Sunni Muslims of the Hanafite and Shafi'ite *madhhab*s (way, interpretation) rejected Islamist Salafist ideology, and in July 1995 the Kyrgyz National Security Council "met to discuss what they called the 'Muslim offensive'" in southern Kyrgyzstan. Members of the Council were "alarmed" by the alleged existence of mullahs with criminal records actively propagating Islam in the region. They argued for the reestablishment of the moribund Committee on Religious Affairs in order to monitor Islamist activities, including those of Islamic charities around Osh at the eastern end of the Ferghana Valley. Osh was home to Kyrgyzstan's Uzbeks, who total some 13 percent of Kyrgyzstan's population, and the bloody ethnic clashes between Uzbeks and Kyrgyz in 1989–1990 had not been forgotten.[34] Years of religious tranquility came to an end, and in the autumn of 1999 *mujahideen* from the Islamic Movement of Uzbekistan (IMU) invaded the mountainous Bakten region of Kyrgyzstan, kidnapping a group of Japanese geologists. It created a *cause célèbre* that brought international publicity to the hitherto unknown local Islamists – Kyrgyz, Uzbek, and Tajik. The Kyrgyz National Security Council at first made conciliatory efforts to reduce ethnic tension between Kyrgyz and Uzbeks in eastern Ferghana, but then moved forcefully to halt the spread of the emerging Salafist movement in the south. It wanted no replication of the tragedy in Tajikistan.

In May 2004 another team of Uzbeks from the Andizhan Uzbekistan Interior Ministry, accompanied by two Kyrgyz from the Osh Interior Ministry, were caught secretly filming people attending Friday prayers at a large mosque in Karasuu. Their cameras and cassettes were seized by the local citizens and handed over to the police, who passed them on to members of HuT present at the scene before they in turn relinquished them to the local government after viewing the film. Since several hundred Uzbeks regularly crossed the border to attend Friday prayers, and the mosque had been the focal point for the gathering of Islamists, it was an indication that even though religious freedom did exist in Kyrgyzstan, the authorities kept a close watch on ethnic Uzbeks who were thought to be most susceptible to Islamist penetration. China, of course, maintained its vigilant military patrols along its border with Kyrgyzstan to prevent Islamist penetration of its western frontier, where in Xinjiang there are more than 18,000 Uighur Muslims in detention.

In April 1996 the Presidents of China, Russia, Kazakhstan, Kyrgyzstan, and Tajikistan met in Shanghai to discuss border security and the serious threat from Afghan-Arabs and Islamists in Afghanistan as they began to infiltrate northward into Central Asia and the western Xinjiang Uighur Autonomous Region of China. In spite of many decades of colonization by ethnic Chinese, the Han remained a minority, accounting for only 38 percent of its population, but the vast resources of Xinjiang – iron, oil, grain, and hydroelectric power – were now to be exploited for the dynamic Chinese economy. China would not tolerate any threat to the security of Xinjiang by militant religious movements. The meeting ended with an agreement for the parties to cooperate and coordinate their activities in order to secure their borders with China. In June 2001 the "Shanghai Five" became six when Uzbekistan, which did not border on Xinjiang, joined the alliance. By then strategy had been expanded from containment into an agreement known as the Declaration of the Shanghai Cooperation Organization to "prevent, expose and halt terrorism, separatism and extremism."[35] "Extremism" was an ill-disguised code word used to define not only Islamists but also the "East Turkestan" separatists who were active in Xinjiang. The following year the signatories met in St. Petersburg to sign the Charter for the Shanghai Cooperation Organization. A proposal for a sweeping anti-terrorist agency was tabled, but the members opened an anti-terrorism center in Tashkent in which the Philippines, Indonesia, and Malaysia were invited to participate.[36]

Transcaucasia

When travel restrictions were eased throughout the Soviet empire during the years of perestroika in the late 1980s, Saudi charitable institutions supported the travel of hundreds of Wahhabi mullahs to proselytize in the Caspian and Caucasus. Their mission was given greater definition and guidance in 1992 when a "Memorandum of Advice" was signed by 107 leading Saudi religious figures that called for the strict enforcement of Islamic law, Shari'a, and the severing of all relations with non-Islamic states. The Saudi royal family reacted with anger to this peremptory attempt to export religious extremism and promptly dismissed from the Saudi Supreme Authority of Senior Scholars those members who refused to condemn the memorandum. It then began to suppress the more radical clerics, many of whom thought it wiser to seek refuge in Central Asia, the Caspian, and the Caucasus mountains, supported by Saudi-sponsored and Saudi-approved charities.

When Azerbaijan became independent in 1991, its Muslim community, two-thirds of whom were Azeri Shi'ites, was under the authority of the Spiritual Administration for Muslims of Transcaucasia with its headquarters in Baku. Led by Shaykh-ul-Islam Allahshukyur Pasha-Sade, it supervised both Shi'ite and Sunni mosques, and maintained a reputation for diplomacy and sensitivity. Freedom of worship was guaranteed by law, and there were no restrictions on the activities of religious charities, either indigenous or foreign. At the time there existed only a very small Islamist movement, the Azerbaijan Islam Party (AIP), which had been founded during the Soviet era, but its financial and religious ties with Iran were of greater concern to the authorities than its subversion of orthodox Shi'ites and Sunnis. It was this very religious freedom that attracted Wahhabi Islamists from the Gulf; they soon discovered, however, that they and their message were not welcome in a country where the Azeri, a Turkic people who had already fought off a decade of Iranian infiltration, did not now want the Wahhabis. In 1994, during the first Muslim campaign against Russian rule in Chechnya, *mujahideen* from Afghanistan began to arrive in Baku by bus from Turkey. Laws were enacted in 1996 and

1998 forbidding foreign citizens to engage in religious propaganda, and although a few Salafists in Baku had sought to create an Islamist political organization, Islamist activities in the "Stans" across the Caspian were more than sufficient to convince the government to terminate their activities in 1997.

At the turn of the twenty-first century the Azeri authorities expanded their investigations of Islamic charities to include Ikraa, then directed by Saleh Abdallah Kamel, President of the Dallah Al Baraka Group of Jidda. Kamel was thought to have been the moving spirit in the Al Riad Foundation, which funded mosques and *madrasa*s in Kazakhstan. In 1999 its affiliate in Azerbaijan, the Foundation for Chechnya, used the Dallah Al Barakah Group to fund Chechen gangs and separatists in Azerbaijan, including two centers that trained Salafist propagandists. The centers were staffed by Islamists from Saudi Arabia and members of the Yemen Islah movement headed by Shaykh Abdul Madjid al-Zindani, an associate of Osama bin Laden and Hasan al-Turabi. The government of Azerbaijan contained the growing Islamist presence by strengthening the indigenous Shi'ite charities, building mosques and *madrasa*s, and maintaining close surveillance on the international organizations. In Transcaucasia the laws governing charitable activities passed in 1994 and improved in 1997 were perhaps the most stringent in all the former Soviet republics. Thus, when NGOs did not follow the legal regulations, their offices were closed and their activities proscribed. The Chagyrush Society and the Kuwaiti Society for the Revival of Islamic Heritage were charged with "propagating religious fanaticism," and using mosques to attract young *mujahideen* to fight in Chechnya. They were told to leave.[37] Finally, after years of questionable activities the Al Haramain Foundation in Azerbaijan was also closed in 2000.

Republic of Georgia

Undoubtedly, the same Saudi and Gulf charitable organizations assisting the transit of Afghan-Arab *mujahideen* to Chechnya were also funding the passage of numerous *mujahideen* into the Republic of Georgia by 1999.[38] When Georgian authorities began investigating their activities, they discovered that Madli, an affiliate of BIF in Chicago registered in Georgia in 1999, was "conducting illegal activities in the Pankisi Gorge." Madli had received at least $850,000 in foreign funds to be used for humanitarian purposes, but many of the 4,000 impoverished local refugees were so frightened by these foreigners that they had little contact with any Islamic charity.

The Pankisi Gorge, an isolated valley surrounded by inaccessible mountains and located in the Republic of Georgia near the Dagestan–Georgia–Chechnya tri-point, had for years served as a base of operations for Chechen-Arabs "who trained new recruits for jihad in neighboring Chechnya." In addition, *mujahideen* were recruited from Lebanon's refugee camps by the Sunni-dominated and Al Qaeda-friendly Usbat Al Ansar (Partisans' League); it used the IIRO operation in the Pankisi Gorge to support jihadist activity in Chechnya.[39] Following 9/11 American-trained Georgian security forces captured fifteen Al Qaeda militants in the Pankisi Gorge, including Saif al-Islam al-Masri, a member of Al Qaeda's *shura*, and turned them over to American authorities.[40] In the elections of 2004 Mikheil Saakashvili replaced Eduard Shevardnadze as President of Georgia. He admitted that Chechen *mujahideen* had indeed been permitted to move freely across Georgia, but he "was determined to put a stop to it." Saakashvili argued that "Wahhabism represented a threat to Georgian secularism," and that some of the villages in the Pankisi Valley had already turned into "centers of Wahhabism where schools were propagating Wahhabism." He promised that foreign funding of "Pankisi-based fundamentalist groups" would be terminated. Georgia was committed to freedom of religion, but those who would propagate Wahhabism could expect no compromise and would be severely punished, for Wahhabism was an "unacceptable, hostile ideology."[41]

Chechnya

Situated in the mountainous southern border of Russia, Chechnya has during the past two hundred years had a history of resistance and tragedy in its relations with Russia. After a long and bloody campaign the armies of the Christian Tsar finally overcame the resistance of the Muslim Imam Shamil in 1859, and Chechnya was incorporated into the Imperial Russian Empire. Sixty years later at the end of the First World War and the upheavals of the Bolshevik Revolution the Chechens experienced a few brief years of independence before once again being overwhelmed, this time by the Red Army. Chechnya became the Chechen Autonomous Region in 1922, and in 1934 it was joined with the Ingush Autonomous Oblast to form the Chechen–Ingush Autonomous Soviet Socialist Republic. During the Second World War when the Chechens and Ingush were accused of collaborating with the Germans, over 425,000 Chechens were deported to Kazakhstan and hundreds of mosques, cemeteries, and Islamic libraries in Chechnya were destroyed. Thousands of the exiles died during transit and in Kazakhstan until they were allowed to return

in 1957 to the Soviet Socialist Republic of Chechnya during the regime
of Nikita Khrushchev.

During the dying days of the Soviet empire a National Congress of the
Chechen people gathered in November 1990 in Grozny, the capital, in
which large expatriate communities from Syria and Jordan participated.
When the Soviet Union collapsed in 1991, the Chechens were prepared
to hold elections in October in which a former general in the Soviet
Air Force, Dzhokar Dudayev, was elected President. In November the
independence of the Republic of Ichkeria or Chechnya was proclaimed,
and in the following year the Ingush minority in Chechnya was granted
its own territorial Republic of Ingushetia. Despite Chechen aspirations
Moscow refused to recognize the independence of either Chechnya or
Ingushetia as it had done for the Muslim republics of Central Asia.
The result was predictable. During the next three years armed groups
of Chechens increased their hold on Chechnya as Dudayev became ever
more defiant of orders from Moscow, where the leadership was divided
as to what to do. It was during these years that Islamic charities began to
support their fellow Muslims and those Afghan-Arabs who came to carry
on their *jihad* against Russia.

After President Mikhail Gorbachev's perestroika had relaxed state control of religion, travel in the Soviet Union and its republics was made easier
for Islamic clerics and Arab visitors, and by 1991 Saudi Arabia was using
its Islamic charities in Chechnya to finance "Wahhabites," a pejorative
term used in Russia to describe the various Islamist movements regardless of their origins. Many of the unemployed Afghan-Arab *mujahideen*,
who had congregated in eastern Afghanistan and Peshawar after the war,
appeared not only in the Sudan and the Balkans but also in Chechnya.
Neither they nor "Wahhabite" clerics, however, were welcome in Chechnya where the universality of Wahhabism antagonized those who had
absorbed local customs into Sufi Islam.

The contradictions between the tribes and regions, flatlands and
mountains of Chechnya, and between "Wahhabites" and the traditional
Muslim Chechens with their Chechnya Sufi brotherhoods became ever
more self-evident by 1992; Islamic clerics were now classified either as
"Traditionalists," who followed the older, more conservative and local
Sufi leadership, or as "Reformers," "Jama'at," or "Al Risala," a small
but militant group of Salafist revolutionaries. Under the influence of
the Uzbek scholar and Islamist Abdur Rahman, the Islamist movement
expanded even more rapidly with the arrival in Chechnya of Shaykh
Fathi (aka Abu Sayyaf), a Jordanian Islamist revolutionary. He urged his
Chechen followers to "take the best from Ikhwan, Salafi, and Tablighi."[42]
Religious tensions soon erupted into armed conflict. In December 1993

Dudayev attended the PAIC in Khartoum where Hasan al-Turabi, Ayman al-Zawahiri, and the Salafists represented the vanguard of the New Islamic Order. Returning to Chechnya, Dudayev infuriated Moscow by urging the Islamic world "to form an alliance against the West." Soon "no less than 75 representatives of the traditional Chechen clergy were killed" as the Salafist Islamists relentlessly drew the Chechens into their orbit, making them hostages to "those committed to destroy the Russian grip on the Caucasus."[43]

Determined that the growing separatist and Islamist movements in Chechnya had to be checked, Russian President Boris Yeltsin ordered 40,000 troops to remove Dudayev and smash the separatists and the Islamists as well. The campaign was poorly planned, and the early promises of a quick victory evaporated in the face of fierce Chechnyan resistance and heavy Russian losses. The capital, Grozny, was eventually captured after its destruction, at a cost of some 30,000–100,000 dead. Hundreds of Afghan-Arab *mujahideen*, now known as "Chechen-Arabs," responded to the *jihad* to fight the *Urus kufr* (Russian infidels). In 1994 an "exploratory group of first-generation Afghan-Arabs led by Amir (Commander) Khattab arrived in Chechnya to assist the outgunned Chechens." Osama bin Laden in the Sudan offered $1,500 to any *mujahideen* for the purchase of a kalashnikov and travel expenses to Chechnya. When the *jihad* in Bosnia had withered after the signing of the Dayton Peace Accords in November 1995, Al Qaeda sent men, arms, and money, and "some Chechens went to Afghanistan" for Al Qaeda military training.[44]

Although the International Islamic Brigade (IIB) of Commander Khattab was never very large, his influence became more pervasive when Shamil Basayev, the most prominent Chechen field commander, declared Khattab his "brother" and began to coordinate activities with IIB.[45] The presence of Chechen-Arabs assured the Chechen resistance access to the financial resources of wealthy Islamic charities. Khattab opened training-camps in southeastern Chechnya where Chechen and foreign *mujahideen* were given military training. He obtained funds through "official" charities such as the Al Haramain Foundation and from other Islamic charities specifically established to support the *jihad* in Chechnya. Quasi-charities such as the Al Kifah Refugee Center in Brooklyn and a new charity, BIF in Chicago, were eager to supply financial assistance. Its popular website indicated how and where one could donate *zakat* for Chechnya that BIF would then transfer in cash and purchase weapons for the Chechnya *mujahideen*.[46]

Amid the growing public outcry against the heavy losses sustained by the Russian army and the failure to defeat the separatist Chechen

rebels, Alexsandr Lebed, then chief of security for Boris Yeltsin, negotiated an agreement in 1996 for a ceasefire. Chechnya was granted substantial autonomy, but not independence. General Aslan Maskhadov,
chief of staff of the Chechnya military, who had swiftly forged a ragtag
army into an effective armed Chechen force, played a dominant role
in the peace negotiations. A pragmatist, he won the respect of both
the Russians and the Chechens, and in the elections of January 1997
defeated his rival, Shamil Basayev. Maskhadov sought to assuage his loss
by appointing him Acting Prime Minister. Nonetheless, the following
year Basayev defected and joined former field commanders who had
degenerated into warlords growing rich from organized crime and kidnapping foreign aid workers and Russian envoys. In religion Maskhadov
was a conservative who encouraged the revival of Chechen religious traditions. He failed, however, to evict or contain the Salafist Islamists.
When told to leave and take IIB to fight elsewhere, Khattab defied
Maskhadov by marrying a Muslim woman from neighboring Dagestan
and joined the anti-Maskhadov resistance. Later, with an $11-million
price on his head, Aslan Maskhadov was trapped and shot by the FSB
in a bunker in Tolstoy-Yurt twelve miles north of Grozny on 8 March
2005.[47]

In August 1999 units of IIB and Chechen Islamists invaded the Republic of Dagestan, which shares a 355-mile border with Chechnya. Overwhelmingly Sunni, during the Soviet era Dagestan had only had one dominant Muslim leader, but perestroika and its subsequent social dislocation
permitted numerous independent Muslim clerics to emerge and win local
followers. Prominent among them were two Sufi theologians with large
followings, Said Chirkeisk and Tadjurin Hasavyut, who advocated strict
interpretation of the Quran, and Maghomed Djeranskyi, who was more
violent than theological in his advocacy. Even more Islamist were the
Vakhabites, who first appeared in the North Caucasus in the 1980s but
only emerged as a serious force in the next decade. The raids were led by
Khattab's deputy, Abu Walid, who set up camps where the Vakhabites and
other Dagestani Islamists could acquire weapons and military training.
Their expectation was to unite the Islamist revolutionaries to fight for the
secession of Dagestan from the Russian Federation as an Islamist state.
The Russians carried out savage airstrikes, for they could not tolerate the
loss of their southern frontier. The Islamists retaliated with a series of
bombings that swept through Moscow with heavy loss of life. In October
1999 the Russians once again invaded Chechnya. Khattab and Abu Walid
became heroes on scores of Islamist internet websites, but tens of thousands of civilians and 10,000 Russian conscripts died. Another 400,000
Chechens fled to refugee camps in neighboring Ingushetia.

In Chechnya Aslan Maskhadov was caught in the schism between the indigenous Chechen religious leaders and the Salafi Islamists. "Powerless in the face of well financed Salafi radicals," he surrendered those regions where field commanders supported radical Salafists.[48] Consequently, in May 2000 President Vladimir Putin imposed direct Russian rule in Chechnya and appointed Akhmad Kadyrov, a separatist-turned-Muslim-cleric, head of the Chechen government. In retaliation for appointing a "puppet" the Chechens launched attacks against Russian targets – at Gudermes, the headquarters of the Russian administration in Chechnya, and in Moscow. During these chaotic years Moscow sought to influence Saudi activity in Chechnya by encouraging Saudi charities to cease funding Chechen *mujahideen*. Kadyrov was welcomed in Riyadh, where he "campaigned hard to have aid funds sent directly to his administration in Grozny." Assassinated in May 2004, his tenure was too short to redirect the use of charitable funds or maintain "Saudi pressure on Islamic charities."[49]

It was no longer any secret that Chechen rebels were receiving financial support through Islamic charities. In 1991 the Al Haramain Foundation opened a branch office, the Foundation for Chechnya, in Azerbaijan, after which funds were filtered through the Al Baraka Bank and the Al Baraka Investment and Development Company of Saudi Arabia to Chechen separatists, including Shamil Basayev. In Saudi Arabia the royal family sponsored a television program to collect funds for Chechnya, and the ruler of Kuwait, Shaykh Jaber al-Ahmed Al Sabah, sent $3 million in a charitable "first installment" to the Chechens. In Qatar the Committee for Charity and the Shaykh Eid-ben Mohammed al-Thani Foundation solicited funds in a program supported by Shaykh Yousuf al-Qaradawi, a notorious member of the Muslim Brotherhood then living in Qatar. Qaradawi issued a *fatwa* allowing *zakat* money to be used for "poor and needy" refugees in Chechnya. Saudi Arabia and the Gulf states were not the only donors. In the UK the Blessed Relief Foundation was busy transmitting funds to Chechnya through Azerbaijan.[50] BIF-US sent some $700,000 to Chechnya during 1999–2000. The Department of Justice would later describe BIF as "a multinational criminal enterprise that for at least a decade used charitable contributions of innocent Americans – Muslim, non-Muslim and corporations alike – to support al Qaeda, the Chechen mujahideen and armed violence in Bosnia."[51] In Russia *Izvestia* disclosed that BIF offices in Chechnya, Ingushetia, Dagestan, and Moscow had spent $1.3 million in 2000–2001 on "projects" in Chechnya and recruited "volunteers" to work in Chechnya. A BIF official, Saif al-Islam al-Masri, was a member of Al Qaeda's military committee and a veteran of its Somalia campaign. When Moscow finally blocked the

Foundation's assets in January 2002, it was "just a small fragment of BIF assistance to the Chechen separatists."[52]

Lost opportunity and investigations

In December 1996 a well-disguised visitor slipped across the Russian border between the Caspian Sea and the Caucasus Mountains. Ayman al-Zawahiri, the leader of EIJ, was in search of a safe haven. He was accompanied by Ahmed Salama Mabrouk, head of the EIJ cell in Azerbaijan, and Mahmud al-Hennawi, an Islamist who was familiar with the clandestine routes west of the Caspian and through the Caucasus. The crossing was perilous but necessary, for Zawahiri desperately needed a secure base. Zawahiri would later write that conditions in Chechnya "were excellent," for the ceasefire of August 1996 had ended two years of fighting and the Russian troops were withdrawing. Near Derbent in Dagestan he was arrested, however, and held for trial. For reasons that remain unclear the Russian intelligence agents never succeeded in penetrating Zawahiri's cover, and the Egyptian terrorist was released in May 1997, a year after the USA had declined to accept a Sudanese/Saudi offer to kidnap Osama bin Laden. Afghanistan and Bin Laden were now his only hope for safety and financial support. Once in Peshawar "Zawahiri became bin Laden's closest confidant and talent scout," and EIJ was soon absorbed by Al Qaeda.[53]

After the renewal of war in Chechnya the FSB uncovered an Islamist network operating in "49 regions of Russia and the Commonwealth of Independent States." All were receiving support from the Muslim Brotherhood to "incite separatist feelings," and the Moscow branch was "working under the auspices of the Kuwait Joint Relief Committee" to provide "ideological, military and financial support."[54] Another Kuwaiti charity, the Society for Social Reform (SSR), one of the most powerful charitable organizations in Kuwait and registered in Russia in 1998, was active in the recruitment and infiltration of the governments of the former Soviet Republics. The Kuwaiti embassy in Moscow, rather disingenuously, claimed that it had never heard of the Society, which certainly was very much alive and well both in Russia and the North Caucasus. In Dagestan, Russian agents investigating the Ikraa charity gathered information on "Wahhabi enclaves" in Dagestan and Chechnya. It monitored the Salvation International Islamic Organization, a satellite whose director in Moscow was an Egyptian, Servakh Abed Saad, with ties to the Saudi intelligence services. Ikraa was staffed with many former Afghan-Arab *mujahideen*, and its offices throughout Asia provided employment for jihadists from Algeria, Egypt, Jordan, Sudan, and Yemen. Despite its declared aim to meet the "social and economic needs of the people," Ikraa provided military training and sponsored radical clerics to preach the Islamist message in Chechnya, while Ikraa *mujahideen* "swelled the ranks" of Chechen jihadists.[55]

After 2000 Russia expelled hundreds of "Wahhabite" clerics "predominantly of Arab origin" from the North Caucasus. This was followed by a crackdown on the Salafists in the Volga region of Tatarstan where Islamists had sought to infiltrate the government-sponsored Central Spiritual Management of the Muslims of Russia and the Spiritual Management of the Muslims of Republics of North Caucasus. "In Moscow, Volgograd, Ulyanovsk, Astrakhan, even in Yakutsia," the Salafist Islamists could not have organized Quranic schools, built mosques staffed by friendly clerics, or founded Islamic cultural centers for the distribution of Wahhabi literature without receiving funds from the Gulf charities. Before fighting resumed in 1999 the Islamists circulated freely, but when the Chechen separatists began their terrorist attacks in Moscow, President Putin was determined "to protect the spiritual space of the country from the subversive influence of the geopolitical oppositors of Russia."[56]

After 9/11, between October 2002 and August 2004, Chechen separatists, now terrorists, had carried out ten attacks including a theater siege and nine suicide truck, train, and airplane bombings. However, when the attack on Middle School Number One in Beslan in North Ossitia on 3 September 2004 killed 330, mostly innocent children, Russia and the world were stunned at the enormity of the atrocity. President Putin declared: "This is a total, cruel and full-scale war that again and again is taking the lives of our fellow citizens." Russia was placed on a war footing, and he promised "entirely new approaches to the way the law-enforcement agencies work."[57] The planning of such a large-scale terrorist operation fit the pattern established by Shamil Basayev in past terrorist attacks, including one on a hospital in Budyennovski in 1995. Three weeks later, on 23 September, Russian Foreign Minister Sergei V. Lavrov announced the new Russian initiative to expand the UN list of terrorists by adding names to the counter-terrorism sanctions, declaring: "Those who slaughtered children in Beslan and hijacked the planes to attack the US are creatures of the same breed."[58]

There can be no doubt of the role that Islamic charities have played in supporting radical religious revolution in Chechnya and the destabilization of both its civil society and its traditional practices. Certainly, the Islamists were able to exploit a conflict that had already begun to systematically destroy Chechnya. Basayev's Salafist Islamist principles were foreign to the region and would have attracted only a small minority of indigenous radical Islamist revolutionaries were it not for ten years of the unenlightened Russian response to Chechen separatism. More positive actions were taken by the three dominant Muslim organizations in Russia, which joined together to combat Islamist extremism, while the Russian government enthusiastically supported an Islamic Center in Moscow where clerics could be trained rather than in Saudi Arabia, Turkey, or at Al Azhar in Egypt. These measures, however, were regarded with contempt by the Islamists as impotent gestures, and they have continued to destabilize the entire North Caucasus. "It is becoming clearer and clearer that the Chechyna conflict is no longer an isolated one, confined to the borders of Chechnya, and it could even be said that the conflict has already lost its original ethnic and geo-geographical localization. The conflict is metastasizing."[59]

8   From Afghanistan to Southeast Asia

> A revolutionary group like ours needs help from foreigners.
>
> an Abu Sayyaf commander, the Philippines, 1999

On a bright, sparkling January morning in 1995 the occupants of the Doña Josefa Apartments, a nondescript rooming-house in a Manila barrio, had reason to be worried. The acrid smoke escaping from an empty apartment was enough to raise the alarm, and firemen responded immediately, for fires in the barrio can spread like the wind. They extinguished the blaze and discovered its source. Antagonistic compounds had been inadvertently brought together and had precipitated a chemical reaction, bursting into flames. The firemen immediately realized that someone in the apartment was making bombs or was attempting to do so, and they called the police.

When the police searched the apartment, they discovered computer hard-drives and lists of telephone numbers that provided sobering information. The three Afghan-Arab occupants were the core of a team of five Al Qaeda members who had entered the Philippines from Singapore in 1994. Their clandestine activities involved the planning of a number of operations, including attempts to assassinate President Clinton during a visit to the Philippines in November 1994 and Pope John Paul II during his visit in January 1995. In addition, the three men were about to launch Operation Bojinka (Arabic slang for explosion), a plot to use suicide bombers to blow up two airliners as they approached Hong Kong. If that plan succeeded, and it was well under way, it would be followed by simultaneous hijacking of eleven US airliners, which would then be used as flying bombs to destroy the World Trade Center, the Pentagon, and other major buildings in the USA.

Operation Bojinka began to unravel after the Philippines police captured Abdul Hakim Murad, one of the three Al Qaeda agents, and the man who started the fire in the Doña Josefa Apartments. After hard questioning, Murad claimed he "served" Osama bin Laden, a mysterious Arab financier living in the Sudan who was generally unknown to the Philippine police. Murad and the captured hard-drives provided sufficient leads to enlarge the hunt for other Al Qaeda members operating in the Philippines. Of particularly interest was the team ringleader, Ramzi Yousef (aka Abdul Basit Karim), a member of the Al Qaeda inner circle. Yousef had founded the Bermuda Trading Company to import from Singapore the chemicals and supplies needed to make bombs, and he had trained members of the Abu Sayyaf (occasionally called Al Harakat al-Islamiyya), a Sunni jihadist movement active on the islands of Mindanao, Jolo, and Basilan.[1] Yousef had been seen in Mindanao in the first months of 1994, and presumably established an Al Qaeda cell. He was relentlessly tracked down to Pakistan, captured, and deported to the USA where he was tried in 1997 and sentenced to life in prison for his leading role in the truck bomb that exploded in the garage beneath the World Trade Center in New York in February 1993.

The third member of the team was Wali Khan Amin Shah. He was also involved in military training in Mindanao, the plot to assassinate Pope John Paul, the bombing of a Philippine Airlines flight in December 1994, the Operation Bojinka suicide mission, and a foiled plot to bomb foreign embassies. All three members of the Al Qaeda cell were under the control of Ramzi Yousef's uncle, an Afghan-Arab terrorist born in Kuwait, Khaled Shaykh Muhammad. Khaled was not only a key player in the various Al Qaeda plots in the Philippines but was also one of the principal participants in the World Trade Center bombing and later in the 9/11 terrorist attack. This very active Manila cell was financed by one "Amin," a Yemeni national, "rich businessman," and veteran of the Afghan war who used a money-changer in Dubai to transfer funds to the Philippine cell, the MWL, and IIRO.[2]

The discovery of the Al Qaeda cell and the information left behind when its members fled from their burning apartment also enabled the police to uncover, much to their surprise, the extent to which the radical Abu Sayyaf terrorist organization had become deeply entrenched throughout the Philippines. In 1994 when Abu Sayyaf had claimed responsibility for a bomb planted aboard a Philippine Airlines flight from Manila to Tokyo that had killed a passenger and injured six others, Philippine officials did not take its claim seriously, thinking Abu Sayyaf was just an indigenous band of criminals. This rather casual opinion dramatically changed when police, peeling the evidentiary onion, began to realize that Abu Sayyaf was an extensive sophisticated Islamist movement of which Al Qaeda was only a part, albeit the most dangerous one. In June 1994 the police launched Operation Blue Marlin designed to find jihadists and expose their revolutionary organizations, and in the years that followed Philippine police and army were able to piece together the cultural, religious, economic, and political organizations devoted to the creation of an Islamic state in the southern Philippines. It also opened a new vista on the old and the new revolutionaries. The old radicals were the Moro Islamic Liberation Front (MILF), originally known as the Moro National Liberation Front (MNLF), which in the early 1970s had started a rebellion in the southern Philippines. It had continued until 1983 before subsequent negotiations led to a series of peace agreements between the various separatist factions and the central government in Manila. The new Islamist revolutionaries had the same objective, an independent Islamist state in the southern Philippines, but its methods were very different, for Abu Sayyaf was quite prepared to use any means necessary, including methodical terrorism.

Moro Islamic Liberation Front

The *jihad* in the Philippines was as old as the conflict between Spaniards and Philippine Muslims that began when the Spanish Captain Miguel Lopez de Legazpi and his four galleons arrived at the island of Cebu in 1565. For the next four hundred years the Muslim Moro of the Sulu archipelago and southwestern Mindanao fought against non-Muslim foreign rulers, and no central government in Manila ever succeeded in imposing complete control over them. Stimulated by the rise of Islamic nationalism, this resistance erupted once more in the 1970s. Led by its founder, Nur Misuari, the Moro National Liberation Front (MNLF) struggled to establish an independent Islamic state comprising Mindanao, Palawan, Basilan, the Sulu archipelago, and the neighboring islands. With Libyan mediation Misuari signed the first peace agreement in Tripoli between his Muslim separatists and the Philippine government; this led to a split in MNLF when Shaykh Salamat Hashim and the traditional leaders refused to accept any compromise with the government in Manila. On 26 December 1977 Hashim announced in Jidda an "Instrument of Takeover" of the MNLF leadership; Misuari charged him with treason. Hashim took refuge in Cairo where he announced the "new MNLF," the Moro Islamic Liberation Front (MILF). Egypt rallied to Hashim; Qaddafi supported Misuari.[3]

Shaykh Salamat Hashim was born on 7 July 1942 in Pagalungan in the Maguindanao region of the Philippines. Inspired by his mother, he could read and had memorized much of the Quran at the age of six, graduated with honors from secondary school in 1958, and joined the Filipino pilgrims on the *hajj*. He remained in Mecca under the tutelage of Shaykh Ayman al-Zawahiri, often called Zawari by Filipino Muslims, while attending the *halaqat* (study group) at the Masjid al-Haram and was a student at the Madrasat al-Sulatiya al-Diniyah. The following year he was in Cairo, at that time the center of political activism in the Middle East, where he enrolled at Al Azhar University. He vigorously pursued his studies, graduating from Al Azhar College of Theology in 1967 with a bachelor's degree in *'aqida* and philosophy. As a postgraduate student he was awarded a master's degree in 1969 but abandoned his doctoral studies to return to the Philippines to organize the Moro revolutionary movement. During his student years in Cairo he had become deeply involved in student politics, which had exposed him to the various revolutionary trends that transformed him from Islamic scholar to Islamist revolutionary. As President of the Philippine Muslim Student Organization and Secretary-General of the larger Organization of Asian Students in Cairo, in the early 1960s he united a clandestine core of Filipino Muslim students to plan the Bangsamoro revolution. It was during these student years that Hashim was profoundly influenced in his Islamist thinking by Sayyid Abu al-'Ala al-Maududi and the writings of Sayyid Qutb, both of whom shaped his Islamist and radical political beliefs.[4]

Upon his return to the Philippines in 1970 Hashim became a founding member of MNLF and served as second-in-command to Nur Misuari during the talks in 1975–1976 with the Marcos government. He broke with Misuari in 1977. Thereafter, as *amir* of the Moro Mujahideen and Chairman of the Moro Islamic Liberation Front (MILF), his goal was the establishment of an independent Islamic state in the southern Philippines, the same as that of the more secular MNLF. Where MILF differed from MNLF was its determination that the new Islamic state would be based on Islamist principles in which its leaders would be Islamist clerics, like Salamat Hisham, who had committed themselves to the complete submission to the Will of Allah in strict conformity to the teachings of the Quran and the Sunna. Whereas MNLF had accepted the secular Philippine constitution and cooperated with the Philippine government, MILF refused to recognize that constitution and carried on its insurgency in what Hashim called "the longest and bloodiest struggle for freedom and self-determination in the entire history of mankind."[5]

The members of MILF of Maguindanaon and Iranun ethnicity were concentrated in the thirteen Muslim-dominated provinces, four cities, and Mindanao. Their leaders, whom Hashim had brought with him at the time of the split with MNLF, were conservative Muslim scholars from traditional and aristocratic families. As soon as he had returned in 1970 Hashim helped establish a string of Bangsamoro training-camps for the first fighting cadres, who would later become the military core of the MILF. Years later Shaykh Hashim openly admitted that Bin Laden sent financial support to MILF, and in return MILF provided a safe haven for Afghan-Arab veterans of the Afghan war. It also supplied a training site for members of the Algerian GIA. MILF was soon granted observer status in OIC, and that organization provided generous infusions of funds to build the necessary infrastructure for "regional self-reliance." For the first time *zakat* (*zakah* in Malay) was paid annually throughout the region, and non-Muslims in areas controlled by MILF were required to pay the *jizya*, the head tax required from the *kafirin*. These indigenous resources, in addition to those supplied by Al Qaeda and OIC, enabled MILF to launch a wave of terrorist attacks in the southern Philippines during the early 1990s. Thereafter, MILF and the central government would negotiate intermittent ceasefires, that were regularly broken after a few months. By the late 1990s MILF had claimed to have 120,000 *mujahideen* and another 300,000 militiamen. The government, however, estimated the strength of MILF at only 8,000 to 15,000 trained jihadists.

Fierce engagements were fought in the southern provinces in February and March 1998. Artillery duels and infantry battles were followed by yet another ceasefire that in turn collapsed in May 2000, precipitating a massive assault by the Philippine army during which MILF military headquarters, Camp Abubaker, was captured. MILF countered with a series of bombings in Manila coordinated with attempts to assassinate the Philippine ambassador to Indonesia.[6] After 9/11 MILF publicly condemned the attack and denied having any link with Al Qaeda despite the fact that hundreds of MILF members from Mindanao had trained in Al Qaeda camps in Afghanistan, and the leader and members of Jammah Islamiyya (JI), a militant Indonesian group, had received training in explosives at MILF camps. When, however, the USA began a joint operation with the Philippine army in its war against terror, MILF agreed to yet another ceasefire and a commitment to open peace talks. This change of direction was not solely motivated by the threat of active American intervention either in the field or at the peace table. Prior to the election of November 2001 in the Autonomous Region in Muslim Mindinao (ARMM) a pro-Manila faction in the old MNLF ousted Nur Misuari, preventing his reelection as Governor. Combatant supporters of Misuari attempted to disrupt the polls and assaulted military outposts throughout western Mindanao as part of the independence struggle, which was crushed by the army. Misuari was arrested and imprisoned. With Misuari behind bars MILF seized this window of opportunity to heal the old breach between the two movements in order to present a united front during peace negotiations with the government.[7]

Muhammad Jamal Khalifa

Two years after Shaykh Salamat Hashim had declared the "new MNLF" and then presided over the birth of the MILF in March 1984, Muhammad

Jamal Khalifa, a Saudi *mujahid* known in Peshawar as Abu Barra and brother-in-law of Osama bin Laden, paid a visit to Manila. A year later he returned at the request of Bin Laden to provide support for the newly formed Abu Sayyaf Group in the southern Philippines. In one important aspect Khalifa was much like Osama bin Laden. When Bin Laden operated from Peshawar "he received reports of how his money had been spent," and when Khalifa operated in Manila he pinched every penny. Unlike Bin Laden, however, whose "desire [was] merely to fund charitable and military operations," nothing more, Khalifa was an Al Qaeda foot-soldier ready to undertake any mission.[8] In Manila he did not attract the attention of the Philippine police, for he easily disguised his illicit activities in legal transactions that could not be traced in the open climate that characterized commercial life in Manila. In 1988 he recruited a Filipino, Abdurajak Abubakar Janjalani, to bring tough, disciplined leadership to the Abu Sayyaf.[9] By 1991 Khalifa was providing a safe haven for Afghan-Arab *mujahideen* and funding directly or indirectly three Philippine Muslim terrorist organizations: MILF, the Abu Sayyaf Group, and the Pentagon Group. The latter was little more than a gang of extortionists, "a creation of the MILF" used to extract funds for the organization.[10]

In its Islamist context the Philippine *jihad* can be dated from 1987 when Muhammad Khalifa decided to settle permanently in Manila. There he founded the Khalifah Trading Industries Ltd., an export–import front. He married two Filipino women and recruited jihadists while devoting his considerable energy to the creation of an Islamist infrastructure in Southeast Asia. In 1988 he launched IIRO's Southeast Asia operation and served as its Regional Director for Indonesia, Taiwan, Thailand, and the Philippines. Operating from Marawi City and sheltered by MWL, he opened bank accounts from Hong Kong to Thailand.[11] The adept Khalifa was soon administering a number of bogus Islamic charities, and at one time or another in his Philippine career he represented the legitimate MWL, the Dar ul-Hijra Foundation, and the Islamic Da'wa Council of the Philippines.

Khalifa personally established the Al Imam al-Shafi'i Center, where the most conservative of the four schools of Islamic jurisprudence, and the favorite Islamic school of law in Southeast Asia, was taught. He also supported the Islamic Students' Association, the Mercy International Relief Organization (MIRO), and he founded the Al Fatiha Foundation in 1992. In Mindanao he launched the Al Makdum University in Zamboanga and assisted Ikhwan charities in Mindanao. Importantly, he also founded BIC, a false-front export–import company that was restructured in 1992 as BIF, a charity whose real purpose was to attack US interests in the Philippines. Consequently, by the time the Bojinka terrorists were uncovered three years later a dozen interlocking charities underpinned the Islamist movement in the Philippines.

Khalifa's genius was organization. His enterprises involved interlocking directorates and were essentially transnational. He was extremely careful to see that his financial transactions could not be traced to the clandestine Al Qaeda cells in the Philippines. Logistical and financial assistance was provided by the International Islamic Alliance of Muslim Missionaries and the Al Islamiyya Revolutionary Tabiligh, many of whose administrators were from Egypt and Pakistan. Additional support came from the Federation of Muslim Student Leaders and the League of Pakistani Islamic Propagation, and if difficulties arose Khalifa could always depend on the powerful Saudi Arabian Department of External Affairs which represented the global IIRO. Perhaps the most important of his many Philippine charities, however, was the Islamic Research and Information Center (IRIC). It was established in 1993, with Khalifa as its very active CEO, and his Malaysian business partner, a Dr. Zubayr, as Chairman of the Board. IRIC was to be the clearing-house for the operations of his other charities, particularly the Philippine branch of IIRO. Little was known of Zubayr aside from the fact that he arrived in Manila in 1985 and may have been on a reconnaissance for Khalifa. The day-to-day management of IRIC and IIRO was the responsibility of Ahmad al-Hamwi (aka Abu Omar), a Syrian who had fled Turkey for the Philippines after he was suspected in a 1986 bombing. He also helped to establish BIC.

By 1993 Khalifa was seeking new worlds to conquer. He sold his Manila furniture business, and in the following year turned over the administration of IIRO to the learned Shaykh Hamoud al-Lahim, another member of the Al Qaeda network and the author of *The Principles of Islam*, published and distributed by IIRO. One of his highest priorities was the multi-million-dollar program for mosque construction in Christian-dominated Luzon. Funds were funneled to al-Lahim through the Dar ul-Hijra organization and the Islamic Studies for Call and Guidance (ISCAG), a charity of former Filipino workers overseas who had converted to Islam in Saudi Arabia, while the costs of mosque and *madrasa* construction were funded by the IDB of Saudi Arabia. In 1995 IRIC created the satellite Islamic Presentation Committee (IPC) to oversee Islamist "education" in regions under rebel control. IPC used a commercial office in Manila, but its headquarters were in Kuwait where its first Director-General, Salah al-Rashid, had a very close relationship with the Ikhwan movement in that country. The Saudi-sponsored Mercy International Relief Organization (MIRO) was yet another charity about whose activities in the Philippines little was known until the bombings in 1998 of the US embassies in Dar es Salaam and Nairobi revealed that it had smuggled weapons and delivered false passports for Al Qaeda. Finally, when Khalifa required legal advice and services, which was quite often, he could depend on the Islamic Wisdom Worldwide mission, funded by MWL and IIRO, to provide legal services and bail money. The Mission also published the *Wisdom Journal*, financed a popular radio program, and was a regular fundraiser for MILF.

The peripatetic Muhammad Jamal Khalifa was also closely connected with the Bangsamoro Youth League (BYL), an important conduit between activists in the field and IIRO. BYL programs included Islamic indoctrination, dissemination of political propaganda, *da'wa*, social work, and community development. It filled the vacuum created by the absence of social services in the southern Philippines.[12] Founded by the Bangsamoro Council (*majlis al-shura*) in 1993, its fifty-one members, many of whom had fought in Afghanistan, promoted unity among the thirteen tribes of the Bangsamoro. Its funds came largely from the annual collection of *zakah al-fitr* and *zakah al-anwal*, and from contacts it had made in Pakistan, Afghanistan, and Sudan, and with the Palestine HAMAS. BYL provided funds for *madrasa*s, built fortified Islamic communities, and helped support many of the 7,000 Bangsamoro *da'wa* missionaries. It recruited jihadists for both MILF and Abu Sayyaf and by 1998 had opened its own military academy.

In 1994 Muhammad Jamal Khalifa traveled to the USA with an associate, Mohammed Loay Bayazid, an Al Qaeda agent who had previously tried to purchase uranium. The true purpose of his visit remains unclear, but Bayazid, who had joined Osama bin Laden in the Sudan and then became President of BIF in 1992, was also a member of the Al Qaeda hierarchy. Two years before, in September 1992, Ramzi Yousef and Ahmad Ajaj had flown to the USA, where they were stopped at customs and a search of their luggage uncovered several manuals on how to make bombs. The literature was marked with the name of Abu Barra, Khalifa's Peshawar pseudonym. A year later one of his business cards was found among the belongings of the blind Shaykh Omar Abd al-Rahman, who helped execute the bombing of the World Trade Center. Then, in 1994, Ramzi Yousef and a team of terrorists moved to Manila with funds provided by Osama bin Laden and funneled through Khalifa and his IRIC. Thereafter, the terrorists were in frequent contact with Khalifa by cell-phones monitored by US authorities. Not surprisingly, he was arrested in December while waiting at the San Francisco airport for his return flight to Manila. The FBI found enough incriminating evidence – manuals for bomb-making and terrorist-training, and telephone numbers for Ramzi Yousef, members of his gang, and Osama bin Laden – in his belongings. In January 1995, when the smoke cleared from the apartment fire in Manila, the terrorists' hard-drives exposed additional and damaging evidence of Khalifa's ties to terrorism. It was not a crime in the USA simply to be in possession of bomb-making manuals. However, Khalifa had previously been tried in absentia and convicted of terrorism in Jordan. In 1989 he had opened the Al Imam al-Shafi'i Center at the urging of Abdailah Kamil Abdullah, a Jordanian jihadist, who was longing for a safe haven from which he could plan attacks on the Hashemite Kingdom. The USA acceded to the requests of the Jordanian government for his extradition. Tried once again in Amman, his first conviction was overturned when a previous key witness recanted, and Khalifa was found innocent and released.

Although Khalifa's troubles in California forced him to relinquish his position in the IIRO-Philippines office, he returned occasionally and was often seen elsewhere in Southeast Asia. In 1998 "under the umbrella organization of the Muslim World League," he founded and administered IIRO's Southeast Asia operations from Marawi City.[13] In addition he was the Regional Director for Indonesia, Taiwan, Thailand, and the Philippines until the organization decentralized and offices were opened elsewhere in Southeast Asia. By the time of his return to Southeast Asia the relationship between his Islamic charities and MILF and Abu Sayyaf revolutionary movements had become thoroughly intertwined. It was the persistent detective work of National Police officer Rodolfo Bauzon Mendoza, Jr. that eventually established the linkage between Muhammad Jamal Khalifa and the various terrorist organizations operating in the Philippines.[14] Consequently, when Shaykh al-Lahim began to have problems with the Philippine authorities, he moved most of the Philippine IIRO operations to Saudi Arabia where he could deal directly with donors, and when they began to question how their money was spent in the Philippines, al-Lahim accompanied them to the ISCAG office and "showed them around." Meanwhile, the Philippine police were convinced that ISCAG was an Islamist front, and although the work of its charities included the establishment of Islamic communities, *madrasas*, and Islamic centers, its funds were "channeled towards the propagation of Islamic terrorist activities."[15] As for Muhammad Jamal Khalifa, after 9/11 he was placed under house arrest in Saudi Arabia where, after an investigation of his affairs, he was allowed to go free after reportedly distancing himself from Osama bin Laden. He reappears from time to time to give interviews proclaiming his innocence before the media.

Abu Sayyaf Group

In 1986 the Philippines had only one significant insurrectionist movement, the separatist Moro Islamic Liberation Front (MILF). The Islamic community, which probably numbered some 5 million people, was generally passive and massively outnumbered by Christians in a nation of 60 million Filipinos. The creation of Abu Sayyaf (Ar. "Bearer of the Sword") in 1986 dramatically introduced a change in the rebel Islamic movement. Abu Sayyaf was predominantly a mixture of Philippine students educated in Egypt and *mujahideen*, who had either served under or were recruited by the Afghan warlord Abdul Rab Rasul Sayyaf (aka Abu Sayyaf, leader in Afghanistan of the Ittihad-i-Islami). After the end of the war in Afghanistan members of the group, some of whom had served in the International Islamic Brigade, the name first used in Afghanistan to describe what later came to be known as Al Qaeda, returned to the Philippines where more than a thousand Filipino jihadists would continue the struggle begun in Afghanistan. Among the first to arrive home was Abdurajak Abubakar Janjalani from Basilan Island, a Libyan-trained Islamic preacher recruited by Muhammad Jamal Khalifa. Janjalani had received his guerrilla training in Syria and Libya and was already a well-known Peshawar Afghan-Arab and a member of the Executive Council of the International Islamic Brigade. Osama bin Laden himself was believed to have visited the Abu Sayyaf base in the Philippines, and if he did not personally order Janjalani to join Khalifa, he must certainly have approved of it.

Janjalani quickly established a close association with MILF. He incorporated into Abu Sayyaf many Filipinos who had worked in Saudi Arabia and the Gulf, where they had converted to Islam before returning home. The pool was large, and by 1990 some 50,000 Filipinos had become Muslims of the Wahhabi faith. Most had participated in the Balik-Islam program, which derived its funds from local Saudi charities and *zakat* where they were active. Muslim employers often gave "zakat to employees who are converts," and numerous Filipino workers found that if they converted to Islam they need not return to the Philippines when their lucrative contracts expired.[16] Those Muslim converts who did return to the Philippines formed their own organization, the Fi Sabilillah, and received support from Muhammad Jamal Khalifa's Islamic charities – ISCAG, the Dar ul-Hijra, which operated under a variety of names, the Islamic Center, and Islamic Wisdom Worldwide. All were registered charities in the Philippines; all were used to funnel funds to MNLF, MILF, and Abu Sayyaf; all had the same aims: *da'wa* and *jihad*. Balik-Islam had its own military units, and its members were the directors of at least six radical organizations. Fi Sabilillah produced radio and television shows, and it publicly admitted that much of its funding came from overseas donations.

Under the leadership of Abdurajak Abubakar Janjalani Abu Sayyaf, often called Al Harakatal-Islamiyya, became operational sometime in

1989. Muhammad Jamal Khalifa served as "adviser to an eight-man core group" that composed its executive council, and the Philippine IIRO reportedly "shouldered the logistics needed" by Abu Sayyaf.[17] Abu Sayyaf and Janjalani established their headquarters in Zamboanga City on Mindanao. By December 1990 Janjalani was preaching, winning supporters in the Basilan, Sulu, and Tawi-Tawi islands, and recruiting young jihadists to join the Islamist revolt. In January 1991 Abu Sayyaf carried out its first operation. In response to Saddam Hussein's "call to all Muslims and Arabs around the world to launch a jihad against western and Israeli targets," two Iraqi operatives attacked the Thomas Jefferson Cultural Center in Makati City. By then Abu Sayyaf had ended its dependence on MILF, perhaps because it was not sufficiently ruthless and revolutionary and had failed to operate its own camps and establish "international linkages for training, finance, and other matters."[18] Another attack on a Philippine military post was soon followed by the arrival of a number of Afghan-Arabs, including Ramzi Yousef who was seen at the Al Madina Camp in 1992. His plan to attack Pope John Paul II "was conceptualized" during his second visit with Abu Sayyaf, in 1993.

During the early years of Abu Sayyaf, Muhammad Jamal Khalifa made certain that donations from sources in the Gulf were used to finance the group despite the fact that there was only one Islamic bank in the Philippines, and it was notoriously unreliable. The Philippine Amanah Bank, established in 1973 by presidential decree, was a feeble response to the growing Muslim unrest in the South. When Khalifa arrived in the Philippines, its headquarters in Zamboanga City had few important overseas contacts and only a small office in metropolitan Manila. It used both western and Islamic banking practices but devoted what resources it possessed to the development of Mindanao, Palawan, and islands in the Sulu chain. Like other Philippine banks its activity was scrutinized closely by the government, which held 60 percent of its shares, inhibiting any laundering of large sums of money. Thus, without the presence of a dependable international bank or widespread use of the *hawala* system, where transactions could be disguised or even hidden, Khalifa was forced to use Al Qaeda couriers who traveled regularly throughout Southeast Asia. In order to provide the necessary support for Abu Sayyaf to establish a base on Basilan Island or on Mindanao, Khalifa used IIRO to open the Zamboanga Islamic Institute of the Philippines, which then employed many Palestinians with Jordanian passports. Elsewhere on the island IIRO opened three branch offices, including an important one at Davao City, where several Jordanian, Pakistani, and Kuwaiti Islamists and bomb-making experts were employed. One of the Pakistani jihadists served as the titular head of all *madrasa*s in the Philippines.

In 1992 Abu Sayyaf attempted to destroy the MV *Doulous*, an international floating bookstore manned by Christian preachers. The explosion, which injured several people, was followed by a series of bombings at the Zamoanga airport and Roman Catholic churches. The following year they detonated a bomb in the cathedral in Davao City, killing seven worshipers. During that same year Abu Sayyaf, seeking ever more funds to expand its operations, began kidnapping people for ransom. A linguist for the Summer Institute of Linguistics in the USA, Charles Walton, was held for nearly a month until an undisclosed sum of money was paid. In 1994 three Spanish nuns and a Spanish priest were taken in separate incidents and ransomed. In April 1995, Abu Sayyaf achieved the notoriety that had previously eluded it by a particularly brutal attack on the predominantly Christian town of Ipil in Mindanao. The jihadists razed the town center to the ground, terrorized its residents, and killed fifty-three civilians and soldiers. That massacre prompted editor-in-chief Marites Daguilan Vitug of the Manila journal *Newsbreak* to launch a personal crusade against this Muslim Islamist terrorist organization.[19]

On 2 September 1996 the government and MNLF signed a peace agreement in Tripoli that led to the cessation of hostilities and the creation of the Autonomous Region in Muslim Mindanao (ARMM), comprising fourteen provinces and nine cities. MNLF renounced its struggle for an independent Moro state, and many MNLF armed units were integrated into the Armed Forces of the Philippines (AFP). Nur Misuari, the founder and Chairman of the original MNLF, was made Chairman of the Philippine Council for Peace and Development and then won the election for Governor of ARMM.[20] This agreement, granting home rule to the southern Philippines, was strongly opposed by Christian politicians from Mindanao and Abu Sayyaf who hoped to sabotage autonomy by continuing to fight the AFP for independence.[21] A definitive ceasefire agreement was signed in 1997, but negotiations over the details of the regional autonomy proceeded very slowly.

In 1998 Abu Sayyaf suffered two major setbacks – the loss of IIRO funding and the death of Abdurajak Abubakar Janjalani. In August 1998 Janjalani was killed in a firefight with police in the village of Lamitan on Basilan Island. The loss was far more than his organizational and military skills, for he had the charisma and rhetoric to define the Islamist religious and political goals, which were now lost in place of terrorist practices that soon degenerated into brutal banditry. Abu Sayyaf appeared a spent force until subsidies from abroad were resumed in 2000. Despite the dearth of funds, however, its offices in the Philippines had continued to provide safe houses for Islamist jihadists, specifically those entering the Philippines illegally from Malaysia.[22]

After a short internal struggle, Abu Sayyaf was reorganized by Janjalani's brother, Qaddafi Janjalani, also an Afghan-Arab. Its nucleus remained the Filipino Muslims who had fought or were trained in Afghanistan and which were now led by the ruthless Ghalib Andang (aka Commander Robot).[23] Robbery, piracy, and kidnapping for ransom now became its chief means to acquire cash for guns. In April 2000 Commander Robot struck as far afield as Malaysia, seizing 140 hostages at a Malaysian diving resort. To secure their release, the governments of Malaysia, Libya, Germany, and France paid Abu Sayyaf millions of dollars. On 30 December Abu Sayyaf terrorists exploded a bomb in the Manila metro. In 2001 they kidnapped three Americans and seventeen Filipinos in the Philippines, again from a resort where two of the American hostages and one Filipino died. The attacks confirmed the decision by the government not to include Abu Sayyaf in the negotiations concluded in Kuala Lumpur in August 2001 where President Gloria Arroyo signed yet another ceasefire with MILF. The two sides agreed to work jointly to "further Muslim autonomy in the southern islands," and Libya, Indonesia, and Malaysia were to act as monitors.[24] After 9/11 when Abu Sayyaf was placed on the US and UN terrorist lists, Manila made it very clear to MILF that it would honor the ceasefire with them, but it would not abandon its determination to destroy Abu Sayyaf. The USA offered, and the Philippines approved, the use of American military advisers to assist in eliminating Abu Sayyaf from their stronghold on Basilan Island, but no direct US military action in Southeast Asia as part of the war on terror was contemplated at that time.

In November 2001 the Philippine government intensified its investigation of its Islamists by launching Operation Green Veil against Abu Sayyaf. Once again Filipino security agents confirmed their belief that Al Qaeda was recruiting Muslim terrorists "through a network of [Islamic] charities." During the early months of 2002 some members of Fi Sabilillah who had become jihadists were arrested in Manila, including a terrorist who had planted a bomb on a ferry that killed more than a hundred people.[25] In January the Philippine police arrested Fathur Rohman al-Ghozi, an Indonesian terrorist who had masterminded a spate of bombings throughout metropolitan Manila. Al-Ghozi (aka Randy Ali) was not only a key member of the MILF Special Operations Group but a leader of Jammah Islamiyya (JI), the Muslim militant group linked to Al Qaeda that operated in Malaysia, Singapore, and Indonesia. In the Philippines al-Ghozi had been assisted by Hadji Onos (aka Muklis), a MILF member, and an Indonesian named Riduan Isamuddin (or Encep Nurjaman), better known as Hambali. Al-Ghozi's capture led to a major weapons cache and opened a trail to Hambali. Hambali, often called "the Osama

Bin Laden of Southeast Asia," was known to have used a Kuala Lumpur condominium belonging to a former Afghan-Arab to plan JI terrorist attacks.[26]

Meanwhile, the AFP offensive against Abu Sayyaf strongholds in the south was equally damaging to the Islamists, and in two years the Philippine army had reduced the number of terrorists from "a few thousand to fewer than 400."[27] On the defensive in Basilan Island, Abu Sayyaf retaliated with terrorist attacks in Manila, and it was joined by a little-known group, the Rajah Sulaiman Movement, planning terrorist attacks on the Christian-dominated island of Luzon in the north, presumably to divert attention from their defeats in the predominantly Muslim south.[28] The government had obtained substantial information from an Egyptian Al Qaeda member and "Muslim missionary," Hassan Mustafa Bakre, who had entered the Philippines from Malaysia in 1999. Captured in Maguindanao early in 2004 he admitted teaching bombing techniques to some 500 Islamist students at a MILF camp in Mindanao. He had numerous accomplices, including seven Indonesians and five Egyptians. In June 2004 the government gave MILF six months to get rid of JI terrorist entanglements and expel the thirty JI terrorists known to be using MILF bases in Mindanao. If MILF refused to comply, it could very well ignite the civil war that had been moribund for years, which would likely provoke the USA to add MILF to its list of designated foreign terrorist organizations. By then there were good reasons to end the conflict in the southern Philippines. A Multi-Donor Trust Fund created by the World Bank and sponsored by the United States Agency for International Development (AID), IDB, OPEC, and the governments of Bahrain, the UAE, Kuwait, Saudi Arabia, and Japan totaling $3.75 billion in grants would become available once a definitive peace accord had been signed by MILF and the Philippine government.

After 9/11 the Philippine authorities began a closer surveillance on some forty Islamic organizations that led to the capture in December 2003 of Commander Robot. His arrest and the death of his key officers in Abu Sayyaf gave Qaddafi Janjalani the opportunity to recover control of jihadists and restore Abu Sayyaf to its original political goal of an independent Islamist state, which had become subsumed by wanton banditry. Qaddafi and his core followers left the traditional Abu Sayyaf boondocks in the Sulu archipelago and on Basilan Island for the Mindanao mainland. This was still the home turf of MILF and its Chairman, al-Hajj Murad Ebrahim. He had succeeded Shaykh Salamat Hashim upon his death from cardiac arrest on 13 July 2003 in a Mindanao MILF military training camp. Ebrahim was determined to negotiate a peace with the government before the increasing numbers of unemployed and dissatisfied young Muslims succumbed to the greater radicalism of Abu Sayyaf. "Once they see some hope, then they will think twice before joining groups that advocate suicide bombing and so on. But when they believe there is no future, they will go to Abu Sayyaf." The leaders of Abu Sayyaf, of course, believed the opposite, that if peace was made with the government, they would inherit the young Muslim firebrands of the southern Philippines. "If this sell-out succeeds, more blood will flow because the young are more determined jihadists. We will soon find out there are more Osama bin Ladens in our midst."[29] Neither of these predictions has come to pass. Abu Sayyaf continued its terrorist attacks despite its shrinking numbers, and Qaddafi Janjalani was reportedly killed in an air raid on 19 November 2004 while meeting with members of JI at Datu Piang in southern Mindanao.

Malaysia

While Muhammad Jamal Khalifa was busy creating an Al Qaeda network in the Philippines, in Khartoum Osama bin Laden and Hasan al-Turabi were preparing to export Islamist ideology to Malaysia. Both men had close ties with the country. The Bin Laden Group of Saudi Arabia had substantial interests in Malaysia, investing in large aquaculture projects in Kedah, the home of Prime Minister Mahathir Mohammed. Al Qaeda operatives used Malaysia as a safe haven, and Osama bin Laden himself had visited it several times. He invested in a Malaysian bank, and "bought a few houses and apartments."[30] Hasan al-Turabi also had close ties to Mahathir and contacts with Darul Arqan, an incipient Islamist movement whose investment practices were similar to those of the Muslim Brotherhood in the Sudan. In 1994 an imperious Mahathir suddenly shut down the movement he could not control.

Muhammad Jamal Khalifa also had "legitimate business concerns" in Malaysia, including a bottled-water enterprise and an import–export company. He had a plethora of contacts among local business concerns, one of which, the Konsojaya Trading Company of Kuala Lumpur, provided yet another bogus import–export front. Konsojaya, founded in June 1994 by Riduan Isamuddin (aka Hambali), funneled funds to Muhammad Jamal Khalifa's IRIC office in the Philippines – funds that were then used to support Ramzi Yousef and Operation Bojinka.

After the death of Abdurajak Abubakar Janjalani in the Philippines, and under increasing pressure from AFP in Mindanao, Qaddafi Janjalani expanded Abu Sayyaf operations into neighboring Malaysia. He formed a close relationship with the Malaysian Moujahedeen Group (aka the Kumpulan Mujahideen Malaysia, KMM), and with the Laskar Jihad

(LJ) of Indonesia, founded in 1998. MILF had established strong ties with jihadists in Malaysia, but neither Abu Sayyaf nor MILF sought to launch terrorist attacks against the Mahathir government.[31] Malaysia was more important as a safe haven. Still, Malaysia had its own rapidly growing indigenous Salafist Islamist movement. The demands of the Pan-Malaysian Islamic Party (Parti Islam SeMalaysia) for an Islamic state could only lead to a split between the Islamist community and the large non-Muslim minority, which included substantial Chinese and Indian minorities, in the dominant United Malays National Organization.

The evolution of the Malaysian Islamist movement owed much to the Islamic school in Sungei Tiram that was the home of the Indonesian exile Abu Bakar Bashir (aka Abu Samad). Bashir was a militant Islamist teacher who had first achieved prominence as an instructor in the Al Mukmin Islamic boarding school located at Solo in Central Java, which had graduated many Islamist jihadists. Its most notorious graduates were the Indonesian cleric Riduan Isamuddin (Hambali) and Fathur Rohman al-Ghozi. Hambali, the son of a peasant farmer, was born on 4 April 1966 in Cianjur in the rice belt of Pamokolan. He was a serious student at his Islamic high school. In 1987 he traveled to Afghanistan to fight the Soviets, where he became close friends with Osama bin Laden. He joined Al Qaeda, and after the war he envisaged building an Islamist caliphate that would embrace all of Southeast Asia, and even northern Australia. Making his headquarters in Sungei Tiram in 1991 along with Abu Bakar Bashir and Abdullah Sungkar, he founded JI. He was a close friend of Muhammad Jamal Khalifa and used his money to establish an import–export shell company, Konsojaya, in Manila in 1994, in which Wali Khan Amin Shah, the financier of Operation Bojinka, was a member of the board of directors. As early as 1993 Hambali had become Al Qaeda's director for Southeast Asia. He established cells in Indonesia and Singapore as early as 1993 and later organized others in the Philippines and Malaysia. "Some funding was obtained locally but much came from Al Qaeda."[32]

In Malaysia Hambali supported terrorists and helped fund JI by collecting hundreds of thousands of dollars through the Pertubuhan al-Ehasan, a charitable institution he created in 1998. Police investigating the charity would later find that in one instance $210,000 "from unsuspecting Malaysians and others all over the world who thought the money was to help needy Muslims" was sent to support the activities of JI.[33] Other funds were obtained through charities to buy weapons, send recruits to Afghanistan and the southern Philippines for military training, and to support Muslim assaults on Christians in Ambon, Indonesia. Charitable funds were also used to finance a safe house for terrorists in Karachi, bomb a train station in Manila, and provide money and documents for Zacarias Moussaoui, a conspirator in the 9/11 attack.[34]

After 9/11, the Malaysian government began to investigate JI and its relationship to Al Qaeda. In January 2002 police arrested members of the KMM that had links to Zacarias Moussaoui and were in contact with him when he was in Malaysia during September–October 2000. KMM, founded in early 1999, included numerous Afghan-trained jihadists who had long-standing ties with Al Qaeda.[35] From a series of safe houses throughout Southeast Asia, particularly one in Auytthaya forty-five miles north of Bangkok, Hambali planned a terrorist attack on the Asia-Pacific Economic Cooperation (APEC) summit to be held in October 2003 when twenty-one heads of state, including President George W. Bush, would meet in Bangkok. On 11 August the Thai police and the CIA, after twenty months on his trail, tracked him to his apartment in Auytthaya, where he was seized along with explosives and firearms. At the age of thirty-seven he was imprisoned in a secret location in the USA.

During their investigations into JI and Hambali the FBI and Malaysian agents discovered that a former Malaysian minister had contributed $10 million to an Islamic organization in the USA. In February 2002 the Chairman of the Islamic Supreme Council of America, Shaykh Muhammad Hisham Kabbani, claimed that an Islamic institution operating in the USA had received such a sum from a Malaysian cabinet minister. Shaykh Kabbani, a Naqshabandi Sufi shaykh, added that the organization, which was not named, had been involved "in extremist movements in the US and abroad," and that the relationship had aroused American suspicions that a member of the Malaysian government was involved in terrorist activities.[36] The announcement created a firestorm of criticism in Malaysian political circles, and demands were made that Kabbani be "deported" to Malaysia to substantiate his allegations. The Shaykh was also challenged by other American Muslim institutions with which he had a running feud. While the storm raged American investigators dug deeper to discover wire transfers between Moussaoui and members of a Malaysian JI cell associated with Al Qaeda.[37] The Malaysian investigations of Islamic charities soon expanded to include the Wisdom Enrichment Foundation (WEFOUND), the Islamic University College of Malaysia, and the Regional Islamic Dawah Council of Southeast Asia and the Pacific (RISEAP), only to find that none appeared to have links with terrorist organizations. Founded in 1981 with headquarters in Kuala Lumpur, RISEAP had achieved renown by sponsoring conferences throughout the region. The Malaysian government had maintained a strong presence in the organization, and the Chief Minister of Sarawak, Malaysia, had served as its President. RISEAP received substantial support from the WEFOUND, yet another Saudi charity and a non-profit Islamic organization with a global Wahhabi mission. WEFOUND supported and organized international seminars, including the International Council for Islamic Information Dawah Workshops held in the Philippines for representatives from Singapore, Malaysia, Thailand, Korea, and Sri Lanka. From June 1999 WEFOUND operated its own global e-mail network, disseminating free articles and lessons on *da'wa*. It worked in conjunction with both WAMY and the International Council for Islamic Information (ICII) in Leicestershire in the UK.

Despite Prime Minister Mahathir's political struggles to retain the secular state, characterized by a thriving multi-ethnic business community, he was unable to contain the expanding influence of the Islamists. The Pan-Malaysian Islamic Party, Malaysia's largest opposition party, declared in 2003 its goal of creating an Islamic state, "with punishments such as stoning and amputation for criminals and a ban on non-Muslims becoming prime minister."[38] The party controlled the local government in Trengannu and Kelantan, two of Malaysia's thirteen states, but had little chance of controlling the national government despite its widespread influence among the Muslim Malay community. Nevertheless, after 9/11 many observers were convinced that Southeast Asia had "now become even more important to al Qaeda's money men . . . where money continues to flow to the terror group through hawala networks." Although ten Malaysian firms controlled by JI "donate 10% of their revenue into the Infaq Sabilallah – Jihad fund," the Malaysian government has been reluctant to "cooperate with the United States in tackling" these firms or other charities or other Al Qaeda fronts including the Om al Qura Foundation, a charity that "established money-laundering fronts in orphanages and nursery schools in Malaysia."[39]

Indonesia

When gathering intelligence on terrorists and their financial ties with Islamic charities in the 1990s, Philippine police discovered many ties between the Islamist jihadists in the southern Philippines and an emerging Salafist movement in Indonesia. That came as no surprise, for the best-selling author V. S. Naipaul had warned of this emerging phenomenon in *Among the Believers*, published in 1981.[40] At the time the police did not identify any specific operations involving Islamists from Indonesia and the Philippines, but the Indonesian origins of JI and its leaders, Hambali and Abu Bakar Bashir, were well known to the authorities. Dar ul-Islam, an early Indonesian Islamist movement, shifted its operations to Malaysia in 1993 and adopted JI. At the turn of the millennium JI had gained significant influence in more than 140 religious boarding schools. It assisted the Moro rebels in the southern Philippines, planned to bomb the American embassy in Singapore, and when that target was not considered sufficiently large, a US ship. Until 9/11, however, Indonesian and Malaysian authorities had categorized JI as a loosely structured clandestine gathering of like-minded Southeast Asian Islamists. They had not understood the depth of their fanaticism, although Bashir had frequently called the US "the number one enemy of Indonesia" and encouraged Muslims to carry out *jihad* "if they believe Christians are attacking Muslims."[41]

Less known was the Indonesian Laskar Jihad (Holy War Militia, LJ), with its headquarters at Degolan north of the resort town of Jogjakarta in Java. Its leader, Ustad (Professor) Ja'afar Umar Thalib, had left the Mawdudi Institute in Lahore, Pakistan, in 1988 to join the *mujahideen* fighting the Soviets in Afghanistan until their withdrawal in 1989. In 2000 this veteran of the Afghan war assumed the leadership of LJ, which served as the military wing of the Forum Komunikasi Ahlus Sunnah wal Jama'ah (Sunni Communication Forum, FKAWJ). The Forum, founded by Salafists in 1998 and dedicated to the promotion of "true Islamist values," had an estimated 10,000 jihadists in 2003. LJ was known to have links "with many terrorist outfits and Islamist fundamentalist organizations based in Saudi Arabia, Yemen, and Jordan," and its website demonstrated "striking similarities" to those produced by other Islamist organizations. JI was especially active in the Moluccas, in which Bin Laden had become interested, and may have been responsible for the significant number of Afghan-Arabs involved with LJ forces in their raids on Christian communities.

Critics have regularly condemned Saudi Arabia for the large infusion of Saudi riyals in support of Wahhabi projects in Southeast Asia that have only brought trouble to Indonesia. An especially contentious establishment has been the Educational Institution of Indonesia–Saudi Arabia in Jakarta. It provides a free five-year education to those who accept the strict Wahhabi regimen, and talented students are guaranteed free scholarships to continue their education in Saudi Arabia. The school is seen as the spearhead of Wahhabi influence in the world's most populous Muslim country, which until the 1990s was "famously relaxed" about the practice of Islam. Consequently, Saudi Arabia was perceived as playing a surreptitious role in Indonesian society under the guise of providing "above-board funds for religious and educational purposes" while it "quietly disbursed funds for militant Islamic groups." One critic bitterly complained that "Saudi money has had a profound effect on extremist groups, allowing some to keep going and inspiring others to start recruiting."[42] The Al Haramain Foundation provides an illustration of this overt/covert duality. It signed an agreement with the Indonesian Ministry of Religion in 2002 that allowed it to finance educational institutions, and when once approved used the Foundation to funnel funds to JI.

The extent of Salafist influence in Indonesia became increasingly clear in January 2002 when Philippine police arrested Fathur Rohman al-Ghozi, who was suspected of a rash of bombings in Indonesia. Although living in the Philippines since 1996, al-Ghozi not only worked with MILF but was a leader of JI militants in Indonesia, and "the main recruiter of Filipino members for Osama bin Laden's Al Qaeda network." He carried six passports, but was thought to be a Canadian citizen. On 18 July 2003 he escaped from the Camp Crane prison, only to be shot three months later at a police checkpoint in Cotabato City. In March 2001 the authorities at Manila's international airport intercepted Agus Dwikarna carrying a suitcase filled with C4 explosives; he was tried, convicted, and given ten years in prison. Dwikarna was an Al Qaeda operative and the representative of the Al Haramain Foundation in Makassar, Indonesia, were he had established a terrorist training camp and led the Laskar Jundullah, an Islamist jihadist movement on Sulawesi Island. In June 2000 he had been training members of Al Qaeda cells in Spain and was in frequent contact with Mohamed Atta, the suspected leader of the 9/11 hijackers. He and Omar al-Faruq had served as guides to Ayman al-Zawahiri during the Egyptian's stay in Indonesia in 2000 in what was subsequently regarded as "part of a wider strategy of shifting the base of Osama bin Laden's terrorist operation from the Subcontinent to South East Asia."[43]

The following month Omar al-Faruq was arrested in Indonesia. Called Al Qaeda's "point man in Southeast Asia," he confessed that a branch of the Al Haramain Foundation was responsible for funding Al Qaeda operations in the region and that "money was laundered through the foundation by donors from the Middle East."[44] Stung by the arrest of a string of Islamist radicals and buffeted by the rising Islamist tide that was particularly conspicuous in the Moluccas and Sulawesi, the Indonesian parliament rejected an attempt by Islamist politicians to impose Shari'a throughout Indonesia; this would have precipitated a sea-change in a nation of 220 million people, composed of 350 ethnic groups, who had mostly accommodated themselves to one another and to Islam. Although Indonesia was 87 percent Muslim there were still 25 million non-Muslims, and any Islamist imposition of Salafist doctrine would have disrupted its traditional ethnic and religious harmony.

After the arrest and interrogation in September 2002 in Singapore of twenty-one domestic terrorists, nineteen members of JI and two from

MILF, the Home Ministry reported that Hambali, the region's most dedicated terrorist, had organized a number of Islamist jihadist groups with roots in five Southeast Asian countries. Hambali had personally forged the Rabitatul Mujahideen coalition, "the objective [of which] was to unify the Islamic militant groups in the regions, with the ultimate goal of realizing an Islamic state comprising Malaysia, Indonesia, and Mindanao, following which Singapore and Brunei would eventually be absorbed."[45] The alliance, three years in the making, was led by Hambali and a council that included the leaders of MILF from the Philippines and the Pattani United Liberation Organization (PULO) from Narathiwat in southern Thailand. Meeting secretly three times between 1999 and 2000 they constructed a long list of possible targets in Singapore to destroy – four embassies, including that of the USA, water pipelines, the Changi airport, a radar station, and a large chemical complex on Jurong Island. They also sought to create chaos among the populace by using disinformation to set Chinese against Malay. MILF was an indispensable ally for Hambali. Since 1997 JI had paid generous "rent" for the use of its combat training base at Abu Bakr camp in Mindanao, and although most of the money came from Islamic charities, the Singapore members of JI "contributed five percent of their salaries to the organization," of which half was "to support JI operations in Malaysia and Indonesia."[46]

At 11:05 p.m. on 12 October 2002 an electrically triggered bomb exploded in Paddy's Bar in Bali, Indonesia. It was followed a few seconds later by a second, more powerful, car bomb of ammonium nitrate that was concealed in a white Mitsubishi van outside the Sari Club, a popular nightspot. Some 202 customers, including 88 Australian holiday-makers, most in their twenties and thirties, were killed and hundreds wounded in what has become known as "Australia's September 11." Suspicion of the "worst act of terror in Indonesian society" immediately focused on JI, but Abu Bakar Bashir denied any involvement. Although he was never charged over the Bali bombing, he was accused in 2003 of plotting to overthrow the government to establish an Islamic state and with "attempting to assassinate Indonesian President Megawati Sukarnoputri." He was sentenced to four years in prison.

Indonesian security forces eventually narrowed their search for the assassins to Solo, a small town in central Java that was home to Perjalanan Ali Gufron (aka Mukhlas), the field commander in the Bali bombing. Gufron had attended the Al Mukmin Islamic boarding school in Solo, the *madrasa* founded in the 1970s "to teach Wahhabi Islam." He had continued his education in Malaysia at Abu Bakar Bashir's Islamic school in Sungei Tiram and was known to be a close associate of Bashir, who had returned to Indonesia in 1999 and to the school at Al Mukmin.[47] He was sentenced to death. His accomplice, Amrozi bin Haji Nurhasyim, had purchased the explosives and the van and was also sentenced to death. Imam Samudra and Ali Imron expressed remorse for their part, which persuaded the judge to commute their sentences to life imprisonment.

In 2003, under pressure from the USA, the Saudi government ordered the Al Haramain Foundation to close all of its overseas offices, including the two-story Al Haramain headquarters in a suburb of Jakarta. Closed it was, but the charity quietly moved to a smaller house just down the street where it continued to supervise the "completion of the charity's expensive new religious boarding school on the outskirts of Jakarta." Saudi money continued to flow to Indonesia, and far from Jakarta funds were distributed by the Darul Istiqamah al-Haramain in Makassar, and from another office in a small town in central Java.[48] In February 1994 the US Treasury reported that the Al Haramain Indonesia office was "either continuing to operate or [had] other plans to avoid these measures." The UN also reported that the charity was still active and had just opened its Islamic school in Jakarta. Consequently, the Treasury froze the assets of six foreign branches of Al Haramain, including its office in Indonesia, and it urged Saudi Arabia to close the charity's main office in Saudi Arabia once and for all. "The branches of Al Haramain that we have singled out today not only assist in the pursuit of death and destruction; they deceive countless people around the world who believe that they have helped spread good will and good works."[49] Not surprisingly, the Saudis argued that if the USA and UN "thought al Haramain is doing something in Indonesia, then it is up to the government of Indonesia to take action, not Saudi Arabia." Cynics wondered if JI wanted to create a regional pan-Islamist state (Daulah Islamiyya Raya) by overthrowing Southeast Asian governments, which was none of Saudi Arabia's business either. Whether by ignorance or design Saudis were certainly using their "charitable" outreach to expand a Salafist jihadist influence throughout Southeast Asia.

Revolt in southern Thailand

The genesis of the Islamist movement in Thailand was the founding of the Pattani United Liberation Organization (PULO) in 1968. Its aim was stark and straightforward: to separate by force the four Malay Muslim provinces of southern Thailand. Throughout the next two decades there were a number of small bombings and acts of arson by PULO rebels. They attacked Buddhist temples, schools, government administrators, and other symbols of what they perceived as Thai political and cultural domination. By the early 1990s PULO seemed a spent force, but many of its Muslim youth had gone to the Middle East for their education where they, like so many other young men in the Islamic world, were deeply influenced by the war in Afghanistan. Thailand was known "to have played host to a plethora of outside religious groupings," including Hizbullah, and Islamists from both Bangladesh and India.[50] Nor had Thailand been ignored by Al Qaeda; Ramzi Yousef created a terrorist cell in Bangkok in 1994, where he plotted to blow up the Israeli embassy. Moreover, the government of Thailand was willing to spend money and military capital to pacify its southern provinces. Members of PULO were constantly under surveillance by the police, and their organization, which probably never attracted more than three thousand jihadists, was constantly harried by joint patrols of Thai and Malay border patrols.

Despite the best efforts of Thai security forces, however, militant separatism survived. About a thousand PULO hardcore remained in hiding, and the demand by the Pattani people for self-determination was popular in the towns and cities. Pockets of highly radicalized Muslims continued to exist, many of whom had been deeply influenced by Wahhabist teachings. In the 1990s PULO began to receive support from transnational Islamist terrorists, including JI, which used Bangkok and southern Thailand as safe havens, and the small but persistent KMM. Thailand was the site for the final meeting of the terrorists before the Bali bombings in 2002 and the refuge for Hambali prior to his capture in Thailand in August 2003 while traveling on a Spanish passport. Despite his arrest Thailand continued to serve as a base for JI plotting to bomb tourist sites and five western embassies. PULO raids continued in the four southern provinces, including one against a Thai army base that left four soldiers dead and more than four hundred weapons looted. That act precipitated major firefights between the Thai military and the rebels, causing hundreds of casualties.[51] The Thai government placed the blame on foreigners and "a flood of funds from Wahhabi fundamentalists in Saudi Arabia."[52] Funds were also traced to the Muslim Salvation Organization of Burma, which operated in Chaing Mai, Thailand, and collected funds for the 30,000–50,000 Burmese Muslims who had been settled in twenty-eight refugee camps in western Thailand.

Even the small Muslim Chan community in neighboring Cambodia was infiltrated by Islamists. The Om al-Qura Foundation had received "huge inflows of cash" to support JI and Hambali.[53] In May 2003 the Cambodian authorities closed a Saudi-financed *madrasa* fifteen miles north of Phnom Penh, arrested an Egyptian and two Thais who were linked to JI and the bombings on Bali, and deported twenty-eight teachers and dependents from Nigeria, Pakistan, Sudan, Thailand, Yemen, and Egypt. In Singapore its elder statesman, Lee Kuan Yew, warned that terrorists from Thailand to the Philippines and Indonesia were still a major threat, and in the months prior to the Bali bombings he was particularly concerned about Indonesia, where Islamist jihadists moved freely. Yew had reason to be troubled. When coalition forces searched the ruins of a bombed Kabul hotel that had housed Al Qaeda members, investigators found a twenty-minute surveillance videotape of Singapore that enabled them to unravel "an extraordinary series of plots by Jamaat Islamiya," including plans to bomb the "US military sites and businesses, diplomatic posts, and the city's subway and water supply."[54] Singapore arrested thirteen suspected terrorists, and then began a crackdown on Muslim institutions and practices, including wearing Islamic headscarves (*tudung*) by girls in schools, and warned parents to avoid those who traveled to Malaysia to raise funds for questionable causes.

Forgotten Bangladesh

In Southeast Asia the Philippines had become the strategic stepping stone in the Islamist infiltration of Malaysia, Indonesia, and Singapore, but in South Asia Bangladesh was not totally ignored by the Islamists who hoped to make it a stepping stone, albeit a lesser one, for the infiltration of Myanmar (Burma) and the half-dozen states of eastern India. After the "War of Liberation" from March to December 1971, Pakistani troops withdrew from Bangladesh, leaving its provisional government, the Mujibnagar government and its president in absentia, Shaykh Mujibur Rahman, to reconstruct a devastated country, with a million dead and 10 million refugees. Bangabandu Shaykh Mujibur Rahman (1920–1975) had long been the active architect and political leader for a separate Bengali state as a student activist in the 1940s. He had been Secretary of the East Pakistan Awami Muslim League and member of the East Bengal Legislative Assembly as well as the Pakistan Second Constituent Assembly in the 1950s. He also wrote his famous six-point program, "Our [Bengalis'] Charter of Survival," which served as the declaration of independence from West Pakistan. From 1958 to 1961 and 1966 to 1969 he had been in and out of prison, followed by his sweeping triumph in the general elections of December 1970 that confirmed his status as the spokesman for East Pakistan. Under Shaykh Mujibur Rahman the process of Islamization and anti-"Hinduism" had gradually evolved in the 1960s, when a program was undertaken to replace the Bengali script with Arabic.[55] The process proceeded gradually under Rahman. Despite being labeled a secularist and a traitor to Islam, the first President of Bangladesh revived the banned Islamic Academy in 1972 and joined OIC in 1974. Following

Rahman's assassination in 1975, the Islamic revival continued apace during the military regimes of General Ziaur Rahman, "Zia" (1975–1981), and, following his assassination in 1981, under General H. M. Ershad (1982–1990). Under Zia the constitution was amended, and the centerpiece of a secular society was replaced by the words "Absolute trust and faith in the Almighty Allah shall be the basis of all action." General Ershad continued the Islamization of the constitution, making Islam the state religion and requiring "Islamiyat" education from the first to the eighth year in the schools.[56]

In 1978 Professor Golam Azam returned to Bangladesh from exile in the UK, carrying a British passport. Like Mujibur Rahman he had been a student activist in the 1940s and Secretary-General of the Hall Union of the famous Fazlul Haque Muslim Hall at Dhaka University, and had played a leading role in the language movement demanding that Bangla, not Urdu, become the official language of East Pakistan. While a professor of political science in Rangpur Kermichle College, he discovered the political and cultural Islamist ideology of "Tamaddun Majlish" and in 1952 founded a branch in Rangpur. He did not support the "War of Liberation," wanting autonomy within a unified Pakistan, not independence. However, soon after the liberation, when the new government, determined to preserve the secular state, began its campaign to uproot Islam, deleting the words "Muslim" and "Islamic" from educational institutions, banning Islamic parties, and arresting prominent leaders and scholars, Professor Azam was deprived of his citizenship and fled into exile in the UK where he played a key role in the establishment of Jama'at-i-Islami in Britain. When Zia's government launched its Islamic program, Azam returned to Bangladesh, ostensibly to visit his sick mother, where he has lived protected by successive Islamic governments and his own "Islamic Guards," despite having no citizenship and being a well-known "collaborator." Here in 1991 Golam Azam was declared the *amir* (leader) of the Jama'at-i-Islami of Bangladesh.[57]

An attempt to establish a political party advocating an Islamic state had been made in the early 1930s by Maulana Sayyid Abu al-'Ala al-Maududi, but it was not until 25 August 1941 at a meeting in Lahore that Jama'at-i-Islami was founded, with Maududi as its *amir*. Under his leadership the party had only a modest influence until the outbreak of the "War of Liberation" in 1971 when large numbers of government officials began to collaborate with the Pakistanis and joined Jama'at-i-Islami to protect their jobs, for they expected the separatist Bengali insurgents would be easily crushed. The student wing of Jama'at-i-Islami was more ideologically motivated to establish active service units of the Al Badr to defend Pakistan and wipe out the Bengali intellectuals. These

razakars ("collaborators") were held responsible for perpetrating thousands of rapes and massacres in the name of Islam and for guiding the
Pakistani army to places of resistance. In order to coordinate this task
of seeking out miscreants and Indian agents, and to assist the armed
forces in destroying them, the Pakistani government formed the National
Peace Committee. Among its leading members was Golam Azam, who
repeatedly exhorted the *razakars* to rid the county of its anti-Pakistani
dissidents. During the early years of the secular independent Bangladesh
the Jama'at-i-Islami was banned. In 1979 it was allowed to remain in the
open, and when Golam Azam became *amir* in 1991 the movement had
won eighteen seats in the Jatiya Sangsad, the Bangladesh Parliament.[58]

Under Professor Azam Jama'at-i-Islami began to receive significant
financial support from Saudi Arabia for the party's youth organization
(Islami Chhatra Shibir, ICS). This enabled it to dominate Chittagong
University and most of the private *madrasa*s in Bangladesh. Funds also
arrived for its Islamic Students' Camp, an organization that teaches
students only Salafist Islamist ideology. The "Arab invasion" led one
Bangladesh nationalist to declare: "The religious mask of the Arab
invader remains intact, his sword has been replaced by his abundant cash.
Through his subsidies to our political parties and their leaders, the Arab
sheikh is trying his best to corrupt the top." He argued in a vein similar to that heard in the Philippines: "The millions of our compatriots
employed by the Saudis and their Gulf vassals are daily indoctrinated
with subtle messages of Arab cultural superiority. Some carry this virus
of indoctrination back home to their friends, family, and neighbors."[59]
When the Awami League, led by Shaykh Hasina Wajed, the daughter of
Shaykh Mujibar Rahman, achieved power in June 1996, the Salafists of
Bangladesh emerged under the aegis of Jama'at-i-Islami. Its rapid growth
had been abetted by financial support from a number of indigenous "pro-
Islamist relief organizations," such as the Association of Preaching Islam
and international organizations including SARCS, Al Haramain, and BIF
of the USA.

When Osama bin Laden issued his *fatwa* on 23 February 1998 calling
for assaults on all Americans everywhere, he announced the founding of
the International Islamic Front for Jihad against the Jews and Crusaders.
Its signatories included the usual cast of terrorist organizations: the EIJ,
the Pakistan Scholars/Ulema Society (Jama'at-ul-Ulema-e-Pakistan), and
the Partisans Movement in Kashmir (Harkat-ul-Mujahideen). Surprisingly a new name was added to the list, the Harakat-ul-Jihad-al-Islami
(Jihad Movement of Bangladesh, HUJI). HUJI was founded in 1992 by
Bangladeshis returning from Afghanistan, and, with the aid of Osama bin
Laden, it would become the most militant Islamist group in Bangladesh

and its "Bangladeshi Taliban," with some 15,000 members, perpetrated assaults on religious minorities, secular intellectuals, and journalists. Its principal recruiting grounds were the some 64,000 *madrasas* – whose students would one day serve as imams for the innumerable mosques in Bangladesh – in which they were susceptible to brainwashing and made "religious fanatics rather than modern Muslims."[60] Its General Secretary, Imtiaz Quddus, declared that HUJI would recruit 5,000 *mujahideen* from the *madrasas* and another 10,000 from the "Rohingyas," Muslim refugees in Myanmar (Burma). The latter were trained in guerrilla warfare in the Rohingya Hills of southeastern Bangladesh adjacent to Myanmar where HUJI had close ties with the Rohingya Solidarity Organization (RSO).[61] Not only did Osama bin Laden urge the *mujahideen* to infiltrate secular Bangladesh and assist HUJI, but he sent some 150 Al Qaeda *jihadi* to HUJI by ship from Pakistan to hasten the process along. In addition to funds from other "Islamic charity groups in Saudi Arabia and the Arab peninsula" for training *mujahideen* Bin Laden himself had personally sent $400,000 to assist some 421 *madrasas* controlled by HUJI.[62] By 1999 HUJI was involved in scores of bombings, and it was charged with two failed assassination attempts on Bangladesh Prime Minister Sheikh Hasina in July 2000. HUJI also had close ties with the Pakistani Harakat-ul-Jihad-al-Islami and Harakat-ul-Mujahideen, which were members of Bin Laden's International Islamic Front.

In the general election of 1 October 2001 two Islamic fundamentalist parties, the Jama'at-i-Islami and the Islami Oikya Jote (Islamic Unity Front), both with links to terrorist organizations, joined a four-party alliance led by Prime Minister Begum Khaleda Zia's minority Bangladesh Nationalist Party (BNP). The Islami Oikya Jote membership replicated that of HUJI and publicly declared its sympathy for Islamists, the Taliban, and Al Qaeda. It created dismay among the secularists because the coalition had become determinedly Wahhabi, having campaigned against theater, films, music, dancing, the consumption of alcohol, and "Hindu" artistic representation. Jihadist leaders "spoke of breathing the Islamic spirit of jihad" into the armed forces, and members carried posters of Bin Laden "with the HUJI slogan: Amra Sobai Hobo Taliban, Bangla Hobe Afghanistan ('We will all be Taliban and Bangladesh will be Afghanistan')."[63]

In July 2003 both the Canadian Security Intelligence Service (CSIS) and the US Department of State warned their citizens and officials posted in Bangladesh to be aware of their circumstance in an increasingly dangerous environment. Al Qaeda had a special relationship with indigenous Islamists, and the government, despite repeated reminders from the international community, had done little to confront the visible presence of

Al Qaeda *mujahideen* operating in and from Bangladesh. Reports of mysterious ships with weapons arriving in Chittagong with scores of bearded passengers elicited little interest, and even after the SS *Mekka*, a rusting tub, made repeated trips from Karachi to Chittagong in 2001, the government seemed to take no notice. The following year the CIA opened an "office" in Dhaka. When an Indonesian Islamist, Omar al-Faruq, provided specific information, Bangladeshi officials arrested four Yemenis, an Algerian, a Libyan, and a Sudanese who were involved in military training at a Dacca *madrasa* operated by the Al Haramain Foundation. After questioning "seven Al Haramain members," security officials searched the five-story Al Haramain office building in Dhaka and thirty-seven branches in Bangladesh. The charity "promptly ceased operations." Many Al Haramain employees who had entered Bangladesh in 1999 were known Al Qaeda members carrying false passports. Arrested and tried, they were mysteriously released and disappeared.[64] Under constant pressure from the US, Saudi Arabia finally closed the Al Haramain Foundation in June 2004, but the Foundation's office in Bangladesh continued its operations as usual, and its director remarked: "It is doing fine, no problem at all," its fourteen foreigner employees were still at work, and "the bank accounts of the charity and flow of funds are undisturbed."[65] Finally, in August the UN included three Bangladesh NGOs on its list of terrorist organizations having links with Al Qaeda: Al Haramain, BIF, and GRF.

By 2004 persistent raids on regional terrorist organizations, Al Qaeda, and other Afghan-trained *mujahideen* had eliminated many important leaders and scattered the Islamist, jihadist forces in East and Southeast Asia.[66] These victories in the war on terrorism resulted in large part from the information shared by the Asia-Pacific Economic Cooperation Counterterrorism Task Force, the Southeast Asia Regional Center for Counterterrorism, the Australian Security Intelligence Organization, and the South Pacific Chiefs of Police Organization of the Southeast Asian Nations Regional Forum.[67] With the support of the UN and the USA, the nations of Southeast Asia have combined to make money-laundering, illegal entry, and the illicit use of charities in support of terrorism much more difficult to sustain.

9   The Holy Land

It's a cheap shot to say our money goes to fund terrorists.
spokesman, Saudi Arabian embassy,
Washington DC, June 2003

On 29 November 1947 a resolution by the recently established UN General Assembly divided the then British Mandate of Palestine into Jewish and Arab states, thus opening another stage in the long and tortuous struggle by the Zionists, on the one hand, to establish a Jewish homeland in Palestine, and the Arab Palestinians, on the other, to preserve their land holdings of many centuries. The Palestinians rejected the partition primarily because the United Nations proposal allotted 55 percent of Palestine to the new Jewish state, when Jewish ownership of the land at the time did not exceed 7 percent. When the British Mandate in Palestine came to an end on 15 May 1948, war erupted, with the Palestinians and their Arab allies fighting against the Jews, who had the support of the international Jewish community and the sympathy of the West for a Jewish homeland in Palestine. Despite the intervention by Arab armies on behalf of the Palestinians, the superior leadership, organization, and military training of the Jewish immigrant population prevailed, so that by the time UN mediation arranged an armistice, the Zionists had seized 77 percent of Palestine, from which some 725,000 Arabs had fled. Thousands scattered throughout the world, but the vast majority of them soon congregated in refugee camps in Lebanon, Jordan, the West Bank, and Gaza, organized and supported by the UN. Meanwhile, the Palestinian Arab refugees were largely ignored by the impoverished Arab states, which had few resources to assist the poverty-stricken Palestinians in their refugee camps. Even the most fundamental type of charity, *zakat*, was infrequently committed to help the Palestinian refugees, for "the Quran is silent on the enforcement of the *zakat* obligation and the disbursement of *zakat* funds."[1] During the subsequent decades the Palestinians' hopes of regaining their lost lands, expropriated by the Israelis, or of establishing a new Palestinian state withered but never died. Despondency in defeat combined with poverty – material, cultural, spiritual – to move the spirit of charitable giving, so deeply embedded in Islamic society to serve the destitute, homeless, unemployed, the sick and infirm, toward a more political purpose in Palestine. During the next twenty years the Palestinian refugees became the wards of the UN Relief for Palestine Refugees program initiated in November 1948, and its successor, UN Relief and Works Agency for Palestine Refugees in the Near East (UNRWA), authorized by UN General Assembly Resolution 302(IV) of 8 December 1949. Other UN agencies, WHO and UNESCO, established sustaining programs, and both the Christian Red Cross and the Islamic Red Crescent Societies (International Commission for the Red Cross/Red Crescent, ICRC) then became involved and formed a peculiar relationship with the indigenous Palestine Red Crescent Society (PRCS). Since only independent states are recognized by ICRC, PRCS could not achieve full official status. Nonetheless, ICRC quietly provided support for PRCS training programs, radio transmissions, and the use of the Red Crescent logo.[2] Other large international charities and NGOs soon joined their efforts. CARE, a US charity established at the end of the Second World War, was active in Gaza as early as 1948. It was followed by a plethora of smaller charitable organizations, both Muslim and Christian, that collected funds throughout the Muslim world for Palestinian refugees, and even in the West.

During the 1950s and 1960s the charities had remained remarkably apolitical, concentrating on alleviating poverty and depression in the refugee camps. This changed dramatically after June 1967 and the end of the Six Day War. The secular Arab socialism of President Gamal Abdel Nasser was a spent force, and the indigenous Palestine Liberation Organization (PLO) began to splinter into factions whose rivalries would last for decades. Some received support from Syria, others from Iraq, but Al Fatah (Palestinian National Liberation Movement; Harakat al-Tahrir al-Watani al-Filastini) led by Yasir Arafat managed to stay independent. Eventually the dynamic Arafat became Chairman of the Executive Committee of PLO in 1969 and its Commander-in-Chief the next year. After he had gained control of Al Fatah Saudi Arabia began to provide generous funding, not only to symbolize its concern for the 200,000 Palestinian refugees in Saudi Arabia, but because Crown Prince Fahd considered Arafat, a former Muslim Brother, much more acceptable than the other secular revolutionaries, whom he deeply distrusted.[3]

Palestine Red Crescent Society

As Arafat consolidated his authority PRCS became the most visible charity in the West Bank and Gaza. Several autonomous Red Crescent

Societies had been established in the Holy Land after 1948, including offices in Nablus (1950) and Jerusalem (1951), and in the West Bank several branches served as satellites of the Jordan Red Crescent Society. Generally, they acted independently of one another, but each individual society still had the mandate to provide emergency medical services and other assistance to its Muslim population. In December 1968, thanks to pleas from Arafat and the intervention of Saudi Arabia, PRCS was granted full membership in the Red Crescent Society, but not the recognition of the International Federation in Geneva. The Palestine National Council then invested it with overall responsibility for medical and social welfare services in the West Bank and Gaza; it was also to work with the Red Crescent Societies of Lebanon and Syria and assist in providing humanitarian health and social services to the Palestinian population in the Diaspora.

In 1993 the role of PRCS was dramatically changed after the signing of the Oslo Accords. At Oslo, Israel and the PLO agreed to the Declaration of Principles that led to the establishment of the Palestinian Authority (PA); during the negotiations Yasir Arafat had refused to sign any agreement unless his PLO was recognized as the sole representative of the Palestinian people. The West agreed; the Israelis did not. Israel refused to recognize Arafat as President of the state of Palestine, accepting him only as the head of the Executive Committee of PLO. The Palestinian Authority without Arafat was the result. The PA was to control all aspects of charitable giving, and PRCS was now called upon to play a leading role in the creation of a new Palestine Ministry of Health and to lay the foundation for the "National Health Plan for the State of Palestine." In 1996 PRCS for the first time met in general assembly to unite all their uncoordinated activities in the Palestinian Territories and the autonomous areas, and although still not officially recognized by the International Federation of the Red Cross and Crescent Societies, it was granted observer status, and the Federation substantially increased its assistance to Palestine. In 1996 PRCS headquarters was moved from Jericho to Al Bireh, ten miles north of Jerusalem, from where it supervised the activities of more than twenty branches and thirty primary health-care centers in the West Bank, East Jerusalem, and Gaza. It also continued to maintain three branches in the Diaspora in Lebanon, Syria, and Egypt.

By 1999 PRCS counted 15,000 volunteers, 3,500 staff, and a vast network of more than 70 hospitals and 300 clinics. Active in the fields of health care, blood banks, social welfare, and disaster preparedness, its presence was most visible through its fleet of ambulances that served the West Bank and Gaza. PRCS has also benefited from an alliance with the Norwegian Red Cross for institutional/capacity development, the

German Red Cross/European Union for community health development, the Australian Red Cross for women's and children's health, and the British Red Cross for special education.

Charities in Palestine

In addition to its support for PRCS the PLO also made certain it controlled the umbrella Palestine Welfare Association (PWA). Established in 1982 shortly after Arafat and the PLO leadership had been driven from Beirut by the Israel Defense Force (IDF), its founders were three wealthy Arabs; two lived in Europe, the third was chairman of the Arab Bank Ltd., often called the "PLO Bank." In addition, PWA received the support of Hasib Sabbagh, considered the "Richest Palestinian on Earth." Registered in Geneva in October 1983 with $30 million, the charity has never sought to disguise its close ties to PLO. Its primary task was to collect funds from wealthy clients and use them to provide humanitarian and health-care assistance. Critics of PWA have often asserted that the funds it spent for humanitarian assistance actually "free up PLO funds for the support of covert and military operations against Israel and the West." To be sure, many wealthy Palestinians annually sent their *zakat* to PWA, which spent it as quickly as possible, but the claim that it supported the covert activities of PLO has never been proven.

Perhaps the most ubiquitous indigenous charity in Palestine was the charitable network created by the Muslim Brotherhood that first appeared in Gaza in 1946. The Ikhwan created a "network of social, charitable and educational institutions linked to the local mosques, which came to be known as *Al Mujamma' al-Islami*, or the Islamic Congress."[4] It built free clinics, centers for the propagation of its doctrines, mosques, and Quranic schools. Since 1967, however, one finds few similarities in Palestine to the activities of public and private charitable institutions found elsewhere in the Islamic world. With Israel in control of the former Arab Palestine, the funds collected worldwide through *zakat*, *saqada*, or from *waqf* foundations have been used first for political purposes and only second to provide direct assistance to the Palestinians. Over time Israel prohibited the activities of thirty Islamic charities on the grounds that they supported terrorist organizations. They included, inter alia, the Zakat Committees of Zenin, Tulkarm, Ramallah and Khan Younis, the Islamic Charity Societies of Nablus, Hebron, and the Gaza Strip, IIRO, and local chapters of the Holy Land Fund for Relief and Development (Holy Land Foundation, HLF).

Although the Saudi royal family had extended its moral approval, it had at first given grudging financial support for the Palestinians until

1970 when the kingdom opened its purse-strings. During the next three decades billions of Saudi riyals were funneled into Palestine, where the notable Shaykh Ahmed Isma'il Yasin benefited the most from Saudi generosity. Nearly blind and a quadriplegic confined to a wheelchair from a sports accident in his youth, he and his family had moved to Gaza after their village had been destroyed in the first Arab–Israeli war of 1948. Despite his paralysis, he studied at Al Azhar where he joined the Muslim Brotherhood. Returning to Gaza, he became a powerful Islamist and successful fundraiser, establishing in 1973 the Mujamma', a welfare charity specifically to collect *zakat*. Although he never attended a *madrasa*, which would have given him the authentic title of "shaykh," his proselytizing skills and determination to halt the spread of western influence in Palestine convinced his followers to confer upon him that honorary title. He preached Islamist values and worked quietly in Gaza mosques, the Islamic University of Gaza, and eventually, with financial assistance from the Muslim Brothers in Saudi Arabia and the Gulf, he built his own mosque in Gaza. Here, he along with Muhammad Taha founded HAMAS in 1987, originally calling it the Palestinian Wing of the Muslim Brotherhood. His chief rival, Yasir Arafat, argued speciously that Yasin was collaborating with the enemy after the Mujamma' received support from the Israeli government and was seen to be in competition with the PLO-dominated PRCS. The Salafist shaykh shrugged off the accusations and continued to provide humanitarian aid while building what would eventually become a dangerous infrastructure designed for terrorism.

Shaykh Yasin was not the only one to benefit from Saudi largesse. After the 1967 Arab–Israeli war a Popular Committee for Assisting the Palestinian Mujahideen (PCAPM) was established in Saudi Arabia; in turn, it created in 1975 the Al Quds (Jerusalem) Committee (aka the Committee for the Support of the Al Quds Intifada), and the following year established the Al Quds Fund. The Al Quds Fund provided hundreds of millions of Saudi riyals for the Palestinians, and untold millions were devoted to maintaining the Fund's *waqf* to support "the struggle and Jihad of the Palestinian people and consolidating their heroic Intifada within their occupied homeland Palestine, and particularly the city of Al-Quds Al-Sharif." At the Ninth Meeting of the Board of Directors of the Al Quds Fund, held in Rabat on 15 October 1990, and at the Tenth Meeting, convened in Jidda on 14 May 1991, member states were called upon "to cover the approved budgets for the Al-Quds Fund and its waqf amounting to a hundred million US Dollars each." A government mass media campaign was launched to encourage the "organization of festivals, exhibitions and charity bazaars at local and Islamic levels."[5]

In addition, Saudi money was used to support the charities of PLO. In the late 1970s PLO expansion had resulted in the exponential growth of the pro-Palestinian movement in the Arab world. Under the PLO banner regional, town, and village charitable organizations flourished. Hundreds of mosques were built, and for the first time direct Saudi funding was substantial. It was a subtle penetration and "by the time the [Israeli] security establishment began to understand what was happening it was too late to halt the process."[6]

The next major move in support of the Palestinians was undertaken by King Fahd bin Abd al-Aziz in 1992 when he issued orders to repair all mosques in Jerusalem at the kingdom's expense. Then, at the Twenty-First Conference of the OIC Foreign Ministers held in Karachi in April 1993, he announced a donation of $10 million to the Al Quds Fund, and Crown Prince Abdullah proposed the creation of yet another charitable mechanism, the Al Aqsa Fund. The latter became the Al Aqsa Foundation, with a capitalization of $800 million, and financed projects to preserve the Arab and Islamic characteristics of Jerusalem. It would also assist Palestinians "to free themselves from dependence on the Israeli economy." And following the international recognition of the Palestinian Authority in February 1994, Prince Salman initiated a nation-wide campaign to enhance support for the Palestinian cause.[7]

HAMAS

In the early 1990s Shaykh Ahmed Yasin used his mosque to preach ever more violent sermons, which precipitated his arrest by Israeli police in 1983 and subsequent imprisonment. Freed in a prisoner exchange in 1985 Yasin was the first to conceive of Palestine as a battlefield in which Israel would be destroyed, to be followed by the founding of an a Islamist state in Palestine by *jihad*. This holy struggle was dedicated to the destruction not only of Israel but of any political movement that might recognize Israel's "right to exist." True to his Salafist Islamist core he "spoke of an Islamic Palestinian state as a stage" in the development of a greater Islamic nation. Yasin proved to be an accomplished fundraiser, but that did not satisfy many of his followers. They declared: "A non-violent charity organization is good for the Arabs, but we have to deal with the Jewish ruler and for that purpose we need to establish a military arm in the organization."[8] When Yasin appeared reluctant to embrace more violent means, the dissidents broke with their mentor and joined the Islamic Jihad Movement in Palestine (Harakat al-Jihad al-Islami fi Filistin, IJMP). IJMP was founded in Gaza in 1980 by Dr. Ahmad Fathi al-Shiqaqi and Shaykh Abd al-Aziz al-Awda, both of whom had been active in the

Muslim Brotherhood at Zaqaziq University in Egypt in the 1970s. Inspired by the Islamist revolution in Iran in 1979, IJMP conceived of revolutionary rather than evolutionary means to their end. It appeared more dynamic, more youthful, and less parochial in its approach to confronting Israel than Shaykh Yasin and his circle. Of all the Islamist movements it was the only one that sought to bridge the chasm between radical Sunnis and Shi'ites in the Muslim world. The Shi'i radical ideology of the Ayatollah Khomeini, not that of the Muslim Brotherhood, became the driving force of their movement.[9]

At its birth, the members of IJMP probably did not number more than 300, with perhaps another 3,000 active supporters, "the believers," whose duty was to purify the Islamic world, but particularly Palestine, of western influence. Since Israel was considered the leading agent of the West, particularly the USA, it would be destroyed by its military wing, the Al Quds Brigades, which were responsible for carrying out *jihad*. IJMP argued that deeds were more important than indoctrination, and by raising the banner of *jihad* by acts of violence, they would inspire others in Palestinian society to create a mass movement that would overwhelm Israel. During the 1980s IJMP carried out a series of spectacular attacks against Israeli soldiers in Gaza that were widely popular among Palestinians who, in December 1987, erupted into a general uprising, or Intifada.[10] It began to solicit funds from American Muslims through the Islamic Committee for Palestine (ICP), a US charity affiliated with the University of South Florida (USF) which was used as a front "for security reasons." In response to IJMP taking the lead in the struggle against Israel and the West, Shaykh Yasin and the Muslim Brotherhood faced a popular challenge to their policy of indoctrination before declaring the holy war, and the shaykh acted decisively. He quickly formed his own militant organization in 1988, the Islamic Resistance Movement in Palestine (Harakat al-Muqawama al-Islamiyya fi Filistin) whose acronym, HAMAS, was soon known throughout the Muslim world.

When Jordan disengaged from the West Bank in November 1988, PLO sought to fill the vacuum caused by King Hussein's withdrawal by issuing a declaration of independence "to ensure that the land [the West Bank] would retain its Palestinian identity." The secular PLO consolidated its position in the West Bank, but Shaykh Yasin would never cease his challenge to PLO for primacy in Palestine. HAMAS survived, gathering strength from its three pillars: Sunni Islam, Islamic charity, and the destruction of Israel. The popularity of HAMAS owed much to the vacuum produced by the exile of PLO leaders to Tunisia during the Israeli occupation of Lebanon in 1982. By 1990 its charities incorporated an extensive network involving education, distribution of food, youth camps, sports activities, elderly care, and scholarships. HAMAS mosques were used to disseminate propaganda, as recruiting centers for jihadists, and as armories to stockpile weapons. Operating from Jerusalem, Judea, Samaria, and the Gaza Strip, it was given political cover by its own Islamic National Salvation Party of which PA disapproved but which it could not fail to recognize. No one knew better than Yasir Arafat that the stronger HAMAS became, the weaker PA, and thus secular authority in the West Bank and Gaza, would become. Ironically, Arafat's conundrum did not seem to bother Saudi benefactors who continued to fund both Arafat and Yasin indiscriminately.

In competition with PLO, Shaykh Yasin sought to frustrate his rival by dividing HAMAS into a political section, with an appearance of rectitude, and a military wing that survived as an underground terrorist organization. HAMAS political representatives inaugurated diplomatic relations with the revolutionary government in the Sudan and then in 1992 opened an embassy in Tehran. The political leaders of HAMAS began to appear at international forums, engage in dialogue with fellow Islamists, and collect funds for its mosques. It operated its own charitable organizations and schools, and maintained an internal intelligence apparatus, Al Majd (Glory). Meanwhile, the Izz al-Din al-Qassam Brigades were its secretive military wing, set up to attack Israeli military forces, Israeli settlements, and arrange for large-scale suicide bombings of Israeli civilians. Together the two halves of a single whole would oppose any peace with Israel, and they cooperated with the Unified National Leadership of the Uprising (UNLU), consisting of the smaller revolutionary factions actively involved in the Intifada.[11]

The Israelis struck back against the Intifada. They arrested, tried, and sentenced Shaykh Yasin in 1988 to life imprisonment, followed in 1990 by the arrest of selected members of the HAMAS hierarchy. The Israelis security forces then confiscated the documents of the Shari'a Court in Palestine, an act that was strongly condemned throughout the Muslim world and considered a violation of international law. The seizure of these records was thought to enable the Israelis to confiscate Islamic *waqf* properties in Jerusalem.[12] The HAMAS command structure was purposely scattered throughout the Middle East. In Amman Mohammad Nazzal, a computer expert and former Afghan-Arab, directed HAMAS operations and maintained contacts with both the Palestine Islamic Jihad and Al Qaeda. In 1991 he helped form the Jaish-e-Muhammad (Muhammad's Army) in Jordan, a terrorist group whose failed attempt to overthrow the Hashemite throne forced it to relocate to Iraq. Other HAMAS leaders were active in Damascus.

HAMAS abroad

Shortly after it was founded, HAMAS emerged in the USA, where it invested some $25 million in housing projects. The funds were said "to have stemmed from Saudi and other Gulf Arab sources as part of an effort to finance HAMAS insurgency operations in the West Bank and Gaza Strip." Soliman Biheiri, an Egyptian national, was the administrator for BMI, the bank that acted as the conduit for Saudi and Gulf funding to Al Qaeda and HAMAS. BMI was a New Jersey Islamic investment bank founded by Biheiri in which Yassin al-Qadi and Musa Abu Marzouk, a HAMAS leader who resided in America until deported in 1997, had considerable interests. Both Qadi and Marzouk were listed as designated terrorists after 9/11.[13] They obtained funds through the Palestinian Occupied Land Fund, established in Los Angeles with a false address and no known headquarters. In 1992, the fund changed its name to the Holy Land Foundation (HLF) and moved to Richardson, Texas, and greater visibility with Shukri Abu Bakar as president. HLF financially assisted a number of Palestinian organizations in the West Bank and Gaza, including the Muslim Youth Society. It also assisted the families of HAMAS terrorists who had been "martyred," killed, wounded, or imprisoned, and thereby actually encouraged terrorism. In fact, Rahman Anati, head of the HLF Jerusalem office, was arrested and indicted on charges of aiding and abetting a terrorist organization.

In 1995 Italian intelligence reported for the first time in Europe the importance of foreign funding for HAMAS operatives in Europe. The Al Taqwa network had financed radical movements in Algeria, Tunisia, and the Sudan, and it had been a major patron of PLO during the 1970s, after which it also began to provide funds for HAMAS. In November 1997 the headline in the *Corriere della Serra* reported the startling news that HAMAS had lost "Half its Finances – Treasure and Terrorism, 50 Billion lire." More than half HAMAS's annual budget had somehow disappeared. Although HAMAS was accustomed to receive annually "approximately $50 million collected from charitable societies, generous donors, and sympathizers of the Islamist cause worldwide," in spring 1997 its leadership discovered that more than $28 million was missing from an account the Muslim Brothers used to provide financial support. An investigation found that the money flow followed a triangular route. Point A were the donors who deposited their funds in branches of Bank Al Taqwa, Point B. Al Taqwa then distributed the money to Point C, "various shell organization in Gaza," corporations in Ramallah, and other HAMAS agencies. The decline in funds had "dramatic political consequences for HAMAS" whose money was already considered

"the real power in the Palestinian autonomous territories." An emissary
was sent to the President of the HAMAS International Committee, who
was then living in Turkey, followed by an audit in London, where most
of HAMAS funds were banked at Al Taqwa, "the financial heart of the
Islamist apparatus."[14] The investigation soon led to the Al Quds Press
and INTERPAL (aka the Palestinian Relief and Development Fund),
both located in London. INTERPAL administrators were reported to
have been skimming funds, and the Al Quds Press, which had its main
office in Beirut, was using two sets of books. At Al Taqwa Youssef Nada
was quick to counter-attack. He denied any culpability in the malfeasance
and rejected the assertion that Al Taqwa itself was an Ikhwan bank. Nada
countered that the Brothers did not exceed 8 percent of the 1,500 shareholders, and nothing should be made of the presence of Ikhwan leader
Shaykh Yousuf al-Qaradawi, Dean of the Faculty of Shar'ia and Islamic
Studies at the University of Qatar, as an adviser to the bank on Islamic
principles. The loss of funds created a storm that soon blew over, and
the door that had been opened to allow a glimpse of HAMAS operations
was quickly shut.

Despite numerous charitable sources it was, in fact, the constant support of the Saudis, mostly through MWL, that had enabled HAMAS
to expand rapidly. Nevertheless, at a press conference held at the Saudi
embassy in June 2003 a spokesman denied that Saudi Arabia gave money
to HAMAS. "Do we as a government give money to HAMAS? No. We
give money to the Palestinian Authority or we give money to the Palestinians through international organizations that are doing relief work in the
territories." When asked if the kingdom had either directly or indirectly
financed HAMAS or Palestine Islamic Jihad, Prince Saud argued that his
government had sent funds only to PLO, as the sole legitimate representative of the Palestinian people. The Saudis did admit, however, that when
their own "charitable organizations were first set up there were no regulatory measures," and "if money reached HAMAS and Jihad from Saudi
individuals, money reached them too from the United States, Britain,
and France." The Saudi government even had the audacity to make the
fatuous claim that it had instituted controls, "and the possibility of money
reaching any illegal organization is non-existent."[15]

Iran also did its part to fund HAMAS, providing up to $30 million
a year. Determined to scuttle the Oslo Accords, it increased support to
IJMP and HAMAS, and "worked to develop a rejectionist front, comprising Hizballah and 10 Palestinian groups based in Damascus, to counter
the Middle East [peace] process."[16] The Muslim Brotherhood in the
Middle East also pitched in. It established the International Muslim Aid
Committee to the Palestinian Nation, which included Ikhwan, HAMAS

activists, and IJMP terrorists. While the Saudi royal family may have believed that this amalgamation portended the cataclysmic *jihad* that would destroy Israel, the jihadists visualized their attacks on Israel as just the beginning of the purification of Islam in the Middle East.[17]

The United States responds

After 9/11 the US Department of the Treasury was not only concerned with Saudi financing of HAMAS, it also investigated a number of international charities and individual donors for the Palestinians whose assets in the USA were soon frozen. They included the Comité de Bienfaisance et de Secours aux Palestiniens (CBSP) of France; Association de Secours Palestinien (ASP) of Switzerland; INTERPAL of the UK; the Palestinian Association of Austria, and the Sanabil Association for Relief and Development of Lebanon. INTERPAL was one of the largest charities in Great Britain, and strongly objected when the UK Charity Commission froze its accounts, accusing it of being "the principal charity utilized to hide the flow of money to HAMAS." Founded in 1994, INTERPAL had raised some $6 million in 2001 alone. Its director, Ibrahim Hewitt, denied any wrongdoing, claiming that "since 1996 we have been in fairly regular contact with the [UK charity] commission. We've tightened up procedures."[18] Thereafter, three more charities based in the West were also closed, including the Palestine Relief and Development Fund (INTERPAL) of the UK, the Al Aqsa Foundation headquartered in Germany with branches in Belgium and Holland, and HLF in France. In the USA, HLF was the largest Islamic charity to provide direct support for HAMAS. Under investigation since 1993, its proscription in the USA following 9/11 was a sharp warning that HAMAS would be treated with "the same severity as Al Qaeda's terrorist network."[19] Also under investigation were two major Islamic charities: Muslim Aid and the Islamic Relief Agency (IRSA), as well as the Jerusalem Fund for Human Services of Ontario, Canada and Medical Aid for Palestine (MAP) of Montreal (formerly the International Relief Association). The Jerusalem Fund provided assistance to the West Bank, Gaza Strip, and Lebanon. MAP in the UK was also investigated. In addition to charities the Treasury also investigated banks operating in Palestine, particularly the Al Aqsa Islamic Bank, described as the "financial branch of HAMAS." Al Aqsa had been established with $20 million in capital by the Saudi Dallah Al Baraka Group led by Saleh Abdallah Kamel, who persistently denied having any association with terrorist organizations. The Treasury also froze the assets of Yassin Abdullah al-Qadi, for the money manager was a HAMAS financial adviser.

In contrast to the USA in the months after 9/11, the EU found the issue of charitable giving to Palestinian causes a difficult problem to resolve. WAMY, IIRO, and the Al Haramain Foundation had all donated money to HAMAS. In May 2002 some 200 new names were added to the European list of terrorist organizations, but Hizbullah and HAMAS were conspicuously absent. The EU simply could not decide if it was possible to disassociate the humanitarian from the political activities of a charitable organization.[20] Finally, in August 2002, Germany was the first to prohibit the Al Aqsa Foundation from sending money to the families of Palestinian suicide bombers and forbade its staff from collecting donations in mosques, Islamic centers, and at "public demonstrations."[21] The following year HAMAS offices in Australia, the Netherlands, and Denmark were closed. In Denmark the Chairman and Vice Chairman of Al Aqsa were detained in January and $164,000 was confiscated. In May the USA and UK followed suit, freezing the assets and blocking payments to the Al Aqsa Foundation, which "fed money to HAMAS, one of the groups which sponsor suicide bombings on civilian targets in Israel." US Deputy Assistant Treasury Secretary Juan Zarate told reporters, "It's a clear signal the US takes very seriously the rejectionist stance of HAMAS and other likeminded terrorist groups that are impeding, in our mind, the [Middle East] peace process . . . [funds donated] with Al Aqsa's knowledge and consent goes to fund suicide bombers and other armed activities by HAMAS."[22]

In 2003 Senator Charles Schumer of New York, a Jew and one of the most outspoken critics of WAMY, which had recently hosted HAMAS leader Khaled Mash'al in Riyadh in November 2002, charged that HAMAS was using the charity "to get financing from the Saudis." Schumer urged the US Attorney General and the Treasury Department to immediately freeze WAMY's assets in the USA and investigate its headquarters in Virginia. Schumer found it especially disturbing that a nephew of Osama bin Laden had founded the charity in Virginia and was especially incensed that WAMY would support HAMAS and its leadership, which included reported terrorists Khaled Mash'al and Shaykh Ahmed Yasin.[23] As for HAMAS, in September 2003 the Department of State reported that it was still using its charities "to strengthen its own standing among Palestinians at the expense of the Palestinian Authority . . . HAMAS' recent suicide bombings demonstrate the organization's commitment to undermining real efforts to move toward a permanent peace between Israel and the Palestinians."[24] By 2004 the USA had used Executive Order 13224 to "designate" five HAMAS charities and six HAMAS leaders and freeze the assets of individuals and entities associated with terrorism, including Shaykh Yasin, Imad al-Alami,

Usama Hamdan, Khaled Mash'al, Musa Abu Marzouk, and Abdel Aziz Rantissi.

Arafat's charitable corruption

Since the Second World War the Palestinians have received more money from charities than any other single group in the world. And during its years in exile, PLO survived thanks to substantial amounts of financial assistance from the Soviet Union, the Arab states, and the European community, and by imposing a 5 percent income tax on all Palestinian workers in Arab League countries. Between 1993 and 2000 the PA received some $1.5 billion from the EU, and from 2000 to 2003 it was given over $1 billion from the Arab League, but the total support from the international community for the Palestinians between 1993 and 2004 has been estimated by the World Bank at $10 billion, "the highest per capita aid transfer in the history of foreign aid anywhere."[25] Arafat personally enriched himself, and in 2000 he maintained accounts in the Cayman Islands, Switzerland, North Africa, and even in the Hashmonaim branch of the Bank Leumi in Tel Aviv. His personal slush fund was estimated to contain anywhere between $300 million (Forbes) and $4 billion (Rawya Shawa of the Palestinian Legislative Council). An investigative report published by the HAMAS weekly *Al Risala* in December 1998 estimated that the Office of the Presidency account held $400 million, "which to date has not been subject to any kind of external review."[26]

Arafat also created scores of monopolies directed by his cronies in the West Bank and Gaza. Inexplicably, despite rampant PLO corruption, in November 1997 the US Overseas Private Investment Corporation (OPIC) chose Arafat's friend Hani al-Masri and his private company, Capital Investment Management Corporation, to supervise a loan to the PA of $60 million.[27] In August 2002 Israeli intelligence estimated Arafat's personal fortune in the billions of dollars.[28] A year later, an IMF study of Palestinian public finance discovered that the presidential office used 8 percent ($74 million) of the PA budget, $40 million of which was spent on administration, the remainder to be personally distributed as Arafat pleased. Moreover, between 1997 and 2003 some $900 million in PA funds had been diverted to overseas accounts, including a reported $10 million to the President's wife, Suha Arafat, who lived with her free-spending mother, Raymonda Tawil, in Paris on a $100,000 monthly stipend from the PA.[29] Since 2000 a great number of documents captured by IDF in the West Bank and Gaza have confirmed PLO corruption, embezzlement, and the use of charitable funds for dubious purposes. Especially reprehensible were the "irregularities in the distribution of foreign humanitarian aid" whereby favored doctors and pharmacists in the Gaza Strip were known to steal expensive medicines and sell them in private health clinics, while officials in the Ministry of Welfare regularly sold aid packages donated by the Gulf states. Even the Director of the Jabaliyya Charity Association of the PA Ministry of Religion was accused by local residents of stealing Saudi aid during the month of Ramadan.

In June 2002 at a meeting in Gaza attended by members of the Jordan Charity Coalition (Aathlaf al-Hir) and a coalition of Islamic associations from Yemen (including the Al Aqsa Charity Foundation and the Wali Mekbal al-Juabirah Association), the Jordanians were represented by "known HAMAS terrorists," including the leader of the Islamic Committee for Support of the Palestinian People (the Jordanian branch of the Charity Coalition). The Coalition served as the umbrella organization regulating the activities of indigenous Islamic charities; its management council consisted of some of the most important Islamists, including Shaykh Yousuf al-Qaradawi from Qatar and chairman of its fundraising apparatus and Azzam Mustafa Yusuf, the Acting Director of the Coalition and former head of UK INTERPAL. It was the successor to the Islamic Movement in Israel; the Movement had been closely scrutinized by the government of Israel and two of its most important major charitable institutions, Islamic Aid and the Committee for Aid to Orphans and Prisoners, were shut down in 1995–1996. In addition, the Islamic Relief Committee of Nazareth was closed in March 1996 for providing direct assistance to families of HAMAS activists. These closures, which were meant to discourage fundraising for HAMAS, failed; by mid-1996 HAMAS had opened new channels to the West and to the Arab states where the donations far exceeded any that had been raised in the past.[30]

In Europe there were three important donors: the Al Aqsa Fund located in Germany, Belgium, and the Netherlands; INTERPAL UK; and "the Committee for Assistance and Solidarity with Palestine" in France, which were legally prorogued by Israel in May 1997. Israel made no distinction between the civic and the terrorist activities of HAMAS, despite the fact that HAMAS had consistently promoted its social welfare programs, especially those teaching the Quran to children, building hospitals, and providing services "to women whose husbands died sanctifying Allah's name, or are held by Israel." HAMAS charities, especially in Gaza, grew in stature and significance. There were three Coalition "fund drives" in the West Bank, and charitable associations from Saudi Arabia, Kuwait, Qatar, Bahrain, Great Britain, and the Netherlands were "complicit with the Charity Coalition." Even the poor Muslims in Bosnia-Herzegovina contributed to a charity association in the West Bank identified with HAMAS. In 2000 the Coalition launched its "101 Days" worldwide Islamic fundraising campaign headed by Shaykh al-Qaradawi for the benefit of Palestinians in the West Bank and Gaza. Eventually its name would be changed to "the Charity Coalition" and serve as "the umbrella organization that encompasses Islamic organizations in the Arabic and Western worlds."[31] It emerged as a powerful HAMAS organization not beholden in any way to the PA.

Reviving the Intifada

Determined to sabotage the Oslo Accords of September 1993 and the establishment of the PA the next year, the Izz al-Din al-Qassam Brigades unleashed a number of suicide bombings against Jewish civilians in Israel proper in February and March 1996, but not against Israeli troops in the West Bank and Gaza, that persuaded the PA to crack down on HAMAS. The PA responded to this challenge to its authority by shutting down the HAMAS fundraising apparatus. Charities were closed, administrators arrested, and documents confiscated. Undeterred, HAMAS proceeded on its murderous way, proudly proclaiming that in replicating and improving on the charitable organizations created by the Muslim Brotherhood their network of institutions had become "the sources of the movement's strength," enhancing its ability "to recruit operatives, including suicide attackers." HAMAS raised "an undisclosed amount of charity [zakat]" that was then made in cash awards to its agents, to "families of terrorists killed," and to the terrorism apparatus itself.[32] The HAMAS bombings that followed certainly contributed to the election of Benjamin Netanyahu, who was prepared to take a hard line against the terrorists. Nevertheless, King Hussein successfully lobbied the Israeli government to release Shaykh Yasin from prison in return for the release of two Israeli intelligence agents who had been captured in a failed attempt in Amman to assassinate HAMAS leader Khaled Mash'al in October 1997. Undaunted, Yasin returned to Gaza and launched a new onslaught against Israeli targets both inside and outside Israel. The PA and Yasir Arafat responded by pressuring HAMAS to cease its support for the policy of suicide bombings that the Izz al-Din al-Qassam Brigades had set in motion in Jerusalem in July and September 1997.[33]

The extent to which HAMAS used charities to support its political and military activities was further clarified by Israeli raids in retaliation for the second major Palestinian insurgency, the Al Aqsa Intifada, in September

2000. On 28 September Ariel Sharon, the leader of the hardline Likud Party, visited Al Haram al-Sharif (the Temple Mount) in Jerusalem and its Al Aqsa Mosque, the third most holy shrine in Islam. This provocative act, accompanied by 1,000 riot police, was followed the next day by a Palestinian demonstration during which Israeli police using live ammunition and rubber bullets killed 6 and wounded 220 rock-throwing but unarmed Palestinians. The fundamental cause was, of course, the continued Israeli occupation of the West Bank and Gaza that now seemed more permanent after the failure of the Camp David Israeli–Palestinian negotiations in July. Thirty-three years of pent-up Palestinian frustration, despair, and rage exploded. As in the first Intifada (1987–1991) the Palestinians began by using non-violence, but after 144 Palestinians had been killed in demonstrations the Al Aqsa Martyrs Brigade and Al Fatah commenced their suicide bombings, at first against the Israeli army and settlers in the West Bank, and then in January 2002 against Israeli civilians. Although Yasir Arafat did not initiate the Intifada, he most certainly gave his tacit approval to armed resistance and terrorism. In April 2002 an IDF raid discovered Arafat's signature on a memo approving thousands of dollars for Fatah's ragtag Tanzim militia operation, which had directed several suicide bombings.[34]

The relentless Israeli raids continued to uncover ever more evidence for the use of charities by HAMAS and Islamic Jihad as they looked for money "sent by Hizbullah, the Lebanese guerrilla group."[35] Despite their political differences, PLO contributed to HAMAS, and Yasir Arafat himself donated $1,000 to the family of a HAMAS member taken prisoner, because HAMAS activists were considered to be the "sons of the PLO."[36] The suicide bombings against civilians were roundly condemned by the international community, but payment for the martyrs became inextricably intertwined with Islamic charities. The Arab summit in Cairo in October 2000 overwhelmingly adopted a recommendation by the Kingdom of Saudi Arabia to give its support to the Al Quds Intifada Fund to assist the families of Palestinian martyrs.

After the outbreak of the Al Aqsa Intifada the Saudis agreed to provide financial aid to families of Palestinian martyrs, and repeated their firm commitment to finance the Al Quds Fund and the Al Aqsa Foundation. In addition to the promised money it "reportedly pledged Palestinians up to $1 billion to finance the continuation of the Intifada," which Saudi officials commonly referred to as "The Jihad."[37] A detailed report prepared by the Middle East Media Research Institute (MEMRI) revealed that Saudi Arabia was not only incredibly generous, but by its own admission much of its aid was directed to "Mujahideen fighters" and "families of martyrs" killed or wounded in operations against the Jewish state.[38] King Fahd personally supported the families of 1,000 Palestinian "martyrs," and a directive was issued requiring the governors of all Saudi Arabian regions "to initiate campaigns for every citizen to donate to the Al-Quds Intifada Fund."[39] An Israeli military-intelligence analysis of captured documents found that Saudi support to Palestianian suicide bombers who died in the calendar year 2001 amounted to $545,000 via a branch office of the Arab Bank to families of 102 terrorists. Despite the fact that some twenty-eight terrorists were known HAMAS, Fatah, and Palestinian Islamic Jihad *mujahideen*, their families received $5,333 for each martyr and $4,000 for each injured Palestinian. Saudi Arabia pledged $400 million in 2001 for the support of "martyrs' families . . . at $5,300 per 'martyr,' that works out to about 75,000 martyrs." Of course, those 75,000 "martyrs" never materialized, but the loss to "martyr families" was perhaps made more bearable by the charitable contributions from the Committee for Support of the Al Quds Intifada, a Saudi agency run by Prince Naif bin Abd al-Aziz, Minister of the Interior.[40]

A nation-wide charitable fund drive was initiated by Prince Salman bin Abd al-Aziz, Governor of Riyadh, and citizens and guest workers were urged to give *sadaqa* and send funds, jewelry, and other valuable items to "Account 98." For years Prince Salman's Popular Committee for Assisting the Palestinian Mujahideen had organized a campaign urging citizens and expatriates to contribute to the Palestinian cause through donations either to its many branches or by depositing their gifts in Account 98, which had been opened in all domestic banks. Account 98 funds were then collected by the Al Quds Committee. The Supreme Council for the Funds of Al Aqsa and the Al Quds Intifada then utilized IDB to transfer funds to the Unified Treasury of the National Palestinian Authority. Funds disbursed through Account 98 were published in the 2001 annual report authorized by Prince Naif, head of the Executive Committee of the Al Quds Intifada. Saudis were informed that the charity drive was led by the king himself "and his stand against the idea of establishing a Zionist state."[41] He personally donated $8 million, calling it support for the Palestinian people in the face of the Israeli aggression against "our Palestinian brethren" fighting to establish a Palestinian state with Al Quds (Jerusalem) as its capital. Prince Naif also responded by encouraging donations from his Ministry, and he ordered the Saudi Ministry of Information to launch a propaganda campaign in support of the charity campaign.[42] Those who responded to the call of King Fahd, Prince Salman, and Prince Naif were, of course, the banks – NCB, Saudi American Bank, Al Rajhi Banking and Investment Corporation,

Saudi-British Bank, Saudi French Bank, and the Al Riyadh Bank. The charitable institutions included the heads of WAMY, Al Haramain Foundation, IIRO, the all-female Nahda Society, and the Al Wafa Women's Charity Association.[43]

The suicide bombers soon implicated PRCS in assisting terrorists. When the first female Palestinian suicide bomber apparently used her status as a field worker for PRCS to gain entry into Jerusalem and carry out an attack that killed one and wounded nearly two hundred, the legitimate charitable community was shocked. Israeli investigators charged that she probably used "a Palestine Red Crescent Society ambulance to get past IDF checkpoints into Jerusalem." Worse, on the same day in February 2002 IDF reported it had captured a Palestinian terrorist disguised in a doctor's uniform and riding in a PRCS ambulance as it tried to pass through a roadblock near Nablus.[44] Next, PRCS vehicles were seen transporting terrorists in Gaza, Ramallah, and Jenin where they were taken to sites from which they could snipe at IDF forces; IDF also claimed that Palestinian terrorists had used a PRCS building near Ramallah to fire on Israeli troops. The ICRC vehemently denied all these allegations, and the local PRCS publicly denounced IDF for their past attacks on sixty-eight Red Crescent ambulances, "leading to one death and 122 injuries." When Israeli investigators concluded that these assertions were false, the Red Cross/Red Crescent officials in Geneva admitted that there had been a problem with the misuse of Red Crescent emblems; Israeli objections appeared to many in Geneva as petulant retaliation against PRCS because Israel's medical society, Magen David Adom (Red Star of David), had been denied membership by secret ballot among Geneva Convention signatories in 1949 and had its membership rejected by the ICRC ever since.

The second Intifada, like the first, was a violent reaction against decades of harassment and humiliation, often accompanied by the ill-concealed contempt of the Israeli authorities for the Palestinians, but it differed from the first by more coordinated organization, greater commitment, and advanced skills in explosives. As the Intifada intensified, killing 125 Israelis and wounding hundreds more, the IDF launched Operation Defensive Shield in March 2002 to destroy the Intifada infrastructure. The IDF stormed four Palestinian banks in Ramallah, and two branches of the Arab Bank were thoroughly searched for evidence that would link suicide bombers to the sources of funds from abroad for HAMAS, Islamic Jihad, and the Lebanese guerrilla group Hizbullah and enable the Israeli authorities to confiscate those funds from the accounts of militant factions that had claimed to have carried out suicide bombings. The offices of an Islamic charity in the West Bank city of Tulkarm were also raided, and computer hard-drives and documents were seized. These documents clearly revealed evidence, from correspondence between the PA and the Saudi government, that the latter had been paying compensatory money to the families of Palestinian suicide bombers. The correspondence also included "a damning letter from the Saudis complaining that the Palestinians had exposed [their] secret financial ties by allowing the publication of a Feb. 19 report in the PA publication *Al Hayat Al Jedida* thanking Saudi Arabia for assisting the families of terrorists killed in attacks on Israelis."[45] A letter written in 2000 to a PA representative claimed that the Saudi committee that transferred contributions to beneficiaries had sent "large sums to radical committees and associations including the Islamic Association which belongs to HAMAS."[46]

In January 2002 $45 million was transferred from the Al Aqsa Foundation and the Al Quds Fund to the Palestinian International Cooperation Minister in a meeting held with the Saudi royal family to "confirm the strategic relationship between Palestine and the Kingdom." It was the phrase "strategic relationship" that angered the USA and elicited an acknowledgment from the Saudi embassy in Washington that the Saudis had indeed helped fund HAMAS. The embassy argued that the funds were relayed to the HAMAS political wing, "for charities they managed in the occupied territories." "Whether these are families that have lost a loved one to violence, we do not know."[47] Another spokesman for the embassy stated that the government of Saudi Arabia did "not fund terrorists," and refused to accept the State Department's classification of HAMAS as a terrorist organization. He refrained from any criticism of the suicide bombings of Israeli civilians. He stressed, rather disingenuously, that Saudi charitable support for the Palestinians used such international organizations as the UNHCR, the International Red Crescent, and the PA.

More charitable support for Palestine and HAMAS

Other Saudi charities had close ties with terrorists. The Al Wafa Humanitarian Foundation (Wafa al-Igatha al-Islamiyya), a powerful charity with offices in Saudi Arabia, Kuwait, UAE, and Peshawar, operated the Al Wafa Rehabilitation and Health Center and nursing homes in Gaza. It had close ties to radical Islamists in the West Bank and Gaza, and to some of the kingdom's wealthiest families. It was thought by some to be an integral feature of the Bin Laden network, assisting the movement of Al Qaeda and Taliban jihadists.[48] The Al Wafa Humanitarian Foundation did "a small amount of legitimate humanitarian work and raised a lot of money for equipment and weapons, but it was reported that Abdul Aziz, a senior

Al Qaeda operative and Saudi citizen, used al-Wafa to finance terrorist activities."⁴⁹ In the USA the Al Wafa Humanitarian Foundation was first on the list of Saudi-sponsored charities designated by President Bush as a "Specially Designated Global Terrorist Entity," and the first to have its assets frozen. Moreover, it was a partner in the Islamic Supreme Council of America. Its Chairman, Shaykh Muhammad Hisham Kabbani, had previously been involved in Islamist activities in Somalia. In Pakistan the Al Wafa office had been designated as "terrorist supporters," and the Council of Foreign Relations reported ominously that while Al Wafa had carried out legitimate work, it had also financed "more suspect groups."⁵⁰ Washington expressed its concern about Al Wafa, whether from centers in UAE, Oman, or Mogadishu, when a senior Al Wafa official captured during the US invasion of Afghanistan in 2001 was found to have close ties to the Pakistani nuclear scientific establishment.

In April 2002 Prince Naif organized a two-day telethon to increase the funding for the Palestinian Intifada. More than $67 million had already been collected, but Prince Naif and Prince Sultan, Second Deputy Prime Minister, were determined to collect even more. Their slogan was "Hundreds of Millions of Riyals for the Palestinian People and their Leadership." Prince Sultan also staged his own three-day telethon organized by the Saudi Committee for the Support of the Al Quds Intifada to reach 200,000 Palestinian families "living in cities besieged by the Israeli occupation forces." The money raised by the telethon totaled $160 million, of which $18 million was given by King Fahd and his circle.⁵¹ In the Gulf UAE launched a weeklong "For You, Palestine" campaign to raise more millions on top of the $86 million already contributed. Chairman of the UAE Red Crescent Society and Minister of Foreign Affairs Shaykh Hamdan ibn Zayed al-Nahyan asked people to give generously as UAE wanted to play "a leading role in the reconstruction of the Jenin refugee camp." Qatar alone raised some $10 million. Mustafa Hashim al-Shaykh Deeb, the Palestinian Ambassador in Riyadh, issued a frank statement: "Our people would not have continued the struggle without the support and backing of their Arab brethren," and the $1 billion "infused" in all Palestinians the "confidence and the spirit to keep up the struggle. The Kingdom's payment of $250 million it had pledged was a decisive factor in the continuation of the struggle." Deeb actually understated the role played by Saudi Arabia, for its payments already totaled $325 million or half "the $668 million pledged by the other Arab countries."⁵²

At the conclusion of the Arab summit in Beirut in October 2002 the Saudi royal family announced that it would augment its donation to the Al Aqsa Foundation and the Al Quds Intifada Fund by another $21 million. This contribution was one of many responses at the summit, whose

resolutions promised additional support of $150 million. Ignoring crit-
icism from the US media, King Fahd and Crown Prince Abdullah
promised to provide "unlimited financial and political support for the
Palestinian people and cause," and promptly deposited $7 million in the
Al Aqsa Foundation account at IDB.[53] The grand total donated by participating states to support the "Jerusalem Intifada" had reached nearly
$700 million. Prince Naif, the General Supervisor of the Committee,
had personally endorsed more than $62 million to benefit some 35,000
people.[54]

When President George Bush raised the issue of Saudi funding to
HAMAS during the summit of Arab leaders held in Sharm al-Shaykh,
Egypt, in June 2003, the Saudi response was quietly diplomatic. In contrast, the Islamist reaction was swift and vitriolic. HAMAS leadership
asserted that the movement was supported by private individuals who
were "not obliged by the resolutions of heads-of-state summits." An IJMP
spokesman condemned the summit arguing speciously: "No Arab regime
provides any assistance to the [Palestinian] resistance."[55] Ironically, his
argument was contradicted by a Saudi Arabian embassy spokesman who
informed the *New York Times* "that it was no secret that large Palestinian
charitable funds existed in Saudi Arabia," but he said they were closely
monitored and channeled through major international organizations.

After 9/11 and the incremental deterioration of the US plan for peace
in the Middle East, Israel moved sharply against the Palestinian authorities and their institutions. A series of raids found further evidence that
incriminated the PA, HAMAS, and Hizbullah in the use of charitable
organizations for military purposes. The Charity Coalition had con-
ducted three "fund drives" in the West Bank and among Israeli Arabs, and
had received substantial funds from charities in Saudi Arabia, Kuwait,
Qatar, Bahrain, the UK, and the Netherlands.[56] The Al Aqsa Foundation in Germany, despite being designated a terrorist organization by
the USA in May 2003, continued to be a "vital source of funding"
for HAMAS. Efforts by the Americans to convince Arab governments
"to help rein in HAMAS" were largely ignored, for the popularity of
HAMAS continued to grow among the Palestinians for the many excellent social services it provided, and it was not until the bus bombing in
Jerusalem that killed twenty-one civilians that the USA redoubled its pursuit of the HAMAS money-trail. Several European countries now cooperated and under great pressure from Washington and UN, the Palestine
Monetary Authority froze the bank accounts of nine Islamic charities,
including HAMAS; the Islamic Young Women's Association; Al Salah
Association (HAMAS); the Social Care Committee; the Palestinian Student Friends Association; the Islamic Charity for Zakat; Al Mujamma'

al-Islami (HAMAS); Al Nour Charity Association; and Al Aqsa Charity Foundation.[57]

Trapped, the PA promised to monitor funds received from outside sources and make certain that the money was used by institutions for "service purposes."[58] Palestinian Prime Minister Mahmoud Abbas publicly asked Saudi Arabia to divert donations that went directly to the Al Jamiya al-Islamiyya and Al Salah, and Crown Prince Abdullah "officially withdrew the kingdom's support for HAMAS in early 2002." Nevertheless, Account 98 continued to function "and fund groups like HAMAS."[58] SAMA announced impressive money-laundering and terrorist financing regulations in May 2003, but they would not be enforced for many months. Meanwhile, the Saudi-based WAMY was still spending $2.7 million annually in support of the Intifada for which Shaykh Yasin publicly thanked the charity just before his assassination in March 2004. Shaykh Yasin was succeeded by his adjutant, Abdel Aziz Rantissi, but after his assassination his successor, Khaled Mash'al, was desperate for cash now that Saudi Arabia could no longer be relied upon for substantial funding.

As summer 2004 approached Israel once again opened a frontal attack on both UNRWA and PRCS, blaming them for providing cover for terrorists. In the USA a Congressional Task Force on Terrorism and Unconventional Warfare report in 2002 had already provided evidence that UNRWA facilities were used "as storage areas for Palestinian ammunition and counterfeit currency factories." Then, in June 2004, an Israeli television station showed photographs of Arab terrorists operating in southern Gaza using an ambulance "owned and operated" by UNRWA. Palestinian gunmen had used the vehicle, with a UN flag flying from its roof, "as getaway transportation after murdering six Israeli soldiers in Gaza City on May 11." Next, it was reported in the USA that an "ambulance-for-terrorism program" had functioned for years, and "humanitarian" officials, including a number of PRCS ambulance drivers, were "willing collaborators."[59] In response, IDF closed the offices of HAMAS "Da'wa" charity organization in Bethlehem and Kalkiya, and in Bethlehem the Orphans' Assistance Association, which had received funds from the Gulf states, was also closed.[60]

The demands on Islamic charities in Palestine, however, have remained greater than ever, for two out of five Palestinian families are utterly destitute and dependent on humanitarian assistance largely because of the rampant corruption within the PA and the Islamic charities operating in Palestinian territories. The EU, which had contributed €4 billion, remained convinced that the PA was the obstacle to political, social, and economic reform, and despite "the highest per capita transfer in the history of foreign aid" the average Palestinian lived on about $2 a day. European funding "had been distributed in a reckless manner, rarely reaching the intended target populations in full."[61]

Lebanon and Hizbullah

One of the oldest of the modern Islamic charities is the Association of Islamic Charitable Projects, a non-profit international organization founded in 1930 in Beirut by the honorable Shaykh Ahmad al-Ajuz. In its early years the Association was more interested in helping the poor of Lebanon socially, educationally, and economically than in the propagation of Islam. When the Lebanese Red Crescent was founded, it was able to expand the health-care facilities of the Association. Until the late 1940s the population of Lebanon had been rather homogeneous, but after the founding of Israel and the 1948 Arab–Israeli war large numbers of Palestinians fled into Lebanon where their refugee camps required an ever-greater humanitarian presence. Consequently, the government of Lebanon allowed PRCS to open a branch office in Beirut and solicit funds locally and through international aid organizations. Yasir Arafat placed his brother, Dr. Fathi Arafat, in charge of the Lebanese branch of PRCS; this enabled him to control the organization's activities until he and his PLO followers were expelled from Lebanon in 1982 during the Israeli invasion called Operation Peace for Galilee. Despite the vicissitudes of PLO, Dr. Arafat somehow managed to survive at the head of the Lebanon branch of PRCS until the start of the second Intifada, when he retired as an honorary member.

At the time of the Israeli invasion in 1982 Palestinian refugees numbered about 10 percent of Lebanon's population. PRCS was responsible for the administration of six major hospitals and thirteen clinics in Lebanon, and with UNRWA and a number of western charities it provided primary health care for 175,000 Palestinian refugees in twelve camps, the largest being Bourj Al Barajneh and Shatilla in Beirut, and another 175,000 scattered throughout Lebanon. Severe restrictions on travel and work made emigration difficult, so the refugee camps and the charities supporting them soon became self-perpetuating. Poverty, unemployment, and depression were the tools that made Palestinian youths in the camps eager recruits for the jihadists from HAMAS, IJMP, and lesser radical groups that followed in the train of PRCS and frequently infiltrated its administration and staff. HAMAS presence was particularly strong in Sidon where one of its charities, the Sanabil Association for

Relief and Development of Sidon, was placed on the US list of terrorist organizations in May 2003.

In addition to the Red Crescent a new independent humanitarian organization was established in southern Lebanon managed by Hizbullah (Party of God), a militant Shiʻa political movement with militias in southern Lebanon, the Bekaa Valley, and the suburbs of Beirut. Launched after the Israeli invasion of southern Lebanon in 1982, its indigenous spiritual guide was Shaykh Muhammad Hussein Fadlallah, a radical cleric and author of *Al Islam wa Mantaq al-Quwa* (*Islam and the Logic of Force*). Iranian support for Palestine's Shiʻite refugees began with the creation of an Iran–Palestine Friendship Society shortly after the end of the Six Day War in 1967. It had existed for more than a decade before the Islamist revolution of the Ayatollah Khomeini, who provided the Shiʻite and Salafist theological foundations for the Hizbullah leadership. The Ayatollah had argued for the establishment of an Islamic Republic in Lebanon that would assist in the destruction of "western imperialism" and work ceaselessly to effect the complete destruction of the state of Israel. To that end, HAMAS and Hizbullah "embassies" were established in Tehran to coordinate their activities despite the historical differences between Shiʻite and Sunni. Both agreed with Khomeini that "the goal of this virus [Israel] that was planted in the heart of the Islamic world, is not only to annihilate the Arab nation. The danger is to the whole Middle East, and the solution is in annihilating the virus. There is no other treatment." All means to this end were legitimate including "the use of charity money" to extirpate Israel.[62] In conception and execution Hizbullah was an Iranian creation whose annual budget in excess of $200 million was subsidized by Al Wali al-Faqih, an Iranian government office, and the Iranian Revolutionary Guard (Pasdaran) Liberation Organizations Bureau.

The Emdad Committee for Islamic Charity (aka Imdad al-Imam) was the single most important charity sponsored by Hizbullah. Registered in Lebanon as an NGO, it was established in 1987 to "alleviate hardship" in that element of the southern Lebanese and Shiʻite population "most affected by Israeli occupation." It had nine branches, administered five schools and two centers for handicapped children, and provided direct benefits to 6,800 students and 3,320 orphans. By May 1998 the charity had registered 50,000 families with 157,000 members. Other Hizbullah charitable organizations substantially funded by Iran were Al Shahid and the Al Mustazafin Fund, which delivered financial assistance "to the families of the Hizbullah martyrs, wounded, and handicapped."[63] Similarly, the Emdad charity could always count on generous donations from Iran and Syria during Ramadan and for the support of the aged and orphans, as can the Martyrs Foundation.[64] Hizbullah managed its own charitable institutions without reference to the government of Lebanon, funding its own schools, health programs, and public works projects. The Jihad al-Bina'a (Holy Struggle for Development) served as its "reconstruction arm," building hospitals, schools, clinics, and agricultural development schemes.

From 1993 to 2003 Iran had delivered more than $1 billion to Hizbullah for military hardware, but "a good portion – supplemented by donations from Muslims around the world, including the United States – was directed to Hizballah's social programs."[65] While most charities "were founded with funding from Iran," by 2000 Hizbullah could claim that independent donations and contributions from the worldwide Islamic community now provided much of the cost of administration. Like HAMAS, Hizbullah has been listed as a terrorist organization by the USA and donations to its charities were prohibited. The US proscription had resulted primarily from the activities of Imad Mugniyah, an elusive terrorist and enigmatic figure who plotted bloody attacks against western targets well before Al Qaeda. He planned the first suicide bombings in the Middle East and was involved throughout the 1980s in a succession of kidnappings. He was also the Hizbullah "security chief" who planned the 1983 suicide bombing of US peacekeepers in Lebanon that killed 241 Marines. Mugniyah was said to have been involved in the bombing of the US embassies in Beirut in 1983 and 1984, which left seventy-seven dead and hundreds injured. He was then charged with criminal acts in a US District Court in 1985 – three years before Al Qaeda was founded. Thereafter, he was charged with masterminding a succession of hijackings and the kidnapping of western officials.

Mughniya managed to survive thanks to the patronage of Iran's Revolutionary Guards, but after planning the bombing of the Israeli embassy in Argentina, which killed 115 people, he vanished. His disappearance coincided with Hizbullah's emergence from the political wilderness. It was Muhammad Fadlallah, supported by Hasan al-Turabi and Iran, who convinced Hizbullah to enter the Lebanese parliamentary elections of 1992. This, of course, was contrary to the teachings of Sayyid Qutb and other Salafists who "urged Islamists to break with the jahaliya, or [pre-Islamist] regimes masquerading as Muslim Governments," and Hizbullah, not surprisingly, won seats in the Lebanese parliament. This gravitation to parliamentary democracy did not, however, alter its commitment to *jihad* against Israel. A conference of Islamic scholars held in Beirut in January 2002 concluded with a statement that Hizbullah, HAMAS, PIJ, "and all resistance forces vividly express the will of the nation" and that *jihad* and the *mujahideen* "represent the honor, pride and dignity of Muslims everywhere and reflect the human ambitions of all oppressed peoples in the world . . . [*Jihad* is the] noblest and most sacred phenomenon in our contemporary history." The OIC meeting held in Kuala Lumpur in April then rejected an effort "to include Palestinian suicide bombers in a condemnation of terrorism."[66] Strengthened by the rejectionists, Islamist activities increased in the mosques in east Jerusalem, and in Judea and Samaria where HAMAS, Islamic Jihad, and the Muslim Brotherhood were all competing for influence. Meanwhile, the US Treasury continued to scrutinize closely other questionable organizations, listing in May 2005 the Alehssan Society, a charity that operated in the West Bank, Gaza, and Lebanon and which supported the PIJ directly.

10   The Islamization of Europe

> If they are brothers, tell them it's for the prisoners. And if they are
> infidels, tell them the money will go to the poor.
>
> Sifaoui, *Inside Al Qaeda*

Muhammad Jaber Fakihi arrived in Berlin in June 2000 to take up his post as Attaché for Islamic Affairs in the Saudi Arabian embassy. A former law student at King Saud University in Riyadh, he had traveled in the West, but once in Berlin he displayed little interest in Germans or Germany. He much preferred the company of a few fellow Arabs who lived in a neighborhood of Middle Eastern immigrants. He ate his meals at a restaurant serving spare Arab fare and spent most of his time at the Al Nur Mosque in Berlin. A "slim man with a bushy beard," he assisted Muslims on the *hajj*, distributed Qurans, and disseminated Islamic religious literature published in German, but he spoke neither German nor English and played no significant role in the Berlin diplomatic community. Although introverted and withdrawn, Jaber Fakihi proved assiduous in organizing and collecting funds for charity. He had "arranged for Saudi government-backed charities to fund the expansion of Al-Nur" including $1.2 million from the Al Haramain Foundation. Fakihi had a grand vision that the mosque would be the center for the expansion of Islamic *da'wa* eastward into Poland, Czechoslovakia, and Hungary. His model was the Islamic Cultural Center and the Central Mosque in London's Regent's Park, then under the direction of Ahmad al-Dubayan, Fakihi's mentor and predecessor in Berlin. In the late 1990s Dubayan had opened the Al Nur Mosque to preachers who, in defending Islam, justified violence.

The world of Saudi diplomacy accommodated innocuous cultural attachés who managed to slip back and forth between postings to an embassy, on the one hand, and placement at a foreign-based Saudi charitable institution, on the other. Dubayan, however, was different. In Germany he had cultivated questionable friends, and after he left the Saudi embassy in Berlin for a London posting he seemed to develop a particular interest in *jihad*. In March 2003 Dubayan returned to Berlin to meet with Fakihi, arriving the day before that diplomat was expelled by the

German government.[1] As Fakihi was a proven associate of known terrorists, German officials were prepared to declare him *persona non grata*.
The Saudi embassy tried but failed to assure the German government that
Fakihi's diplomatic activities had been thoroughly proper, but a month
after his departure the German Office for the Protection of the Constitution (BfV) placed "the Saudi embassy, its consulates and other facilities
in Germany under surveillance." German officials were concerned that
the Saudi Ministry of Religion was providing "tacit support" for radical *mujahideen*.[2] In one case, the King Fahd Academy, a Saudi school in
Bonn with close ties to militant Islamists, was ordered to reform or close.

   Although the Fakihi episode elicited harsh criticism of the Saudis in
the German media, it was not the first "diplomatic incident" involving a
Muslim. In 1993 another Saudi "diplomat," Dr. al-Fatih Ali Hassanein,
had set up TWRA in Bavaria from where he organized his pipeline to ship
arms from friendly Muslim countries to the Balkans. Although thirty
Bosnians and Turks had been quietly indicted in Munich on weapons
and racketeering charges, the German authorities did not intervene in
the activities of TWRA, nor did they interfere with the UN-sponsored
Malaysian and Turkish troops who were using a Turkish charity to smug-
gle weapons from Croatia into Bosnia. The Turks were a sensitive issue in
Germany. Two-thirds of the 4 million Muslims in Germany were Turkish
and for forty years had been an important presence, despite the fact they
could not become German citizens. Their strongest institutional representation was the International Humanitaire Hilfsorganization (International Humanitarian Relief Organization, IHH). IHH, an overseas arm of
the Turkish Prosperity Party (RAFAH), first appeared in Zagreb in 1993.
It smuggled *mujahideen* into Bosnia, and later Algeria. It also worked
closely with Al Kifah, a bogus humanitarian organization founded in
Germany by the Al Qaeda operative Kamar Eddin Kharban, an Algerian Afghan-Arab who worked out of Croatia. It competed with the more
legitimate Diyanet Isleri Turk Islam Birligi, a Turkish government agency
whose representatives regularly spent five-year tours in Germany, and
with the Islamische Gemeinschaft Milli Gorus, a German NGO founded
in 1978 as an association for migrant Turkish workers.[3] The latter is now
in the forefront of the battle against secularization in Germany and is a
powerful funding agency.

   In early 1996 General Asad Durrani, the Pakistani Ambassador to Germany and former chief of ISI, was forced to return home in order not to
answer questions from BfV about the weapons traffic through Germany to
the Islamist jihadists in Algeria. HCI in Europe was the principal financier
for the Algerian GIA through which the Pakistani embassy facilitated the
transfer of weapons. Strangely, the Algerian Islamist leadership "thought

it unnecessary to waste one's time and energy building charities that could reach out to the grassroots." As one observer dryly remarked, they lived in "a fantasy of the Afghan jihad, where it seemed violence was enough."[4]

Muslim Europe

There are 20 million Muslims in the EU, and their growth has been rapid and greater than the indigenous European population. In thirty years the Muslim population in the UK rose from 82,000 in 1970 to 2 million in 2000. France has another 5 million Muslims, mostly North Africans; there are a million Muslims each in Italy and the Netherlands, and a half-million in Spain. By 2000 nearly one in ten babies born in the EU countries was Muslim, and the percentage promised to grow through immigration and the significantly higher birth-rate. By 2020 Muslims will account for 10 percent of Europe's population, and most will likely be living in distinctly Muslim neighborhoods, ghettos, such as those through which Jaber Fakihi circulated. As they tend to congregate in ethnic exclaves, Moroccans with Moroccans, Algerians with Algerians, European investigators have found it extremely difficult to trace the collection and distribution of *zakat* and *sadaqa*, whether inside or outside the local community. What transpires in Europe's mosques remains somewhat of a mystery if for no other reason than that a new mosque has been opened somewhere in Europe every week since 1980. Germany has 8,000 mosques; France has about 10,000, most of them little more than prayer rooms.[5]

The Islamization of Europe began after the Second World War, and grew into a massive migration by the end of the twentieth century. The migrants were mostly poverty-stricken North Africans and Turks seeking work, a higher standard of living, and security from civil strife at home. They settled within their own segregated communities where they could enjoy their own language, culture, and religion. They were mostly law-abiding visitors who quietly continued to abide by the religious practices of Islam. The beginning of the spread of an Islamist doctrine can perhaps be dated from the Third Islamic Summit Conference of Kaaba in 1981 and its "Mecca Declaration" by which *da'wa* was to be used "to propagate the precepts of Islam and its cultural influence in Moslem societies and throughout the world." At first this Islamist ideal had little appeal, until the *mujahideen*'s war against the Soviet Union in Afghanistan, after which the Islamists made determined efforts to spread their ideology into the heartland of Europe, first during the Balkan wars in the 1990s and then embedded within the massive tide of Muslim immigration that followed.[6]

In addition to TWRA the Muwafaq Foundation of Sudan also acted as a cover for illegal activities in Germany. Registered in Karlsruhe in March 1995 but with headquarters in Munich since 1996, the Muwafaq Foundation was involved in illegal financial transfers and arms shipments to *mujahideen* in Bosnia. When interrogated by German police, its Lebanese director, Shafiq Abbadi, admitted his relationship with Yassin al-Qadi, from whom the Foundation had received substantial funding through one of his companies in Istanbul. On his release, Abbadi thought it wise to relocate to Britain, and settled in London. In the late years of the 1990s BfV steadily increased its investigations of Islamic charities to include Khaled bin Mafouz and the Human Appeals International (HAI, Hayat al-Amal al-Khayriyya) charity, which had close ties with Muwafaq. Other investigations involved IHH and the Qatar Charitable Society, but it was not until after 9/11 that the German and other European governments began to work in concert to close down suspect charities. Within a month after 9/11 the fifteen-member EU had frozen the assets of twenty-seven Islamic organizations and individuals linked to terrorism. In all, more than $90 million of suspected terrorist assets were blocked in Britain, France, and Germany.[7] Europe immediately began to enforce old anti-terrorist laws and enact new ones. France restored a 1986 law that allowed special judges to investigate heinous crimes and the police to detain suspects for at least four days without evidence. In Britain, the Terrorism Act of 2000 greatly expanded a 1974 law that prohibited radical groups. In Spain, terrorist suspects could be held for five days without charge, and in Germany laws were passed making terrorist activities a criminal offense.[8]

Germany's problem

The German government also proposed legislation that would have made it difficult for immigrants to enter Germany illegally, stay in Germany illegally, or claim political asylum. The minority Green Party in the Schroeder government refused to support it, however, and thus no penalties were imposed on the Al Nur Mosque in Berlin despite taped phone calls that implicated Fakihi in plans to bomb various German facilities.[9] The possibility that Germany was harboring dangerous jihadists seems only to have been taken seriously when an Algerian member of Al Qaeda was tracked in 1999 to Sydney, Australia, where he was detained and questioned. He was released because Australian officials found it "impossible to determine if the man was engaged in terrorist activities or establishing cells in Australia"; nevertheless, they informed the German government that he was a member of IHH, an aid organization that "was a front for al-Qaeda."[10]

For years the German authorities had been quite content to toler-ate the activities of indigenous Muslim movements. They knew that the *Haus des Islam* in the small town of Lutzelbach near Frankfurt "had been set-up in the 1980s with cash smuggled into the country from the Middle East."[11] The Turkish RAFAH collected *zakat* throughout Germany without any official interference. In the aftermath of 9/11, how-ever, the Germans could no longer remain passive when a Syrian busi-nessman, Muhammad Galeb Kalaje Zouaydi, was found to be connected to an Al Qaeda cell in Germany. Zouaydi also sent money to Mamoun Darkazanli, a Syrian-born financier and suspected "major player in Al Qaeda's European network," who operated an export–import business in Hamburg where he maintained contact with Mohamed Atta of World Trade Center notoriety.[12] Zouaydi was arrested in Spain in April 2002 after the transfer of some $600,000 to the Bin Laden network was discov-ered, and another $211,000 was sent to the Director of the Global Relief Foundation (Fondation Secours Mondial) charity in Belgium. GRF, founded in Chicago in December 1992 by five Muslims, had by 2000 become one of the largest Muslim charities in the USA. It opened satel-lite offices in Pakistan and France, and in 1995 Nabil Sayadi, a Lebanese Belgian citizen, had opened its Brussels office to carry out relief work in Bosnia and the Balkans. Prior to settling in Belgium Sayadi had been for years an associate of Wadih al-Hage, the Bin Laden lieutenant convicted in the Tanzania and Kenya embassy bombings, and he had continued to meet with the terrorist during the 1990s.[13]

During the summer of 2002 the German police finally launched a crackdown on Islamic charities in Germany. In July they raided the Al Aqsa Charity Foundation in Aachen, seized more than 150 crates of documents, and froze $300,000 in its account. The Al Aqsa offices in Aachen and Cologne had been under surveillance "for some time," but the police had refrained from staging a raid until a law had been passed forbidding religious organizations that supported extremists or terror-ism. A few days later the Al Aqsa offices in Solingen and Braunschweig were also raided and more documents and computers were confiscated. The Al Aqsa lawyers insisted that the charities only "provided assistance, such as food medicine and clothing, to needy Palestinians." The German Minister of Interior, Otto Schily, replied coolly that "documents found in the group's headquarters support the government's belief that the charity was assisting HAMAS."[14] Nevertheless, a year later in July 2003 the Leipzig federal court lifted the ban and allowed Al Aqsa to resume fundraising among the German Muslim community. Schily declared their decision "incomprehensible," and the Bavarian state Interior Minister was equally apoplectic, arguing that the verdict of the court "would ren-der terror combat impossible."[15]

In December police raided three more Islamic organizations operating in Baden-Württemberg: the Islamic Workers' Union in Mannheim, the Islamic Community in Germany in Stuttgart, and the Islamic Union of Freiburg. The last was suspected of preparing forged passports and identity cards. The Islamist chase continued into the new year when German agents arrested Yemini Shaykh Mohammad Ali Hassan al-Moayad, the Imam of the Al Ihsan Mosque in Sanaa. Moayad was an important leader of the Yemen Islah Party and the Director of the Yemen office of the Al Aqsa International Foundation (AAIF). Ironically, he was arrested in Germany, not for his activity in conjunction with AAIF, but as the result of an indictment issued in the USA that charged him with providing arms, communications equipment, and *jihad* recruits for Al Qaeda. Moayad and his assistant fought extradition, but the German Federal Constitutional Court ruled he could be bound over. In November 2003 both were indicted in a Brooklyn court for conspiring to provide material support to Al Qaeda and HAMAS, and for supplying Osama bin Laden with $20 million that included funds solicited from members of the Al Farouq Mosque in Brooklyn. On 10 March 2005 a New York jury found him guilty of "providing support and resources to the foreign [Al Qaeda] terrorist organization."[16] German intelligence and security services dramatically increased their surveillance of "semi-state Saudi institutions," a euphemism for Islamic charities, and on "functionaries and private individuals" including the arrival and departures of Muslim diplomats.[17]

Muslims in Italy

Of all the European nations Italy offered the least hospitable environment for immigrant Muslims. The first mosque built in Italy was not opened (in Catania, Sicily) until 1980. Surprisingly, the Vatican, which one would expect to view Muslim migration with suspicion, was more sympathetic to the religious needs of Muslims than were local authorities in Italian cities and towns; it did not object to the construction of the impressive Monte Antenne Mosque financed by the late King Faisal of Saudi Arabia that opened in Rome in 1995. Among the 60 million Italians the Muslim population of Italy was estimated between 800,000 and 1 million in 2000, 100,000 of whom were illegal residents. Islam, however, was not officially recognized by the Italian government, and mosques were under surveillance by the Italian authorities. They would instantly be closed, as in Cremona, if there were any questionable activities.[18] Most Muslim families in Rome and Milan, the two major centers of Italy's Muslim population, remained poor, living in substandard housing, without subsidies or tax benefits. Except for the question of education most parents paid greater attention to events in the Muslim world than the internal affairs of Italy or Europe. There were no state contributions for Muslim schools, and Arabic was taught only through middle school, after which Muslim parents seeking higher education for their children had to send them to their country of origin or elsewhere in the Muslim world. Only 50,000 Muslims are currently registered to vote in Italy.

After Rome, Milan has the highest percentage of Muslim migrants, one in five of whom arrived during the large influx of Muslims in the late 1980s. In order to preserve their own cultural and religious identity they organized their own associations and maintained charities. Some 5,000 Muslim students attended public schools in Milan and the surrounding region; their presence has precipitated vigorous and often hostile debate over Muslim-only classes and the wearing of the headscarf by female students. However, both before and after 9/11 the Milan Muslim community was sharply divided theologically and culturally. The Al Rahman Mosque, opened in 1988, is traditional and apolitical, and welcomes all Muslim immigrants and converts. In contrast, the Viale Jenner Mosque, which takes its name from the street it faces, is located in a rundown section of town and appeals to those Muslims who resist any assimilation. The Jenner Mosque appears to have had few resources, but in July 1996 the editor of *Corriere della Sera*, Guido Olimpio, exposed it as the financial heart of the Egyptian Islamist network. The logistical and banking ties of its radical leadership to Osama bin Laden were discovered, and after 9/11 its bank account was frozen. Nevertheless, it continued to provide a meeting place for Islamic revolutionaries in Europe.

Although the Muslim community in Milan had its own newspaper, *Il messagero del Islam*, it was culturally as well as theologically divided between two cultural associations. The moderate Italian Muslim Association had rejected the Islamist firebrands and considered the Wahhabis a "menace." In contrast, Milan's Islamic Cultural Institute trafficked in arms to support *mujahideen* in the Balkans, maintained close ties with jihadists in Yemen and Peshawar, and was called the Al Qaeda "station house" in Europe, moving weapons, men, and money around the world. The Institute had also provided support for the 1998 bombings of US embassies in Kenya and Tanzania. It also had ties to the Charitable Society for Social Welfare (CSSW), founded in the American Midwest in the mid-1990s, ostensibly to aid the victims of the civil war in Yemen.[19] Funds solicited by CSSW went directly to the Yemen Society for Social Welfare, a charity founded in 1990 and considered to be the first voluntary organization of its kind in Yemen. CSSW also had ties to Yemeni Shaykh Abdullah Satar, a cleric who had visited mosques in Brooklyn and Manhattan, and who was an occasional visitor to the Islamic Cultural Institute in Milan.

After the bombing of the Khobar Tower in 1996 cooperation steadily increased between Italy and the USA. Two years later the Italian police arrested Al Qaeda activists, and in February 2002 a Tunisian suspected of "criminal association" and heading Osama bin Laden's European logistics operations received "the first guilty verdict in Europe related to al-Qaida since September 11."[20] Six months later the USA and Italy designated twenty-five "New Financiers of Terror" who had ties to Al Qaeda, blocked their assets, and submitted their names to the UN 1267 Sanctions Committee.[21] Included on the list were eleven individuals active in Italy and tied to the Algerian terrorist Salafist Brigade for Call and Combat, a faction of the Algerian GIA that operated in Italy, Spain, and North Africa and planned to bomb the US embassy in Rome. Another charity in which the Italian press showed particular interest was Al Awda (Palestine Right to Return Coalition), a charity with its headquarters in Carlsbad, California. Its members were present at the meeting of Islamist militants held in Assisi in September 2003 where the most radical members of the pro-Palestinian militants indicated "a growing alliance between Italy's leftist radicals and Islamists."[22] After the Italian government supported the invasion of Iraq in 2003 five major Muslim organizations issued a position paper in April 2004 entitled "Against the War and Terrorism."[23] This irresolute document demanded an end to the invasion of Iraq, the return of Italian troops, and, almost as an afterthought, an end to terrorism. Thus, it only reinforced the concern that, although the Italian Islamic community was generally conservative and law-abiding, there was a thin stratum of Salafists, including members of the Union of Muslim Organizations of Italy (UCOII), seeking to radicalize the Italian Muslim community while serving as a front for the Muslim Brotherhood.[24]

One of the principal financiers of terrorism in Italy was Bank Al Taqwa. Although its operations have been examined (see chapter 3), it was the center for the commercial network organized by Youssef Mustafa Nada and Ahmed Idris Nasreddin that constituted an extensive financial web in support of terrorist-related activities in Italy. Nada often traveled on an Italian passport, and was well known at the Islamic Center of Milan. Ahmed Idris Nasreddin, a mysterious Ethiopian businessman who reportedly at one time worked for the Bin Laden family construction company, served as the honorary consul of Kuwait in Milan. He had houses in Switzerland, Morocco, and Italy where he was a member of the board of directors of the Milan Islamic Center. He was also President of the Islamic Community of Ticino, a Swiss canton on the Italian border, and used a small Italian enclave, Campione d'Italia on Lake Lugano, as a base for the Nada–Nasreddin business empire in northern Italy and Milan. His empire included the Gulf and African Chamber in Lugano, the Gulf Center SRL, the Nasco Business Residence Center, the Nasreddin Company (Nasco SAS), and the Nasreddin International Group, Ltd. In addition, the Nada–Nasreddin network also held interests "in one or more hotels in Milan." Both men used the Asat Trust to establish yet more shell companies in Liechtenstein, "where no record was kept of activities or transactions on behalf of the companies."[25]

On 7 November 2001 fourteen businesses owned or controlled by either Nada or Nasreddin were designated in the USA and listed by the UN "to disrupt their use of assets under their ownership or control that could be used to finance terrorist activities." The listings were the result of "the collaborative and cooperative efforts" of Italy, the USA, the Bahamas, and Luxembourg. The Nada–Nasreddin network had been financing a plethora of radical groups including HAMAS, Algeria's GIA, Tunisia's Al Nahda, Osama bin Laden, and Al Qaeda. In December 2001 a Zurich paper published an article "concerning a 50 page report by the private Geneva Organisation du Crime Organisé that linked Al-Taqwa to private 'humanitarian' networks."[26] Also drawn into the Nada–Nasreddin net was a Syrian, Baha Eldin Ghrewati, the leader of Italy's Muslim Brotherhood and the brains behind its front organization, UCOII. Ghrewati maintained two homeopathic health centers in Milan and another in Rome that was "used exclusively for closed door meetings by members of the Muslim Brotherhood." He had been a frequent visitor to the Sudan. In 2005 the Nada–Nasreddin empire was still under investigation in Italy, Switzerland, and the USA.

Islam and France

France, historically the most determinedly secular nation in Europe, was by 2000 home to the largest Islamic community in Europe, estimated at between 5 and 8 million Muslims, or roughly 10 percent of its population. Given the disproportionate birth-rates of Muslims compared to non-Muslims in France and the burgeoning growth of legal and illegal immigration, Muslims are likely to be in the majority by the year 2040. From the 1990s the number of militant ideologues, the "Islamist Intelligentsia" as one expert labels them, grew quickly, and their determination and persistence managed to submerge the more moderate Muslims in France.[27] Praise for Osama bin Laden was heard in the mosques; anti-Semitism festered. Some nine of ten imams were foreign born. More than half could not speak French and, despite the efforts of the government to work with the Muslim Council of France to strengthen the Francophone Muslim community, little progress was made. The number of new mosques under construction continued at a rapid pace, and from the ornate Institute of the Arab World in Paris to the most humble mosque in the suburbs, nearly all received some Saudi financial support.

For years the French had sought to establish a single acceptable authority to supervise Islamic activities, and in 1990 it launched the Conseil de Reflexion sur l'Islam de France (CORIF), an umbrella organization that gathered within its folds the numerous and often contentious Muslim associations. That endeavor soon failed, CORIF was disbanded, and the Great Mosque in Paris then became the center for all the diffuse Muslim groups. When chaos ensued, the Minister of the Interior, Nicolas Sarkozy, convened a meeting of Muslim leaders in December 2002 and gave them two days to form a representative body of French Muslims acceptable to the government. The Conseil Français du Culte Musulman (CFCM) was the result of their deliberations, chaired by Dalil Boubakeur, the aging Rector of the Great Mosque. A CFCM Council was elected in April 2003, and despite the fact the Council was more radical than Sarkozy had hoped, the government now had a single organization through which it could monitor the activities of French Muslims. Boubakeur, however, was not neutral. He owed his position and salary to the military government of Algiers and that, from the point of view of the Islamists, vitiated his claim to authority over the Muslim community in France.

Indeed, Sarkozy was already fighting a losing battle to gain control of the powerful and independent Union des Organisations Islamiques de France (French Union of Islamic Organizations, UOIF). UOIF received substantial funding from Saudi "foundations," and was dominated by the Muslim Brotherhood in Europe led by Tariq Ramadan, the Swiss-born grandson of the Egyptian founder, Hasan al-Banna. Sarkozy also could do little to influence the Islamic Countries Educational, Scientific, Cultural Organization (ICESCO), which also received substantial financial assistance from Saudi Arabia and was very active in France. ICESCO proposed to finance a school in France to educate imams that would most certainly result in the spread of the Wahhabi indoctrination of Muslim society in France and the radicalization of a community that was once the province of the more moderate immigrant imams from Algeria.

In Paris, along the Rue du Faubourg Saint-Denis in the Tenth Arrondissement Turks, Algerians, Pakistanis, Tunisians, and Moroccans, who live in low-rent apartments in this decaying enclave, converge on its mosque every Friday around 13:30 and pray for the victory of the Muslim renaissance. It is one of 1,685 mosques that the government officially recognizes and is probably included among the fifty radical mosques that the two domestic intelligence agencies, the Renseignements Généraux (RG) and the Direction de la Surveillance du Territoire, a counter-intelligence agency, watch very closely. Muslim sources, on the other hand, claim that the number of mosques and prayer rooms is at least five times greater than the official figure, mostly located in empty buildings, shabby rooms, basements, and garages where many self-styled imams hold forth. After prayers donations are received on behalf of the "Islamic Salvation Front, Jama'at-Islami, Tanzeem-Islami, Sunni Tehrik, Jamiat Ulema, and the Kashmir Muslim Front."[28] Some donations are delivered directly to International Islamic Aid (IIA) in France. Charities such as IIA are registered in accordance with a 1901 law dealing with charitable organizations, and their accounts can be scrutinized by government officials, but rarely are. There are more than six hundred Islamic associations of one sort or another active in France and most receive little attention, often for political reasons. One such is the very active Pakistan Muslim Welfare Association, a "global network" that receives the support of the Pakistani embassy and was designed to assist immigrant Pakistanis with problems of cultural integration. Less threatening are the regional associations such as the Association des Musulmans de la Gironde and des Alpes Mari in Nice, whose charitable collection and distribution of donations is unusually transparent.

By 1991 the Faubourg Saint-Denis Mosque, which received subsidies from the Saudis, Iraq, UAE, and Kuwait, had attracted the attention of the French authorities. It had become the center for Salafists from Algeria at a time when the political situation in Algeria was deteriorating and Wahhabi ideology was growing among the more than 1 million Algerians living in France. The prospect of the first free national elections in Algeria had precipitated riots in Algiers by the supporters of the Islamic Salvation Front (FIS) of Shaykh Abbasi Medani. FIS, which had been receiving Saudi financial support until Medani endorsed the1990 Iraqi invasion of Kuwait, had substantial numbers of Afghan-Arabs and a network of mosques and Islamic charities that enabled it to win the first phase of the elections in December 1991. When it became apparent that the Islamists were about to triumph in the final vote, the military intervened and the elections scheduled for January 1992 were canceled. A military dictatorship followed. Over the next decade more than 100,000 Algerians perished in the subsequent civil war between the Algerian military and Salafist insurgents that included the infamous "Afghan Legion" trained in Al Qaeda camps. Although many Algerian revolutionaries escaped to France where they joined Al Qaeda cells and kept to themselves, their leaders were not welcome. Algerian rebel leader Abdelkader Benouis fled Algiers for Saudi Arabia, from where he was soon expelled for collecting funds for Al Qaeda. Benouis next appeared in France, but when he began soliciting funds for Islamist movements, he was arrested and expelled. He fled to Pakistan and then Belgium before taking refuge in the UK where from 1998 onward he was under constant surveillance.

In a more recent case, Abdelkader Bouziane, an Algerian-born imam from Lyon, had lived in France for twenty-five years and achieved notoriety for advocating wife-beating and the stoning of women in cases of marital infidelity. When the French courts prevented his expulsion, Sarkozy's successor at the Interior Ministry, Dominique de Villepin, changed the law, and Bouziane was soon deported with the blessing of the Rector of the Great Mosque. M. de Villepin had no illusions about the Islamists. "We need a strong policy to combat radical Islam. It is used as a breeding-ground for terrorism. We cannot afford not to watch them very closely."[29] His anti-Islamist policy was two-pronged. The first was zero tolerance for the slightest incitement to violence by Islamists, which would be met by repressive force. The second sought to gain the initiative by promoting moderate and secular Muslims by a foundation to replace CFCM, which had fallen under the control of the radicals.

Islamic charities, Algerian Islamists, and Palestinians

The "Wahabbi invasion" of Islamic charitable institutions in France began when MWL opened its Paris office in 1979. At the time MWL was principally interested in providing financial assistance for the construction of mosques and *madrasas* and in the 1980s a number of other Saudi charities opened branch offices in France. A decade later a host of obscure Islamic charities sponsored projects "in war-torn countries," particularly Algeria and Palestine. By then the French Ministry of Interior had acknowledged that it had difficulties overseeing the outreach activities of Muslim charities. The Comité de Bienfaisance et Secours aux Palestiniens (CBSP), founded in 1990 in Nancy by members of the Muslim Brotherhood, soon established a powerful presence in France. CBSP was the first charity to use an internet site (www.islamiya.net) to collect *zakat* and *sadaqa*, and it was soon followed by other Islamic charities, giving greater unity to Muslims in France by the click of a computer mouse. A second charity, Secours Islamique (Islamic Relief), founded in 1992, soon supported five offices in the West Bank and Gaza and was considered an especial favorite of the Saudis. In contrast to the questionable activities of such charities as Muwafaq and Al Haramain Foundation, the Nimatullahi Sufi order worked diligently and openly in France. Founded in Persia in the fourteenth century, its successful fund drives enabled the construction of two centers, one east of Paris, the other in a suburb of Lyon. Like Nimatullahi, the other Sufi orders in France were historically ill-disposed to Salafist ideology and Wahhabism; most of their

followers came from the former French colonies in West Africa and
had little interest in supporting revolutionary movements. Many of their
preachers belonged to the Mouride *tariqa*, a dominant force within Sene-
galese Islam that emphasized the virtue of hard work and whose members
paid little attention to the anti-Semitic or pro-Salafist propaganda that so
moved Muslims from the Middle East.

Paris became the favorite European city for numerous Pakistani
Islamists, including Dr. Israr Ahmad, the Islamic revolutionary and *amir*
of Tanzeem-e-Islami since its founding in 1975. Dr. Ahmad first visited
Paris in September 1993 as the guest of an Islamic center operated by
Algerian and Moroccan fundamentalists in the Tenth Arrondissement,
a center that had been under surveillance by the French authorities for
some time. In September 1995 he would address the annual convention
of the Islamic Society of North America in Columbus, Ohio, to warn
Muslims to "prepare themselves for the coming conflict" with the West.[30]
Next, Senator Qazi Hussain Ahmed, Secretary General of Pakistan's
largest Islamic party, the Jama'at-i-Islami, visited Paris from Peshawar
in June 1994 "to meet Algerian FIS members and other Maghrib-
ian fundamentalist activists." Qazi would eventually succeed in uniting
Pakistan's major religious parties in the Muttahida Majlis-e-Amal coalition, and became its Acting President. His enemies have tried to link him
to the Al Rashid Trust and Al Akhtar Trust, two charities later designated
by the USA as sponsors of terrorism.

A month after Qazi's arrival in Paris French police arrested in Perpig-
nan four terrorists from Tangiers. The leader, Hallal Ahmed al-Hamiani,
an Algerian, was a member of Al Kifah, the notorious "humanitarian"
organization and an offshoot of Al Qaeda. The team was preparing to
attack American and Jewish targets in the Barcelona region. In March
1995 Maulana Fazlur Rehman, President of the Pakistani parliamentary
Foreign Relations Committee, visited Paris to meet with the President of
the Pakistan Muslim Social Welfare Association in France. A veteran of
the Afghan war, Maulana was a director of the Da'wa Jihad University
in Kakarkhel near Mardan, which was supported by substantial funding
from the Saudis and UAE. The USA would later accuse the institution
of running terrorist training centers.

All this Islamist activity had not gone unnoticed by the Parisian press.
In August 1993 *La Vie* published an article, "Islamists Give Condi-
tional Food," that questioned the legitimacy of Islamic Relief (Secours
Islamic). Islamic Relief demanded a public apology and threatened to
bring suit; *La Vie* was forced to print an apology and pay legal costs.
When *Le Point* also published a defamatory article against Islamic Relief
on 14 August 1993, the courts ruled against the newspaper, and when

Liberation published an article the following year, August 1994, it too lost a similar suit to Islamic Relief, as did two other newspapers. These setbacks momentarily discouraged investigative journalism by the Parisian press despite the suspicion that Islamic Relief was involved in weapons deals with Bosnia.[31] After a series of bombings in and near French train stations from July to October 1995, the press renewed its inquiries into Algerian Islamists, to discover that as early as 1994 the French Interior Minister had complained to Riyadh about the transfer of Saudi funds for Algerian terrorists.[32] In August 1995 the conservative Paris daily *Le Figaro* reported that French security services were aware that Algerian Islamists had already "set up a security network across Europe with fighters trained in Afghan guerrilla camps and [in] southern France, while some have been tested in Bosnia."[33]

Immediately after the outbreak of the bombings French police were able to attribute them to various Maghrebian Islamist organizations. More than a hundred Islamists, Islamic mosques, charities, and institutions were placed under close scrutiny, and in October and November 1995 additional numbers of Algerian suspects were arrested. The French intelligence service attributed the attacks to Osama bin Laden and to Afghan-Arab sleeper cells that were soon ferreted out by the French security services. In September 1997 the Paris office of CBSP was the subject of a "violent attack" that led the international Islamic Human Rights Commission of France to protest to the French authorities.[34] The Commission's report argued that CBSP was "one of the four charities currently being targeted by the Israeli government." The organizations claimed that the attack was carried out by GSC, known in the Middle East as the Zionist Action Group and called a branch of the Jewish Defense League, a terrorist organization that had emerged in New York during the late 1960s.

By 2002 Palestine had replaced Afghanistan as "the number one cause célèbre of the year" for Islamic charities in France. However, after years of activity there still existed "no official records of the checks sent to local mosques and Islamic charities to rebuild shattered Palestinian communities, nor charitable donations received by other denominations." It was common practice for donations received at the PLO office in France to be forwarded "to charity bank accounts in the Palestinian territories" without recording them. The imam of the Paris Mosque, the de facto leader of the Islamic community in France, continued to urge the collection of *zakat* and participation in charitable works through *sadaqa*, but he limited "direct appeals to prayer" in order to avoid "anything inflammatory that would further divide the Muslim and Jewish communities in France."[35] President Jacques Chirac for years had maintained a very close relationship with Yasir Arafat, and then with Leila Shahid, PLO representative in Paris, and was thus loath to move against the Palestinian activists or HAMAS-related charities. Nonetheless, France had begun to freeze the assets of pro-Palestinian charities by August 2003, and Chirac warned Arafat that "time is of the essence and if nothing is done, France will soon be all alone as the only country supporting you."[36]

When Jacques Chirac visited the Great Mosque in 2002 to meet with the imams of Paris and other cities and with a delegation from the Muslim community, it was the first time that a President of France had visited the Great Mosque since its opening in 1926. Chirac came "to address a message of confidence and gratitude to the Muslim community and its representatives who condemned the September 11th attacks and called for the use of calm, understanding, and dialogue during the current crisis." He stressed the importance of "establishing dialogue between the authorities and Muslim's representatives in France and noted that he has always been in favor of establishing an organization that represents all Muslims with transparency under the umbrella of respecting the laws and principles of the Republic."[37] Time, however, appeared to be on the side of the imams, for a study prepared by French domestic intelligence had found that at least half of the 630 Muslim-dominated suburbs had already drifted far from the mainstream. They had become, the report warned, "separate ethnic communities," ghettoes isolated from mainstream French society that "could encourage radical Islam to take root." Not surprisingly, these suburbs suffered from high unemployment and crime, while "a growing number of Islamic prayer rooms, as well as frequent anti-Western and anti-Semitic graffiti" were omnipresent. Moreover, the French language was rejected by many Muslims. Attendance at Friday prayers had increased, and *zakat* and *sadaqa* were openly donated, not for domestic purposes but for international causes. For decades, France had hoped that its immigrants and their children would simply integrate into secular French society. Instead, the opposite was happening, "with the divide becoming ever greater."[38]

The Netherlands, Belgium, and the Danes

The Netherlands and Belgium, two of the smallest nations of Europe, are considered the most tolerant of varied lifestyles and religious practices. For years they have served as safe havens for Islamists, many of whom would willingly betray their hospitality. The Netherlands was the preferred home for most, and by 2000 there were about 800,000 Muslims and an unknown number of illegal residents living among 16 million Dutch. In the mid-1990s Al Qaeda, the Algerian GIA, and HAMAS were operating freely in Rotterdam, Amsterdam, and Eindhoven. Ayman al-Zawahiri had spent much of 1998 traveling on a Dutch passport, and he returned to visit under the name of Sami Mahmoud al-Hifnawi. The Muwafaq Foundation was active in Breda in southern Holland, and members of the board included its founder, Yassin al-Qadi of Saudi Arabia, and its Director, Chafiq Ayadi of Tunisia, both of whom were later named "designated nationals" on the US Treasury's list. By 1998 the Dutch intelligence agency (Binnelandse Veiligheidsdienst, BVD) had linked the Al Waqf Al Islami Foundation to "extremist" Islamist causes, using the Al Furqan Mosque in Eindoven to solicit *sadaqa* and spread the Wahhabi message. The history of the Al Furqan Mosque, one of the most infamous in Europe, was interwoven with that of the Al Waqf Al Islami Foundation and Ahmed Cheppih, a wealthy Moroccan immigrant who had received political asylum in the 1970s. Cheppih helped found the Al Furqan Mosque in 1989, and using the Al Waqf made it an important center for seminars on Islamic law and other Islamist topics that would attract "several thousand students a year during the 1980s and 1990s." Curiously, in Bulgaria, half a continent distant, Al Waqf Al Islami was, thanks to an infusion of Saudi funds, sponsoring the construction of mosques and schools wherein Wahhabi teaching would dominate. During 1993–1994 it paid for more than a dozen mosques before being expelled without explanation in 1994. Also without explanation, it was allowed to reemerge following 9/11; shortly thereafter a close tie to Eindhoven was discovered. A member of the Eindhoven Al Waqf Al Islami board of directors was Hamad al-Hussein, brother of Abdullah Osman Abdul Rahman al-Hussein, the Director-General of Al Waqf Al Islami itself. The latter had initiated operations in Bulgaria and was named among the participants in the Golden Chain.

At the Al Furqan Mosque the seminars were almost always held in Dutch, "but the message was imported from Saudi Arabia, via Saudi books and lecturers who taught a strict, orthodox interpretation of Islam."[39] They "drilled extremist messages into the heads of thousands of young Muslims from across the Continent," and among its most famous graduates were a "half a dozen members of the group of young men from Hamburg, Germany, who plotted the Sept. 11 attacks" on the USA.[40]

Cheppih's son, Muhammad Cheppih, had been educated in Saudi Arabia, and when he returned to the Netherlands in 2000, he did so as a representative of MWL. Shortly afterward, the Dutch General Intelligence and Security Service (AIVD, formerly BVD) alleged that Cheppih's elementary schools spread "extremist beliefs." When questioned, the elder Cheppih expressed ignorance as to the extent of Al Waqf funding in Eindhoven or for the six primary schools it sponsored. He did admit, however, that MWL spent $50,000 a year to offer courses on Islamic law and beliefs in Rotterdam and Amsterdam. Muhammad Cheppih also represented for a time the Arab–European League (AEL), an immigrant Islamist institution founded in Belgium with Saudi funds by the rabble-rousing Dyab Abu Jahjah, a known Hizbullah terrorist. In Holland the secret service was convinced that AEL was a security risk, but it did not investigate its funding or halt the charity's activities.

After 9/11 the Dutch began to crack down on Islamic charities. The Al Aqsa Foundation, which helped fund many Palestinian causes, was closed and its assets frozen while the government sought to find any links it had to terrorist groups. The Al Haramain Foundation was also under suspicion. Linked to the 1998 attacks on US embassies in Africa, it was represented in Amsterdam by the Al Tawhid Mosque and Foundation, another major Saudi charity. The Al Haramain Director, Uqayl bin Abdul Aziz al-Uqayl (Aqeel al-Aqeel), a strong supporter of the Islamic struggle in Chechnya, served on its board.[41] While Al Haramain continued to operate in the Netherlands, the Dutch authorities discovered that Al Qaeda was using the Funds Beyond Frontiers Foundation internet website (www.qoqaz.nl) to collect charity in support of the *jihad* in Chechnya. It praised "brother Osama bin Laden," and urged Muslims "to learn firearms skills at shooting clubs and to join karate clubs." Jihadists were especially encouraged to join the Dutch army in order to receive proper military training.

By 2002 Dutch police estimated that the Taliban movement in Afghanistan could count on some one thousand sympathizers in the Netherlands, some of whom served on the boards that governed the activities of Islamic schools. The number seemed small, but in Amsterdam, where 88,000 Muslims constituted 13 percent of its 600,000 inhabitants, there was deep concern by many Dutch that, given the high birth-rate among Muslims, in twenty years half of all children under the age of eighteen would be Muslim.[42] Anti-Muslim sentiment played a significant role in the election of the flamboyant Pym Fortuyn, a politician who was often labeled a bigot or racist for expressing the opinion that Muslim immigrants were playing too great a role in Dutch affairs. He appealed to those Dutch who wanted to limit or halt entirely Muslim immigration and prevent any aspects of the Shari'a creeping into Dutch law. Not surprisingly, he received widespread support in Rotterdam. Stung by the growing enthusiasm for Fortuyn, Dutch officials began to investigate Islamic schools, to discover that many were funded by an "intolerant Islamic foundation in Saudi Arabia," others had ties to HAMAS, and most were supported by other Islamic charities. "It has become evident that the objectives of the World Islamic Call Society, the Al Waqf al

Islam Foundation, and the Diyanet [the Government of Turkey religious affairs directorate for 320,000 Turks in Holland] are damaging the Dutch democratic order."[43] In May 2002 Fortuyn was assassinated by an ethnic Dutch animal rights activist who was, to the great relief of politicians and public alike, neither Muslim nor an immigrant.

Although many Dutch regarded Fortuyn's assassination an aberration, they could no longer remain indifferent or tolerant after a second political murder. The people of the Netherlands were deeply shocked by the November 2004 assassination of the well-known provocative film director Theo van Gogh, and by the way it was done. A twenty-six-year-old *jallaba*-clad Moroccan, Muhammad Bouyeri, emptied a magazine of bullets into his victim, stabbed him as he lay dying, and then finished by leaving a note pinned to his body with a knife. He had been murdered as he was cycling to his studio to edit a film about Pim Fortuyn. Van Gogh had been an outspoken critic of Islam, and had called the radical Islamists "a fifth column of goatfuckers." The assassin was arrested along with another thirteen Islamists, all of whom were members of the "Hofstad Network" whose spiritual leader was a forty-three-year-old Syrian, Redouan Issar.

The gulf between the 16 million ethnic Dutch and 1 million Muslims now appeared irreparable. "The jihad has come to the Netherlands," declared Jozias van Aartsen, a leading Christian Democrat. Mosques and Muslim schools that were attacked retaliated with strikes against Christian churches and street battles in The Hague. The government tightened immigration controls, but many Dutch were convinced that the idea of building a multicultural society had failed. Their solution was integration. Thus, it was now high time for the 1 million Dutch Muslims, 95 percent of whom were moderates, to isolate some 50,000 potential Islamists by adopting the Dutch language, culture, and way of life – voluntarily or, if necessary, by force. On 23 December 2004 the Dutch Ministry of the Interior did the unthinkable by publicly singling out the Muslim community in an AIVD report, *From Dawa to Jihad*, describing militant Islam and examining how to meet its very serious threat to Dutch society.[44]

In Belgium, virtually no effort was made by the authorities to investigate Muslim organizations. The government, in fact, was even more resolute than the French in its support of the Palestinians and was one of the few that publicly criticized the USA for its tough stand on terrorism. Although there were active Al Qaeda cells in Belgium, the government only moved to close them down or extradite their leaders when it could no longer ignore their presence. Meanwhile, the government continued to support the Executive Commission for Belgian Muslims financially.[45] An example of the unwillingness of the Belgian authorities to crack down on radical Islamists or their charities was its reluctance to interfere in the activities of Fondation Secours Mondial (FSM), the GRF branch in Belgium. It had been the recipient of some $600,000, which was later used in support of an Al Qaeda network managed by the Syrian businessman Muhammad Zouaydi, a "senior Bin Ladin financier." On another occasion, $205,853 was sent to Nabil Sayadi (aka Abu Zaynab), the GRF Director of Operations for Europe and "the head of the Global Relief Operations in Belgium."[46] After Sayadi had opened the GRF office in Belgium, between 1995 and 2001 he handled $1.6 million, half of which came from the Chicago office. Although Belgian authorities would eventually freeze the GRF accounts, no criminal charges were brought against Sayadi or the charity. Instead, Sayadi was granted Belgian citizenship despite the fact that he was a close friend of Rabih Haddad, another notorious Al Qaeda member and GRF official arrested in the USA in 2002. The Belgian authorities did not appear to appreciate creeping terrorism in Europe even after the attack on the Belgian consulate in Casablanca in May 2003. "The fact that the terrorists tried to attack the diplomatic facility of one of the most Muslim friendly countries in the West should make it clear that they do not hate the West for its alleged pro Israel bias or its colonial past: They simply hate it for what it is and for the values for which it stands."[47] Liberal Belgium could escape neither its European heritage nor its Christian past, even in denial.

Despite the growing Muslim unrest in Belgium's major cities, its politicians and media refused to be drawn into the debate over Muslim immigration that was sweeping through Europe. Belgians have been proud to welcome the surge of immigrants from Muslim countries during the past forty years. However, there now exists a second generation of Muslims, many born in Belgium, who, unlike their parents, have found acculturation difficult or even impossible. Not surprisingly, they too demand Islamic schools and the acceptance of Arabic as multilingual Belgium's fourth official language, even though its 400,000 Muslims comprise only 5 percent of the population. Whether the government wished to acknowledge it or not, "Belgium was a recruiting ground for Islamic militants with at least one in ten mosques used to spread anti Western ideas."

The radical Islmists were concentrated mostly in Antwerp, the home of AEL where its leader, the Hizbullah *mujahid* Dyab Abu Jahjah, advocated "a form of separatism for Belgian Muslims." They believed time was on their side, for "fifty seven percent of the children born in Brussels are Muslims, which means that Belgium will be a completely different country in a few decades."[48] AEL led marches, inflamed Muslims by preaching anti-Semitism, and opened its first branch in the Netherlands, which many in Holland thought "ill considered."[49] Moreover, the Belgian government, despite appeals from Washington, refused to take any action against GRF.[50] After all, a royal decree had recognized Islam as a religion respected in the country and recognized in its laws. Some 800 Muslim teachers had been appointed by the Executive Commission for Belgian Muslims despite the fact that thirty of the 300 mosques in Belgium were dominated by Islamists who openly supported Bin Laden and Salafists. However, liberal Belgium has not been without its anti-immigrant faction. The Vlaams Blok Party, the most popular party in Flanders, particularly in Antwerp and Mechelen, was determined to halt the flood of immigrants and to curtail the benefits automatically granted to Muslims once they reach Belgium, legally or illegally. Still, the mainstream parties have resisted working with its leaders and on 9 November 2004 the Belgian Appeal Court banned the party for violating anti-racism laws.

Like the Netherlands and Belgium, Denmark had to confront many of the same problems produced by Muslim immigration. It had a substratum of Salafist clerics and a very active Islamic Center that opened in 1999 and was financed by the Shaykh Zayed bin Sultan al-Nahayyan Charitable and Humanitarian Foundation of the UAE. Throughout the 1990s Denmark had been a popular stopover for Al Qaeda members and for a time the residence of Ayman al-Zawahiri. During the European crackdown on the Al Aqsa Charity Foundation after 9/11, however, the Copenhagen police seized $539,000 from Al Aqsa that had been collected from Muslims in Denmark and used by the charity to finance terrorist operations in the Middle East.[51] In February 2003 the director of the Al Nur Islamic Information office was arrested in Denmark for photographing sensitive security installations. The Al Nur press was used by such radicals as the Jordanian Abu Muhammad al-Maqdisi to spread the Takfiri ideology, the ultimate Salafist doctrine. The Hizb ut-Tahrir in Denmark also underwent a lengthy probe resulting from certain anti-Semitic statements, even though there were only 6,000 Jews in Denmark among the 5.4 million Danes and 200,000 Muslims. The case was dismissed by the Justice Ministry in January 2004 after an eighteen-month investigation, but Muslim immigration was a major issue in the Danish elections that resulted in a center-right coalition defeating the Socialists for the first time in more than seventy years. To become a permanent resident an immigrant must now live in Denmark for seven years, and in 2004 a fifteen-year-old agreement that permitted the Turkish Dayanet to send imams to Denmark was canceled.[52]

The United Kingdom

Prior to 9/11 the UK had already established a system for the regulation of charities far superior to any other country in Europe. The Charity Commission for England and Wales was granted extensive regulatory powers, including the ability to audit, review correspondence, freeze bank accounts, remove directors, and investigate and rectify the misuse of funds. Similar regulatory powers devolved to the Scottish Charities Office and in Northern Ireland to the Police Service of Northern Ireland and the Department for Social Development. In the early 1990s the authorities were permitted to investigate charities that might be involved with terrorist organizations, and they could request criminal prosecution if warranted. Between 1980 and 2000 Islamic charities sprouted like mushrooms. Among the many, the Kurdish Cultural Centre (KCC) was created in 1985; the Al Furkan Islamic Heritage Foundation in 1988; the Waqf Al Birr Education Trust in 1992; the United Kingdom Islamic Education Foundation in 1994. Muslim Aid, established in 1985, assisted Muslim victims of poverty, war, and natural disasters. Islamic Relief Worldwide of the UK, founded in Birmingham in 1984, concentrated on international relief and development in response to famines in Ethiopia and the Sudan. Muslim Hands was established in 1993 to help the needy of the world by medical and educational programs and emergency relief. The IQRA Trust Prisoners' Welfare worked to promote a better understanding of the needs of Muslim inmates in British prisons. Muslim immigrants were responsible for the creation of the Yemeni Development Forum, a non-profit British-registered organization determined to alleviate poverty and enhance development. The Turkish Advisory and Welfare Centre assisted the Turkish community in the Lewisham Borough with health services, education, welfare, and housing. By 9/11, Muslim charities in the UK were many and varied, and much of their work was devoted to religious education and the strengthening of the Muslim identity.

One of the oldest charities in the UK is the Welfare Association (Ta'awoun), a private, non-profit foundation established in 1983 in Geneva with offices in the UK. For years it sustained Palestinian emigrants in the Diaspora. Likewise, the Palestine Relief and Development Fund (INTERPAL), a non-political, non-profit, and independent charitable organization concerned with providing support for poor and needy Palestinians in the West Bank, Gaza Strip, and refugee camps in Jordan and Lebanon. Medical Aid for Palestine (MAP) was a UK charity established in 1984 to provide medical facilities to the survivors of the Sabra and Shatilla refugee camp massacres in West Beirut. Save the Children charity had created Eye to Eye, a well-known NGO that gave assistance to young Palestinian refugees in Lebanon, Gaza, and the West Bank funded by the International Programme of the National Lottery Charities Board.

The proliferation of Islamic charities went largely unnoticed in Britain because officials were confident their monitoring was very effective; thus they saw no cause for alarm. Nevertheless, even among the best Islamic charities there were those that became "problems" and required careful surveillance. First and foremost was Islamic Relief Worldwide. A welfare organization founded in 1984 by Dr. Hany El Banna with headquarters in Birmingham and linked to the Muslim Brotherhood, it maintained regional offices in Albania, in the north Caucasus, and in Montreuil, a Paris suburb and home to many Algerian Salafists. The Director of the Al Haramain Foundation, Khaled al-Fawaz, was regularly questioned by Scotland Yard after September 1998.[53] The website azzam.com was located in the UK, and it shopped for funds with the appeal that the Taliban needed to raise $10 million a month "in order to repel a chemical weapons attack on Afghanistan by the United States." The site was managed by Babar Ahmad, who was later arrested and faced extradition charges related to "soliciting funds for use in terrorism."[54] Established in 1984, Islamic Relief Worldwide was collecting donations as early as 1988 to support Muslim refugees fleeing Serbia. It opened an office in Albania in 1992 where it provided for refugees. In 1999 alone it had closely supervised the distribution of more than £1.8 million ($3.4 million) for food, clothing, bedding, and medical supplies, and at one time it met the needs of about 5,000 refugees at a camp in Shkodre, Albania. Muslim Aid also collected donations from a broad spectrum of donors – mosques, Jewish centers, and Christian charities – in support of Kosovar refugees. In 1989 alone it allocated £1.5 million ($2.8 million) for food and medicines to assist refugees in Albania, Macedonia, and Montenegro.[55]

While the Charity Commission could monitor Islamic charities in the UK, the authorities had less success in keeping track of dubious individuals who took advantage of the ease with which Islamists from Egypt, Saudi Arabia, Pakistan, Kashmir, and India obtained political asylum in Britain. Newcomers could disappear in mosques, *madrasas*, and charities and attract little attention. For example, in December 1995 British police raided the London residence of an Algerian expatriate who had "disappeared." There they found communications from GIA, already suspected of seven bombings in France that had killed seven and wounded 180, and bank transfers that were traced to Khartoum and the headquarters of Osama bin Laden.

When the Committee for the Defense of Legitimate Rights was banned by Saudi Arabia in May 1993, Muhammad al-Maasari, its founder, moved the organization to London. Here Maasari was joined by Kahled al-Fawaz from Khartoum, and the two began to receive substantial funding from unknown sources. They created a radical Islamist telecommunications network that, among other things, translated and distributed Osama bin Laden's 1996 *fatwa* declaring war against the USA. Maasari, however, was not the only friend Osama bin Laden had in London.

Abu Qutada, born Omar Mahmud Othman on 13 December 1960, was a Palestinian of Jordanian origin and a veteran of the Afghan war. In London he directed the recruitment for Al Qaeda and became the spiritual leader of GIA. In the late 1990s he edited the Islamist journal *Al Ansar*, and was a close associate of Abu Dahdeh, the leader of the Al Qaeda cell in Spain. In London Abu Qutada made no effort to disguise his belief that Islamic charity should be given directly to support *mujahideen* and not to the mosques. When Abu Qutada was finally arrested in South London in October 2002 the police found $200,000 in cash; he was thought to have been the mastermind behind the transfer of funds from European terrorist cells to *mujahideen* and was wanted in France and Spain. The British authorities confiscated his passport and placed him in detention without trial.

Dr. Ayub Thakur, Kashmiri expatriate and President of the World Kashmir Freedom Movement, arrived in London in 1986 and soon became the director of Mercy International Relief Organization (MIRO) in the UK. Registered in Switzerland and led by Sahid Shaykh, MIRO had been used as cover by Al Qaeda terrorists who bombed the US embassies in Kenya and Tanzania. In 1993 Thakur was accused by the government of India of funding Kashmiri *mujahideen*, and he was implicated in a spate of *hawala* scandals that had plagued India. His passport was impounded in the UK, and after his death in March 2004, the British Charity Commission decided to investigate the questionable movement of MIRO funds, especially to its office in Srinagar.[56] Other charities were dealt with more severely. In 2002 the International Development Foundation was closed because of its ties to Osama bin Laden, and one of its donors, Khaled bin Mahfouz, was labeled "not the sort of person we would want connected to a charity in this country."[57] Outlawed in Israel in 1997 for supplying support to HAMAS, the UK INTERPAL office was named a Specially Designated Global Terrorist organization and closed, and in October 2002 the Chancellor of the Exchequer, Gordon Brown, froze the accounts of BIF UK, which was "extensively" involved in fundraising in support of international terrorism.

Following 9/11 the public learned that many young British Muslims had died in Afghanistan, fighting alongside the Taliban. Scores had traveled to Kabul, many explaining to friends that they were involved in "humanitarian work." In the UK itself, Pakistanis were generally opposed to that war; in one poll taken, 90 percent of respondents claimed they would not take up arms for the UK, although half said they would do so for Islam.[58] The Pakistani-dominated and self-selected Muslim Council of Britain, founded in 1997 and considered the voice of moderate Islam, was then scrutinized by the authorities. Subsequently, it was found that the organization, which sponsored numerous charitable works, was in fact closely tied to the radical Jama'at-i-Islami of Pakistan.

Finsbury Park Mosque

After 9/11 Scotland Yard became ever more interested in Al Muhajiroun (the Emigrants, AM), a charitable society founded in the UK on 16 February 1996 by a Syrian, Omar Bakri Muhammad. Educated at Al Azhar and a Muslim Brother, Omar Bakri had been expelled from Saudi Arabia in 1986. He took refuge in Britain where he and Farid Kasim, a fellow Syrian, founded Hizb ut-Tahrir UK. They soon had the reputation "as the most vocal, visible, and active Islamist organizers in the UK," particularly on university campuses. Bakri split from the Hizb ut-Tahrir movement in 1996 when he founded AM. He became its self-proclaimed spiritual leader and by 1997 was widely known as the "Tottenham Ayatollah." Bakri established a National Da'wa Committee, proclaimed himself "a judge of the self styled British Court of Shariah," and founded Al Khilafah Publications. Numerous AM fronts were founded, including the Society of Muslim Lawyers and the Society of Converts to Islam. Dummy corporations were created, including Info 2000 Software for "raising money through donations." It and the Muslim Cultural Society of Enfield and Haringey, a registered charity established in May 1994, were closed by British authorities in November 1999. AM jihadists were "taught by the organization that Israel, the Jews and the West are evil and that it is their Muslim duty to fight them."[59] The center of AM activity was the Finsbury Mosque Trust, a registered charity located in north London.

The Trust was registered in August 1988, "to advance and promote the knowledge of the religion of Islam in the UK and abroad." Nearly a decade later, in May 1998, when the Charity Commission sought to investigate complaints about the Trust, the commissioners were not allowed to enter the mosque to evaluate the collection of funds raised during Friday and other prayer meetings. Investigators found Muslims living in the mosque itself in violation of the terms of the Trust. In fact, the Finsbury Park Mosque had been occupied by an Egyptian, Abu Hamza al-Masri (aka Mustafa Kemal), a jihadist and founder of the Supporters of Sharia and AM. Abu Hamza, a one-eyed fanatic who had lost both hands in Afghanistan, issued tapes, gave fiery sermons at Friday prayers, and recruited jihadists prepared to kill westerners living in Muslim countries. He used the dilapidated Finsbury Park Mosque for meetings of Supporters of Sharia and AM that were political rather than charitable. Outsiders were not welcome. In June 1998 an inquiry was begun by the

Charity Commission, and by November it had obtained an agreement with Abu Hamza to return the mosque to its trustees on the condition that he be permitted to preach.

Even before 9/11, the UK had received scores of protests from foreign governments, both in the West and in the Middle East, concerning "Britain's protection of, and refusal to extradite, known terrorists." The government appeared "to have taken the view that Islamic terrorism affected Israel and the Arab countries, but not Britain, so Britain could afford to ignore it." Former Taliban were "being accorded not just asylum, but British taxpayer legal aid, to claim, and be granted 'asylum' in Britain."[60] After 9/11, however, the Charity Commission hurriedly undertook inquiries into the activities of a number of Muslim charities – the Margate Muslim Association, Muslim Girls' and Young Women's Association, the Muslim Cultural Society of Enfield and Haringey, the Ahmadiyya Muslim Association, Muslim Welfare House, the Muslim Association of Thanet, and finally the Finsbury Park Mosque. Within a month of 9/11 the Charity Commission had received a tape of an Abu Hamza sermon that "was of such an extreme and political nature as to conflict with the charitable status of the Mosque." Still the government refused to close it down. Instead, the feckless mosque trustees were ordered to prevent Abu Hamza from using it for political activities. Finally, in April 2002 Abu Hamza was "suspended," and the mosque's bank account with Barclays Bank PLC frozen, but Abu Hamza continued to live in the mosque.

By January 2003 the British government had lost all patience with Abu Hamza and the trustees. Police raided the mosque, to discover it was being used to support terrorist activity – which should have come as no surprise. The Charity Commission declared that the Finsbury Park Mosque trustees "had lost effective control," for Abu Hamza and his supporters contemptuously ignored them while planning and participating in illegal activities. The trustees had not been allowed to audit financial transactions, "nor did they possess the accounting records needed to enable them to compile accounts" despite the Commission's orders in September 1999 that such records be made available to the trustees.[61] Despite an official government report that claimed "the UK is recognized to have one of the best systems for regulating charities in the world," the government remained reluctant to end activities in the mosques that supported the Islamist jihadists.[62] Instead, it created two new security agencies: a branch of the traditional security service (MIS) and the National Terrorist Financial Investigation Unit (NTFIU) within the Special Branch at New Scotland Yard to assist the Terrorist Finance Unit of the National Criminal Intelligence Service (NCIS), which was determined to staunch the flow of funds to terrorist organizations. "After eavesdropping for months on his nightly praise of the 9/11 highjackers and of suicide bombings," by January 2005 Scotland Yard's patience was finally exhausted, and it decided to deport the leader of AM, the largest Muslim organization in the UK, known simply as Shaykh Omar.[63] By 2004 the UK had frozen the assets of more than a hundred organizations, mostly charities, and 200 individuals.[64] Finally, Abu Hamza himself was arrested in May 2004 in response to a warrant of extradition by the USA. On 19 October 2004, he was charged in a sixteen-count indictment of "soliciting or encouraging persons [jihadists] to murder those who did not believe in Islam."[65]

Yet some good came out of the Finsbury Park follies. The trustees of all British charities with incomes over £10,000 per annum have ten months from the end of the charity's fiscal year to submit its audited accounts to the Commission. Ostensibly, any charity that does not meet its legal obligations is subject to closure. Moreover, the UK has strongly supported the UN Counter Terrorism Committee and provides it technical assistance, and the Philippines, for one, has asked the British Charity Commission to help them create its own organization to emulate the British in controlling its charities. Still, in the UK problems continued to surface. In February 2005 the US Treasury listed the Birmingham-based Islamic Relief Agency (IRSA) for reportedly funding both Al Qaeda and HAMAS. Although it had long-standing ties to the notorious Islamic African Relief Agency (and was considered its successor), the IRSA office in the UK continued to function as British officials undertook their own investigation.

Despite these warnings the British public continued to believe that they were immune to Muslim extremists, and that their relationship with the Muslim immigrant community was one of mutual respect and appreciation for Britain's willingness to give generous asylum to Muslims thereafter protected by the fortress of British law. This complacency was shattered suddenly and violently during the morning rush hour of 7 July 2005 when three bombs exploded on the London Underground and a fourth on a bus, killing 56 people and injuring another 700. Al Qaeda claimed responsibility. On 21 July a second series of explosions erupted, but miraculously there were no fatalities or injuries. As in the USA after 9/11 and the swift passage of the Patriot Act, Prime Minister Tony Blair immediately proposed a raft of stringent anti-terrorism measures. Whether and in what form this controversial legislation is enacted, there now remains widespread agreement in the public, press, and Parliament that Britain cannot return to the blissful days before 7/7.

11   Islamic charities in North America

> O, brothers, after Afghanistan, nothing in the world is impossible for us
> anymore. There are no superpowers or mini-powers – what matters is
> the will power that springs from our religious belief.
>
> Shaykh Abdullah Azzam, Islamic training center, Oklahoma City, 1988[1]

The few Americans present at the meeting between President Franklin
Delano Roosevelt and King Saud bin Abd al-Aziz al-Saud aboard the
USS *Quincy* in Great Bitter Lake in the Suez Canal on 14 February 1945
did not realize that it was the beginning of a political tapestry between
the USA and the Kingdom of Saudi Arabia that would build, fray, but
never unravel in an alliance that would endure for more than fifty years.
Although the US Department of State has been much involved in the
affairs of the Middle East since that meeting, by and large Americans
have paid little attention to the growing Saudi influence or the Islamic
presence in their country.

In 1970 the Islamic Center of Washington DC was the only mosque in
the greater Washington area; a quarter-century later a network of mosques
had been established around the capital. In the Dar Al Hijrah Mosque in
Falls Church and the Islamic Center in Herndon the faithful listened to
clerics preaching in the revolutionary tradition of the thirteenth-century
Islamist Ibn Tamiyya for Muslims to return to the purity and virtue of
early Islam.[2] As elsewhere in the non-Islamic world, the financial foundations for this expanding Islamic network came from Saudi Arabia. In
the USA and Canada an estimated 8 percent of all Islamic establishments
received some Saudi financial support for many years. The Muslim Students' Association of the United States and Canada (MSA) was founded
with Saudi money as a branch of MWL and consequently was Wahhabi
in its propagation of Islam from its chapters in some 175 colleges and
universities.[3] By 1995 the MSA website at Ohio State University was
computer friendly and Salafist in tone and message. MSA also helped to
raise money for a number of Muslim charities that were later accused of
being fronts for financing terrorism abroad.

The radicalization of the campus chapters and young Muslims who had previously been concerned with good works, religious studies, and leftist international politics was now being undertaken by Salafist Islamists whose influence spread from MSA into other hitherto benign Islamic organizations, including the important Islamic Society of North America (ISNA). ISNA operated more than 320 of the 1,200 mosques in the USA, and the important Council of American–Islamic Relations (CAIR), both of which were beholden to the Saudi Arabian embassy.[4] By the mid-1990s, however, MSA had become thoroughly infiltrated by Salafist radicals hostile to the Saudi royal family, and they were moving the goals of MSA in a direction hostile to their Wahhabi paymasters. By 9/11 the majority of MSA chapters had been taken over by Islamists and were anti-American and anti-Saudi royal family; their agenda exuded intolerance and rejected American values. Even after 9/11 when MSA sought to moderate its image, it was difficult to reverse course given the strident rhetoric that dominated its meetings and its computer website. In the USA the tragic events of 9/11 dramatically destroyed the tolerant complacency toward Islam. New initiatives were devised to make America more secure, and Title III of the Patriot Act enacted on 26 October 2001 included specific provisions against money-laundering and terrorist financing that soon led investigators to Islamic charities.

Investigating charities

Despite a 1996 anti-terrorism law that made it a crime to provide material support to any group designated a terrorist organization, the investigations of suspect Muslim charities were few and prosecutions rare. Grand juries had been impaneled in Illinois, New York, and Texas, but the only indictments issued prior to 9/11 were against those refusing to testify. It was only in the immediate aftermath of 9/11 that the White House moved with alacrity to freeze the assets of Muslim charities. Executive Order 13224, signed on 23 September 2001 by President George W. Bush, invoked the International Emergency Economic Powers Act and thereby established the legal framework needed to investigate the active terrorist infrastructure in the USA. Another executive order authorized US financial institutions to issue "blocking orders" that froze the assets of 321 individuals and organizations amounting to some $125 million. Included were those Islamic charities affected by 501(c)(3) of the Internal Revenue Service (IRS) Code that governs non-profit charitable or educational institutions. The Treasury Department specifically sought the financial records of eight Islamic charities including those of Islamic Relief

Worldwide of Burbank, the Islamic Center in Tucson, Care International, Inc. (no relationship to CARE International) of Boston, GRF, BIF, and the Islamic Association for Palestine (IAP), all with offices in Illinois. Banks and financial institutions that, wittingly or unwittingly, supported terrorist organizations were investigated, and state association regulators were instructed to maintain files on charities that would include income tax returns, state incorporation records, and audits, if any.

In a curious way, the very secular IRS publicly supports one of the essential pillars of Islam, *zakat*. Just like *zakat* committees, IRS permits US citizens giving to worthy causes a financial deduction not dissimilar to the annual voluntary contribution of *zakat*. These alms, for that is what they are, can be donated to support religion, education, citizenship, veterans' groups, public health, combat disease, etc., but the recipient charities must submit a yearly tax return open to public scrutiny. Ironically, government prosecutors had long used charges of racketeering and tax evasion against drug traffickers and mafia bosses that could now be used against directors of charities. Yet to investigate a well-known drug lord or mafia chieftain was one thing; to examine the books of religious charities was quite another. To apply such statutes to any religious denomination was virtually unheard of, and it troubled those determined to maintain the separation between church and state, defend religious freedom, and preserve the human rights of religious donors. Moreover, the silent invasion of Islamic charities had largely gone unnoticed by a government that only kept data on legal immigrants by country and knew virtually nothing about its Muslim community. For years the government had failed to investigate any linkage between questionable donations and Islamic charities, especially since the Muslim community was evolving into a powerful voting bloc in the USA with Muslims numbering some 5.2 million in 1991 and more than 8 million a decade later. Moreover, the investigation of suspected Islamic charities was no easy task. There were more than 1,200 mosques/Islamic centers and 426 Muslim associations in the USA, and most were actively collecting and distributing *zakat* and *sadaqa*.[5] Virtually every major Islamic charitable institution in the USA and Canada, however, had been infiltrated by Islamists. Thus, the Holy Land Fund for Relief and Development (Holy Land Foundation, HLF) of Texas, BIF, Al-Nasr International, and GRF all of Illinois, World and Islamic Studies Enterprise (WISE) of Florida, Islamic African Relief Agency (IARA) of Missouri, the Al Haramain Foundation of Oregon, the Islamic Assembly of North America of Michigan, and the SAAR Foundation of Virginia would all be investigated.

Ironically, in 1999 the Muslim community had presented the Clinton administration with guidelines acceptable to the Islamic charities.

They would have strengthened mainline Muslims against the increasing attacks upon them by the Islamists. The leaders of the Muslim community were willing to adopt "a policy of complete transparency," and they appeared "eager to show the government where their money comes from and what they use it for."[6] The move was long overdue. An effort had been made in 1993 to identify those charities connected with HAMAS, but the subsequent investigation by the FBI elicited no change in policy or action.[7] In 1995 President Clinton was urged to create a "President's List" of terrorist organizations, "their members and donors," and to warn the Muslim community that "well intentioned donations" could be funneled to terrorist groups. A year later he was advised to prohibit certain Islamist fundraising. Clinton rejected these recommendations, and FBI agents "were prevented from opening either criminal or national-security cases," for fear that such activities would be regarded as "profiling Islamic charities."[8] And when the Muslim community again came forward after 9/11 seeking "federally sanctioned guidelines" in order "to conduct a thorough legal and financial audit, one that will provide a clean bill of health," nothing happened.[9]

In designing anti-terrorist legislation Congress has relied heavily on the annual State Department report, *Patterns of Global Terrorism*. First published in October 1986, it listed and described worldwide state-sponsored terrorism and terrorist organizations. In addition, the State Department issued other occasional reports including a 1996 short history on Osama bin Laden. After 9/11 the FBI and the Treasury Department, both of which had been slow to gather data on Islamists in the USA, quickly joined the hunt for terrorists.[10] Unfortunately, many Muslims in America regarded the government attack on suspicious Islamic charities as an attack on Islam. Charity is one of the most respected basic tenets of Islam, and by closing its charities the government had given Americans the false impression that American Muslims were supporting terrorists. It had also given the Muslim world a similarly false impression that America was intolerant of a religious minority.

There was a danger that the American public would lump all Muslim charities in the same boat, but questions were bound to surface that demanded answers: Did suspected officials of the various charities know one another? Did they coordinate their efforts? Was there a larger conspiracy at work in the USA? In fact, many Islamists did indeed know one another. They met at important gatherings held in New York in 1988 and Chicago in December 1989 at a meeting sponsored by the Islamic Committee for Palestine (ICP) attended by Bashir Nafi, a founder of EIJ, and Abd al-Aziz Odeh, the financial and spiritual leader of Palestine Islamic Jihad (PIJ). All the major Islamists visited the

USA, including Ayman al-Zawahiri on numerous occasions and Hasan al-Turabi at Tampa and Washington DC in 1992. Musa Abu Marzouk lived in the USA; Abdullah bin Laden and Shaykh Abd al-Rahman were regulars at various conferences; Shaykh Qaradawi attended the HAMAS Conference in Kansas City in 1989; Shaykh Abdullah Azzam arrived at an Islamic training center at Oklahoma City in 1988, and Shaykh Mubarik Ali Gilan, a Pakistani visitor and founder of the radical Muslims of the Americas, arrived in 1990. Shaykhs Zindani and Maasari were rumored to have visited the USA on fundraising missions at one time or another prior to 9/11. Only Osama bin Laden stayed away, first because he was building an organization, originally in Afghanistan and then in the Sudan, and also because he may have been "spooked" by being named a co-conspirator in the March 1993 World Trade center bombing.

When the Bush administration froze the assets of BIF, GRF, and HLF, other Muslim leaders were concerned that the Muslim community would reduce its charitable giving. When HLF was investigated at Rancho Penasquitos, San Diego, California, it was regarded as an affront to the imam, Mohammad al-Mezain, Director of the prosperous American Muslim Coalition of San Diego county, with fourteen mosques and 100,000 Muslims. Al-Mezain was recognized as a popular HAMAS fundraiser, and for years the American Muslim Coalition of San Diego had sent its *Islam Report* to likeminded internet websites, listing its bank account for potential donations.[11] This was an expensive operation, and any diminution of funds was bound to curtail its numerous questionable activities.

BIF and GRF[12]

The Benevolence International Foundation (BIF) was a derivative of the Islamic Benevolence Committee (Lajnat al-Birr al-Islamiyya, LBI), one of the thirteen major Middle Eastern charities in Peshawar in the 1980s. Founded around 1987 by Saudi Shaykh Adil Galil Abdul Batargy, it maintained branches in Saudi Arabia and Pakistan. "One of the purposes of LBI was to raise funds in Saudi Arabia to provide support for the mujahideen then fighting in Afghanistan" and to provide "cover for fighters to travel in and out of Pakistan and obtain immigration status."[13] BIF was constituted in the USA in 1992 when a Syrian Afghan-Arab, Enaam Arnaout, opened an office of the Islamic Benevolence Committee (IBC) in Plantation, Florida; the name was soon changed to the original Benevolence International Foundation (BIF). In Florida Arnaout married an American woman, thereby obtaining US citizenship, and moved BIF headquarters to Chicago in 1992 and began to collect funds for

Al Qaeda – supposedly to purchase food for families impacted by wars in Afghanistan and the Balkans.

In December 2001 US agents raided the Chicago office of BIF but found little more than videos and literature glorifying martyrdom. In January 2002 Bosnian authorities, working on information from the USA, searched the BIF office in Sarajevo and seized weapons, booby-traps, false passports, and plans for making bombs. They also discovered the seminal historical document that described "the origins, growth and expansion of his al-Qaida network in the 1980s and 1990s" and the close relationship between Arnaout and Bin Laden. Another document, entitled "Osama's history," disclosed that "Al Qaida military leaders were paid salaries from Muslim charity proceeds and purchased weapons with money from charity leaders." Other handwritten notes provided a detailed description of the founding of Al Qaeda, including minutes of the 11 August 1988 meeting in which Bin Laden and his associates discussed the establishment of a new militant group. Quotations from Bin Laden's own statements included one boasting that Al Qaeda had received "huge gains" from Saudi donors. In April Arnaout was arrested for denying under oath that he had ties to terrorists. There was no longer any doubt that Arnaout was an Al Kifah veteran, associate, and long-time friend of Bin Laden.

In October 2002 Enaam Arnaout was charged with conspiracy to provide material support for terrorists. He had signed documents listing a senior Al Qaeda member, Mamdouh Salim, as a BIF director when the latter traveled to Bosnia, and Mohammed Bayazid, a Bin Laden agent seeking to procure nuclear and chemical weapons for Al Qaeda, had used the BIF address as his residence on an application for a driver's license. A month later BIF was listed on the Terrorist Designation Lists.[14] In February 2003 Arnaout pleaded guilty to providing boots, tents, and uniforms for rebels in Chechnya and Bosnia, but a plea bargain dropped the charges related to Al Qaeda and the prospect of a long prison term. In return Arnaout agreed to provide prosecutors with a history of Al Qaeda and the jihadist presence in the USA and abroad. When Arnaout was sentenced in 2003 to eleven years in federal prison for defrauding donors, a supercilious judge gave him a longer term than the eight to ten years in the sentencing guidelines because he "deprived needy refugees of important aid."[15]

In July 2003 Rabih Sami Haddad, a Lebanese citizen, was ordered to be deported from the USA. Haddad was the co-founder of the international Global Relief Foundation (GRF) and another Afghan-Arab who had been closely associated with MAK and Shaykh Azzam in Peshawar. At the end of the war in Afghanistan he had moved to Kuwait. There he conceived of a new charitable foundation. Using an associate, Muhammad

Chehade, GRF opened for business in suburban Chicago in 1992. The following year Haddad moved to Chicago to become the Chairman of GRF. In the first year GRF collected over $700,000, and during its first ten years raised about $20 million. The charity had received $3.6 million in 2001 alone, and when its accounts were frozen, it had over $900,000 in cash and tangible assets of $1.7 million. In December 2001 a presidential executive order was issued against GRF accusing the charity of diverting contributions to help bankroll terrorism; between June 2000 and September 2001 GRF had received $1.4 million in wire transfers from a Swiss bank that was "co-mingled" with funds collected in the USA. Haddad was arrested in December 2001 and accused of having links to the Al Qaeda network. Never charged, after being held for a year he was deported by an Immigration Court judge in November 2002 and sent to Lebanon.[16] In addition, the Treasury Department was convinced that GRF had close ties to Al Qaeda and to Wadih al-Hage, previously convicted of being involved in the 1998 bombings of the US embassies in Kenya and Tanzania. Ironically, reporters from the *New York Times* were subject to investigation by the FBI because they may have alerted the GRF office the day before it was raided by federal agents. Whoever tipped them off, the charity staff shredded many documents, destroying incriminating evidence.[17] A year later, in November 2002, GRF was officially designated a financier of terrorism by the Treasury Department and so charged under Executive Order 13224. It was also bankrupt.

Al Kifah and Al Haramain

Although many have perceived a vast conspiracy involving Islamic charities, neither in the USA nor Europe has anyone unearthed any grand design that united all questionable charitable activities in a single conspiratorial purpose. Much of the belief in an Islamic conspiracy was generated by the fact that the leading Islamists lived in a closed world in which they all knew one another, attended conferences together, and communicated among themselves to raise funds for common causes such as HAMAS or Al Qaeda. The futile pursuit of that elusive conspiracy began at the Islamic Center of Tucson, Arizona. Founded in 1971 by Muslim students at the University of Arizona, it was the first American Islamic charitable institution to provide direct support to the Afghan-Arabs in Peshawar. By 1986 the Center had become closely associated with the Al Kifah movement founded in Pakistan, and its Director, Wael Hamza Julaidan, had been President of the Tucson Center in 1984–1985. He was a founding member of Al Qaeda and became Osama bin Laden's chief of logistics. Wadih al-Hage also spent time at the Tucson Center during the 1980s when it was raising money for the cause in Afghanistan. The Islamic Center of Tucson was the host for the IAP conferences and raised money for HLF. It was the first campus center to distribute the Islamist tracts and booklets prepared by Shaykh Abdullah Azzam, founder of MAK in Peshawar.

On the East Coast the Al Kifah Refugee Services center in Brooklyn was the first charity in the USA whose primary purpose was to support Osama bin Laden and his Afghan-Arabs. Its beginnings can be traced to the arrival in Santa Clara, California, of two members of EIJ, Ali Mohammed and Khaled Abd al-Dahab. Abd al-Dahab had left medical school and in 1984 was in Egypt on his way to Afghanistan when he met Mohammed, who persuaded him to accompany him to California. In the USA Abd al-Dahab worked quietly but efficiently collecting funds in mosques and dispatching money to terrorists throughout the Middle East. He maintained contact with Dr. Ayman al-Zawahiri, the leader of EIJ, and worked as a troubleshooter for that organization. He later moved to Brooklyn where in a tiny first-floor office in the Al Farouq Mosque he founded the Al Kifah Refugee Services center in 1987. Al Kifah relentlessly developed an international network with scores of centers around the world, including Tucson and thirty other cities in the USA. Although mostly small storefront operations, they still managed to raise millions of dollars to support the Afghan resistance, and the Al Kifah centers in New York and New Jersey regularly recruited American Muslims to fight in Afghanistan. By 1989 the Brooklyn center had become the meeting place for jihadists, and a year later Shaykh Abd al-Rahman, the blind Egyptian cleric and holy warrior, arrived and began planning terrorist attacks in the USA.[18] Their first strike was in November 1990 when an Egyptian terrorist assassinated Meir Kahane, a radical rabbi, after his fiery speech in a New York hotel. The assassin later admitted that he and others, including Shaykh Abd al-Rahman, were planning to bomb tunnels and landmark buildings in New York City. The shaykh was eventually captured, tried, and sentenced to a long prison term.

The Al Haramain Foundation-USA was founded in 1997, and its legal adviser and administrative director, Soliman al-Buthe (aka Suliman Albuthi), worked out of Ashland, Oregon. Perhaps it was the remote location, but it would be years before the Treasury Department discovered its direct link to Osama bin Laden and Chechen terrorists. Its assets were frozen in February 2004. In fact, the Al Haramain Foundation-USA proved to be a rather ineffectual organization. Ironically, after being shut down in February 2004, its name continued to appear on the "website of the Friends of Charities Association (FOCA)," an organization founded and registered by the same Soliman al-Buthe in January 2004.[19]

American Muslims also gave alms to the Chechen–Ingush Society of the USA; Eritreans gave to the Al Ehsan charity of Washington DC; Algerians supported the Algerian Relief Foundation and Algerian Relief Fund; the Iraqis of Michigan gave to a host of Iraqi causes; Afghans gave to the Afghan Refugee Aid Committee and the Afghanistan Rescue Effort; Palestinians donated to a spectrum of Palestinian refugee organizations, including the Islamic-American Zakat Foundation of Bethesda, Maryland. Most of this money undoubtedly went to support the humanitarian objectives of these charities. In the end the FBI found no great conspiracy, no organization that centralized collection for each country or region. It was assumed that even though administrators of questionable charities knew one another, each worked in its own way. After all, there was always room for the individualist who for himself or his own favorite cause would skim off unaccountable funds. Adham Amin Hassound was such a "lone wolf." He had entered the USA on a student visa and then remained as an illegal resident. Arrested in South Florida in 2002 for recruiting jihadists, he had registered with the Florida branch of BIF in 1993; he then used BIF to collect funds for the Palestinian *jihad*, working as a freelance with no accountability to the foundation.[20]

Holy Land Fund for Relief and Development

The Holy Land Fund for Relief and Development (HLF) was perhaps America's most perfectly disguised Islamic "charity." Founded in 1987 as the Occupied Land Fund, it was registered in Los Angeles under the IRS regulation [501(c)(3)] governing non-profit, tax-exempt charitable organizations. Founded by Palestinian immigrants, HLF was designed to help "victims of the Palestinian uprising." It opened its first office in Culver City, California, in January 1989 and soon became well known throughout the Palestinian community in southern California and the USA. In 1992 the Occupied Land Fund received its first substantial donation when Musa Abu Marzouk deposited $200,000 in the charity's bank account. The mysterious Marzouk, a native of Gaza, had been attending college in Louisiana when the Fund was launched. At the time he was already active in the founding of the United Association for Studies and Research (UASR), a "think tank" incorporated in Illinois in 1989 as a front for HAMAS. He may have attended the first important HAMAS fundraising in Kansas City in 1989 at which the radical Shaykh Yousuf al-Qaradawi from Qatar and the Chief Financial Adviser of Bahrain, Shaykh Ahmed al-Qattan, were present. In 1991 UASR moved to Springfield, Virginia, and Marzouk departed for Jordan as head of the HAMAS political bureau.[21] According to one Occupied Land Fund official, Marzouk was just an average, unimpressive individual. "When he turned out to be a so-called chief of HAMAS political wing, I said, 'Poor HAMAS.' I had no clue, and I think the [US] government had no clue back in 1991, 1992."[22]

In 1990 Marzouk opened a bank account in Virginia on behalf of the Islamic Association for Palestine (IAP) of Richardson, Texas, a suburb of Dallas, which was actively raising funds for HAMAS. He deposited $125,000 both that year and the next.[23] Although IAP would later deny any relationship with HAMAS, Marzouk had been a member of the IAP advisory boards and its Chairman in 1988–90. IAP had been founded as a pro-Palestinian organization in the early 1980s and in the years before HAMAS had operated from the Islamic Center of Tucson, Arizona. By the early 1990s, IAP was publishing a HAMAS communiqué asking for contributions "to be sent to the Occupied Land Fund in Los Angeles" and distributing paramilitary training videos.[24] In 1993 Ghassan Elashi, IAP's Chairman, whose wife was a cousin of Marzouk, renamed the Occupied Land Fund the Holy Land Fund for Relief and Development, and moved from Los Angeles to Richardson, the headquarters of IAP. As a protective cover Elashi and HLF became founding members of the Texas chapter of the Council of American–Islamic Relations (CAIR), the Muslim lobbying agency in Washington DC. While Elashi and his four brothers preferred to remain quietly anonymous, Shukri Abu Bakar assumed the presidency of HLF to launch an aggressive fundraising campaign in support of the Palestinian Intifada. In a Ramadan appeal in March 1993 the pledge card declared: "Yes. I can and want to help needy families of Palestinian martyrs, prisoners and deportees."[25] After the bombing of the World Trade Center in 1993 HLF began to attract attention. One of its directors, Ahmed bin Yousef (aka Yousef Salah), was a member of the HAMAS "inner circle" that served as the political command of HAMAS in the USA and reported directly to Musa Abu Marzouk.[26] In the wake of the bombing, when investigations curtailed his aggressive fundraising, he bitterly complained that "there is nothing that can be concealed in this world anymore" despite the best efforts of HAMAS, HLF, and IAP.[27] In August 2004 Marzouk's UASR was still under investigation because Ismael Elbarasse, "a high ranking HAMAS leader" with ties to UASR, used banks in the eastern USA to launder money, the "amounts ranging from tens to hundreds of thousands of dollars from various foreign sources including Saudi Arabia."[28]

Shortly after HLF had moved to Texas Israeli authorities arrested two HAMAS leaders, both of whom held US citizenship. During their interrogation, they provided critical information regarding the role that Musa Abu Marzouk had played in HAMAS. It was shared with the US Treasury

Department, which then opened its own investigation of HLF. Treasury agents quickly learned that HLF regularly sponsored the entry into the USA of "religious workers," an amorphous immigration category that allowed the entrants to raise funds and be given a "green card" permitting legal employment. Officials at HLF admitted sending money to Palestinian refugees in the West Bank and Gaza, and it had on numerous occasions welcomed HAMAS fundraisers to the USA. However, they argued strenuously that the funds had been distributed on the basis of need, not ideology. The government did not press the matter, and the charity continued its activities and even expanded them. In October 1993, the three principal members of HLF, including President Shukri Abu Bakar and Ghassan Elashi along with several important members of IAP, met in a Philadelphia hotel with senior HAMAS leaders to discuss the means to increase funds for "Samah," a reversal of HAMAS and a codeword for the *jihad* in the Holy Land. The Philadelphia meeting was followed several months later by a strategy session in Mississippi during which HLF was designated as the primary fund raising HAMAS affiliate in the USA.

Thereafter, HLF paid the expenses for innumerable visits to America by HAMAS delegations, one of which attended a conference organized by the Muslim Arab Youth Association (MAYA) in a Los Angeles hotel from 30 December 1994 to 2 January 1995 during which the HLF Director for California, Mohammad al-Mezain, told the organizers that the Foundation collected funds "strictly for HAMAS terrorists." At the conference he received $207,000, a significant portion of the $1.8 million reportedly collected for HAMAS in 1995. Coincidentally, Shaykh Muhammad Siyam happened to be traveling throughout America in search of funds. Siyam was introduced as the head of the HAMAS military wing, and at one event exhorted the crowd: "Finish off the Israelis. Kill them all. Exterminate them. No peace ever."[29] Despite even more provocative statements by Islamists associated with HLF and President Clinton's Executive Order of 23 January 1995 designating HAMAS a terrorist organization, the FBI made no attempt to block HLF assets. In the same year Rita Katz, then a neophyte analyst investigating suspicious Islamic organizations, wrote that she could prove HLF was providing support to nine organizations that transferred funds to families of HAMAS terrorists.[30] In response to President Clinton's Executive Order, however, Congress enacted anti-terrorist legislation that enabled the Justice and Treasury Departments to freeze terrorist assets; unperturbed, HLF blithely continued its fundraising. Attorney-General Janet Reno made no effort to intervene "even after a connection between the foundation and Osama bin Laden was revealed."[31]

At the IAP Convention in 1996 Abd al-Rahman Alamoudi, the Executive Director of the American Muslim Council, leader of the Islamic Institute, a supporter of both HAMAS and Hizbullah, and an Islamist who had "high level contacts with the Clinton White House in late 1995 and early 1996," acknowledged: "If we are outside this country we can say, 'Oh, Allah destroy America.' But once we are here, our mission in this country is to change it."[32] The actions of the HAMAS militants provoked Congresswoman Nita Lowey into demanding that the IRS revoke the tax-exempt status of HLF; she protested that there was ample "proof of the foundation's support for terrorism." Her accusations elicited no action, and HLF not only continued "business as usual," but rapidly expanded. It began to advertise itself as the largest Islamic charity in the USA, and opened offices in California, Illinois, and New Jersey now to collect funds for Chechnya and Kosovo as well as Palestine.

While the FBI was loath to move against HLF, the Israelis were not. They raided the HLF office in Jerusalem in 1997 and found a cache of documents that contradicted the claims by the charity's US officials that funds were collected strictly for humanitarian purposes. The evidence clearly associated HLF with a satellite, the Islamic Relief Committee of Nazareth. Its Jerusalem Director, Rahman Anati, was arrested for distributing cash to family members of suicide bombers, and in May 1997 Israel closed HLF-Palestine, its satellite, and three other charities. Despite the evidence, the FBI still refrained from action against HLF, but it continued its surveillance of the charity, begun in 1992.[33] In reality those FBI agents who were building the case against HLF privately admitted that they were stonewalled by the Justice Department and the Clinton White House, both of whom "didn't want to come off as Muslim bashers."[34] Congress, however, was more aggressive. It authorized the formation of a Commission on National Security/21st Century. Chaired by former Senators Gary Hart and Warren Rudman, the Commission held its first meeting in October 1998 and then in September 1999 released its first report, warning that America was vulnerable to terrorism, and that terrorists were probably infiltrating the USA to destroy domestic targets. Surprisingly, there was no mention of the role that Islamic charities played in financing these Islamist movements.

HLF continued its work unmolested. When IAP organized a conference at Brooklyn College in May 1998 entitled Palestine: 50 Years of Occupation, HLF joined with CAIR, the Islamic Society of North America (ISNA), and the Islamic Circle of North America to sponsor American Muslim speakers whose anti-Jewish rhetoric in Arabic was as intense as any found in the West Bank or the Gaza Strip. The following year HLF hosted a conference entitled Rebuilding Shattered

Lives, which featured representatives from WAMY, INTERPAL, and the Netherlands's Al Aqsa Foundation, a pro-Palestinian organization with headquarters in Yemen. In that same year the Attorney-General for the State of New York wrote to the IRS challenging the charitable status of HLF, as it was raising funds "not explicitly mentioned in the group's request to solicit funds in New York." Predictably, the IRS did nothing. It was no secret that the Clinton administration was seeking votes within the Muslim community, and also no secret that Vernon Jordan, friend and golfing partner to the President, was the attorney for HLF.[35] The IRS, however, was not alone. The Immigration and Naturalization Service (INS) refused to deport immigrants affiliated with HLF and IAP. Perhaps it was too busy; in fiscal year 2000 alone the Department of State approved "an astounding 493,473 temporary or non-immigrant US visas" for citizens from states already included on its own "watch list."[36]

Meanwhile HLF quietly continued to expand. It raised more than $5 million in 1998, $6 million in 1999, and $13 million in 2000.[37] Finally, it took a lawsuit filed in the USA by the family of an American killed in Israel seeking damages from HAMAS to prod the US government into action. In August 2000 the State Department ordered its satellite, the Agency for International Development (AID), to withdraw its recognition of HLF for its ties with HAMAS and activities "contrary to the national defense and foreign policy interests of the United States." AID, reluctantly and with glacial speed, "started to review how it registers charities and relief groups that work overseas." [38] In the weeks after 9/11 an investigation of suspected Islamic charities by the FBI resulted in a devastating report by its Director for Counterterrorism in November. A month later the assets of HLF were frozen and its offices promptly closed.

Although the evidence collected left no doubt that HLF was the principal US charity supporting HAMAS, it was another year before arrests related to HLF funding practices were made.[39] In December seven men were arrested in Texas and Lackawanna, New York, including four members of the Elashi family, and another seven in Dearborn, Michigan, for reportedly funneling $50 million to Yemen in a money-laundering scheme.[40] Musa Abu Marzouk, the senior HAMAS leader, was indicted in Texas for violating the ban on financial dealings with terrorists, and with what seemed excessive force, the North Texas Joint Terrorism Task Force of the FBI, Department of Commerce, IRS, INS, the Secret Service, the Customs Service, the State Department, and the police departments of Dallas, Addison, Plano, and Richardson, Texas, rounded up the Elashi family and permanently shut down HLF. [41] Marzouk, his wife, the Elashi brothers, and InfoCom were charged with violating the 1979 International Emergency Economic Powers Act (IEEPA), which permitted the

President to "investigate, regulate or prohibit any transactions in foreign exchange," the transfer of funds through banking institutions, and the export or import of currency and securities.[42] After a decade of dithering, in July 2004 Ghassan Elashi, Shukri Abu Bakar, and three other officials of HLF were placed under arrest, and the government unsealed a forty-two-count indictment and prepared to prosecute.[43]

Canadian connections

Before 9/11 there was little difference between the operations of Islamic charities in Canada and the USA. In both countries they could be easily established, and once founded they received little oversight, if any. Canada was even more reluctant than the USA to enact legislation governing the distribution of charitable funds for international causes, and both were extremely lax concerning funds raised to be sent abroad. Muslims, however, could establish refugee status in Canada much more easily than in the USA, and few security checks were ever made by Canadian officials.

Human Concern International (HCI) of Canada was the first Islamic charity in North America to provide funds to Afghan-Arabs. Founded in 1979 in Calgary by Abudhamid Abdulrahim (aka Abu Obeida), it established a presence in Peshawar, providing scholarships for Afghan-Arabs to attend the University of Islamabad, a school favored by Shaykh Abdullah Azzam. A few years later HCI moved to Ottawa where in the 1980s it evolved into the most important Islamic charity in Canada. As a recognized international NGO, HCI received at least $250,000 in grants from the Canadian International Development Agency (CIDA) from 1988 to 1997. One critic later complained that HCI was "simultaneously receiving Canadian taxpayer funding and working with Al Qaeda."[44] In Peshawar the director of the HCI office was Ahmed Said Khadr (aka Abu al-Kanadi), the ranking member of EIJ and among the founders of Al Qaeda. Khadr had immigrated to Canada in the 1970s, and after the Soviet invasion of Afghanistan he had joined HCI and soon left for Peshawar. His presence there enabled HCI to convince the Canadian government to fund projects for Afghan refugees, funds that were then used to support Al Qaeda and Islamic Jihad. Ahmed Khadr, who would be killed by Pakistani forces in October 2003, was in fact the leader of the most important jihadi family in Canada. Three of his four sons were Al Qaeda members: one was killed; one was badly injured; one was interned at Guantánamo Bay after 9/11; and one gave up the jihadist struggle.[45]

In Peshawar Ahmed Khadr certainly consorted with Enaam Arnaout, a fellow founder of Al Qaeda. Arnaout, who later became director of

BIF in Illinois, had opened an office in Ontario, Canada, in 1992 to raise money for Al Qaeda in Canadian mosques and through university student groups. Although each of these charities jealously guarded its independence, there appears to have been close cooperation between HCI and BIF until 1995. Then, the bombing of the Egyptian embassy in Islamabad led Pakistani officials to HCI and the Khadrs who had financed the terrorist attack. Ahmed Khadr was arrested, but he was released after the intervention of the Canadian Prime Minister, Jean Chrétien, who was presumably protecting a Canadian citizen. In 1996 Khadr returned to Canada where he and his wife created in Toronto a new charity, the Health and Education Project International. It was responsible for the construction of five clinics and two hospitals in Peshawar. The next year, 1997, CIDA finally stopped giving aid money to HCI, and in June 1998 the Canadian Security Intelligence Service (CSIS) reported that HCI was one of several charitable organizations that used Canada's ethnic communities as a source of funding for terrorist groups that had established themselves in Canada "seeking safe haven, setting up operational bases, and attempting to gain access to the USA." Claude Pacquette, the police investigator who wrote the report, asserted that "loose immigration controls and interagency fumbling have turned Canada into 'a Club Med for terrorists.'"[46] After the Khadrs had left Canada, never to return, the board of directors of HCI joined Health Partners International in a new charitable enterprise fully committed to humanitarian assistance. Ironically, the name of Ahmed Kadr later surfaced during the prosecution of Enaam Arnaout, but the investigators appeared to be ignorant of the close ties between Khadr and Arnaout, Osama bin Laden, and the founding of Al Qaeda. The amount of money the Khadrs may have used in support of Islamist movements has never been disclosed, but in 2003 when HCI reorganized with Health Partners International the charity had received at least $34 million over its twenty-three years in existence.

Canada, like the USA, was considered a haven for Islamist fundraisers. Not all were as active as the Khadrs, but in one interesting case a Sudanese citizen, Qutbi al-Mahdi, a University of Khartoum law school graduate and follower of Hasan al-Turabi, arrived in Canada in the 1980s as an employee of the IARA office in Montreal. An Islamist militant, he became a Canadian citizen, traveled on a Canadian passport, and "was a top figure of the North American branch of the Muslim Students Association." He worked at the Centre for Muslim Studies at McGill University in Montreal and on occasion played host to Turabi during his visits to Canada.[47] After the 30 June 1989 coup d'état and revolution in the Sudan he returned to become the hardline Sudanese Ambassador to Iran, and in November 1996 he was appointed Director of the External

Security Organization. In 1998 the Canadian War Crimes Unit Director confirmed that his office was reviewing the case of Qutbi al-Mahdi. The investigation of HCI had raised his cause for concern that Canada was "being used as a base to raise money to support the war effort in Sudan."[48] In the same year CSIS learned that the Sudanese embassy staff in New York, London, and Rome collected cash for Osama bin Laden, established budgets to finance terrorism, and issued diplomatic passports that allowed Al Qaeda personnel to travel freely. The alleged agreement involved Ayman al-Zawahiri, Sudanese Islamists, and jihadists from Eritrea, Uganda, Yemen, and Egypt.[49]

A more intensive scrutiny of Islamic charities in Canada was now begun by the authorities. The Canadian Customs and Revenue Agency revoked the charity status of the Canadian branch of MWL established in Etobicoke, Ontario, for not meeting "the filing requirements of the Income Tax Act." Nevertheless, it was not held responsible for terrorism. The Financial Intelligence Branch of the Royal Canadian Mounted Police (RCMP) would finally conclude in 2003 that "the main sources of funding of al-Qaeda are charities, NGO, and commercial enterprises . . . The money is given by supporters and is funneled to al-Qaeda through the *hawala*, the international underground banking system."[50] When the publication in 2003 of *The Trouble with Islam* by the Ugandan feminist Irshad Manji stoked the fires under the simmering debate in Canada about the nature of Islam, Canadian Muslims appeared quite capable of sorting out their own future.[51] The President of the Canadian Islamic Congress argued persuasively that the Muslim congregation was determined to prove that "Canadian Muslims are, above all, Canadians. And Canadians are nice folks, with the best sense of decency in the world."[52]

WISE

When Sami al-Arian, a Kuwaiti with a doctorate in engineering from an American university, was hired by the University of South Florida (USF) in January 1986, no one paid much attention. Yet this innocuous computer science professor was soon to become the very personification of terrorism's fellow-traveler. After the eruption of the Intifada in 1987 he became deeply involved in Palestinian causes, and thereafter sponsored numerous Palestinian students at USF. In 1988 he founded the Islamic Concern Project, an umbrella organization that included the Islamic Committee for Palestine (ICP), and subsequently, the World and Islamic Studies Enterprise (WISE), an Islamist "think tank" on the Florida campus. Al-Arian was helped by Dr. Bashir Nafi, an Egyptian biologist with a doctorate from the University of Cairo and a US resident. He arrived in Tampa in June 1991, after which he worked at WISE with Ramadan Abdullah Shallah, a fellow Egyptian and a founder of EIJ for whom Al-Arian had arranged a teaching position at USF; Shallah was also the Director of WISE and a member of the board of directors of ICP. In 1991 Nafi and Al-Arian used WISE to sponsor various conferences in which such Islamist luminaries as Shaykh Abd al-Rahman and Hasan al-Turabi were eager participants.

WISE attracted little attention outside the Islamist world until 1994, when the production of Steven Emerson's television documentary *Jihad in America* described Al-Arian as the head of PIJ in North America. Thereafter, the activities of ICP, which included a large fundraising drive in south Florida, were under surveillance "until the FBI shut it down in 1995" in the wake of White House criticism of fundraising in the USA for Palestinian radical groups.[53] Al-Arian's office and home were searched, but he was charged with no crime. In the following year, however, his petition for citizenship was rejected when it was discovered that he had voted illegally in American elections; next, his brother-in-law was arrested as an illegal alien. Meanwhile, Shallah, whose hatred of the USA seemed limitless, left Florida following the death of PIJ leader Fathi Shiqaqi and surfaced in Damascus, where he became the new Secretary-General of PIJ.[54]

After 9/11 WISE and Sami al-Arian found themselves in yet more trouble, facing a fifty-count indictment in February 2002 including the use of an Islamic charity and an academic think tank to provide financial support for PIJ; the indictment held WISE responsible for the suicide bombings in Israel in which American citizens had been killed. Al-Arian was also accused of managing PIJ money and property. The radical Islamist mosques in the USA rallied behind al-Arian, collecting money for his defense, but he was discharged by USF in December 2002. His arrest and indictment led the FBI to his close friend Fawaz Damra, imam of the largest mosque in Ohio and a well-known Islamist. Damra, a Palestinian and veteran of the Al Kifah Refugee Center in Brooklyn, was arrested in 2004 and charged with lying about his ties to PIJ and ICP. He was then deported. Al-Arian remains in federal prison in Florida awaiting trial in 2005 for, among other crimes, "Conspiracy to Commit Racketeering, Conspiracy to Murder, Maim or Injure Persons at Places outside the United States," collecting funds for the "benefit of Specially Designated Terrorists" (i.e. PIJ and HAMAS), and facilitating the entry of terrorists into the USA by helping them to obtain entry visas.[55]

SAAR Foundation

Interest in the Suleiman Abd al-Aziz al-Rajhi (SAAR) Foundation at 555 Grove Street, Herndon, Virginia, a small city twenty miles south of

Washington DC, began after a raid on the WISE offices in 1995 produced documents disclosing the close ties between SAAR and WISE. As early as 1993 funds were being sent from Virginia to Florida, and one message declared: "We consider you a part of us and an extension of us . . . All your institutions are considered by us as ours . . . We make a commitment to you; we do it for you as a group, regardless of the party or facade you use the money for."[56] The SAAR Trust (later Foundation) had been founded in 1984 by a Palestinian, Yaqub Mirza, who had just received his doctorate in physics from the University of Texas. He had used money provided by Suleiman Abd al-Aziz al-Rajhi, the patriarch of the Al Rajhi Banking and Investment Corporation, to establish an organization that gave to charities, "invested in companies, and sponsored research, all with a goal of fostering the growth of Islam." Over the years the SAAR network had grown to include more than a hundred branches, including Muslim think tanks, charities, and companies. SAAR owned property in downtown Washington DC, and its officers lived in houses purchased in 1987 by SAAR in Herndon. Many of its branches were linked by overlapping boards of directors, shared office space, and were involved in what was called by federal investigators the circular movement of money.

It was not until 1998, however, that NSC pressed the FBI to intensify its investigation of SAAR, but the Bureau declined to become involved in what it perceived to be "ethnic profiling."[57] Although the SAAR Foundation headquarters had been ordered closed in 2001, it was not until March 2002 that 150 Treasury agents of Operation Green Quest raided the offices of SAAR Director Jamal Barzinji, the nearby Safa Trust, and the International Institute for Islamic Thought (IIIT), all of which were suspected of laundering money for Al Qaeda, HAMAS, and other terrorist groups. Elsewhere, in Falls Church, the task force searched the combined office of MWL and IIRO, whose Palestine Charity Committee headed by Nadir al-Nuri had long been under suspicion of sending funds to HAMAS.[58] Included among fourteen Islamic charities and businesses was IIIT, a Muslim think tank, which was located across the street from the SAAR Foundation. Its Islamist founder, Ismail al-Faruqi, a Palestinian immigrant who taught for many years at Temple University in Philadelphia, had regularly predicted since 1983 that America would one day reject its Christian past and accept a great American Caliphate.

The raid was the most important yet undertaken by government officials to expose the "money trail" of Islamic charities and Muslim commercial firms in the USA. It was, however, a decade overdue, for Rita Katz, a skillful and persevering investigator, had earlier and alone uncovered the "nameplate" SAAR operations at 555 Grove Street in Herndon. When Katz began checking the SAAR tax records, she discovered an accounting labyrinth that only an Ikhwan financier schooled in 1960s banking dispersions would understand. At Herndon SAAR, Safa Trust, and IIIT accounts were intermingled. Charities that ostensibly lived off donations did not bother to proselytize. SAAR and Safa Trust had invested in Mar-Jac Investments, a poultry producer in Georgia which was also raided by Operation Green Quest agents. Although it had tangible assets, Mar-Jac also operated from a storefront at 555 Grove Street. So too did the Al Aqsa Foundation, a HAMAS front. By the time Katz was finished she had found 130 interrelated organizations, from the African Muslim Agency to the York Foundation, that wove the bewildering SAAR spider-web. To complicate matters, outside organizations, such as WISE, received most of their funding from IIIT, and the relationship between IIIT and SAAR itself was hopelessly opaque. What the FBI did know, however, was that Tarik Hamdi, an IIIT employee, had personally sent communications gear to Osama bin Laden.[59]

What was SAAR? Tax records demonstrated a direct connection between the SAAR Foundation and five related organizations: IIIT, Safa Trust, Sterling Management Group, Sterling Charitable Gift Fund, and Mar-Jac Investments. Money "was flowing freely in all directions," and much of it disappeared in accounts on the Isle of Man.[60] In 1995 the government had listed SAAR-controlled charities in Virginia among eighty groups in the USA suspected of diverting cash to Islamist terrorists overseas. The SAAR Foundation, however, had managed to avoid any intense scrutiny because of the close links between the Saudi royal family and its patron, the Saudi banker Shaykh Suleiman Abd al-Aziz al-Rajhi. Saudi financiers such as al-Rajhi, Khaled bin Mahfouz, and Yassin al-Qadi were all major instruments in the expansion of Wahhabism, and their paths repeatedly lead back to Northern Virginia, where it was claimed they didn't "play for small stakes."[61]

The SAAR Director, Jamal Barzinji, was well known in Washington. He had first achieved prominence in the USA in 1980 when he began to represent WAMY, and he seemed especially close to Sami al-Arian and WISE. Barzinji was also director, officer, or chairman of a number of financial operations, including the Makkah Mukarramah Charity Trust, Inc., Mena Investments, Inc., and Reston Investments, Inc. He was listed with the Amana Mutual Funds Trust, a growth and income mutual fund headquartered in Bellingham, Washington, and appears to have become involved with the infamous Youssef Nada and his network by helping to set up Nada International in Liechtenstein. He was also a member of the board of directors of IIIT, and the Graduate School of Islamic and Social Sciences (GSISS), which received substantial support from the Saudi government; GSISS was the institution approved by the Department of Defense to certify Muslim chaplains in the US military. SAAR activities were not only well disguised, its directors were powerful and immensely wealthy Saudis, led by Suleiman Abd al-Aziz al-Rajhi and his brother Saleh Abd al-Aziz al-Rajhi, owner of a major construction and real-estate firm.

Above all SAAR was particularly expert in the clandestine movement of money, including an inexplicable donation of $1.7 billion that SAAR had received in 1998, a donation reported in 2000 without any explanation "for this bit of accounting sorcery." SAAR disputed the sum, claiming an accounting error whereby three zeroes had been added to the account without reason.[62] The SAAR Foundation was abruptly dissolved in December 2000 and was immediately replaced by the Sterling Charitable Gift Fund. No official reason was given for its closing, but Dr. Cherif Sedky, an American lawyer who lived in Jidda, represented Khaled bin Mahfouz, and had joined the SAAR Foundation board of directors in the mid-1990s, wryly mentioned that the SAAR Foundation had few board meetings. Loosely administered, SAAR had been the instrument through which more than $26 million had been sent overseas. It was a powerful organization with many powerful friends, and it was linked to the Safa Group whose Safa Trust funded many charities, both in the USA and throughout the world. The SAAR/Safa empire helped finance such institutions as the African Muslim Agency, Heritage Education Trust, IIIT, the York Foundation, and then the Sterling Charitable Gift Fund.[63] Another SAAR official who attracted attention was Ahmad Totonji, an Iraqi – now Saudi – citizen and prominent Islamist. He helped found MSA in the USA and was its second President. He then became an SAAR official and Vice President of the Safa Group. The Operation Green Quest raid also resulted in the arrest of Soliman Biheiri, an Egyptian educated in Switzerland, resident of New Jersey, an Egyptian financier, and the banker for the Muslim Brotherhood in the USA. Biheiri had established Mostan International to raise money for HAMAS and Al Qaeda from such wealthy investors as Musa Abu Marzouk, Yassin al-Qadi, and Youssef Nada.[64]

In 2003 a Virginia grand jury charged Soliman Biheiri with three counts of immigration violations. Although the charges appeared innocuous, Biheri was the central figure in a complex terrorism investigation spanning two decades. He had founded BMI, an investment company based on Islamic principles, in January 1985. Advertising in popular Muslim magazines distributed throughout America, BMI offered financial services and a variety of real-estate investments in Maryland and Virginia. In 1985, Biheiri met and became close friends with Suliman al-Ali, who also lived in New Jersey. Four years later al-Ali left for Saudi Arabia, where he became a successful fundraiser for IIRO. Impressed, IIRO sent him back to the USA in 1991 to open an IIRO office around Washington DC. At the time the structure of Saudi relief was shifting from Afghanistan to the Balkans, and over the next few years al-Ali raised funds for Bosnia while investing in BMI. In August 1998, only days after the bombings of US embassies in East Africa, Biheiri received a call from Hassan Bahzfulla, secretary of the investment committee of IIRO, inquiring about BMI and Suliman al-Ali. Days later, Biheiri received a personal letter from the Secretary-General of MWL, a man he described as the "Pope of the Muslims," ordering him to cancel "all [IIRO] accounts with your firm." Shortly afterwards, an FBI investigation discovered that BMI was involved in funneling money to HAMAS. Eventually, Biheiri was subpoenaed, by which time the FBI had learned that among his silent investors were Musa Abu Marzouk and Yassin al-Qadi. The BMI probe continued into 2004 as federal investigators explored the links between Biheiri, Mercy International, IIRO, MWL, and the East African bombings.[65] Soliman Biheiri was finally charged in 2003, not for laundering money, but for immigration fraud.[66]

As the investigations by Operation Green Quest continued it was impossible to separate the Safa Group from SAAR, now the Sterling Charitable Gift Fund, for Barzinji was the director of various Safa Group enterprises and charities including the Child Development Foundation of Herndon, the Sana-Bell Al Kheer, Inc., the Fiqh Council of North America, Inc., and the Heritage Education Trust, Inc. Moreover, Safa received revenue in rent from MWL and IIRO, whose headquarters were also in Herndon and Leesburg, Virginia.[67] The Falls Church office of MWL was searched by the FBI in 2002, with no charges being filed. The office, however, was placed under scrutiny, and raided again in July 2005. The employee who was working as Publicity Director, but was actually Director of the charity's operations, was arrested and charged with immigration fraud. Although some fifty Islamic enterprises were raided, closed down, or had their assets frozen by federal authorities because of suspected ties to terrorists, no one could be quite sure that Operation Green Quest had "inflicted serious injury on the Wahhabi lobby, the Saudi-backed extremist network that largely controls Islam in America," but it did uncover the magnitude of monies being passed through SAAR enterprises.[68] There was the $100,000 donation from Pathfinder Investments, a Netherlands Antilles company controlled by the Mahfouz family, to the Success Foundation, a Virginia charity. SAAR had also moved another $20 million to Bank Al Taqwa and Akida Bank Private Ltd., controlled by Youssef Nada and Ahmed Idris Nasreddin. There was the unexplained $9 million transfer of funds from the Humana Charitable Trust, an Isle of Man front, to SAAR; also on the Isle of Man

284   Alms for *jihad*

a private, unregistered trust, Happy Hearts, received substantial sums from SAAR. The *Washington Post* reported that in the mid-1990s "the Saudi government, upset with its inability to control the SAAR network, pressed contributors to stop giving money." If that were true, it has never been proven.[69]

Epilogue

The Department of State had been the first agency of any government to name terrorist organizations, list them as such, and proscribe the delivery of funds to them or their charities. In 1995, the Treasury Department initiated investigations into the shady dealings between a number of Saudi US charities and suspected extremist groups. Inexplicably, the investigation was summarily closed by the Clinton administration. Had this and similar investigations been allowed to proceed US security agencies may well have unraveled the terrorists' networks and the charitable sources of their funding before the tragedy of 9/11 that signaled the end of Saudi spending in support of Wahhabi Islamist movements throughout the world. The Saudis had good reason to be furious with Bin Laden for his attack on America, for 9/11 revealed the hidden elements of Saudi policy in the USA, and that most of the suicide bombers were Saudis. On 15 August 2002, relatives of those killed in 9/11 filed a lawsuit in the US District Court in Washington, a 258-page complaint accusing international banks, eight Islamic foundations and charities, the government of Sudan, and a multitude of individuals of helping finance Osama bin Laden's terrorist network and demanding $100 trillion in damages.[70] There was little likelihood that the plaintiffs would succeed, but that was not the issue. One plaintiff probably spoke for all: "It's not the money. We want to do something to get at these people."[71]

During the past three decades the Saudis had created numerous enterprises, institutions, and charities whose resources and members were the agents for the spread of Salafist, Islamist Wahhabism throughout the world. MWL, WAMY, and the Al Haramain Foundation were all under the control of and financed by the government of Saudi Arabia. As the oil spigots opened, the petrodollars flowed to hundreds of other Saudi Islamic organizations, large and small, but Riyadh paid special attention to those propagating Wahhabism among western societies. Over these three decades Saudi funds were used to build and administer over 1,500 mosques, 210 Islamic centers, and dozens of academies and schools in non-Muslim, mostly western, countries. Official Saudi sources have reported that between 1975 and 1987 Saudi "overseas development aid" averaged $4 billion per year, and that level was maintained, if not increased, during the next decade. Some of that aid certainly went to international development projects, but at least half, $50 billion in twenty-five years, and perhaps as much as two-thirds, was used to finance strictly "Islamic activities." "Compared to these numbers, the massive Soviet external-propaganda budget (estimated at $1 billion annually) at the peak of Moscow's power looks modest indeed."[72]

Today, Salafist Islamist ideologies have gained a significant following among American Muslims, largely through the efforts of Saudi-supported charities that should be discouraged if not suppressed, for Islamist extremism is not a matter of religion but of criminal sedition. The Islamists should not be tolerated any more than were the Nazis. The instinctive response is to employ all the agencies of law enforcement to crush seditious organizations, but force is not always the most effective instrument in combating ideologies. Radical Islam is best dealt with by ideological and political means, and the Islamists are very vulnerable on two issues that the western world should exploit: the ideology of *jihad* and the nature of Wahhabi subversion not only in the West but in the Islamic world as well. The ideology of *jihad*, which is the psycho-religious engine driving Islamist terrorism, is not representative of Islam practiced by the vast majority of Muslims, who reject it. Today in the USA many of the important organizations claiming to represent American Muslims are financed and controlled by Wahhabis who have attempted to silence those who speak for mainstream Islam. The long alliance between the USA and Saudi Arabia has contributed in no small measure to the credibility of that condition and, by implication, the reach of its ideology, yet to end that close relationship with Riyadh would hardly solve the problem. Rather, the USA must take the lead in forging a Muslim alliance against extremism and provide the resources to sustain it. In the Islamic world today there is a growing backlash against the Islamist extremists that the USA should strongly support.[73]

Islamist extremism has not yet become the dominant force in Islam, but there is no doubt that in the 1980s Saudi money brought Wahhabi Islam to the small and impoverished Muslim community in the USA and provided it with the resources to build an infrastructure by which Wahhabism could be spread and Islamist ideology could be expressed without challenge. Some 80 percent of all mosques and Islamic institutions and schools established in the USA and Canada appear to have received support from Saudi sources, principally charities. The mosques became centers of radical Islam, and the Muslim schools became nurseries for intolerance, both supported by Saudi charities. Since 9/11 the US government has used its security agencies and legal authority to halt the use of mosques, charities, and Islamist institutions as a conduit for

Muslim youth to join *jihad* organizations active in Bosnia, Chechnya, Kashmir, and the Philippines. The FBI and other intelligence agencies have immobilized internet sites that promote violence, recruit jihadists, or use charitable fronts to raise money. Undoubtedly, the most important and decisive goal is for the administration, Congress, and their friends in the Muslim community to isolate the prominent radical and Islamist organizations and thus de-politicize Islam. There can be no greater force to marginalize the Islamists than the rational Muslim organizations of mainstream Islam, which should receive unwavering support from America, predominantly a Christian nation. American Muslims and their organizations should, therefore, embark upon a new strategy as soon as possible. While the Muslim community has legitimate religious concerns related to the institution of charitable giving, the Islamic community must understand the necessity, given the social, political, and religious cultures of the USA, for greater transparency in their charitable institutions to satisfy the Islamic community, the federal government, and the American public.

Daniel Pipes has written that Islamism is not so much a distortion of Islam as a radically new interpretation. The painful fact is that Muslims alone are susceptible to the lure of Islamist extremism. While safeguarding the civil rights and religious freedoms of Muslims, steps must be taken to diminish their unique susceptibility to this totalitarian ideology.[74] In order to protect the rights of Muslim charities, banks, and other institutions, and the rights of Muslims devoted to Islam and the precept of *zakat* in America, perhaps the only way is to employ a Cold War practice: "Trust, but verify."

12   Conclusion

The Moving Finger writes; and having writ,
Moves on: nor all your Piety nor Wit
Shall lure it back to cancel half a Line,
Nor all your Tears wash out a word of it.

The Rubáiyát of Omar Khayyám, st. 72

At the beginning of this illusive and intricate saga a very clear distinction was made between those Islamic charities – some several score – which supported *jihad* to achieve the Islamist state and the many thousands devoted to humanitarian and religious purposes throughout both the Islamic and non-Muslim worlds. Although few in number, those charities with an Islamist agenda were not only the largest but the wealthiest Islamic charities, which enabled them, through the disbursement of a great deal of money, to support the religious commitment and objectives of the small Islamist minority among the world's Muslims by *jihad*, including the use of terror. This very complex tale of intense religious belief to justify the wanton disregard for human life and the manner by which it was carried out has been the subject of this book.

It begins after 1973 with the acquisition of an enormous amount of wealth by the members of OPEC, particularly Saudi Arabia, in return for petroleum to quench the insatiable thirst of the West, particularly the United States, for oil. The primitive financial institutions in Saudi Arabia and the Islamic world at that time were slow to respond to the management of such large sums of revenue. They had neither the trained staff nor experience in banking, and the Islamic restriction against interest on borrowed money, the very foundation of western banking, spawned new and fragile systems of fiscal management by Islamic banks to complement the traditional institution of *hawala* to transfer large sums with little accountability. Consequently, wealthy donors were increasingly inclined to satisfy their *zakat* obligation and to distribute their excess wealth as an act of religious piety (*sadaqa* and *waqf*) through donations to the traditional institution of the Islamic charity. This abundance of charitable giving produced, in the late 1980s and early 1990s, an astonishing proliferation of new charities established by wealthy Saudis, which had, however, a more specific agenda – to promote the Wahhabi Islam of Saudi Arabia – unlike the older, less ideological charities, which promoted Islam by humanitarian relief and the construction of mosques and schools, but not *jihad*.

The invasion of Muslim Afghanistan by the *kafirin* communists of the Soviet Union was greeted with outrage throughout the Muslim world, and sparked a determination to defend Islam, providing an opportunity for the new Islamic charities to use their wealth to fund *jihad* in Afghanistan, where its distribution was increasingly managed by Islamists to promote their ideological objectives by any means, cloaked in the mantle of Wahhabism. When the disintegrating Soviet Union withdrew from Afghanistan in 1989, the Islamist leadership was determined not to remain solely in that country, which had plunged into civil war, but to seek their objectives throughout the world by utilizing the veteran Afghan-Arab *mujahideen* ready to die for the Islamist faith by *jihad*. From Afghanistan – or, more precisely, Peshawar – the *mujahideen* under numerous leaders scattered in cells throughout the globe, for they could hardly return to their homelands, whose secular governments would have instantly incarcerated or killed them.

At first they found a safe haven in the Sudan, whose revolutionary Islamist government had come to power in 1989, the year that the Afghan war ended. Here they were welcomed, and accommodated in a score of jihadist training camps scattered in the semi-arid desert surrounding Khartoum, financed by a spate of new – mainly Saudi – charities, which had suddenly appeared in the capital. These Afghan-Arab *mujahideen* could not resist the call for military assistance by the beleaguered Bosniaks in the Balkans. Other Islamist jihadists,with support from Islamic charities, went to assist the Muslims of Central Asia, Transcaucasia, and Chechnya, while a separate group had returned directly from Peshawar to the Philippines and elsewhere throughout Southeast Asia. While the use of *jihad* in the Holy Land may have had intellectual roots similar to those of the Salafist Islamists, its primary aim, expressed by the Intifada and suicide bombers and supported by Saudi charitable giving, was to destroy Israel, and only then to establish the Islamist state in Palestine. Finally, *jihad* by the use of terror and funded by Islamic charities arrived in Europe, its Islamist proponents submerged within the great wave of Muslim immigration, and took the form of terrorist attacks in Amsterdam, Madrid, and London; but the greatest confrontation between jihadist Islamist terrorists and the West had already succeeded in the destruction, with great loss of life, of the World Trade Center in New York on 9/11.

It was this act that galvanized the United States to mobilize the resources, not only of its allies, but, slowly and painfully, those of other Muslim countries, against terrorism; and President Bush has declared that "money is the lifeblood of terrorism." One reporter claims that " 'Financial Jihad' (*Al Jihad bil-Mal*) has funded more than 26,000 terror attacks, including 144 suicide attacks."[1] Whether this is an exaggeration is, of course, not the point; the point is that jihadist Islamist terrorism remains very much a reality, and a danger to innocent civilians in Muslim as well as non-Muslim countries. Consequently, scores of national and international agencies have been created to interdict and disrupt the flow of financial resources required to sustain terrorism, with mixed results. The United States has been the most aggressive in this pursuit of the financial sources of terrorism and has curtailed or closed the activities in America of the large and wealthy MWL, IIRO, the Rabita Trust, and especially the Islamic Society of North America, with surprisingly little reaction from the Saudi government and relative silence about attacks in the US media on Saudi "missionaries" disseminating egregious Wahhabist propaganda in American mosques.

After two decades, funding for the Islamist movement by specific Islamic charities appears to be in sharp decline. Certainly, the vast financial networks that have been erected throughout the world to combat terrorism are responsible for the constricted flow of money laundered through Islamic charities; but the Islamists have had considerable experience and skill in acquiring and moving money, and no sooner has one network been disabled than another usually appears, in a different form and using different methods. The efforts to impede the flow of charitable funds to Islamist jihadists has also been greatly facilitated by "103 charities suspected of raising funds for terror [that] have been shut or otherwise neutralized in Afghanistan, Pakistan, Saudi Arabia, Yemen and Kuwait alone."[2] In October 2005 Saudi Arabia announced that King Abdullah, Custodian of the Two Holy Mosques, had called for an Extraordinary Islamic Summit to be held in Mecca in December 2005 under the aegis of the OIC. Among the issues for the fifty-seven Muslim nations to consider was the creation of a poverty fund as one significant step in response to the difficulties encountered in achieving greater transparency regarding the purposes for which the billions of dollars of charitable donations are used throughout the Muslim world. Never known for taking strong stands on unpleasant subjects, the OIC would now have the mandate to distinguish between the many thousands of humanitarian and good works performed by Islamic charities and those that would be considered criminal. Whether the OIC will pass such a resolution and then enforce it remains to be seen. "In faith and hope the world will disagree, but all mankind's concern is charity."[3]

Notes

INTRODUCTION

1. Ayman Al-Zawahiri, "Loyalty and Enmity, an Inherited Doctrine and a Lost Reality," FBIS report, Washington DC, February 2003, p. 21.
2. See the annual reports, *Patterns of Global Terrorism*, US Department of State, Washington DC, and its list of *Foreign Terrorist Organizations Designations* compiled every two years since 1997.
3. In 1997 the Muslim Students' Association of the United States (MSA) listed forty-three Muslim agencies located in the USA for soliciting donations for charities operating overseas: see www.msa-natl.org/resources/Relief_Orgs.html.
4. M. E. Hamdi, *The Making of an Islamic Political Leader*, Boulder, CO: Westview Press, 1998, pp. 108–110.
5. See Mansour al-Nuqaydan, "The Islamist Map in Saudi Arabia and the Question of Repudiation," *Al Wasat*, Manama, 28 February 2003, FBIS translation from the Arabic GMP2003022800126, Washington DC, 28 February 2003.
6. See Quran, Sura 62; Mahmoud Haddad, "Salafiyya Movement," in Philip Mattar (ed.), *Encyclopedia of Modern Middle East and North Africa*, Farmington Hills, MI: Thomson Gale, 2004, vol. III, pp. 1973–1975; T. P. Hughes, *Dictionary of Islam*, London: W. H. Allen, 1885, pp. 548–549; "Indonesian Background: Why Salafism and Terrorism Don't Mix," International Crisis Group, Asia Report, No. 83, Brussels, 13 September 2004; for a history of Salaf and pertinent definitions see www.salafnotkhalaf.com.
7. As to the definition of terrorism and the definition used by the US Federal Emergency Management Association, see www.mema.domestic-prepardness.net/glossary.html.
8. "Bin Laden's Money Takes Hidden Paths to Agents of Terror," *Washington Post*, 21 September 2001, p. A13.
9. "New Treasury Unit to Track Terrorist Funding Methods," US Department of the Treasury report, 14 September 2001, available at www.usconsulate.org.hk/usinfo/terror/2001/091401.htm.
10. Kenneth W. Dam, "The Financial Front of the War on Terrorism – the Next Phase," address delivered to the Council on Foreign Relations, New York, 8 June 2002.

11. See Matthew Levitt, "Charitable and Humanitarian Organizations in the Network of International Terrorist Financing," testimony before the Subcommittee on International Trade and Finance, Committee on Banking, Housing, and Urban Affairs, United States Senate, 1 August 2002.

I THE THIRD PILLAR OF ISLAM:*ZAKAT*

1. A. Rahman, *Subject Index of Quran*, Lahore: Islamic Publications (PVT) Limited, 1988.
2. Abu Bakr quoted in Shaykh Musa Abdulmajeed et al.," Declaration of Jihad against African Sudanese," *fatwa* issued from Kordofan, El Obeid, 27 April 1993.
3. From Sayyid Abu al-'Ala Maududi, "Islam: Its Meaning and Message," in M. Tariq Quraishi (ed.), *Islam: an Introduction*, Indianapolis: American Trust Publications, 1988; see also "Application of Islamic System of Zakat," islamzine.com/pillars/Zakat.html.
4. Faisal Raja," The Significance of Zakat," *Khilafah Magazine*, December 2001, www.khilafah.com.
5. Tajuddin B. Shu'aib, *The Essentials of Ramadan, the Fasting Month*, Los Angeles: Da'awah Enterprises International, Inc., 1991; see also Talut Mujahid, "42 Ways of Supporting Jihad," www.homescurityus.net.
6. Khilafah Rashidah, "The Significance of Zakat," uploaded on 10 December 2001 at khilafah.com. *Fi sabeelillah*, "In the Way of Allah," is a general term meaning all good causes that has become today more specifically defined to mean "those who fight in the cause of Allah against the enemies of Islam." See Abduallah Tariq, "Our Dialogue," *Islamic Voice*, vols. 13–14, no. 156, December 1999.
7. Janine A. Clark, *Islam, Charity, and Activism: Class Networks and Social Welfare in Egypt, Jordan, and Yemen*, Bloomington: Indiana University Press, 2004.
8. "Second Opinion," *Daily Times*, Pakistan, 1 October 2004. See also Michael Bonner, Mine Ener, and Amy Singer (eds.), *Poverty and Charity in Middle Eastern Contexts*, Albany: State University of New York Press, 2003.
9. For instance, see "Use Zakah for Investment, Employment, Cottage Industries," from the Fifth International Conference on Zakah held in Kuwait, in *Islamic Voice*, India, December 1998.
10. "Conference Calls for Including Zakat (Alms) in Law, Regional Politics," www.ArabicNews.com 11/2/1998; "Use Zakah for Investment."
11. Mohammad Akhtar Saeed Siddiqi, *Early Development of Zakat Law and Ijtihad: A Study of the Evolution of Ijtihad in the Development of the Zakat: Law during 1st Century AH*, Karachi: Islamic Research Academy, 1983; Monzer Khaf, "The Performance of the Institution of Zakah in Theory and Practice," International Conference on Islamic Economics, Kuala Lumpur, 26–30 April 1999.
12. Nimrod Raphaeli, "Commentaries on Islamic Economic Discipline and Islamic Banking," *Middle East Economic News Report*, no. 19, 10 (August 1987).

13. Youssef M. Ibrahim, "Mosque and State," *Wall Street Journal,* 10 August 1987.
14. Abd al-Muem al-Gusi, "Contemporary Governmental Application of Zakat in Sudan," Seminar on Contemporary Applications of Islamic Economics, Casablanca, Morocco, 5–8 May 1998; Muhammad Bashir Abdulqadir, *Nizam al-Zakah fi al-Sudan,* Omdurman: Omdurman Islamic University Printing and Publishing, Sudan, 1992, p. 192.
15. Holger Weiss, *Obligatory Almsgiving: An Inquiry into Zakat in the Pre-Colonial Bilad al-Sudan,* Helsinki: Helsinki Oriental Society, 2003, p. 26.
16. "Awkaf: Seeing it from the Socio-Economic Perspective," OICexchange.com at www.oicexchange.com, 18 March 2004.
17. Research Center for Islamic History, Arts and Culture (IRCICA), www.islamic-world.net/economic/waqf/ waqaf_mainpage.html, p. L.
18. S. Balman, "Saudis, US Fail to Limit Extremist Funding," UPI, Washington DC, 18 August 1997.
19. MEMRI Special Dispatch No. 360: www.memri.org.
20. Interview with *Al Sharq Al Awsat,* a Saudi-owned London daily and reported in *Ayn Al Yaqeen,* Saudi Arabia, 20 September 2002.
21. "WASHINGTON, Insider Notes," UPI, 2 January 2004; see Yusuf al-Qaradawi, *Yusuf, Fiqh al Zakah* (English translation by Dr. Monzer Khaf), Center for Research in Islamic Economics, Jeddah, 2000.
22. M. Isikoff and M. Hosenball, "Jihad's Long Reach," *Newsweek,* 18 September 2003.

2 SAUDI ARABIA AND ITS ISLAMIC CHARITIES

1. "Prince Salman bin Abdul Aziz: Rejects Charges against Saudi Charitable Societies," *Ayn Al Yaqeen,* Saudi Arabia, 8 November 2002.
2. "Knights under the Prophet's Banner," *World News Connection,* 29 October 2003, translated from an article published in *Sawt al-Jihad* that first appeared in *Al Sharq Al Awsat,* London, October 2003.
3. *Ayn Al Yaqeen,* at www.ain-al-yakeen.com, and report at www.memri.org/, MEMRI Special Dispatch No. 360.
4. Anthony Cordesman, "Saudi Arabia: Opposition, Islamic Extremism, and Terrorism," www.csis.org, also in *SUSRIS Newsletter,* www.saudi-us-relations.org.
5. "Reflections from a Saudi Prince," *Business Week Online,* 9 November 2001.
6. "Saudi Arabia Announces Counter-Terrorism Measures: Official Statements and Press Briefings," press release, Embassy of Saudi Arabia Information Office, 3 December 2002.
7. Saudi Red Crescent Society website (www.srcs.org.sa) and news releases, al-Dhabab Road, Riyadh, Saudi Arabia.
8. "Government Evidentiary Proffer Supporting the Admissibility of Co-Conspirator Statements," *United States of America* v. *Enaam M. Arnaout,* US District Court, Northern District of Illinois, Eastern Division, Case No. 02 CR 892, 6 January 2003.
9. "The Making of a Terrorist," *The Straits Times,* 23 September 2001.

10. Abdullah Azzam interview. See "Testimony of Steven Emerson with Jonathan Levin," US Senate Committee of Governmental Affairs, 31 July 2003, pp. 11–13.
11. "Family, Friends Tell of the Man behind bin Laden," *USA Today*, 12 October 2001; "Bin Laden Underling Raised Money in US," UPI, 11 October 2001; "Testimony of Steven Emerson"; "Usama Bin Laden – a Millionaire Finances Extremism in Egypt and Saudi Arabia," *Al Rose Al Yusuf*, Egypt, 17 May 1993.
12. "Government Evidentiary Proffer."
13. "Khattab's Brother Interviewed on Khattab's Life, Death in Chechnya," *Al Sharq Al Awsat*, Saudi Arabia, 2 May 2002.
14. "Pakistan Deporting 89 Arab Aid Workers," AP, 6 October 2001.
15. *The New York Times Report*, 26 September 2003, quoted in Josh Lefkowitz and Jonathan Levin, "Kingdom Cover," www.nationalreview.com, 11 February 2004.
16. "Usama Bin Laden – a Millionaire Finances Extremism"; see also Muhammad Basil, *Al-Ansaru Arab fi Afghanistan,* pamphlet published by the Committee for Islamic Benevolence Publications, 1991, p. 26.
17. *New York Times*, 26 September 2003; "Charity and Terror," *Newsweek*, 9 December 2002.
18. "Testimony of Steven Emerson," pp. 23–24.
19. Andrew Higgins and Christopher Cooper, "CIA-Backed Team Used Brutal Means to Break up Terrorist Cell in Albania," *Wall Street Journal*, 20 November 2001.
20. Compass Newswire, Copenhagen, 27 June 1995.
21. Dore Gold, "Saudi Arabia's Dubious Denials of Involvement in International Terrorism," Jerusalem Center for Public Affairs, Position Paper No. 504, 1 October 2003.
22. Cordesman, "Saudi Arabia."
23. "The Saudi Connection," *US News & World Report*, 15 December 2002.
24. N. P. Walsh, "Al-Qaida Men Handed to US, Says Georgia," *Guardian*, 23 October 2002.
25. Article 7, *Ayn Al Yaqeen*, Saudi Arabia, 1 November 2002.
26. "In Brief," *Ayn Al Yaqeen*, Saudi Arabia, 12 September 2003.
27. R. Kuppchinsky, "Spotlight: The Moscow Metro Bombing," *RFE/RL Analytical Reports*, vol. 4, no. 8, 12 March 2004; "Chechnya News," Maktab al-Jihad, www.maktab-al-jihad.com, 10 February 2004.
28. *Monthly Digest*, Society for Humanitarian Research, 30 August 2000.
29. Alex Alexiev, "Terrorism: Growing Wahhabi Influence in the United States," Center for Security Policy postion paper, US Senate Subcommittee on Terrorism, Technology and Homeland Security, 26 June 2003.
30. *Treasury News*, Office of Public Affairs, 11 March 2002, PO-1087.
31. "Lawyers Seek to Freeze Saudi Assets in US," MENAFN.COM Middle East North Africa – Financial Network, www.arabnews.com, 30 August 2002; "Al-Haramain Charity is Suspected of Aiding al-Qaeda's Network," www.middle-east-online.com, 23 January 2004.

32. "Al-Haramian Shuts 3 Offices Abroad; 4 More to Close," ArabNews.com, 16 May 2003; "Saudis Admit Funding Hamas," WorldTribune.com, Washington DC, 13 June 2003; Gold, "Saudi Arabia's Dubious Denials."

33. "Al Haramain Islamic Foundation Welcomes Retraction; *Washington Times* Apologizes for Inaccuracy," PR Newswire (New York), 26 November 2003; "IRS Officials Execute Search Warrant against Al Haramain Foundation," press release, United States Embassy, Tokyo, Japan, 19 February 2004; *United States of America* v. *Al Haramain Islamic Foundation*, US District Court of the District of Oregon, February 2005.

34. "The First Forum for Charitable Societies Ends its Session," *Ayn Al Yaqeen*, Saudi Arabia, 8 November 2002; "Prince Salman Ibn Abdul Aziz: Rejects Charges."

35. "Youth's Drug Problems Discussed," *Monthly Digest of Society for Humanitarian Research*, 30 August 2000.

36. Stewart Bell, "US Links Toronto Group to Bin Laden," *National Post*, Canada, 19 September 2003.

37. Greg Palast and D. Pallister, "Crimes against Civilization," *Guardian*, 7 November 2001.

38. "WAMY Keen to Boost its Activities Despite Smear Campaign: Wahhabi," *Al Jazeera*, www.aljazeerah.info, 27 August 2002.

39. "WAMY to Offer Ramadan *Iftar* (Breaking of the Fast) Meals for Impoverished Muslims in 40 Countries," Saudi Arabia Ministry of Culture and Information website, www.saudinf.com, 26 October 2003.

40. "Al-Anzy, the First Arab POW Returns from Afghanistan," IslamOnline.net, Kuwait, 9 February 2002.

41. Laurie Cohen, G. Simpson, M. Maremont, and P. Fritsch, "Bush's Financial War on Terrorism Includes Strikes at Islamic Charities," *Wall Street Journal*, 25 September 2001; J. Mintz, "From Veil of Secrecy, Portraits of US Prisoners Emerge," *Washington Post*, 15 March 2002, p. A3.

42. "Terrorism Weighs on US–Saudi Relations," *Washington Times*, 26 November 2002; Steve Emerson, "Fund-Raising Methods and Procedures for International Terrorist Organizations," House Committee on Financial Services, Subcommittee on Oversight and Investigations, 12 February 2002.

43. M. Boettcher, "Evidence Suggests al-Qaeda Pursuit of Biological, Chemical Weapons," CNN.com World, 14 November 2001.

44. E. J. Lake, "US Demands Data on Islamic Charities," UPI, 22 March 2002.

45. See www.treasury.gov/terrorism.html for Wafa listing.

46. Mintz, "From Veil of Secrecy."

47. "Benevolence International Foundation," www.rotten.com.library/history/terrorist-organizations/b-i-f/.

48. "Benevolence International," www.en.wikipedia.org/wiki/Benevolence-International-Foundation.

49. C. Freeze, "Islamic Charity May See Assets Frozen," *Globe and Mail*, Toronto, 1 October 2001; T. Hays, "Feds Link Money Smuggler to Outlawed Muslim Charity," *Sacramento Bee* via AP, 27 November 2003.

50. J. Miller, "US is Said to See Links between Terrorism and Islamic Charities," *New York Times*, 19 February 2000.
51. "Saudi Arabia Announces Counter-Terrorism Measures."
52. Lefkowitz and Levin, "Kingdom Cover."
53. "In the Wake of the Riyadh Bombings," MEMRI Special Dispatch Series – No. 514, 1 June 2003, *Al Sharq Al Awsat*, London, 17 May 2003.
54. "Saudi Arabian Monetary Agency Implements New Regulations Regarding Charities," *Saudi Arabia News*, Saudi–US Relations Information Service, www.saudi-us-relations.org, 21 July 2003.
55. "Threatened Humanitarian and Charity Societies Prepares [*sic*] for First Conference," www.ArabicNews.com, 4 January 2003.

3 THE BANKS

1. *United States of America* v. *Enaam M. Arnaout*, various documents, including Government's Evidentiary Proffer, Case No. 02 CR 892, US District Court, Northern District of Illinois, Eastern Division, 6 January 2003.
2. "Les documents originaux de la Golden Chain," www.investigateur.com.
3. A. Fuer, "Bin-Laden Group had Extensive Network of Companies, Witness Says," *New York Times*, 13 February 2001.
4. *Ottawa Citizen*, 12 October 2001, noted in Frontline Fellowship, www.frontline.org.za/articles/terrorism_ persecution.htm.
5. R. Woodward, "Bin Laden Said to 'Own' the Taliban," *Washington Post*, 11 October 2001.
6. D. Benjamin and S. Simon, *The Age of Sacred Terror*, New York: Random House, 2002, pp. 292–293.
7. J. Winer and T. J. Roule, "Fighting Terrorist Finance," *Survival*, vol. 44, no. 3, Autumn 2002, p. 99.
8. See the reports of OFAC on www.treas.gov/offices/enforcement/ofac/.
9. See www.fbi.gov/congress/congress02/lormel021202.htm.
10. "Financial Action Task Force (FATF) Cracks Down on Terrorist Financing," US Consulate, Hong Kong: www.usconsulate.org.hk/usinfo/terror/2001/103101.htm, 31 October 2001.
11. K. W. Dam, Deputy Secretary of the Treasury, "The Financial Front of the War on Terrorism – the Next Phase," address delivered to the Council on Foreign Relations, New York, 8 June 2002.
12. Robert O'Harrow Jr., David S. Hilzencath, and Karende Young, "Bin Laden's Money Takes Hidden Paths to Agents of Terror," *Washington Post*, 21 September 2001, p. A13; see also testimony of Matthew A. Levitt, US House of Representatives Subcommittee on International Trade and Finance, Committee on Banking, Housing and Urban Affairs, Washington DC, 1 August 2002.
13. "Following the Terrorists' Money," *Business Week Online*, 1 October 2001.
14. See US Department of the Treasury, www.treas.gov/offices/enforcement/ofac/actions/index.html, for updates.
15. J. M. Dorsey, "Saudi Arabia is Monitoring Key Bank Accounts," *Wall Street Journal*, 6 February 2002.

16. "Saudis Issue Order to Freeze Terrorist-Linked Assets," USATODAY.com, 3 March 2003.
17. Matthew Levitt, "Targeting Terror," position paper, Washington Institute for Near East Policy, 2002. See also "Subversion from Within: Saudi Funding of Islamic Extremist Groups Undermining US Interests and the War on Terror from within the United States," testimony of Matthew Levitt, Senate Judiciary Committee, Subcommittee on Terrorism, United States Senate, 10 September 2003, Washington DC.
18. R. Lacey, *The Kingdom: Arabia and the House of Saud*, New York: Harcourt Brace Jovanovich, 1981, p. 323.
19. "Banking in the Kingdom," *Gulf States Newsletter*, no. 515, 17 July 1995.
20. The Muslim Brotherhood Movement homepage for 2001 provided substantial information: www.ummah.org.uk/ikhwan/index.html.
21. Pierre Pean, *L'Extremiste François Genoud, de Hitler a Carlos*, Paris: Fayard, 1996.
22. C. M. Henry, "Guest Editor's Introduction," *Thunderbird International Review of Business*, special issue on Islamic finance, July 1999.
23. F. E. Vogel and S. L. Hayes III, *Islamic Law and Finance: Religion, Risk, and Return*, The Hague and Boston: Kluwer Law Intl, 1998, p. 176.
24. First Islamic Banking Conference, Toronto, Canada, 25 May 1995, co-sponsored by the Islamic Society of North America, Zafar & Associates, and the *American Journal of Islamic Finance*.
25. "Sudan: Islamic Banking," http:reference.allrefer.com for the Sudan, 1991.
26. "Moves Begin to Set up Sharia Bank in UK," www.zawya.com, 10 November 2002.
27. "Banking in the Kingdom"; see also Andrew Cunningham, *Banking in the Middle East*, London: Financial Times Publishing, 1995.
28. "Written Testimony of Jean-Charles Brisard," US Senate document: www.senate.gov/~banking/_files/brisard.pdf, 2003.
29. Clement M. Henry, *The Mediterranean Debt Crescent: Money and Power in Algeria, Egypt, Morocco, Tunisia, and Turkey*, Cairo: American University Press, 1996.
30. Henry, "Guest Editor's Introduction."
31. Marc Roche, "La Grande discretion des banques 'islamiques,'" *Le Monde*, 18 September 2001.
32. No mention is made of Kaki involvement in either M. Potts et al., *Dirty Money*, Washington DC: National Press Books, 1992, or P. Truell and L. Gurwin, *False Profits*, New York: Houghton Mifflin Co., 1992.
33. "Banking in the Kingdom."
34. "The Press on the BCCI–bin Mahfouz–bin Laden Intelligence," *Boston Herald*, 11 December 2001.
35. See articles in the *Boston Herald* for 14 October, 10 and 11 December 2001.
36. "The Press on the BCCI–bin Mahfouz–bin Laden Intelligence Nexus."
37. Seth Stern, "Can a Trillion-Dollar Lawsuit Stop Saudi Terror-Cash Flow?" *Christian Science Monitor*, 20 August 2002; "Families of September 11 Victims to Sue Alleged al-Qaeda Paymaster," *Middle East Times*, issue 33, August 2002.

38. G. Simpson and R. Wartzman, "US Probes Saudi Conglomerate for Links to Islamic Militants," *Wall Street Journal*, 2 November 2001.
39. "The United States and Italy Designate Twenty-Five New Financiers of Terror," US Department of the Treasury, Office of Public Affairs, www.ustreas.gov/press/releases/po3380.tm, 29 August 2002.
40. Translation from the German: "Report: Al-Taqwa Finance Company Searched," *Neuen Zurcher Zeitung* (www.nzz.ch), 8 November 2001.
41. Lucy Komisar, "Shareholders in the Bank of Terror?" Salon.com, 15 March, 2002; Mark Hosenball, "Terror's Cash Flow," *Newsweek*, 25 March 2002.
42. Testimony of Juan C. Zarate, Deputy Assistant Secretary, US Department of the Treasury, House Financial Subcommittee on Oversight and Investigations, 12 February 2002.
43. Komisar, "Shareholders in the Bank of Terror?"
44. M. Huband, "Bankrolling Bin Laden," *Financial Times*, 29 November 2002.
45. "The United States and Italy Designate Twenty-Five New Financiers of Terror."
46. "Saudi Front Divided in the War on Terrorism," *Gulf States Newsletter*, no. 672, 17 October 2001.
47. Komisar, "Shareholders in the Bank of Terror?"
48. P. W. Rasche, "The Politics of Three – Pakistan, Saudi Arabia, Israel," www.druckversion.studien-von-Zeitfragen.net, 2002.
49. "Bin Laden's Money Takes Hidden Paths to Agents of Terror."
50. The bibliography for *hawala* is not large, but perhaps the most succinct analysis is in Patrick M. Jost and Harjit Singh Sandhu, "The *Hawala* Alternative Remittance System and its Role in Money Laundering," www.interpol Int/Public/FinancialCrime/MoneyLaundering/hawala/default. Asp, 6 June 2004. See also Thomas H. Kean (Chair) and Lee H. Hamilton (Vice Chair), *9/11 Report: National Commission on Terrorist Attacks upon the United States with Reporting and Analysis by the* New York Times, New York: St. Martin's Press, 2004, chap. 2.
51. M. Falkov, "The Wahhabites' Anti-Eurasian Crimes," *Arktogaia Forum on Geopolitics and Politology*, Moscow, 11 April 2001.

4 AFGHANISTAN BEGINNINGS

1. See Quran, Sura 62; Mahmoud Haddad, "Salafiyya Movement," in P. Mattar (ed.), *Encyclopedia of the Modern Middle East and North Africa*, Farmington Hills, MI: Thomson Gale, 2004, vol. III, pp. 1973–1975; T. P. Hughes, *Dictionary of Islam*, London: W. H. Allen, 1885, pp. 548–549; "Indonesian Background: Why Salafism and Terrorism Don't Mix," International Crisis Group, Asia Report, no. 83, Brussels, 13 September 2004.
2. "Holy War on the World," *Financial Times*, FT.com, 17 April 2004.
3. J. Calvert, "The World is an Undutiful Boy: Sayyid Qutb's American Experience," *Islam and Christian–Muslim Relations*, vol. 11, no. 1, 2000, pp. 87–103; M. Ruthven, *A Fury for God: The Islamist Attack on America*, London: Granta, 2002, p. 83.

4. P. Berman, "The Philosopher of Islamic Terror," *New York Times Magazine*, 23 March 2003.

5. "Robert Irwin on Sayyid Qutb, the Father of Modern Islamist Fundamentalism," *Guardian*, 1 November 2001.

6. J. Adams, *The New Spies*, London: Hutchinson, 1994, pp. 180–181; B. R. Rubin, *The Search for Peace in Afghanistan*, New Haven: Yale University Press, 1995.

7. "Arab Veterans of Afghanistan War Lead New Islamic Holy War," Compass News Service, London, 28 October 1994; see also J. K. Cooley, *Unholy Wars: Afghanistan, America and International Terrorism*, London, Sterling, VA: Pluto Press, 2000; M. Griffin, *Reaping the Whirlwind: The Taliban Movement in Afghanistan*, London, Sterling, VA: Pluto Press, 2001.

8. "The Striving Sheik": Abdullah Azzam," *Nida'ul Islam*, no. 14, www.speednet.com.au/~nida, July–September 1996. Azzam's most influential work is *Ilhaq bi l-q filah* (Join the Caravan), Pakistan, 1986.

9. W. B. Quandt, *Saudi Arabia in the 1980s*, Washington, DC: Brookings Institution, 1981, pp. 42–43.

10. "The Striving Sheik."

11. M. J. Grinfeld, "Mental Health Consequences of Conflict Neglected," *Psychiatric Times*, vol. 19, no. 4, April 2002.

12. "Mujahid Usamah Bin Ladin," *Nida'ul Islam*, no. 15, www.speednet.com.au/~nida, October–November 1996.

13. V. Loeb, "A Global, Pan-Islamic Network: Terrorism Entrepreneur Unifies Groups Financially, Politically," *Washington Post*, 23 August 1998.

14. L. Bergman and M. Smith, *Hunting Bin Laden*, PBS TV, Washington, DC, 21 March 2000.

15. F. Symon, *Analysis: The Roots of Jihad*, BBC News, 16 October 2001.

16. Paul Harris and Martin Bright, "Saudi Envoy in UK Linked to 9/11," *Observer*, 2 March 2003.

17. Rohan Gunaratna, *Inside Al Qaeda*, New York: Berkeley Books, 2002, pp. 26–27.

18. M. Weaver, "Blowback," *The Atlantic Online*, May 1996.

19. "Arab Veterans of Afghanistan War Lead New Islamic Holy War."

20. S. Emerson, "Abdullah Assam: The Man before Osama Bin Laden," International Association for Counterterrorism and Security Professionals, www.iacsp.com/itobli3.html.

21. "Attack on Terrorism – Inside al-Qaeda: Holy War on the World," *Financial Times*, special report, 28 November 2002.

22. A. Marshall, "Terror 'Blowback' Burns CIAS," *The Independent*, London, 1 November 1998.

23. B. Whitaker, "Egyptian Doctor who Laid the Foundations for Global Jihad," *Guardian*, 20 March 2004.

24. L. Wright, "The Man Behind bin Laden," *The New Yorker*, 16 September 2002.

25. C. T. Miller, "The Alleged Brains behind bin Laden," *Los Angeles Times*, 2 October 2001.

26. T. Valdmanis, "Egyptian Masterminds Behind bin Laden," *USA Today*, 11 October 2001.
27. N. Raphaeli, "Radical Islamist Profiles: Ayman Muhammad Rabi' al-Zawahiri: The Making of an Arch Terrorist," Special Dispatch, MEMRI, 11 March 2003.
28. David Ignatius, "US Fears Sudan Becoming Terrorists' 'New Lebanon,'" *Washington Post*, 31 January 1992, p. 13; Tarun Basu, "Pakistan Called an 'Incubator' of Terrorism," *India Abroad*, 1 December 1995; Cooley, *Unholy Wars*, pp. 33 ff.
29. Weaver, "Blowback."
30. "Islam on Trial: The Case of Sheikh Omar Abdul-Rahman," azzam@panther.netmania.co.uk.
31. E. A. Gargan., "Afghan President Says US Should See him as Ally against Militant Islam," *New York Times*, 10 March 1992. In 1999 Afghanistan accounted for 4,500 tons of opium or 75 percent of the world's production that year, worth $183 million at the farmgate. See Ahmad Rashid, "The Year in Afghanistan: 2000," *Afghanistankomiteen: Norge*, Oslo, 2001.
32. R. Weintraub, "Afghanistan to Allow Outside Refugee Aid," *Washington Post*, 17 May 1988.
33. "The Striving Sheik."
34. J. Millard Burr and Robert O. Collins, *Revolutionary Sudan: Hasan al-Turabi and the Islamist State, 1989–2000*, Leiden: Brill, 2003, pp. 69–73.
35. Miller, "The Alleged Brains behind bin Laden."
36. "Treasury Department Statement on the Designation of Wa'el Hamza Julidan," Department of the Treasury, Office of Public Affairs, 6 September 2002.
37. Zachary Abuza, *Militant Islam in Southeast Asia: Crucible of Terror*, Boulder, CO: Lynne Rienner, 2003.
38. Simon Reeve, *The New Jackals: Ramez Yousef, Osama bin Laden, and the Future of Terrorism*. Boston: Northeastern University Press, 1999.
39. "Khadr Tied to al-Qaeda as Far Back as 1988," *National Post*, Canada, 1 February 2003.
40. "Arab Veterans of Afghanistan War Lead New Islamic Holy War."
41. "Trial Testimony, *USA v. Usama bin Laden*," US Federal Court, New York City, January–May 2001.
42. A. Martin and M. J. Berens, "Terrorists Evolved in US," *Chicago Tribune*, 11 December 2001.
43. *Khaleej Times*, Saudi Arabia, 8 September 2002.
44. "Confusion over Linking Saudi Businessman with Osama," *Dawn*, Pakistan, 9 September 2002.
45. "Saudi Spy Chief 'Surprised' over Action against bin Laden Associate,"AFP, 7 September 2002.
46. See www.satp.org/satporgtp/countries/pakistan/. This site provides information on other trusts supporting terrorist organizations.
47. "US Designates Al Akhtar Trust," US Department of the Treasury, Office of Public Affairs, 14 October 2003.

48. Mahmood Zahman, "Blood, Sweat, Tears," *Dawn*, Pakistan, 11 September 1997.

49. After 9/11 Pakistan banned the Al Rashid Trust and Akhtar was reportedly "whisked off" to the Gulf by "one of his Arab friends" after the Taliban defeat in 2002. See also "The Great Banuri Town Seminary," *Friday Times*, Lahore, Pakistan, 20–26 February 2004.

50. P. Escobar, "The Roving Eye: Anatomy of a 'Terrorist' NGO," *Asia Times*, 26 October 2001.

51. South Asia Analysis Group, paper no. 330, 27 September 2001.

52. "Al-Qaeda Still Spreading, Warns UN Group," smh.com.au, *Stanley Morning Herald*, Australia, 2 December 2003.

53. "How Charity Begins in Saudi Arabia," *Asia Times* online, www.atimes.com, 16 January 2004.

5 ISLAMIC CHARITIES AND THE REVOLUTIONARY SUDAN

1. Francis M. Deng, *War of Visions: Conflict of Identities in the Sudan*, Washington, DC: Brookings Institution, 1995, p. 16.

2. On BADEA see Dunstan M. Wai, "African–Arab Relations: Interdependence or Misplaced Optimism?" *Journal of Modern African Studies*, vol. 21, no. 2, 1983.

3. K. Gannon, "Pakistan Deporting 89 Arab Aid Workers," AP, Peshawar, 6 October 2001.

4. B. Mudawi, "How Islamic Banks can Aid Governments," *Arabia*, January 1984, pp. 58–59; B. Mudawi, "Islamic Bank in Africa," *The Muslim World*, 23 July 1983, p. 5.

5. R. Labeviere, *Dollars for Terrorism: The United States and Islam*, New York: Algora Publishing, 2000, p. 85.

6. "The Banking System: Its History in Sudan," *Sudanow*, June 1991.

7. "Sharia Support Fund: Guaranteeing Justice and Welfare," *Sudanow*, March 1991.

8. "Muhammad al-Bashir Muhammad al-Hady, the Secretary of the Sudanese Information Ministry to 'Nida'ul Islam,'" *Nida'ul Islam*, www.islam.org.au/articles/17/sudan.htm, pp. 2–3, 1997.

9. Sudan 1991: *USA* v. *Ali Mohamed*, Guilty Plea in US Embassy Bombings, Court Reporters Office of the Southern District of New York, 24 October 2000.

10. 1996 US Department of State Report, Washington DC

11. "Usama bin Laden: A Legend Gone Wrong," *The Muslim Magazine*, vol. 1, no. 4, 1998.

12. "Frontline," www.pbs.org/wgbh/pages/frontline/shows/binladen/who/family.html, 2001.

13. R. Woodward, "Bin Laden Said to 'Own' the Taliban," *Washington Post*, 11 October, 2001.

14. R. Sale, "Collapse of BCCI Shorts Bin Laden," UPI, Washington DC, 1 March 2000.

15. J. Kenny, OP, "Arab Aid and Influence in Tropical Africa," Consultation of the Christian Councils in West Africa on Christian–Muslim Relations,

Monrovia, 25–28 November 1984, in *Christianity and Islam in Dialogue*, Cape Coast: Association of Episcopal Conferences of Anglophone West Africa, 1987, pp. 77–83.

16. "Saudi-Arabian stiften Koran-Exemplare"; "Islamische Welt-Liga: Hauptanliegen bleibt die Verkundigung"; "Islamische Liga entsendet Prediger in alle Welt," all in *Deutsche Welle-Kirchenfunk*, 20 April 1983, p. 4; 29 June 1983, p. 1; 30 May 1984, p. 2, respectively.

17. News of the Day Section, *Wall Street Journal*, 16 March 1992, p. 10.

18. "Sudan: Munadamat al Da'wah Al Islamiyah (Islamic Call Organization)," Qatar News Agency, 24 April 1997.

19. D. D. Akuany, *Can There be a Sustainable Peace, Democracy, and Development under Sectarian Political Islam? Experience from Sudan*, New Sudan African Society publication (pamphlet), 2003.

20. "Islamic African Relief Agency," *The Muslim World*, 10 September 1983, p. 2.

21. O. H. Kasule, "Islamic Da'wa in Africa: Methods and Strategy," *The Universal Message*, May 1984, pp. 6–9.

22. "Islamic African Relief Agency."

23. Gannon, "Pakistan Deporting 89 Arab Aid Workers."

24. "Saudi Commitment to Establishing Islamic Centers, Mosques and Institutes," Saudi Arabian Information Resource, 15 February 2002.

25. Kenny, "Arab Aid and Influence in Tropical Africa."

26. "Islamic African Centre, Khartoum," *Al-Islam*, June 1983.

27. Akuany, *Can There be a Sustainable Peace, Democracy, and Development?*

28. "Comprehensive Da'awa Programme Targets Social Renewal," *New Horizon*, Khartoum, 4 August 1994, p. 2; "Salih Lashes Out at Population Conference," *New Horizon*, Khartoum, 7 September 1994, p. 4.

29. "Islam, Democracy, the State and the West; Roundtable with Dr. Hassan Turabi," *Middle East Policy*, vol. 1, no.3, 1992, pp. 49–61; see also "Tourabi, Hassan Al," *Agence Europe*, European Institute for Research on Mediterranean and Euro-Arab Cooperation, April 2004; J. Miller, "Faces of Fundamentalism: Hassan al-Turabi and Muhammad Fadlallah," *Foreign Affairs*, no. 11–12, 1994, p. 127.

30. See D. Hurst, "Dark Times Loom for Visionary Sudan," *Guardian*, 26 May 1997.

31. Y. Bodansky and V. S. Forrest, "Iran's European Springboard?" Congressional Task Force on Terrorism and Unconventional Warfare, US House of Representatives, Washington DC, 1 September 1992.

32. S. Lautze, "International and National Islamic NGOs in Sudan," *Sudanow*, Khartoum, November 1992.

33. "The Connection," *Tampa Tribune*, 28–29 May 1995.

34. Hasan al-Turabi, "Islamic Fundamentalism in the Sunna and Shia World," speech, Madrid, Spain, 2 August 1994.

35. Y. Bodansky, "Arafat – Between Jihad and Survivalism," *The Maccabean*, May 1997.

36. "Islam, Democracy, the State and the West."

37. *Al Wasat*, London, 14–20 December 1992, pp. 22–25; on HAMAS, Fatah, and the Khartoum connection, see *Al Watan Al Arabi*, 30 October 1992, pp. 21–22.
38. J. Flint, "Under Islamic Siege," *Africa Report*, September/October 1993, p. 26.
39. "Dudaev Calls for Islamic Alliance against West," *Radio Free Europe/Radio Liberty Research Institute Daily Report*, Washington DC, no. 226, 26 November 1993.
40. Bodansky and Forrest, "Iran's European Springboard?"
41. S. Gangadharan, "Exploring Jihad: The Case of Algeria," *Strategic Affairs*, issue 0014, 1 February 2001.
42. "Algerian Terrorism," in *Patterns of Global Terrorism 1993*, Office of the Coordinator for Counterterrorism, US Department of State, April 1994.
43. R. Rahal, "Charities Thriving Despite US Warnings," *Middle East Times*, issue 18, 2002.
44. J. M. Burr and R. O. Collins, *Requiem for the Sudan*, Boulder: Westview Press, 1995.
45. R. Block et al., "US Targets Saudi Accounts," 3 March 2003, www.globetechnology.com/archive/20011015/WJFEAT.html.
46. "Sudan/Egypt: Calling the Shots after Addis Ababa,"*Africa Confidential*, vol. 3b, no. 14, July 1995, pp. 11–14.
47. Ibid.; also "Saudi Says he Has Not Given Money to Bin Laden," www.cnn.com/2001/WORLD/meast/10/15/inv.saudi.frozen.assets, 15 October 2001.
48. "Middle East: Bin Laden 'Received UN Cash,'" BBC News, 20 October 2001.
49. "Saudi Says he has Not Given Money to Bin Laden."
50. M. Yared, "Soudan. le Sabre et le Coran," *Jeune Afrique*, 33: 1674, 4 January–10 February 1993, pp. 24–26, at p. 4.
51. SUNA Radio, Khartoum, 16:37 GMT, 12 January 1993; "Near East and South Asia," FBIS, 15 January 1993, p. 1.
52. R. Sale, "Analysis: The Man behind Bin Laden," UPI, Washington DC, 25 March 2004.
53. W. Millward, "The Rising Tide of Islamic Fundamentalism (II)," Canadian Security Intelligence Service, Commentary No. 31, April 1993.
54. J. Parmalee, "Waltzing with Warlords," *Washington Post*, 20 June 1993.
55. Millward, "The Rising Tide of Islamic Fundamentalism."
56. "Sudanese–Iranian Relations Shift up a Gear," *Sudan Democratic Gazette*, London, February 1993, p. 4; "Relapse to Clan Warfare," *The Middle East*, January 1992, p. 25.
57. Jerry Seper, "KLA Rebels Train in Terrorist Camps," *Washington Times*, 4 May 1994.
58. *Horn of Africa Bulletin*, derived from an *Indian Ocean Newsletter* report, 6 March 1993.
59. K. Allard, "Somalia Operations: Lessons Learned," National Defense Publication, Institute for National Strategic Studies, January 1995; "Usama bin Laden: A Legend Gone Wrong."

60. "Somali Group Claims Victory in NW," AP, 15 June 1997.
61. D. Bricker and L. Leatherbee, *Balancing Consensus and Dissent: The Prospects for Human Rights and Democracy in the Horn of Africa* (pamphlet), Horn of Africa Program, New York: Fund for Peace, January 1994.
62. K. Kelley, "Saudi Charity Accused of Plotting to Bomb Zanzibar Hotels, US Charges," *The East African*, Nairobi, 26 January 2004.
63. "Uganda: Some ADF Rebels Reportedly Trained under Bin-Ladin Auspices," BBC Monitoring Service, 18 October 2001, from *The New Vision*, Kampala.
64. "Saudi with Royal Links Seized in CIA Terror Swoop," www.timesonline. co.uk/article/0,2089–736695,00.html, July 2003.
65. H. Weiss, "Zakat in Pre-Colonial Sub-Saharan Africa. A Tentative Survey, Part Three" (private distribution).
66. Kenny, "Arab Aid and Influence in Tropical Africa."
67. "Islamic Foundation in Nigeria," *The Muslim World*, 5 March 1983, p. 4.
68. "NGO in Nigeria for Promoting Islam," Abeokuta, Nigeria, www.islam-online.net, 26 January 2002.

6 ISLAM AT WAR IN THE BALKANS

1. A. Izetbegovic, *Le Manifeste islamique*, Beirut: Al Bouraq, 1999.
2. A. Cerkez-Robinson, "Bosnia," AP Sarajevo, 23 March 2002. In 1996 the SJRC changed its name to the Saudi High Relief Commission (SHCR), but the major patrons and administrative staff remained the same.
3. Ibid.
4. "Polish Press Reports on Training of Mujahideen in Bosnia," TANJUG, Yugoslavia, 16 December 1997.
5. "Bosnian Leader Hails Islam at Election Rallies," *New York Times*, 2 September 1996.
6. "Muslim Chief Hints at the Use of Chemicals," *New York Times*, 31 October 1992.
7. "Islam's Legion Seeks Blood in Bosnia," *Observer*, London, 18 October 1992.
8. "Help from the Holy Warriors," *Newsweek*, 5 October 1992.
9. "Islamic Nations will Take it upon Themselves to Arm the Bosnians," Staff Reporter, *Wall Street Journal*, 3 December 1992.
10. Michael R. Gordon, "Weapons Shipment Intercepted on Way to Bosnia," *New York Times*, 26 January 1993.
11. Tony Horwitz, "Bosnia Muslims Threaten to Quit Geneva Talks," *Washington Post*, 28 January 1993.
12. James Risen and Doyle McManns, "US Had Options to Let Bosnia Get Arms, Avoid Iran," *Los Angeles Times*, 1 July 1996.
13. See Y. Bodansky, *Target America, Terrorism in the US Today, Terror, the Inside Story of the Terrorist Conspiracy in America, Offensive in the Balkans*, Alexandria, VA: International Strategic Studies Association, 1995.
14. R. Fisk, "Anti-Soviet Warrior Puts his Army on the Road to Peace," *Independent*, London, 6 December 1993.

15. "The Role of Austria in Financing the Moslem Government," *Serbia Today*, 2 April 1996.
16. IRNA, Vienna dateline, 23 June 1993.
17. "Austrians Intent on Balanced Trade with Iran Says Ambassador," IRNA, 1 September 1993.
18. "Tehran–Khartoum Ties Principled: Sudanese Parliament Speaker," IRNA, Tehran, 18 August 1993.
19. JPRS-TOT-94-026-1, 7 July 1994, from a TANJUG Radio report in English, 24 June 1994, and derived in part from the Turkish daily *Milliyet*.
20. By 1997 the UAE Red Crescent had devoted 134,012 million dirhams (approximately $50 million) to Bosnia, its largest contribution for any state (see http://uae.dmedia.co.kr). Two UAE banks kept "cadres of staff whose sole job is to cater to individual cash demands, which could be anything" from $500,000 to $2 million (*Financial Times*, FT.com, "Arabia Bridles at Americans' Insistence on al-Qaeda Cash," 19 February 2002).
21. K. Hechtman, "Charitable Acts of War," *Montreal Mirror*, 21 November 2002.
22. Fisk, "Anti-Soviet Warrior Puts his Army on the Road to Peace." His interview with Turabi appeared in the *Independent* on 3 December 1993.
23. "Bin Laden's Balkan Connections," Centre for Peace in the Balkans, September 2001; "Bin Laden was Granted Bosnian Passport," AFP, Sarajevo, 24 September 1999. Other Al Qaeda leaders who traveled on Bosnian passports included the Tunisian-born Mehrez Aodouni, who was arrested in Istanbul in September 1999.
24. "Hostages to a Brutal Past," *US News & World Report*, 15 February 1993, p. 56.
25. "Kabul is Khartoum's Latest Arms Supplier," *Sudan Democratic Gazette*, London, October 1993, p. 6.
26. *Foreign Report*, London: Economist Newspaper Ltd., 1 July 1993.
27. "CIPF Investment Contacts," *New Horizon*, Khartoum, 29 November 1994.
28. See Bodansky, *Target America*.
29. "New Peace Bid," *New Horizon*, Khartoum, 1 June 1994, p. 1.
30. *Vecernje Novosti*, Yugoslavia, 2 April 1996.
31. J. Pomfret, "Arms-Supplies for Bosnia: How Bosnia's Muslims Dodged Arms Embargo," *Washington Post*, 22 September 1996.
32. Ibid.
33. Ibid.
34. See www.yugoslavia.com – Serbia Bulletin – October 1996; "Experts in Fear," *Politika* through TANJUG, Tel Aviv dateline, 5 October 1995.
35. Published in the economic journal *Wirtschafts Woche*, Austria, October 1995; see also "Fingerprints: Arms to Bosnia, the Real Story," *New Republic*, 28 October 1996.
36. G. Bradic, "Muslim Humanitarian Organization Delivered Arms to Bosnia-Herzegovina," TANJUG, Vienna dateline, published in the *Serbian Bulletin*, October 1996.
37. Other charities: Bosnia Relief Fund, USA Inc. (Elk Grove, IL); Bosnian–American Cultural Association (Northbrook, IL); Holy Land Foundation

for Relief and Development (Richardson, TX, and Patterson, NJ); ICNA Relief; Albanian Islamic Cultural Center – Kosovo Relief (Staten Island, NY) collects for Macedonia under the name The Light; IKRE Fund (Sunnyside, NY); Jerrahi Order of America (Chestnut Ridge, NY); Mercy International-USA, Inc. (Plymouth, MI) with an office in Albania, three offices in Bosnia, and one in Croatia: Save Bosnia Now, Ummah Relief International (Elgin, IL), and Al Haramain Educational Center (Ashland, OR) were also active in Bosnia. In Canada one found the Bosnian Children Relief (Toronto); Bosnian–Canadian Relief Association (Toronto); and World Humanity Fund, Inc. (Napean, Ontario).

38. F. Schmidt, "Refugees Return to Bosnia from Macedonia," *OMRI Daily Digest*, vol. 1, no. 108, 5 June 1995.
39. "Velayati: OIC Plan," IRNA, Tehran, 14 July 1993.
40. Senate Select Committee Report on Iran/Bosnia Arms Transfers, United States Senate, November 1996.
41. R. Fox, "Iran's Cases of Cash 'Helped Buy Muslim Victory in Bosnia,'" International News, Electronic *Telegraph*, London, www.telegraph.co.uk, 1 January 1997.
42. *United States of America* v. *Aldurahman Muhammad Alamoudi*, US District Court for the Eastern District of Virginia, Criminal Case No. 03-A, 22 October 2003.
43. J. Smith, "A Bosnian Village's Terrorist Ties," *Washington Post*, 11 March 2000.
44. Fox, "Iran's Cases of Cash 'Helped Buy Muslim Victory in Bosnia.'"
45. In March the USA began arming the Bosnian military with light weapons. See M. Mihalka, "News," *Serbia Today*, 2 April 1996; M. Mihalka, "Mujaheddin Remaining in Bosnia: Islamic Militants Strongarm Civilians, Defy Dayton Plan," *Washington Post*, 8 July 1996.
46. Saudi Public Affairs Reports "On the Bosnian Situation," Embassy of Saudi Arabia, Washington DC, 26 September 1996; see also "Kingdom Assists Bosnian Refugees," 3 September 1996.
47. B. Whitmore, "Bosnian Charities Tied to Terror," *Boston Globe*, 3 July 2002, http://www.bostonglobe.com.
48. "Islamic Charity, Leader Charged," *Chicago Tribune*, 14 May 2004.
49. J. Brisard, "Written Testimony of Jean-Charles Brisard, International Expert on Terrorism Financing and Lead Investigator, 9/11 Lawsuit," www.senate.gov/~banking/_files/brisard.pdf.
50. M. Vickers and J. Pettifer, *Albania: From Anarchy to a Balkan Identity*, New York: New York University Press, 1997.
51. Ibid., p. 105.
52. S. Rodan, "Central European Diary: Kosovo Seen as New Islamic Bastion," *Jerusalem Post*, 14 September 1998.
53. Ibid.
54. A. Higgins and C. Cooper, "CIA-Backed Team Used Brutal Means to Break up Terrorist Cell in Albania," *Wall Street Journal*, 20 November 2001.
55. Rodan, "Central European Diary."

56. S. Trifkovic, "The Balkan Terror Threat," *The Greco Report*, http://www.grecoreport.com, 2003.

57. *Sunday Times*, London, 22 March 1998; *Washington Times*, 4 May 1999.

58. Higgins and Cooper, "CIA-Backed Team."

59. "Third Egyptian Accused of Terrorism Arrested in Tirana," Albanian Telegraphic Agency, Tirana, 21 July 1998.

60. Higgins and Cooper, "CIA-Backed Team."

61. A. Bala, "Albania: Officials Crack Down on Terror Suspects," Radio Free Europe/Radio Liberty, 27 January 2002.

62. Isa Blumi, "Indoctrinating Albanians: Dynamics of Islamic Aid," *International Institute for the Study of Islam in the Modern World Newsletter*, November 2002.

63. "Kosovo Asks for US, UN Help to Keep Serbs from Attacking," *Chicago Tribune*, 17 February 1993.

64. T. Siefer, "Same 'Charities' Follow CIA & Bin Laden to Kosovo & Chechnya," www.libertyforum.org/showflat.php?Cat =&Board=news_news & NuSynopsis, 23 July 2003.

65. Rodan, "Central European Diary."

66. C. Stephen, "US Tackles Islamic Militancy in Kosovo," *Scotsman*, 30 November 1998.

67. B. Williams, "Jihad and Ethnicity in Post Communist Eurasia," *The Global Review of Ethnopolitics*, vol. 2, March/June 2003.

68. Siefer, "Same 'Charities' Follow CIA."

69. "Sudan Plans Relief Flight for Kosovo Moslems," AFP, Khartoum, 30 April 1999.

70. M. Epstein and B. Schmidt, "Operation Support-System Shutdown," *National Review Online*, 4 September 2003.

71. Review of his memoirs *Inescapable Questions: Autobiographical Notes*, www.angelfire.com/dc/mbooks/izetbovic.html.

72. D. Pallister, "Terrorist Material Found in Sarajevo Charity," *Guardian*, 23 February 2002; M. Levitt, "Tackling the Financing of Terrorism in Saudi Arabia," *Policywatch*, no. 609, Washington DC: Washington Institute for Near East Policy, 11 March 2002.

73. A. Dragicevic, "Bosnian Official Says al-Qaida Planned Attack on Embassy," *North County Times*, San Diego, California, 24 March 2002.

74. Whitmore, "Bosnian Charities Tied to Terror."

7 RUSSIA AND THE CENTRAL ASIAN CRESCENT

1. "The Taliban is our Ally" (translated from the Russian), *Novy Peterburg*, St. Petersburg, no. 55, 13 December 2001.

2. "Russia's Mufti Council," *Pravda*, 19 July 2001.

3. "Chechnya: The Paths to Settlement," "Islamic Threat or Threat to Islam," *Eurasia*, All-Russian Social Political Movement Conference, Moscow, 28 June 2001.

4. M. Karim, "The Revival of Islam in Central Asia and Caucasus," www.renaissance.com.pk/ferefl.html, 1995.

5. D. Fairbairn, "Islam in the Soviet Era," *East–West Church & Ministry Report*, vol. 2, no. 4, Fall 1994.

6. A. Khamidov, "Countering the Call: The US, Hizb-ut-Tahrir, and Religious Extremism in Central Asia," *US Policy Towards the Islamic World*, Analysis Paper no. 4, Brookings Institution, 4 July 2003.

7. *Hizb ut-Tahrir*, London: Al-Khalifah Publications; see also Suha Taji-Farouki, *A Fundamental Quest: Hizb ut-Tahrir and the Search for the Islamic Caliphate*, London: Grey Seal, 1996.

8. Press conference release by Hizb ut-Tahrir in Denmark, www.hizb-ut-tahrir.info/english/, 21 January 2004; on the origins of HuT see "Al-Muhajiroun in the UK: An Interview with Sheikh Omar Bakri Muhammad," www.al-muhaajiroun.com/articles/interview.htm.

9. A. Cohen, "Hizb ut-Tahrir: An Emerging Threat to US Interest in Central Asia," *Backgrounder*, no. 1656, Heritage Foundation, 30 May 2003.

10. M. Whine, "Al-Muhajiroun: The Portal for Britain's Suicide Terrorists," International Policy Institute for Counter-Terrorism, 21 May 2003.

11. "Russian Troops Drop CIS Figleaf, Will Stay in Tajikistan," *Monitor*, Jamestown Foundation, 8 April 1999; "Russia Obtains Military Basing Rights in Tajikistan," *Monitor*, 21 April 1999.

12. K. Parshin, "Tajik Government Fears Fundamentalist Spread," Transitions Online, 27 March 2001, www.eurasia.net.org/departments/insight/articles/eav032701.shtml.

13. "Tajik Government Fears Spread of Call of Hizb-ut-Tahrir," www.hizb-ut-tahrir.org, 31 March 2001; "Tajikistan Court Sentences Nine Islamists to Death," *Daily Times*, Pakistan, 27 February 2003.

14. "Chechnya: The Paths to Settlement," and "Islamic Threat or Threat to Islam," All-Russian Social Political Movement Conference, *Eurasia*, Moscow 28 June 2001.

15. M. Falkov, "Arktogaia Forum April 2001: The Wahhabites' Anti-Eurasian Crimes," policy paper, Arktogaia Forum on Geopolitics and Politology, 11 April 2001.

16. V. Ilyain and I. Radzhabov, "Soviet Legacy Cannot Help Bothering the West," *Defense and Security*, no. 42, 12 April 2002.

17. The complexities of this struggle focused on the Ferghana Valley are beyond the scope of this work. See *Calming the Ferghana Valley*, New York: Center for Preventive Action, Century Foundation and Council on Foreign Relations Books, 1999.

18. J. Balfour, "Bukharans Shun Radical Islam," Institute for War and Peace, London, report no. 30, 17 November 200.

19. Ibid.

20. D. Frantz, "Central Asia Braces to Fight Islamic Rebels," *New York Times*, 3 May 2001.

21. G. Curtis, "Drug Funded Terrorist/Extremist Groups in Central Asia," in *A Global Overview of Narcotics-Funded Terrorist and Other Extemist Groups*, Washington DC: Federal Research Division, Library of Congress, May 2002.

22. Whine, "Al-Muhajiroun."
23. IRIN, www.irinnews.org, Tashkent, 24 May 2004.
24. "Uzbekistan: Uneasy Calm Reigns after Attacks," Institute for War and Peace, London, report no. 275, 6 April 2004; "Uzbekistan: Affluent Suicide Bombers," report no. 278, 20 April 2004; "No Place for Uzbek Muslims," report no. 213, 1 July 2003, respectively.
25. S. Jumagulov, "Kyrgyzstan's Cautious Mullahs," Institute for War and Peace, report no. 279, Washington DC, 23 April 2004; A. Nuritov, "Musharraf Vows to Extradite Uzbek Militants," *Arab News*, 7 March 2005.
26. "Turkmenistan: No to Foreign Education," Institute for War and Peace, London, report no. 285, 18 May 2004.
27. "Experts: Religious Persecution Rife in Turkmenistan, Washington, DC – May 20, 2004," Radio Free Europe/Radio Liberty, 21 May 2004.
28. "Niyazov Addresses Youth Meeting, Reads Excerpts from his New Book," ITAR-TASS news agency, Moscow, in Russian, 08:51 GMT, 7 May 2004. See also www.eurasianet.org/Turkmenistan, "Weekly News Brief on Turkmenistan," "Turkmenistan Marks Remembrance Day on May 8," "Turkmen President Donates 100,000 Dollars to War Veterans," 7–13 May 2004.
29. "Resolution by the President of Turkmenistan on Deeming Invalid the Resolution by the Turkmen President Issued on 23 March 2004," Turkmen government website, Ashgabat, BBC in Russian, 13 May 2004.
30. See www.gateway2russia.com/columns.js, 1 February 2004; "Paper Says 'Terrorist' Body Funds Southern Kazakh College," *Gateway to Russia*, *Kazakhstanskaya Pravda*, 28 January 2004.
31. "Islam in Central Asia," www.cimera.org/files/ CP/CP1/4EAlniyasov.pdf.
32. D. Dosybiev, "Kazakstan Tackles Hizb ut-Tahrir," Institute for War and Peace, Washington DC, report no. 276, 14 April 2004.
33. "Islam in Central Asia," p. 87.
34. D. Nissman, "Central Asia's Political Leaders Struggle to Control Islamic Influence," *Prism*, Jamestown Foundation, Washington DC, 22 September 1995.
35. "Preventing Another 'Great Game' in Central Asia," Washington DC: Center for Defense Information, January 2001; A. Higgins, "Bloc Including Chinas, Russia Challenges US in Central Asia," *Wall Street Journal*, 18 June 2001.
36. P. Romero, "China to Push Formation of Asian Anti-Terror Alliance," *Star*, Manila, 1 September 2003.
37. *Press Club Weekly*, no. 15, Yerevan, 25 January 2002. The suspect Kuwaiti charity had already been active in Egypt. See Youssef M. Ibrahim, "Saudis Strip Citizenship from Backer of Militants," *New York Times*, 10 April 1994.
38. P. Baker, "15 Tied to Al Qaeda Turned Over to US," *Washington Post*, 22 October 2002. On Chechnya in 2002 see Seven Lee Myers, "Russia Recasts Bog in Caucasus as War on Terror," *New York Times*, 5 October 2002.
39. "Georgian Security Minister Unveils Classified Details on Pankisi," *Civil Georgia*, www.civil.gelcgi-bin/newsprof/fullnews.cgi; P. Quinn-Judge, "The Surprise in the Gorge," *Time*, 20 October 2002; Dore Gold, "Saudi Arabia and Global Terrorism: From Al Qaeda to HAMAS," Subcommittee on

the Middle East and Central Asia hearing, US House of Representatives, Washington DC, 15 July 2003.

40. "Government Launches Probe into Islamic Charity after FBI Tip," AP, Tbilisi dateline, 10 November 2002.
41. "Georgia: Saakashvili Sees in 'Wahhabism' a Threat to Secularism," Georgia in the Foreign Press, www.kvali.com, 14 June 2004.
42. A. Nokhchi, "Islamic Movement in Chechnya," 21 June 2001, www.deja.com.
43. "Dudayev Calls for Islamic Alliance against the West," Radio Free Europe/Radio Liberty Research Institute, Daily Report, no. 226, Washington DC, 26 November 1993; B. G. Williams, "'Chechen Arabs: An Introduction to the Real al Qaeda Terrorists from Chechnya," policy paper, Jamestown Foundation, Washington DC, vol. 1, no. 9, 15 January 2004.
44. J. Corbin, *The Base. In Search of Al Qaeda*, London: Simon & Schuster, 2002, p. 55. See also Williams, "'Chechen Arabs"; A. Lievan, "Al Qaida at the Fringe of a Bloody National Struggle," *Guardian*, 26 October 2002.
45. Williams, "'Chechen Arabs"; David Holley, "Chechen Separatist Leader is Slain: The Death of Aslan Maskhadov, a Relative Moderate, Dims Hopes for Peace with Russia," *Los Angeles Times*, 8 March 2005.
46. The website was accessed through http://www.benevolence.org.
47. Williams, "'Chechen Arabs.'"
48. "Salafism (as-Salafiyya) Factor in Central Asia and Northern Caucasus," *Bakhtiyar Mirkasymov*, 2002.
49. A. McGregor, "Khan of the Kremlin: Charm and Murder in the Middle East," position paper, Canadian Institute of Strategic Studies, May 2004.
50. "CIA Stresses Russian Role in Proliferation; Moscow Focuses on Terrorism Financing," *Russia Reform Monitor*, no. 1003, American Foreign Policy Council, Washington DC, 10 January 2003.
51. "Charity Director Charged with Aiding al Qaeda," CNN News, 9 October 2002.
52. "Report on Chechnya," www.islamicvoice.com/January 2000; *Izvestia* broadcast, Russia, 08:00:33 PDT, 18 October 2000, from *Russia Reform Monitor*, no. 1003, American Foreign Policy Council, Washington DC, 10 January 2003.
53. A. Higgins and A. Cullison, "Saga of Dr. Zawahiri," *Moscow Times* via *Wall Street Journal*, see www.themoscowtimes.com/stories/2002/07/04/203.html.
54. "ISN – Information Services Security Watch," Center for Security Studies, Zurich, Switzerland (from *Moscow Times*), July 2000.
55. "Ikraa – Activities of Arab Extremists," *Defense and Security*, Russian Monitoring Agency, no. 42, 12 April 2002.
56. Falkov, "Arktogaia Forum 2001."
57. "Russia's Horror," *Economist*, 11–17 September 2004, p. 9.
58. "Russia to Propose Expanding UN List of Terrorist Groups," *Los Angeles Times*, 24 September 2004, p. A5.
59. Nickolai Silayev, quoted in "Chechnya's Borders Can't Contain Conflict," *Los Angeles Times*, 26 February 2005, pp. A1, 8, 9.

8 FROM AFGHANISTAN TO SOUTHEAST ASIA

1. Z. Abuza, *Militant Islam in Southeast Asia: Crucible of Terror*, Boulder, CO: Lynne Rienner Publishers, 2003, p. 104.
2. Ibid., p. 178.
3. Shaykh Abu Zahir, "The Moro Jihad: A Continuous Struggle for Islamic Independence in Southern Philippines," *Nida'ul-Islam*, no. 23, www.islam.org.au, April–May 1998.
4. "MIFL Leader to *Nida'ul-Islam*," *Nida'ul Islam*, no. 23, www.islam.org.au, April–May 1998.
5. Ibid.
6. Reyko Huang, "Moro Islamic Liberation Front," *Printer-Friend*, 15 February 2002, www.cdi.org/terrorism/moro, cfm+.
7. Reihana Mohideen, "Philipines: Moro Islamic Liberation Front Rejects 'Terrorist' Slander," *Green Left Weekly*, Chippendale, New South Wales, 28 July 2004.
8. "A Legend Gone Wrong: Researched and Compiled by Shaykh Muhammad Hisham Kabbani and Mateen Siddiqui," *Muslim Magazine*, vol. 1, no. 4, 1999.
9. Rodolfo Bauzon Mendoza, Jr., *Philippine Jihad Inc.*, Philippine National Police publication, 11 September 2002, p. 27.
10. Ibid., p. 44.
11. Ibid., pp. 34–36.
12. D. Z. Sicat, "Abu's Long-Standing Ties to Global Terrorism Bared," *Manila Times Internet Edition*, www.manilatimes.net, 15 February 2002.
13. Abuza, *Militant Islam*, pp. 24, 67, 92, 94, 115.
14. Mendoza, *Philippine Jihad Inc.*; on Khalifa's life in Saudi Arabia, see "A Blueprint for 9/11," CBS Evening News, 17 January 2003.
15. Mendoza, *Philippine Jihad Inc.*, pp. 61–62.
16. M. D. Vitug, "The New Believers," *Newsbreak*, Manila, 27 May 2002.
17. Mendoza, *Philippine Jihad Inc.*, p. 30.
18. *Middle East Intelligence Wire Gulf News*, 29 September 2001.
19. Vitug, "The New Believers."
20. On this struggle, see Thomas McKenna, *Muslim Rulers and Rebels: Everyday Politics and Armed Separatism in the Southern Philippines*, Berkeley: University of California Press, 1998.
21. *Middle East Intelligence Wire Gulf News*, 29 September 2001.
22. R. Abou-Alsamh, "Is Gemma-Cruz a Terrorist?" *Manila Moods*, www.manilamoods.com/archive/160800.shtml, 16 August 2000.
23. S. Elegant, "The Return of Abu Sayyaf," *Time* (Asia), 23 August, 2004.
24. E. Van Dalen, "Philippines Move a Step Closer to Peace Tuesday," *RN Asia*, Radio Netherlands, www.rnw.nl, 7 August 2001.
25. Elegant, "The Return of Abu Sayyaf."
26. "The Abu Sayyaf–Al Qaeda Connection," ABCNEWS.com, New York, 20 December 2001.
27. J. Gomez, "In Philippines, Islamic Militants Regroup," AP, 24 April 2004.

28. "Terrorists 'Seek Muslim Converts,'" CNN News, CNN.com, 9 May 2004.
29. R. Landingin, "Philippines Uncovers al-Qaeda Linked Operation," *Financial Times*, 6 May 2004.
30. M. G. G. Pillai, "The Bin Ladens and a Kedah Prawn Farm," *KM2* reports, http://lamankm2c.tripod.com/ccgi-bin/form.cgi, 15 April 2002.
31. Jay Solomon, "Manila Suspends Talks with Rebels after Allegations of al-Qaeda Links," *Wall Street Journal*, 12 March 2002.
32. *Terrorism in Southeast Asia and International Linkages*, Usindo Open Forum, United States–Indonesia Society, Washington DC, 4 December 2002; "Riduan Isamuddin," www.nationamaster, com/encyclopedia/Riduan-Isamuddin+Riduan+ &hl=en.
33. "Hambali Used RM2 mil Collected from Donations to Fund his Extremist Operations," *The Star*, Malaysia, 1 January 2003.
34. See www.fbi.gov/congress/congress02/lormel021202.htm.
35. "Nik Adli Identified as Militant Group Leader," *The Star*, Malaysia, 9 August 2001.
36. "Hambali Used RM2 mil."
37. FBI periodic reports on terrorism can be found at www.fbi.gov/congress/congress02/lormel021202.htm, 2 December 2002.
38. S. Young, "Muslims Seek Islamic State," *Washington Times*, 13 November 2003.
39. Z. Abuza, "Asia Hasn't Stopped the Terror Funding," *Asian Wall Street Journal*, 1 October 2003.
40. V. S. Naipaul, *Among the Believers: An Islamic Journey*, New York: Alfred A. Knopf, 1981.
41. "Profile: Jemaah Islamiah – Shadowy Advocate of Islamic Caliphate," Reuters, Jakarta, 16 October 2002.
42. J. Perlez, "Saudis Quietly Promote Strict Islam in Indonesia," *New York Times*, 5 July 2003.
43. "Indonesian Linked to al Qaeda Cell," CNN.com/World, http:edition.cnn.com/2002/World/, 19 July 2002; "Intelligence Report: Bin Laden Sought Indonesian Base," CNN.com/World, http:edition.cnn.com/2002/World/, 9 July 2002.
44. M. Levitt, "Combating Terrorist Financing, Despite the Saudis," *PolicyWatch* no. 673, Washington DC: Washington Institute for Near East Policy, 1 November 2002; M. Levitt, "How Al Qaeda Lit the Bali Fuse: Part I," *Christian Science Monitor*, 17 June 2003.
45. A. Sipress and E. Nakashima, "Militant Alliance in Asia is to Seek Regional Islamic State," *Washington Post Foreign Service*, 19 September 2002.
46. Dana Priest, "A Nightmare, and a Mystery, in the Jungle," *Washington Post*, 22 June 2003; "Bin Laden Named in Asian Terror Plots," *Washington Post*, 27 June 2003; "Indonesian Army's Upper Hand," *Washington Post*, 26 June 2003.
47. D. Murphy, "A Village in Java Tells Story of Militant Islam's Growth," *Christian Science Monitor*, 23 January 2003.
48. Perlez, "Saudis Quietly Promote Strict Islam in Indonesia."
49. US Department of the Treasury, press release, 19 February 2004.

50. A. Holt, "Thailand's Troubled Border: Islamic Insurgency or Criminal Playground?" Article appeared in the Jamestown Foundation, www.jamestown.org/index.php; Terrorism Monitor, reproduced by the Asia Pacific Media Network, www.w3.org/, 20 May 2004.

51. "Thailand: Arrests Block Islamic Terror Plot," *St. Petersburg Times*, Russia, 11 June 2003.

52. "THAILAND: Separatism Rising in Southern Thailand after Years of Peace," *New Straits Times*, www.nst.com.my, 5 April 2004; "Thai Violence Rages on as PM Visits Restive South," AFP, Krong Pinang, Thailand, 7 May 2004.

53. "Cambodia Boots Saudi Religious School," *Las Vegas Sun*, 28 May 2003.

54. "The Inside Story of How US Terrorist Hunters are Going after al Qaeda," *US News & World Report*, 2 June 2003.

55. E. Sohail, "Poems of the Tresses: The Arab Assault on our Culture," www.paktoday.com/poems.htm, 27 February 2004.

56. B. Raman, "Bangladesh: A Bengali Abbasi Lurking Somewhere?" South Asia Analysis Group, paper no. 232, 23 April 2001.

57. "Professor Gulam Azam," www.islam-bd.org/GolamAzam/, 10 April 2004.

58. B. Raman, "Bangladesh."

59. Ibid.

60. S. Babar, quoted in "Is Religious Extremism on the Rise in Bangladesh?" Asia Pacific Media Services Ltd., www.asiapacificms.com/articles/, 10 May 2004.

61. A. Roy, "Bangla Outfit Recruits Cadres for Jihad," *Telegraph*, Calcutta, 7 July 1999.

62. B. Raman, "Bangladesh and Jihadi Terrorism – an Update," South Asia Analysis Group, paper no. 887, 7 January 2004; S. Page, "Death of Evangelist Highlights Growing Tension in Bangladesh," Project Open Book, www.domini.org, Dublin, Ireland, 23 May 2003.

63. Raman, "Bangladesh and Jihadi Terrorism."

64. A. Perry, "Deadly Cargo," *Time*, Asian Magazine, http://time/asia/magazine/0,13764,5011021,00.htm.

65. "Saudi Charities Do Not Die," Reuters, 5 June 2004.

66. "Letter Dated 1 December 2003 from the Chairman of the Security Council Committee Established Pursuant to Resolution 1267 (1999) concerning Al-Qaida and the Taleban," UN Security Council, S/2003/1070, 2 December 2003, pp. 3, 8.

67. "Patterns of Global Terrorism, 2003," Office of the Coordinator for Counterterrorism, US Department of State, Washington DC, 29 April 2004.

9 THE HOLY LAND

1. Timur Kuran, "Islamic Redistribution through *zakat*: Historical Record and Modern Realities," in Bonner et al. (eds.), *Poverty and Charity in Middle Eastern Contexts*, p. 278.

2. In May 2001 ICRC began to pay the costs of PRCS's ambulance fleet and salaries for its 220 employees.

3. W. B. Quandt, *Saudi Arabia in the 1980s*, Washington DC: Brookings Institution, 1981, pp. 32–33.
4. *HAMAS, Islamic Jihad and the Muslim Brotherhood: Islamic Extremists and the Terrorist Threat to America* (pamphlet), New York: Anti-Defamation League, 1993.
5. United Nations Information System on the Question of Palestine: Division for Palestinian Rights, vol. XIV, Bulletin no. 9, September 1991.
6. Ilil Shahar, "The Israel Connection," *Maariv International*, 7 July 2004.
7. Fadhl al-Naqib, *The Palestinian Economy in the West Bank and Gaza*, Jerusalem: Center for Palestinian Studies, April 1997.
8. Ilil Shahar, "The Israel Connection," *Maariv International*, 25 July 2004.
9. Y. Barsky, *Islamic Jihad Movement in Palestine*, New York: American Jewish Committee, 2002, pp. 9–12.
10. Anti-Defamation League, *HAMAS, Islamic Jihad, and the Muslim Brotherhood*.
11. The organizations comprising the Unified National Leadership of the Uprising included the Popular Front for the Liberation of Palestine – General Command; Palestinian National Liberation Movement – Fatah (Abu Musa faction); the Islamic Jihad Movement in Palestine; Al Saiqa Forces; the Popular Front for the Liberation of Palestine; the Democratic Front for the Liberation of Palestine; the Revolutionary Palestinian Communist Party; the Palestine Popular Struggle Front; the Palestine Liberation Front; and HAMAS.
12. From the Islamic Solidarity, Concord and Unity meeting held in Dakar, Senegal, 9–11 December 1991.
13. "HAMAS Invests in US Real Estate," *Middle East Newsline*, Washington DC, 23 May 1999; M. Epstein and B. Schmidt, "Operation Support-System Shutdown," *National Review Online*, www.nationalreview.com, 4 September 2003.
14. Labeviere, *Dollars for Terrorism*, pp. 144–145, footnote 31.
15. L. T. O'Brien, "US Presses Saudis to Police Accounts Used to Aid Palestinians," *New York Times Online*, www.nytimes.com/24 June 2003; "Saudis Admit Funding HAMAS," WorldTribune.com, Washington DC, 13 June 2003.
16. "Patterns of Global Terrorism," Office of the Coordinator for Counterterrorism, US Department of State, Publication 10136, April 1994; on Iranian funding see "Testimony of Michael A. Sheehan, US Department of State Coordinator for Counterterrorism," Senate Foreign Relations Subcommittee on Near Eastern and South Asian Affairs, 2 November 1999.
17. "The Metamorphosis of HAMAS," *Jerusalem Report*, 14 January 1993.
18. "Muslims Fight On over Banned Charity," BBC News, UK, www.w3.org/TR/REC-html40/loose, 11 September 2003.
19. D. Sanger and J. Miller, "Bush Freezes Assets of Biggest US Muslim Charity," *New York Times*, 5 December 2001; C. H. Schmitt et al., "When Charity Goes Awry," *US News & World Report*, 29 October 2001.
20. D. Gold, "Saudi Arabia and Global Terrorism: From al-Qaeda to HAMAS," presentation to Subcommittee on the Middle East and Central Asia, US House of Representatives, 15 July 2003; E. Alden and M. Mann, "Brussels

Moves to Block Assets of 11 Terrorist Organizations," *Financial Times*, 3 May 2002.

21. "Germany Bans 'Pro-HAMAS' Charity," CNN.com/World, 5 August 2002.

22. "UK and US Freeze Islamic Charity," BBC News, UK, 30 May 2003.

23. "Schumer: Virginia Charity Linked to HAMAS and Saudis has Escaped Federal Charges," Senate Office of Senator Charles Schumer, Washington DC, 17 September 2003.

24. "The HAMAS Asset Freeze and Other Government Efforts to Stop Terrorists Financing," E. Anthony Wayne, Assistant Secretary for Economic and Business Affairs, Department of State, to the House of Representatives Committee on Financial Services, 24 September 2003.

25. D. Frankfurter, "The Sad Joke of 'Palestinian Aid,'" FrontPageMagazine. com, 2 March 2005.

26. S. Lakind and Y. Carmon, "The PA Economy," *Inquiry and Analysis Series – No. 11*, MEMRI, 8 January 1999, footnote 8.

27. "OPIC Signs Protocol for $60 Million Private Equity Fund in Gaza, West Bank and Jordan Projects," *Forward*, 11 December 1998; OPIC press release, 17 November 1997; "OPIC's Politically Connected Investors Can't Lose as US Taxpayers Shoulder the Risks," Center for Responsive Politics, 15 January 1998.

28. A. Kushner, *Disclosed: Inside the Palestinian Authority and the PLO*, Jerusalem: Pavilion Press, 2004; "Getting Past Arafat," *Jerusalem Post*, http://info. post.com/C003/Supplements/FSB/030905, 9 May 2003.

29. For IMF documents on Palestine and public finance see www-wds.worldbank.org., report for 14 April 2004.

30. "The HAMAS – Background," www.fas.org/irp/world/para/HAMAS.htm, August 1997.

31. Documents can be accessed at: "Arafat Knew: Charity Money Forwarded to Terror Infrastructure," Centrum Informatie en Documentatie Israel, Netherlands, www.cidi.nl, 25 January 2003.

32. A. Lerner, "HAMAS Leader Abu Hamdan – Interview in Hamshahri," *IMRA Review*, 24 August 1997, from *Hamshahri*, Iran, 21 August 1997.

33. "Peace Process – HAMAS," *Middle East Security Report*, vol. 1, no. 38, 1 October 1997.

34. "Getting Past Arafat."

35. W. Amr, "Israeli Troops Hit Banks in Raid on Arafat HQ City," Reuters, Ramallah, 25 February 2004.

36. "In Brief," *Ayn Al Yaqeen*, Saudi Arabia, 31 March 2000.

37. "Kingdom Will Never Fight Islamic Trends Says Prince Ahmed," *Arab News*, 15 January 2003.

38. MEMRI, www.memri.org/bin/. See article SR 1703#_edn4.

39. J. Dougherty, "Saudi Royals Funding Palestinian Jihad," www.worldnetdaily. com, 9 July 2003.

40. Ibid.

41. "The Custodian of the Two Holy Mosques Approves the Establishment of Al Quds Center at King Abd Al-Aziz Foundation," *Ayn Al Yaqeen*, 21 September 2001; "Scholars and Experts Praise King Fahd Approval for the

Establishment of the Al Quds Center for Studies and Researchers," *Ayn Al Yaqeen*, 12 October 2001.

42. "Editorial: Saudi Arabia and the Palestinian Issue," *Ayn Al Yaqeen*, 25 May 2001.
43. "The Kingdom of Saudi Arabia Stands by the Palestinian People, their Rights and Defending the Holy Places," *Ayn Al Yaqeen*, 20 October 2000.
44. International Christian Embassy Jerusalem report, 10 February 2002, footnote 57.
45. K. R. Timmerman, "Documents Detail Saudi Terror Links," *Insight*, 20 May 2002, www.insightmag.com.
46. C. Brisard, "Written Testimony of Jean-Charles Brisard International Expert on Terrorism Financing Lead Investigator, 9/11 Lawsuit," Senate of the United States, http://www.senate.gov/~banking/_files/brisard.pdf.
47. "Saudi Arabia and the Arab Countries Insist on Holding the Arab Summit in Beirut on Time," *Ayn Al Yaqeen*, 11 January 2002.
48. "Al-Anzy, the First Arab POW Returns from Afghanistan," IslamOnline.net, Kuwait, 9 February 2002.
49. L. P. Cohen et al., "Bush's Financial War on Terrorism Includes Strikes at Islamic Charities," *Wall Street Journal*, 25 September 2001; J. Mintz, "From Veil of Secrecy, Portraits of US Prisoners Emerge," *Washington Post*, 15 March 2002, p. A3.
50. "Terrorism Weighs on US–Saudi Relations," *Washington Times*, 26 November 2002.
51. "SR410 Million Collected in Cash during the Saudi Telethon Campaign in Support of the Palestinians," *Ayn Al Yaqeen*, 19 April 2002.
52. "Kingdom's Support for Palestine Remains Exemplary," *Saudi Gazette*, 22 March 2002.
53. "Kingdom Supports Palestinians with Extra Money," Saudi Press Agency, 31 October 2002; "The Kingdom of Saudi Arabia and the Palestinian Cause," *Ayn Al Yaqeen*, 3 January 2003; "Saudi Arabian Information Resource Aid for Palestine," www.saudinf.com/main/y4066.htm, 8 January 2003.
54. "Saudi Committee for the Support of the Al Quds Intifada Executes 27 Programs and Projects," Saudi Press Agency, 1 May 2003.
55. A. R. Ali, "HAMAS, Jihad Defy Sharm el-Shaykh Summit," IslamOnline.net, Kuwait, 4 June 2003, footnote 71.
56. IDF spokesman, "Text of Arabic Document: Arafat Knew: Charity Money Forwarded to Terror Infrastructure," Tel Aviv: Kokhaviv Publications, 23 January 2003; Arabic original posted at www.idf.il/newsite/. Ronni Shaked, former Israeli General Security Service (Shin Bet) official and Arab Affairs editor of *Yedioth Ahronoth*, commented at length on HAMAS fundraising in a book based on interviews with imprisoned HAMAS operatives. The book, *HAMAS: Me-emunah be-Allah le-derekh ha-teror* ("From faith in Allah to the path of terror"), was a limited printing and could not be located by the authors.
57. "Palestinian Authority Freezes Funds of Islamic Charities," *USA Today*, 28 August 2003; "Muslim Groups' Funds Frozen," AP, Gaza City, 29 August 2003.

58. M. A. Levitt, "Charity Begins in Riyadh," *Weekly Standard*, 2 February 2004.
59. M. Malkin, "Ambulances for Terrorists," www.frontpagemag.com/Articles/ReadArticle.asp?ID=13627, 2 June 2004.
60. M. Dudkevich, "Army Seals Offices of HAMAS Charity Organizations," *Jerusalem Post*, online edition, www.jpost.com, 8 July 2004.
61. "UN Report: 63 Percent of Palestinians Below Poverty Line," Reuters, Beirut, 30 August 2004.
62. "Iran Increases Funding and Training for Suicide Bombings," MEMRI Special Dispatch Series, no. 387, 11 June 2002.
63. Ibid.
64. M. Karouny, "Lebanon's Hizbullah Serves Needy, Gains Support," Reuters, Beirut, 28 February 2003.
65. Hanson Hosein, NBC News, 10 May 2003, as reported in www.moqawama.tv.
66. A. W. Same, "Tehran, Washington and Terror: No Agreement to Differ," *Middle East Review of International Affairs*, vol. 6, no. 3, September 2002.

10 THE MUSLIM INVASION OF EUROPE

1. D. Crawford, "How a Diplomat from Saudi Arabia Spread his Faith," *Wall Street Journal*, 10 September 2003.
2. "The Saudis Withdrew Berlin Diplomat after Germans Cite Possible Militant Link," *Gulf Wire Digest*, issue no. 208, pp. 4–10, 28 April 2003; "Saudi Installations under Surveillance in Germany, Report Says," http://www.aarialink.com, *Khaleej Times Online*, 2 August 2003.
3. Turkish expatriates commonly access Diyanet Isleri Turk Islam Birligi at its website, www.diyanet.org.
4. G. Kepel, "The Trail of Political Islam," http://opendemocracy.net, 7 March 2002.
5. S. Trifkovic, "Jihad's Fifth Column in the West," FrontPageMagazine.com, 7 January 2003; S. Trifkovic, *The Sword of the Prophet*, Boston: Regina Orthodox Press, 2002; on data see A. de Borchgrave, "Al Qaeda's US Network," *Washington Times*, 13 August 2004.
6. H. Brucker et al., "Managing Migration in the European Welfare State," in *Third European Convention of the Debenedetti Foundation*, Trieste: Debenedetti Foundation, June 2001.
7. S. Wheeler, "EU to Freeze Terror Assets," BBC News, Strasbourg, 4 October 2001.
8. E. Ganley, "Europe Uses Drastic Laws to Beat Terror," AP, 23 September 2001.
9. "Berlin Terror Trial Witness Names Saudi Diplomat, Journal Says," Bloomberg.com, 2 June 2004.
10. See articles by M. Forbes in *The Age*, Australia, www.theage.com.au, 11–13 July 2003.
11. I. Johnson and D. Crawford, "A Saudi Group Spreads Extremism in 'Law' Seminars," *Wall Street Journal*, 15 April 2003.

12. M. Robinson, "Attorney Denies Muslim Charity's European Director Aided Osama bin Laden's Terror Network," AP, Chicago, 6 May 2002.
13. C. Simpson et al., "Bin Laden Aide Tied to Bridgeview Group," *Chicago Tribune*, 6 May 2002.
14. "German Police Raid Arabic Charity," AP, Berlin, 16 August 2002.
15. Posted on IslamOnline.net, dateline Bonn, 25 July 2003.
16. "Al-Qaeda Suspects Extradited to US," AP, New York, 17 November 2003; for details see www.usdoj.gov, 17 November 2003; "Yemeni Cleric Assistant Convicted of Terror-Funding Charges," http://edition.cnn/2005/LAW/03/10/Yemeni.cleric.terrorism/11 March 2005.
17. M. Trevelyan, "Germany Probes Islamist Backers, Saudi Link Cited," Reuters, Berlin, 17 May 2004.
18. M. Trevelyan, "Muslims Find Recognition Elusive in Catholic Italy," Reuters, Milan, 26 June 2004.
19. P. Smucker, "Out of Honey Business, Bin Laden Still Profits," *Christian Science Monitor*, 23 October 2001.
20. D. Pallister, "Terrorist Material Found in Sarajevo Charity," *Guardian*, 23 February 2002.
21. "From the Office of Public Affairs, Press Release," US Department of the Treasury, Washington DC, 29 August 2002.
22. L. Vidino, "Italy's Fifth Column," www.frontpagemag.com, 20 November 2003.
23. "Iraq: Italian Muslims, against the War and Terrorism," position paper, AGI, Rome, 23 April 2004.
24. See the works of Magdi Allam, Italian journalist of Coptic Christian (Egyptian) origin: *Bin Laden in Italia: viaggio nell'islam radicale*, Milan: Mondatori, 2002 and *Kamikaze: Made in Europe*, Milan: Mondatori, 2004.
25. United Nations Security Council, S/2003/1070, 2 December 2003; see p. 57 for wiring diagram of the "Nada and Nasreddin networks," and pp. 21–22 for additional information.
26. Ibid.
27. Kepel, "The Trail of Political Islam."
28. "Big Dominique and his Struggle against the Islamists," *The Economist*, 18–31 December 2004, pp. 73–74; Imam Akbar Syed, "Geopolitics of Fundamentalism," *South-West Asia Revue*, isayed@pratique.fr.
29. "Big Dominique."
30. B. Raman, "Al Qaeda's Clone," South Asia Analysis Group, paper no. 729, 2 July 2003.
31. Labeviere, *Dollars for Terrorism*, pp. 72–73; "French Courts Vindicate Islamic Relief," Islamic Relief homepage, suaaf@csv.warwick.ac.uk, Islamic Society, University of Warwick, United Kingdom.
32. D. E. Kaplan, "The Saudi Connection," *US News & World Report*, 15 December 2003.
33. "Clinton-Approved Iranian Arms Transfers Help Turn Bosnia into Militant Islamic Base," US Senate Republican Policy Committee, Washington DC, 16 January 1997.

34. "Violent Attack on Muslim Charity in France," Islamic Human Rights Commission, France, 10 September 1997.
35. L. Bryant, "Mideast Conflict Mobilizes Jewish, Muslim Community in France," Voice of America, Paris, 8 August 2002.
36. O. Guitta, "France's Everlasting Love for the PLO," *The American Thinker*, www.americanthinker.com, 2 August 2004.
37. "Article 10," *Ayn Al Yaqeen*, Saudi Arabia, 19 April 2002.
38. C. Wyatt, "Europe: France 'Forming Ethnic Ghettoes,'" BBC News, 6 July 2004.
39. I. Johnson and D. Crawford, "A Saudi Group Spreads Extremism in 'Law' Seminars," *Wall Street Journal*, 15 April 2003.
40. Ibid.
41. "Bin Laden's Terror Networks in Europe," Mackenzie Institute, Washington DC, www.mackenzieinstitute.com/default.htmli; (see also footnote 19). The Mackenzie Institute study provides many Dutch sources for what one article has called "De Politieke Islam in Nederland": in *Binnenlandse Veiligheidsdienst*, Leidschendam, 1998, p. 11; see also R. Abela and K. Bessems, "Terreurfondsen in Nederland," *Trouw*, 17 October 2001, pp. 1, 13.
42. "Islam First Religion in Amsterdam," IslamOnline.net, 30 July 2002; "Islamic Charity Slams Freeze on Assets in Hague," IslamOnline.net, 5 June 2002.
43. "Islamic Hatred in Europe," Religious Freedom Coalition newsletter, Washington DC, March 2002.
44. "Another Political Murder," *The Economist*, 6–12 November 2004, pp. 51–52; "After Van Gogh," *The Economist*, 13–19 November 2004, pp. 55–56; *Los Angeles Times*, 14 November 2004, p. A3; *Van dawa tot jihad. De diverse dreigingen van de radicale islam tegen de democratische rechtsorde*, The Hague: Ministerie van Binnenladse Zaken en Koninkrijksrelaties, 2004.
45. On this and similar phenomena the US Department of State has issued an annual "International Religious Freedom Report" since 2001 that includes individual country chapters on the status of religious freedom worldwide.
46. A. Mullen, "Haddad Breaks his Silence," *Metro Times*, Detroit, 17 March; A. Mullen, "The Terrors of Puptte," *Metro Times*, Detroit, 24 March 2004.
47. L. Vidino, "Belgium Ought to Look Within," National Review Online, www.nationalreview.com, 25 June 2003.
48. Ibid.
49. A. Amory, "Islamofascism Rising in Holland," www.frontpageMag.com, 6 March 2003.
50. M. Robinson, "Attorney Denies Muslim Charity's European Director Aided Osama bin Laden's Terror Network," AP, Chicago, 6 May 2002.
51. "Copenhagen Mosque Suspected of Terror Ties," *Copenhagen Post Online*, www.cphpost.dk, 1 February 2003.
52. J. Klausen, "Rogue Imams," *Axess Magazine*, www.axess.se/english/archive/2004/nr1/.
53. "Who Really Wants to Stop Bin Laden?" *Intelligence Newsletter*, Indigo Publications, 16 March 2000.

54. J. M. Berger, "Al Qaeda-Linked Web Site: $10 Million a Month Needed for Taliban in 2001," www.intelwire.com, 8 August 2004.
55. See *The Muslim News*, muslimnews.co.uk, 15 April 1999.
56. "Kashmiri Separatist Ayub Thakur Dies," www.rediff.com, 10 March 2004.
57. "UK Assets of Islamic Charity Frozen," www.rediff.com, 16 January 2002.
58. H. Gibson, "Traitors or Martyrs?" *Time*, www.time.com/time/europe/, 12 November 2001.
59. M. Whine, "Al Muhajiroun: The Portal for Britain's Suicide Terrorists," International Policy Institute for Counter-Terrorism, 21 May 2003.
60. V. MacQueen, "Britain's Indigenous Terror," www.frontpagemag.com, 5 May 2003.
61. United Kingdom Charity Commission report, www.charitycommission.gov.uk, 1 July 2003.
62. "PDF File of Combating the Financing of Terrorism: A Report on UK Action," Foreword by the Chancellor of the Exchequer, Rt. Hon. Gordon Brown MP and the Home Secretary, Rt. Hon. David Blunkett, www.hm-treasury.gov.uk, October 2002.
63. D. Van Natta Jr. and L. Bergman, "Militant Imams under Scrutiny across Europe," *New York Times*, 25 January 2005.
64. A list of all organizations and individuals whose assets have been frozen is available at the Bank of England website, www.bankofengland.co.uk.
65. "Abu Hamza: Controversial Muslim Figure," CNN.com, International Edition, London, 27 May 2004; "Radical Cleric in Britain Charged with Urging Murder of Non-Muslims," AP, London, 19 October 2004.

11 ISLAMIC CHARITIES IN NORTH AMERICA

1. From a transcript of Steven Emerson's *Jihad in America*, a video presentation on television, 21 November 1994, p. 8.
2. Personal experience of J. Millard Burr.
3. For a study of MSA on campus see E. Stakelbeck, www.frontpagemag.com, 23 April 2003.
4. On MSA see Hamid Algar, *Wahhabism: A Critical Essay*, Oneonta, NY: Islamic Publications International, 2002.
5. An interesting anecdote concerning the personal importance of *zakat* in America can be found in A. M. Muhahid, "Where is Aisha Today? The Mother of Homeless in Chicago," www.soundvision.com/info/poor/aisha.asp, August 2004. The website provides tips on *zakat* and its use.
6. Salam al-Marayati, "Muslim Charities and Religious Freedom," www.mpac.org/NEWS/, Los Angeles, 11 October 2002.
7. D. McManus, "FBI Steps up its Scrutiny of Hamas Backers," *Los Angeles Times*, 2 February 1993.
8. D. Horowitz, "How the Left Undermined America's Security before 9/11," www.frontpagemag.com, 24 March 2004.
9. Al-Marayati, "Muslim Charities."
10. D. Sanger, and J. Miller, "Bush Freezes Assets of Biggest US Muslim Charity," *New York Times*, 5 December 2001; 9/11 Report: Joint Congressional Inquiry, 24 July 2003, www.news.findlaw.com/ndoes/dots/911/rpt/.

11. A. Knight, "Meet your Muslim Neighbor," *San Diego News Notes*, May 2002.
12. A full description of the founding and operations of BIF can be found in chapter 2, "Saudi Arabia and its Islamic charities," and the activities of GRF in chapter 10, "The Muslim invasion of Europe." The sections here pertain specifically to their activities in the USA.
13. M. Levitt, "Combating Terrorist Financing, Despite the Saudis," *Policy-Watch*, no. 673, Washington DC: Washington Institute for Near East Policy, 1 November 2002.
14. "Treasury Designates Benevolence International Foundation and Related Entities as Financiers of Terrorism," Office of Public Affairs, Department of the Treasury, 19 November 2002; Foreign terrorist organizations can be found on the State Department website: www.state.gov/documents/organizations.
15. "Head of Charity Imprisoned for Diverting Funds to Militants," *Washington Times*, 19 August 2003.
16. "Leader of Muslim Charity in US is Said to Have Been Deported," Reuters, 16 July 2003.
17. S. Schmidt, "Reporters' Files Subpoenaed," *Washington Post*, 10 September 2004.
18. Andre Martin and Michael J. Berens, "Terrorists Evolved in US," *Chicago Tribune*, 11 December 2001.
19. R. Ehrenfeld, "Doing Business with Terrorists," www.frontpagemag.com, 21 September 2004.
20. C. McKerney, "Palestinian Activist from Sunrise Charged with Perjury, Obstruction of Justice," *South Florida Sun-Sentinel*, Fort Lauderdale, 5 March 2004.
21. S. Wheeler, "Alleged Terror Threat Operates in DC Suburb," CNSNews.com, 12 July 2004.
22. "Money Freeze a Long Time Coming," CBS News, New York, 5 December 2001.
23. S. McGonigle, "Memo Outlines Links to Hamas," *Dallas Morning News*, 6 December 2001.
24. *Jihad in America*, an award-winning documentary, was first broadcast on 21 November 1964; See S. Emerson, "Jihad in America: Part II," www.blessedcause.org/Patriot%20Progress/Steve%20Emerson%202.htm, 2002; S. Emerson and C. D. Sesto, *Terrorist*, New York: Villard Books, 1991.
25. *The Holy Land Foundation for Relief and Development* (pamphlet), New York: Anti Defamation League, 2001.
26. J. Miller, "Israel Says that a Prisoner's Tale Links Arabs in US to Terrorism," *New York Times*, 17 February 1993.
27. "Hamas: Iranian Funding Reports 'Incorrect,'" *Filistin Al Muslimah* (in Arabic), London, February 1993, pp. 16–17.
28. "More Alleged Hamas Operatives Linked to DC-Area Think Tank," CNSNews.com, www.townhall.com/news/politics, 26 August 2004.
29. S. Hettena, "FBI Links California Islamic Charity to Hamas," *North Coast Times*, San Diego, California, 7 December 2001.
30. Anonymous [Rita Katz], *Terrorist Hunter*, New York: HarperCollins, 2003.

31. "Money Freeze a Long Time Coming."
32. G. Simpson, "Holy Land Foundation Allegedly Mixed Charity Money with Funds for Bombers," *Wall Street Journal*, 27 February 2002.
33. L. Auster, "The Clintons, Abdurahman Alamoudi and the Myth of 'Moderate' Islam," NewsMax.com, 6 November 2000; F. Gaffney, "A Troubling Influence," www.frontpagemag.com, 9 December 2003.
34. Simpson, "Holy Land Foundation."
35. P. Bedard, "Washington Whispers," *US News & World Report*, 6 February 2002.
36. C. Limbacher, "Clinton Protected Terrorist Charity from FBI Shutdown," *Newsmax*, 6 February 2002.
37. Joseph D'Agostino, "7000 Men Recently Entered from Al Qaeda 'Watch' Countries," *Human Events*, 17 December 2001, p. 6.
38. R. Mank, "Feeding the Children of 'Martyrs,'" www.Salon.com, 11 July 2000.
39. J. Miller, "US Contends Muslim Charity is Tied to Hamas," *New York Times*, 25 August 2000.
40. Mike Allen and Steven Mufson, "US Seizes Assets of Three Islamic Groups: US Charity Among Institutions Accused of Funding HAMAS," *Washington Post*, 5 December 2001.
41. "Senior Leader of HAMAS and Texas Computer Company Indicted for Conspiracy," US Department of Justice press release, Washington DC, 18 December 2002.
42. In 1980 President Carter used IEEPA to block Iranian assets in the USA. See US Code, Title 50: War and National Defense, Chapter 35: International Emergency Economic Powers.
43. Eric Lichtblau, "Jailed Islamic Charity Figures Accused of Funding Terrorists," *New York Times*, 28 July 2004, p. A3.
44. D. Pipes, "Canada's First Family of Terrorism," *AmericanDaily*, www.ameircandaily.com/article/630, 17 March 2004.
45. "Canadian Admits al-Qaida Link," http://cnews.canoe.ca, 4 March 2004.
46. Lamar Smith, "Hearing on Terrorist Threats to the United States," Subcommittee on Immigration and Claims, House Committee on the Judiciary, Washington DC, 25 January 2000.
47. "Qutbi Al Mahdi (Sudan/Canada)," *Indian Ocean Newsletter*, 28 November 1998.
48. M. Jimenez, "Canada Investigates Sudanese Official Passport Use Probed," *National Post*, 25 November 1998.
49. G. Dimmock, "Sudan Aiding Bin Laden: CSIS: Used Embassy Staff to Raise Funds, Provide Credentials, Brief Says," *National Post*, 28 September 2001.
50. S. Bell, "Ottawa Pulls Saudi Group's Charity Status. Muslim World League Being Sued by 9/11 Families," *National Post*, 1 December 2003.
51. Irshad Manji, *The Trouble with Islam: A Wake-up Call for Honesty and Change*, Mississauga, Ontario: Random House of Canada, 2003.
52. M. Elmasry, "Islam Needs No Defense against Manji's Book, but Perhaps Muslims Do," *The Ottawa Muslim*, www.ottawamuslim.net, 5 October 2003.

53. "A Pro-Terrorist Rally at Ohio State?" www.frontpagemag.com, 7 November 2003.

54. Elaine Silvestrini,"al-Arian Wiretap Captured Poem of Hate for America," *Tampa Tribune*, 2 August 2005.

55. E. Boehlert, "Is Sami al-Arian Guilty of Terrorist Plots?" Salon.com, 21 February 2003; S. Shields, "Sami al-Arian and the Dungeon: A Fable for our Time?" *Common Dreams News Center*, CommonDreams.org, 16 November 2003.

56. J. Seper, "Clinton White House Axed Terror-Fund Probe," *Washington Times*, 2 April 2002; "Head of U.S. Muslim Charity Indicted," Reuters, 9 October 2002.

57. Steve Emerson was the first to focus on SAAR and the 555 Grove Street connection. See S. Emerson, *American Jihad: Terrorists Among Us*, New York: Free Press, 2002.

58. "All Forms of Suppression Rejected: Firm Support for Uprising," *Kuwait Times*, 6 November 2000.

59. J. Miller, "Raids Seek Evidence of Money-Laundering," *New York Times*, 21 March 2002.

60. Anonymous [Katz], *Terrorist Hunter*, pp. 280–294. Ironically, many Muslim expatriates and J. Millard Burr, the co-author, tried as early as 1993 to interest authorities in the happenings in Herndon, Virginia. The super-secret and ineffectual Foreign Intelligence Service Act (FISA) personnel of the FBI may have been collecting information, but nothing has ever been published about their activities.

61. M. Burgess, "The Trouble with Guantanamo," Position paper, Center for Defense Information, 24 October 2003.

62. S. Schwartz, "Saudis Actively Sponsoring Terrorism," *Weekly Standard*, 8 April 2002.

63. For a US government report on Safa holdings, see www.usdoj.gov/usao/vae/ArchivePress/OctoberPDFArchive/03/safaattachc102003.pdf.

64. J. Seper, "NJ Firm Backed Terrorists Linked to Hamas, al Qaeda," *Washington Times*, 29 March 2004.

65. M. Epstein and B. Schmidt, "Operation Support-System Shutdown," National Review Online, www.nationalreview.com, 4 September 2003.

66. D. Farah, "Terror Probe Points to Va. Muslims," *Washington Post*, 18 October 2003.

67. On US government findings, see www.usdoj.gov/usao/vae/ArchivePress/OctoberPDFArchive/03/safaattache102003.pdf, Attachment E.

68. S. Schwartz, "Wahhabis in the Old Dominion," *Weekly Standard*, 8 April 2002.

69. D. Farah and J. Mintz, "US Trails Va. Muslim Money, Ties," *Washington Post*, 7 October 2002.

70. "Lawyers Seek to Freeze Saudi Assets in US," www.arabnews.com, Jidda/Washington, 30 August 2002.

71. L. Kellman, "More than 600 Sept 11 Victims' Families Sue Saudis, Banks," AP, 15 August 2002.

Notes to pages 285–290

72. A. Alexiev, "The End of an Alliance: It's Time to Tell the House of Saud Goodbye," *National Review*, 28 October 2002.
73. A. Alexiev, "Confronting Saudi Lies, Extremism and Subversion for the Benefit of All," Position paper, United States Committee for a Free Lebanon, 21 November 2002.
74. Daniel Pipes, "Protecting Muslims while Rooting out Islamists," *Daily Telegraph*, London, 14 September 2001.

12 CONCLUSION

1. Rachel Ehrenfeld, *Saudi Dollars and Jihad*, FrontPageMagazine.com, 24 October 2005.
2. Amir Taheri, "Losing Battle for Islamists," *Arab News*, 26 March 2005.
3. Alexander Pope, *Essay on Man*, Epistle 1, 303.

Select bibliography

Abdulqadir, Muhammad Bashir, *Nizam al-Zakah fi al-Sudan*, Omdurman: Omdurman Islamic University Printing & Publishing, 1992.

Ahmad, Dr. Ziauddin, *Islam, Poverty and Income Distribution*, Leicester: Islamic Foundation, 1991.

Allam, Magdi, *Bin Laden in Italia: viaggio nell'islam radicale*, Milan: Mondatori, 2002.

Kamikaze: Made in Europe, Milan: Mondatori, 2004.

Anonymous (Rita Katz), *Terrorist Hunter: The Extraordinary Story of a Woman who Went Undercover to Infiltrate the Radical Islamic Groups in America*, New York: HarperCollins/Ecco, 2003.

Ariff, Mohamed (ed.), *The Islamic Voluntary Sector in Southeast Asia: Islam and the Economic Development of Southeast Asia*, Pasir Panjang, Singapore: Institute of Southeast Asian Studies, 1991.

Arjomand, S. A., "Philanthropy, the Law, and Public Policy in the Islamic World before the Modern Era," in Warren. F. Ilchman, Stanley N. Katz, and Edward L. Queen II (eds.), *Philanthropy in the World's Traditions*, Bloomington: Indiana University Press, 1998.

Benjamin, Daniel and Steven Simon, *The Age of Sacred Terror*, New York: Random House, 2002.

Benthall, Jonathan and Jerome Bellion-Jourdan, *The Charitable Crescent: Politics of Aid in the Muslim World*, London: I. B. Tauris, 2003.

Bonner, Michael, Mine Ener, and Amy Singer (eds.), *Poverty and Charity in Middle Eastern Contexts*, Albany, NY: State University of New York Press, 2003.

Burr, J. Millard and Robert O. Collins, *Revolutionary Sudan: Hasan al-Turabi and the Islamist State, 1989–2000*, Leiden: Brill, 2003.

Carrere d'Encausse, Helene, *Islam and the Russian Empire: Reform and Revolution in Central Asia*, preface by Maxime Rodinson, Berkeley: University of California Press, 1988.

Clark, Janine A., *Islam, Charity, and Activism – Class Networks and Social Welfare in Egypt, Jordan and Yemen*, Bloomington: Indiana University Press, 2004.

"Women, Gender and Islamic Charitable Associates: Arab States," *Encylopedia of Women and Islamic Cultures*, Leiden: Brill, 2003.

Cunningham, Andrew, *Banking in the Middle East*, London: Financial Times Publishing, 1995.

Emerson, Steven, *American Jihad: Terrorists Among Us*, New York: Free Press, 2002.

Ener, Mine, *Managing Egypt's Poor and the Politics of Benevolence, 1800–1952*, Princeton, NJ: Princeton University Press, 2003.

Final Report of the 9/11 Commission, Report of the Joint Inquiry into the Terrorist Attacks of September 11, 2001, the House Permanent Select Committee on Intelligence and the Senate Select Committee on Intelligence, 24 July 2003, Washington DC: US Government Printing Office, 2003.

Al-Ghazzali, Abu Hamid Muhammad *Ihya Ulum al-Din (The Mysteries of Alms Giving)*, trans. Nabih Amin Faris, Lahore: Shaykh Muhammad Ashraf, 1974.

Hasan, S., *Principles and Practices of Philanthropy in Islam: Potentials for the Third Sector*, CACOM monograph series, 53, Sydney, Australia: University of Technology, 2001.

Henry, Clement M., *The Mediterranean Debt Crescent: Money and Power in Algeria, Egypt, Morocco, Tunisia, and Turkey*, Cairo: American University Press, 1996.

Kramer, Martin, "The Mismeasure of Political Islam," in *The Islamist Debate*, Tel Aviv: Moshe Dayan Center, 1997.

Kuran, Timur, *Islam and Mammon: The Economic Predicament of Islamism*, Princeton, NJ: Princeton University Press, 2004.

Kuster, M. J., "The Market of the Prophet," *Journal of the Economic and Social History of the Orient*, vol. 8, no. 3, January 1965.

Labeviere, Richard, *Dollars for Terrorism: The United States and Islam*, New York: Algora Publishing, 2000.

Lacey, Robert, *The Kingdom: Arabia and the House of Saud*, New York: Harcourt Brace Jovanovich, 1981.

Lubin, Nancy and Barnett R. Rubin, *Calming the Ferghana Valley: Development and Dialogue in the Heart of Central Asia*, New York: Center for Preventive Action, 1999.

McChesney, Robert D., *Charity and Philanthropy in Islam: Institutionalizing the Call to Do Good*, Essays on Philanthropy, 14, Indianapolis: Indiana University Center on Philanthropy, 1995.

Mills, Paul S. and John R. Presley, *Islamic Finance: Theory and Practice*, London: Palgrave Macmillan, 1999.

Mitchell, Richard P., *The Society of the Muslim Brothers*, New York: Oxford University Press, 1993.

An-Nabahani, Taqiuddin, *The Islamic State: Hizb ut-Tahrir*, London: Al-Khilafah Publications [n.d.].

Poliakov, Sergei Petrovich and Martha Brill Olcott, *Everyday Islam: Religion and Tradition in Rural Central Asia*, Armonk, NY: M. E. Sharpe, Inc., 1992.

Presley, John and Rodney Wilson, *Banking in the Arab Gulf*, London: Macmillan, 1991.

Al-Qardawi, Yusuf, *Fiqh al-Zakah*, Jidda: Center for Research in Islamic Economics, 2000.

Ruthven, Malise, *Islam: A Very Short Introduction*, New York: Oxford University Press, 2000.

Islam in the World, New York: Oxford University Press, 2000.

A Fury for God: The Islamist Attack on America, London: Granta, 2002.

Sabra, Adan, *Poverty and Charity in Medieval Islam*, Cambridge: Cambridge University Press, 2000.

Sfeir, Antoine, *Les Réseaux d'Allah: Les Filières islamistes en France et en Europe*, Paris: Plon, 2001.

Siddiqi, Mohammad Akhtar Saeed, *Early Development of Zakat Law and Ijtihad: A Study of the Evolution of Ijtihad in the Development of the Zakat: Law during 1st Century AH*, Karachi: Islamic Research Academy, 1983.

Sifaoui, Mohamed, *Inside Al Qaeda*, London: Granta Books, 2003.

Taji-Farouki, Suha, *A Fundamental Quest: Hizb ut-Tahrir and the Search for the Islamic Caliphate*, London: Grey Seal, 1996.

Tritton, A. S., "Notes on the Muslim System of Pensions," *Bulletin of the School of Oriental and African Studies*, vol. 16, no. 1, 1954.

Udovitch, Abraham L., *Partnership and Profit in Medieval Islam*, Princeton, NJ: Princeton University Press, 1970.

Vogel, Frank E. and Samuel L. Hayes, III, *Islamic Law and Finance: Religion, Risk, and Return*, The Hague/Boston: Kluwer Law International, 1998.

von Dohnanyi, Johannes and Germana, *Schmutzige Geschäfte und Heiliger Kreig*, Zurich: Pando Verlag, 2002.

Yaqub, Abu Yusuf, *Abu Yusuf's Kitab al-Kharaj (Taxation in Islam*, vol. III), trans. and intro. A. Ben Shemesh, Leiden: Brill; London: Luzac, 1969.

Zayas, Farishta G. de, *The Law and Philosophy of Zakat: The Islamic Social Welfare System*, intro. Omar A. Farrukh, Damascus: A. Z. Abbasi, 1960.

Index

NB page numbers in bold refer to maps and tables.